STRATEGIC INSTINCTS

Princeton Studies in International History and Politics

G. JOHN IKENBERRY, MARC TRACHTENBERG, WILLIAM C. WOHLFORTH, AND KEREN YARHI-MILO, SERIES EDITORS

Strategic Instincts

THE ADAPTIVE ADVANTAGES OF COGNITIVE BIASES IN INTERNATIONAL POLITICS

{➤➤➤W➤➤➤}

Dominic D. P. Johnson

PRINCETON UNIVERSITY PRESS

PRINCETON & OXFORD

Published by Princeton University Press
41 William Street, Princeton, New Jersey 08540
6 Oxford Street, Woodstock, Oxfordshire OX20 1TR

press.princeton.edu

Library of Congress Cataloging-in-Publication Data

Names: Johnson, Dominic D. P., 1974- author.
Title: Strategic instincts : the adaptive advantages of cognitive biases in
    international politics / Dominic D.P Johnson.
Description: Princeton, New Jersey : Princeton University Press, 2020. |
    Series: Princeton studies in international history and politics |
    Includes bibliographical references and index. |
Identifiers: LCCN 2020011549 (print) | LCCN 2020011550 (ebook) |
    ISBN 9780691137452 (hardback) | ISBN 9780691185606 (ebook)
Subjects: LCSH: International relations—Psychological aspects. |
    International relations—Decision making. | Strategy—Psychological aspects. |
    United States—History—Revolution, 1775-1783. | Munich Four-Power Agreement (1938) |
    World War, 1939-1945—Campaigns—Pacific Area.
Classification: LCC JZ1253 .J65 2020 (print) | LCC JZ1253 (ebook) | DDC 327.01/9—dc23
LC record available at https://lccn.loc.gov/2020011549
LC ebook record available at https://lccn.loc.gov/2020011550

British Library Cataloging-in-Publication Data is available

Editorial: Bridget Flannery-McCoy and Alena Chekanov
Production Editorial: Nathan Carr
Jacket/Cover Design: Pamela L. Schnitter
Production: Erin Suydam
Publicity: Kate Hensley and Julia Hall
Jacket/Cover Credit: The Nike of Samothrace, goddess of victory. Rhodian marble statue,
ca. 190 BC. From Rhodes, Greece / Erich Lessing / Art Resource, NY

This book has been composed in Miller

Printed on acid-free paper. ∞

Printed in the United States of America

10 9 8 7 6 5 4 3 2 1

For Gabriella

CONTENTS

ACKNOWLEDGMENTS

THIS BOOK began a long time ago. The utility of strategic instincts is not always obvious and not always immediate, and I am glad that I seized the strategic opportunity to sign a contract with Princeton University Press when I was still at the Princeton Society of Fellows way back in 2007. The reason the book took so long has often puzzled me, but observant others have helpfully chalked it up to a marriage, two children, three transatlantic moves, four jobs, five schools, being at sixes and sevens over the book's structure, eight houses, and the decision to write another book in the middle (don't do that). All this makes me even more grateful than usual to the press, to colleagues, to friends, and most of all to family who must have wondered when (or if) this would ever see the light of day and I would stop claiming I was working on it.

Despite my overconfidence, I knew I'd get it done eventually. My sincere appreciation goes to all three editors who stuck with me throughout: Chuck Myers, for seeing the light in the original idea; Eric Crahan, who guided and advised at several International Studies Association conferences over the years, in cities across America; and Bridget Flannery-McCoy, who has, somehow, made me finish. Thanks are also due at the Press to Alena Chekanov for her patience and terrific organization, Nathan Carr for expertly seeing the book through production, and to Jennifer Backer for her thorough and brilliant copyediting of what became a very long argument. A special thank you also to my illustrations researcher, Erica Martin, who found things I thought might never be possible, and with incredible efficiency and speed at the eleventh hour.

Although it now seems in the dim and distant past (although still with a warm glow), I thank the Society of Fellows and the Woodrow Wilson School of Public and International Affairs at Princeton University, where this book was conceived and took shape. Thank you to my bosses and supporters there, especially Anne-Marie Slaughter, Leonard Barkan, Michael Wood, Mary Harper, Simon Levin, and all the fellows. I am also grateful to the Department of Government at Harvard University, where I spent a wonderful year working on the book, and especially to Stephen Peter Rosen and Richard Wrangham for their guidance, insight, and good company.

Having moved back to the United Kingdom, I thank colleagues first at the University of Edinburgh, particularly Elizabeth Bomberg and the late John Peterson, who so warmly welcomed me and a young family into a wonderful social and intellectual community in Scotland. I was helped by many colleagues there, especially Mark Aspinwall, Roland Dannreuther, Cecil Fabre, Ian Hardie, Charlie Jeffery, Juliet Kaarbo, Sean Molloy, Glen Morangie, Andrew Neal, and Susan Orr, among too many to name.

At Oxford, among numerous colleagues in the Department of Politics and International Relations and beyond, I thank especially Richard Caplan, Janina Dill, Louise Fawcett, Liz Frazer, Todd Hall, Andrew Hurrell, Eddie Keene, Desmond King, Neil MacFarlane, Walter Mattli, Kalypso Nicolaidis, Andrea Ruggeri, and Duncan Snidal for their help and support. I also thank my brilliant research students, who have in fact inspired and taught me: Robert Bognar, Stuart Bramwell, Laura Courchesne, William James, Jordan Mansell, Christine Pelican, Zoey Reeve, Paola Solimena, Silvia Spodaru, Adrienne Tecza, and Sara Usher. At St. Antony's College, immense thanks are due to Roger Goodman, Margaret MacMillan, and all the fellows and staff for their constant backing and a home from home. I also owe a special thanks to Lord John Alderdice, Annette Idler, Rob Johnson, Sir Hew Strachan, and Peter Wilson at the Changing Character of War Centre in my alma mater Pembroke College, who have provided so many opportunities to engage in strategic thinking at Oxford, and with remarkable people from beyond the ivory tower.

Other colleagues and scholars, scattered around the world, who have immensely helped or inspired me over the years with the ideas in this book, although they may not realize it, include Clark Barrett, Emily Barrett, Dan Blumstein, Terry Burnham, Lars-Erik Cederman, Jonathan Cowden, Oliver Curry, Dan Fessler, James Fowler, Giovanni Frazzetto, Malcolm Gladwell, Jonathan Hall, Martie Haselton, Michael Horowitz, Robert Jervis, Ferenc Jordan, Alex Kacelnik, Joshua Kertzer, Yuen Foong Khong, Jack Levy, Anthony Lopez, David Macdonald, Rose McDermott, Matthew McIntyre, Ryan McKay, Kenneth Payne, Steven Pinker, Michael Price, Jonathan Renshon, Ronald Rogowski, Rafe Sagarin, Richard Sosis, Terence Taylor, Bradley Thayer, Dominic Tierney, Dustin Tingley, Monica Duffy Toft, Robert Trivers, Mark van Vugt, Nils Weidmann, Harvey Whitehouse, and David Sloan Wilson.

All books take immense effort, I keep forgetting, not merely from the author but from all the people who support us and give life meaning in good and bad times. I am grateful for the love and support of my parents, Roger and Jennifer Johnson, and my sister Becci and her family, Andrew, Milo, and Alex. Gigantosaurus-sized thanks are due to my children, Lulu and Theo Johnson, my two main interlocutors over the last few years, who as well as their patience have given me a special appreciation of the amazing strategic instincts of the human brain—and how to get what you want from your dad without him realizing it. Thomas Schelling often referred to his children when explaining the sometimes strange logic of strategic interaction, and I finally know what he means.

Lastly and most importantly, I thank Gabriella de la Rosa, the rock in my life. Nothing happens without the tireless support I get at home, the intellectual curiosity and laughter we share, and the love I feel wherever I may be. Thank you.

STRATEGIC INSTINCTS

Our Gift

The intuitive mind is a sacred gift, and the rational mind is a faithful servant. We have created a society that honors the servant and has forgotten the gift.

—ALBERT EINSTEIN

STARDATE 2821.5. EN route to deliver urgent medical supplies to the New Paris colony, the *USS Enterprise* encounters a novel star formation. Spock and six others take the shuttle *Galileo* to investigate but are knocked off course and forced to make an emergency landing on nearby planet Taurus II. Their communications are down and they have no way to signal to the *Enterprise*, which can only afford to wait a few hours for the missing crew to reappear. Hounded by alien life forms while they make repairs, the crew of *Galileo* eventually get it airborne and out into orbit, but with minimal power and without enough fuel to rejoin the *Enterprise*. After an episode focusing on Spock's cold, calculating logic, he suddenly makes a rash decision as the *Galileo* struggles to escape the planet's gravity. Spock dumps all of the shuttle's remaining fuel and then ignites it—a desperate cry for help that creates a flare in the darkness of space but sends the helpless shuttle on a death spiral to be burned up in the atmosphere of Taurus II. The still silent *Enterprise* is already moving off. Miraculously, however, Lieutenant Sulu happens to notice the tiny streak of light. Kirk turns the ship around, and the survivors are beamed aboard at the last moment. Safely back on the *Enterprise*, Kirk interrogates Spock about his impulsive decision to dump the fuel:

KIRK: There's really something I don't understand about all of this. Maybe you can explain it to me. Logically, of course. When you jettisoned the fuel and ignited it, you knew there was virtually no chance of it being seen, yet you did it anyhow. That would seem to me to be an act of desperation.

SPOCK: Quite correct, Captain.

KIRK: Now we all know, and I'm sure the doctor will agree with me, that desperation is a highly emotional state of mind. How does your well-known logic explain that?

SPOCK: Quite simply, Captain. I examined the problem from all angles, and it was plainly hopeless. Logic informed me that under the circumstances, the only possible action would have to be one of desperation. Logical decision, logically arrived at.

KIRK: I see. You mean you reasoned that it was time for an emotional outburst.

SPOCK: Well, I wouldn't put it in exactly those terms, Captain, but those are essentially the facts.

KIRK: You're not going to admit that for the first time in your life, you committed a purely human emotional act?

SPOCK: No, sir.

KIRK: Mister Spock, you're a stubborn man.

SPOCK: Yes, sir.[1]

The crew of *Galileo* owed their survival to Spock relinquishing his austere, dispassionate reason in favor of an all-too-human act of impulsive behavior. As he himself explains, under the circumstances this reversion to an "act of desperation" offered them a chance of success when all seemed lost. *Star Trek*'s enduring attraction is in large part the different perspectives provided by the steadfast but emotional human, Captain James T. Kirk, and the logical but unfeeling Vulcan, Mr. Spock. Typically, the episodes end with a hair-raising escape from the perils of aliens or space itself, thanks to the instinctive human nature or emotional acts of Kirk, Doctor McCoy, or Scotty the engineer, winning out over Spock's cold and calculating logic that might make sense on paper but fails to win the day. The message is that, however clever and knowledgeable one may be, and regardless of whatever amazing technology we may have at our disposal, we still rely on trusty human instincts to get us through tough times.

Writer Julia Galef warns us not to be taken in too easily by what she calls the "Straw Vulcan."[2] Spock is not just rational but actually tends to conform to so-called "hyper-rationality," an overly restrictive version of rationality that assumes complete information and perfect knowledge, which can be easy to falsify as an optimal decision-making approach in the real world (or beyond!). However, the idea that, sometimes, humans make better decisions than machines or rational actors is a familiar notion not only in literature and movies but also in our everyday experience. Often, our intuitions lead to good decisions, not bad ones. Our gut reactions and first impressions often prove correct. And our automatic responses to events and in interactions with other people are often faster and more reliable than more calculating alternatives.

These are what I call "strategic instincts." Strategic instincts are rapid, adaptive decision-making heuristics that we all have as human beings. And we do not have them by accident. We have them because they helped to keep us alive and successful over the many millennia of human evolutionary history—especially in fast-moving situations of uncertainty, often with limited information—and were thus favored by natural selection. They are tools of survival. The question of this book is a simple one: Do these same strategic instincts continue to serve as tools of survival, not just for individual human beings but also for the nations they lead, especially in times of crisis and war?

Demise of the Vulcans: Rationality and the Rise of Psychology

One of the most important findings in recent decades of scientific endeavor is that humans have numerous "cognitive biases"—quirks of the human brain that cause our judgments and decision-making to deviate markedly from what we would expect if people weighed up the costs, benefits, and probabilities of different options in an evenhanded way.[3] This should be no surprise to astute observers of human beings, as Plato, Shakespeare, Freud, and many laypeople could tell us. Bertrand Russell once remarked: "It has been said that man is a rational animal. All my life I have been searching for evidence which could support this."[4] But with the rise and spread of rational choice theory in academia during the latter part of the twentieth century, we have had to prove this intuition to ourselves, through painstaking experimental research. Scholars in political science and other fields used to take psychology seriously (if sometimes flawed in how they did so), with a strong influence of approaches based on human nature, psychoanalysis, and behaviorism. Rational choice swept all that away—for some good reasons as well as bad. Now, psychology is making a long overdue comeback as a more rigorous science. After many decades in a wilderness dominated by the study of a fictitious *Homo economicus* at the expense of the study of *Homo sapiens*, we have now more or less arrived at a consensus that human cognitive biases are real, pervasive, and important.[5]

But how people *explain* these phenomena remains a major problem. Perhaps unsurprisingly, given the long dominance of the rational choice paradigm as a benchmark standard for evaluating behavior in economics and political science, cognitive biases tend to be seen as errors or mistakes.[6] There remains a widespread idea across the social sciences that rationality is the normative ideal (even if recognized as empirically false), and human brains are prevented from achieving this ideal because of cognitive limitations. Cognitive biases are thus seen as liabilities of the human brain that must be guarded against if

Table 1.1. Disciplinary differences in the interpretation of cognitive biases

Characteristics of Cognitive Biases	Social Scientists	Evolutionary Scientists
What are they?	Cognitive limitations, errors, or mistakes	Cognitive adaptations (context-specific problem-solving mechanisms)
Are they useful?	No	Yes
What do they cause?	Failures, disasters, conflict	Behavior
What are their sources of variation?	Little consideration	Proximate biological mechanisms, contingent on social and ecological context
What are their origins?	No consideration	Natural selection

we are to avoid costly misjudgments, misperceptions, mistakes, crises, policy failures, disasters, and wars. Cognitive biases are bad, and their consequences are bad.[7]

However, in other fields—most notably evolutionary biology—the same cognitive biases are seen in a remarkably different light (see Table 1.1). Far from mistakes, they are considered useful dispositions that serve important functions. Cognitive biases can be good, and their consequences can be good. An evolutionary perspective suggests that cognitive biases are *adaptive* heuristics that evolved to improve our decision-making, not to undermine it. They may contribute to mistakes and disasters at some times (as indeed can rational choice) but not always. If cognitive biases can be useful, we should find out how. This book is about whether and when cognitive biases cause or promote success in the realm of international relations. It turns out that, in the real world, *Homo sapiens* is often a better strategist than *Homo economicus*, especially given that we have to deal with other *Homo sapiens* (not other *Homo economicuses*). Japanese psychologist Masanao Toda pointed out a long time ago that "man and rat are both incredibly stupid in an experimental room. On the other hand, psychology has paid little attention to the things they do in their normal habitats; man drives a car, plays complicated games, and organizes society, and rat is troublesomely cunning in the kitchen."[8] When we move from the lab out into the field, cognitive biases find a new lease on life. They work well. Social scientists have, therefore, been focusing on the wrong end of the stick, with potentially significant oversights for the field. As is now recognized in other disciplines and in everyday life, biases are often better thought of, in psychologist Gerd Gigerenzer's slogan, as "heuristics that make us smart."[9] Seeing biases as mistakes impairs our understanding, predictions, and recommendations for both theory and practice in politics and international relations.

Demons of the Field: A Predilection for Disaster

The interpretation of cognitive biases as mistakes may be only natural for fields without a grounding in life sciences, but in international relations it appears to be exacerbated by two additional tendencies: focusing on disasters (bad-outcome cases) and looking at isolated events (one-off cases). If instead we look at a broader range of outcomes, and at multiple events over time, a different picture emerges. Let us look at each of these problems in turn.

First, international relations scholars often tend to focus on explaining prominent crises, policy failures, disasters, or wars—unusual events that draw special attention and probing. As Robert Jervis, father of the application of psychology in international relations, acknowledged, "There is an almost inescapable tendency to look at cases of conflict, surprise, and error. When things go wrong, they not only attract the actors' attention, they also attract ours."[10] He warns that this makes "analysis of causation difficult," risks assigning causes to "constants rather than variables," and fails to "discriminate between good decisions and bad ones."[11] Tracing back through the causes of calamitous and complex events, involving numerous actors and organizations, examples of bias can nearly always be found. We are more likely to *seek* and more likely to *report* biases when they precede negative events.

By contrast, politics-as-normal, closely averted disasters, and even many successes are rarely noticed or reported, let alone studied. When everything goes right, we spend less time scrutinizing how that happened. Nobel Laureate Daniel Kahneman, reflecting on his life's work on cognitive biases, also found that "it's easier to identify bad decisions and bad decision makers than good decisions and decision makers."[12] This asymmetry represents a major problem if biases are present in both failures and successes but we only ever look at the former. As Jervis urged, "We need to know more about successes."[13] This book aims to redress the balance.

Until now, research has tended to focus on identifying the *presence* of biases and neglected examining their actual *effects*—effects that can be good as well as bad. When found, biases are automatically assumed to have had a detrimental influence on decisions, and thus to have contributed to the negative event. Jack Levy lamented back in 1983 that "theories of foreign policy and crisis decision-making provide a comprehensive analysis of the *sources* of misperception, but are generally not concerned with their consequences."[14] Although research in political psychology has bloomed since then, there is still a strong tendency to focus on where psychological factors have led leaders and states astray, rather than where they may have helped and led them to success. This omission was also recognized by Jonathan Mercer, who noted the "ubiquitous yet inaccurate belief in international relations scholarship that cognitive biases and emotion cause only mistakes."[15] He points out that logically this can only be the case if we make some bizarre assumptions, such as that "rationality must be free of psychology" and that "psychology cannot explain accurate judgments."[16] Both are patently false but persist as unstated assumptions in the literature.

Now for the second problem. Much social science scholarship focuses on isolated case studies, or a small sample of them, which is fair enough given the depth of work needed to understand the complexity of historical events and the methodological traditions of the field. Nevertheless, this approach is always at risk of downplaying or ignoring the bigger picture—the effects that phenomena such as cognitive biases have on average, in *many cases* over the long term. Behavioral scientist Robin Hogarth argued that "several biases identified in discrete incidents result from heuristics that are functional in the more natural continuous environment."[17] As an example, World War I has become a kind of test case for major theories of the causes of war, but any of the cognitive biases that compellingly contributed to disaster in 1914—overconfidence, attribution error, group bias, or many others—could actually have been useful at other times, or on average over the preceding decades or centuries, if they led to more effective deterrence, bargaining, or coercion. The odd mistake—even a big one—does not invalidate the utility of a general propensity. Of course, many social scientists do look at multiple cases and the broad sweep of history.[18] My point is simply that we need to start looking at the role of *cognitive biases* from this perspective as well.

If we look at the long-term outcomes of cognitive biases in many decisions over time, we might find that they are generally useful rather than generally detrimental. In fact, even if a bias were only beneficial on rare occasions, it could still bring important advantages if those occasions are critical ones for a state's security. For example, the United States is argued to have repeatedly overestimated the USSR's aggressive intentions during the Cold War, but this very bias encouraged Kennedy to make a firm stand against Khrushchev in the 1962 Cuban Missile Crisis.[19] Who's to say that wasn't a useful outcome of what seemed like hype at other times? We need to tease apart the *presence* of cognitive biases from the more important *costs* (and indeed benefits) of those biases in different circumstances.

To summarize, if cognitive biases are a source of success as well as a source of failure, then they may sometimes—or even usually—bring benefits as well as costs, potentially generating *net* benefits over time. The occasional failure may be a price worth paying for a bias that works well on average, or very effectively in times of crisis. Even frequent failures may be worth enduring for a bias that brings a major coup at critical junctures. Biases may make us better at setting ambitious goals, building coalitions and alliances, bargaining effectively, sending credible signals, maintaining resolve, and persevering in the face of daunting challenges, and they may make us more formidable when it comes to conflict, deterrence, coercion, crisis, brinkmanship, and war.

Cognitive biases, therefore, might offer political and strategic *advantages*. This seems—at minimum—an interesting idea, but we don't know if it is true or not because no one has looked. This book takes up that challenge.

Plan of the Book

This book examines the strategic advantages of three cognitive biases: overconfidence, the fundamental attribution error, and in-group/out-group bias. These biases were chosen for several reasons: (1) they are among the most important influences on human judgment and decision-making; (2) they are empirically well established in experimental psychology; (3) they have been widely applied to explain political phenomena; and (4) they are commonly cited as contributory causes of crises and wars, such as the world wars, the Cold War, the Vietnam War, and the Iraq War. While these biases may indeed cause disasters at some times and in some contexts, at other times they may bring strategic *advantages*, promoting ambition and boldness, alertness and suspicion of potential rivals, and cohesion and collective action, furthering the aims of the leaders and groups that hold them—whatever those aims may be.

In separate chapters, I outline the scientific research on each bias, its hypothesized adaptive advantages in human evolution, historical examples where the bias caused disasters or mistakes, and then, critically, contrary historical examples where the bias seemed to have lent strategic advantages and caused *successes* instead (see Table 1.2).

Before launching into our exploration of the adaptive advantages of specific cognitive biases, chapter 1 explores the notion of "adaptive biases" and "strategic instincts" in more detail. I compare social science and life science approaches to understanding human behavior, ask why cognitive biases evolved in our evolutionary past, whether they continue to be adaptive today,

Table 1.2. Cognitive biases and historical case studies explored in the book

Cognitive Bias	Case Study	Argument
Overconfidence	American Revolution	Overconfidence increased ambition, resolve, and perseverance
Fundamental Attribution Error (FAE)	Appeasement of Hitler *(Reverse case)*	The FAE *would* have increased recognition of the threat, preparations for war, and alliance seeking
In-Group/Out-Group Bias	Pacific Campaign of World War II	In-group/out-group bias increased collective action, unit cohesion, and offensive action

and why a bias can be better than accuracy. In chapter 2, I take a step back to consider how and why international relations might benefit from an evolutionary approach at all. Evolutionary biology has a long history of misunderstanding and resistance in the social sciences, not least since the "sociobiology" debate of the 1970s, and it is important to review how the natural and social sciences have both moved on since then, as well as the promise for a future of mutual collaboration. That allows us to turn to strategic instincts themselves.

Chapter 3 examines the strategic role of overconfidence. Most mentally healthy people exhibit: (1) an overestimation of their capabilities; (2) an illusion of control over events; and (3) a perceived invulnerability to risk (three widely replicated and robust phenomena collectively known as "positive illusions").[20] Of course, overconfidence has long been noted as a cause of disasters and wars. For example, Geoffrey Blainey, Barbara Tuchman, and Stephen Van Evera all blamed false optimism as one of the key causes of World War I.[21] In the contemporary world, there has also been considerable discussion of the role of overconfidence in, for example, U.S. planning for the 2003 Iraq War and the 2008 financial crisis.[22] However, overconfidence can also offer adaptive advantages—increasing ambition, resolve, and perseverance.[23] The question of this chapter is not when and where does overconfidence cause failure but when and where does it cause success? Evidence for positive as well as negative effects of overconfidence is presented from laboratory experiments, field studies, agent-based computer simulations, and mathematical models, all of which reveal some fundamental advantages of overconfidence under well-defined conditions. Overconfidence is important, pervasive, and increasingly well understood. The outstanding question addressed here is when it hurts or helps us.

In a case study of the American Revolution, chapter 4 suggests that George Washington and the birth of the United States benefited in no small measure from a remarkable confidence—arguably overconfidence—that inspired Washington to fight and sustain the revolution despite the formidable odds stacked against them and repeated setbacks along the way. In a long and grueling war in which Americans lost most of the battles and struggled to even keep an army in the field, ambition and boldness paid off handsomely.

Chapter 5 examines the strategic advantages of the fundamental attribution error (FAE). People tend to attribute the behavior of *other* actors to intentional action (their "dispositions") but behavior of *their own* as dictated by circumstances ("situational constraints").[24] This is thought to be an important reason why nations fail to cooperate, descend into arms races, escalate conflicts, and ultimately end up at war, since they fail to appreciate the constraints acting on others, overestimate the threat they pose, and—in mirror image— underestimate the threat they themselves pose to others. The FAE does not mean that we always perceive others as threatening but rather that we will *perceive apparently threatening behavior as intentional.*[25] For example, the buildup of armies and armaments by European states prior to 1914 was widely considered a menace to security, while individual states considered their own buildups to be an unfortunate but essential defensive response.[26] The FAE suggests that we systematically *overestimate* the threat from other states because we are biased to assume that their actions reveal their intentions. Often this will reduce cooperation and increase conflict. However, the FAE has clear *adaptive* features as well. In a hostile environment with conflicting information, the FAE aids in the detection of threats, preparations for war, and the formation of alliances, which together help to strengthen deterrence and avoid exploitation.[27] The question of this chapter is not when and where does the FAE cause failure but when and where does it cause success? The FAE is a bias that encourages us to err on the side of caution when dealing with other actors and states, and assume the worst. In dangerous environments, the FAE may at least sometimes be useful.

In the case study in chapter 6, I examine British perceptions of Hitler's intentions in the 1930s. This offers a reverse case, in which those in power maintained beliefs *opposite* to those predicted by the FAE. Prime Minister Neville Chamberlain strongly resisted attributing dispositional causes to Hitler's behavior and instead emphasized situational causes: the German desire to redress the restrictions of the Treaty of Versailles, attain territorial security, and unite the German-speaking peoples. In the face of mounting contradictory evidence, Chamberlain continued to give Hitler the benefit of the doubt, leading to the disastrous policy of appeasement and the Munich Crisis of 1938. This raises an unusual question: Where was the FAE when we needed it? Other actors whose beliefs did align with the FAE—not least Winston Churchill—insisted that Hitler was acting out of offensive intentions to expand German power and vigorously opposed appeasement. If the bias had been stronger among leaders at the time, Britain would have stood up to Hitler earlier and more effectively.

Chapter 7 examines the strategic advantages of the in-group/out-group bias. People have a powerful tendency to favor their own in-group and its members, while disparaging out-groups and their members.[28] The bias is so strong and prevalent that it forms a bedrock foundation in social psychology, critical to social identity and intergroup relations. Such group prejudices, however, can have appalling human consequences in the bias's contribution to the oppression of minority groups, ethnic conflict, and genocide—for example, it has been implicated for its role in fanning the flames of the Balkan wars, the Rwandan genocide, and the Israeli-Palestinian conflict.[29] However, in other circumstances the bias has highly adaptive features. For example, the in-group/out-group bias increases cohesion and collective action, as well as coordinated action against other groups, which together can increase survival and effectiveness in competition and conflict.[30] The question is not when and where does group bias cause disasters but when and where does it cause success? The in-group/out-group bias can lift the motivation and effort of citizens, soldiers, and leaders alike, as well as be exploited by elites to rally support. In-group/out-group perceptions may be wrong (both materially and morally), but in times of lethal competition they can nevertheless serve to increase public support and solidarity, bolster the war effort, and boost the willingness to sacrifice self-interest and fight for the wider group.

In the case study in chapter 8, I argue that the United States was able to persist and prevail in the long and brutal Pacific campaign against the Japanese in World War II in no small part as a result of the in-group/out-group bias helping to boost support for the war effort among citizens at home, the cohesion of soldiers, sailors, and airmen in the field, and the commitment and determination of leaders.

In chapter 9, I consider an important caveat about the adaptive advantages of cognitive biases. The argument of the book is not that biases are always good in all settings. Rather, the argument is that biases can be advantageous as long as they are manifested *in appropriate settings* and *in moderation*. Biases that become extreme or arise in the wrong contexts are liable to be counterproductive and result in disaster. In general, human cognitive biases are not extreme. They are tendencies that marginally steer our behavior in some particular way. But they nevertheless vary from person to person and situation to situation, meaning that sometimes they will be too weak, and at other times they will be too strong. This chapter considers how strong biases "should" be, to be effective, and the consequences when they become overbearing. To explore the red lines beyond which strategic instincts go too far, I revisit the Pacific campaign in World War II. That brutal conflict illustrates that although the in-group/out-group bias serves to promote cohesion, collective action, and offensive action, the bias can become extreme, to the point that it begins to impose material—as well as moral—costs on the war effort, potentially negating the benefits it may bring to military effectiveness.

Chapter 10 presents a summary of the findings and explores the implications of this new evolutionary perspective on cognitive biases for international relations. The key conclusions are that: (1) *cognitive biases are adaptive*— "strategic instincts" that help not only individuals but also state leaders and nations achieve their goals (whatever those goals may be); (2) effective strategies often *differ radically from those predicted by conventional paradigms*, such as rational choice theory; (3) the approach, as demonstrated in the case studies, offers *novel interpretations of historical events*, especially the American Revolution, the British appeasement of Hitler in the 1930s, and the United States' Pacific campaign in World War II; and (4) the approach suggests *novel and often counterintuitive strategies* for leaders and policymakers to exploit strategic instincts among themselves, the public, and other states.

This final chapter also considers the future. The mismatch between our evolved psychology and the increasingly technological and globalized world we inhabit is widening ever further. This presents new dangers. We must avoid

creating decision-making protocols, political institutions, and military doc-
trines that leave traps into which our evolutionary dispositions are likely to
fall. But we have seen that biases can be good too. Where they promote our
strategic goals, how can we harness and make best use of them? How do we
ensure that the positive aspects of our strategic instincts are not swamped by
cumbersome decision-making procedures, conflicting training and experience
based on rational choice, or philosophical ideals that may be nice in principle
but deadly when in lethal competition? Kahneman reminds us that cognitive
biases are essential in helping us perform numerous daily tasks, and strategic luminary Carl von Clausewitz stressed the vital importance of intuition
in times of war in particular. Our "adaptive unconscious" is by definition—
and by design—something we are barely aware of, and thus we also are barely
aware of how and when we may be interfering with it. Every day, in life, business, sports, politics, and war, confidence can help promote our ambition
and resolve, the fundamental attribution error can keep us alert to our rivals'
intentions, and the in-group/out-group bias can help to foster cohesion and
collective action, as well as effective performance in competition with other
groups. These are ancient challenges and ones that will always remain important—regardless of social and technological change, as even Kirk and Spock
found far in the future—but for which evolution already gave us the gift of our
strategic instincts.

CHAPTER ONE

Adaptive Biases

MAKING THE RIGHT MISTAKES IN INTERNATIONAL POLITICS

Despite widespread claims to the contrary, the human mind is not worse than rational (e.g., because of processing constraints)—but may often be better than rational.

—LEDA COSMIDES AND JOHN TOOBY

The purist might be appalled at the arbitrary mixture of politics, sociology, economics, psychology, and history that regularly influences decisions in crises and combat, never mind the great contributions made by intuition and hunch.

—SIR LAWRENCE FREEDMAN

CASTING ONE'S EYE OVER any historical textbook, one does not get the impression that history was populated with and shaped by particularly rational agents. From Julius Caesar to Jeanne d'Arc, from Henry VIII to King George III, from Hitler to Trump, momentous decisions and turning points in history have hinged on the quixotic beliefs and perceptions of individual human beings—both leaders who chose courses for their country and citizens who supported or opposed them. More or less rational individuals and decisions can be found too, of course, but it is hard to argue that history has been a linear march of rationality and good sense. People have lived and died, or sacrificed others, not only for material gains but also for ideology, religion, principle, justice, pride, honor, revenge, and glory. As David Welch was moved to remark, "To read the classic texts of international relations theory, one would never suspect that human beings have right brains as well as left; that in addition to being selfish, they also love, hate, hope, and despair; that they sometimes act not out of interest, but out of courage, politeness, or rage."[1] Even when they *have* fought for more rational material interests, such as for wealth or power, in so doing people have been influenced by misperceptions and biases along the way. Often, this has led to disaster. Barbara Tuchman's *March of Folly*, for example, offers a litany of examples of states that managed to act against their self-interest, with personalities and psychological influences helping to bring down governments, cede territory, and lose wars.[2]

Recent scholarship suggests that in international politics, rational choice is in fact empirically rare, even at the top of the decision-making elite where one might—if anywhere—expect it to occur. While certain individuals are recognized for having apparently high levels of rationality, such as nineteenth-century statesman Otto von Bismarck, famous for his cold, calculating logic of realpolitik, it seems they stand out precisely because they buck the norm. More typically, leaders engage in all sorts of non-rational behavior instead. Brian Rathbun in particular has heralded, counter to common theoretical assumptions, "the rarity of realpolitik" and argues that, in contrast to the rational choice model, the preferences and decisions of national leaders tend to be characterized by alternative non-rational ways of thinking, such as pursuing visionary and idealistic goals.[3] With rational choice in doubt both in practice as well as in theory, the bigger question that remains is what the *consequences* of non-rational behavior are for international relations. While non-rational decision-making undermines the "ideal" of rational behavior, leading at times to disaster, at other times might it also in fact bring its own advantages?

For every instance of personalities and psychological factors bringing disaster, one can offer a counterexample of other (or indeed the same) personalities and psychological factors bringing triumph. Alexander the Great was extraordinarily ambitious and sometimes reckless, but who's to say this did not help him create one of history's largest empires—and by the age of thirty? Julius Caesar was imperious and self-assured yet became one of Rome's most successful military leaders and ultimately emperor, likened no less to a god. Napoleon is argued to have harbored an insuppressible ambition, but this was no doubt part of the reason he attempted to conquer most of Europe and succeeded in doing so. Winston Churchill is thought to have suffered from bipolar disorder, swinging from manic highs to depressive lows. While often debilitating, it may well have contributed to both his deep ruminations and his bold decisions. General George Patton was well known for his abrasive and aggressive character, but those very traits appear to have been part of why he was so successful as a war leader in the brutal days of World War II.

History is replete with remarkable individuals with all-too-human characteristics—Kirks rather than Spocks. And it is precisely remarkable and quirky individuals, rather than robotic rational ones, that often appear to shape that history (as well as make it more interesting). This may be no coincidence. As George Bernard Shaw suggested in his *Maxims for Revolutionists*, "The reasonable man adapts himself to the world: the unreasonable one persists in trying to adapt the world to himself. Therefore all progress depends on the unreasonable man."[4] While historians disagree on the relative influence of individual human actors (versus broader social and economic forces) in how history unfolds, few would dispute the fact that many or a majority of the most important figures across the ages do not fit the model of a perfectly rational actor. History is a human story. And being human has brought stunning accomplishments as well as lamentable tragedies.

Strategy as Instinct: A New Approach for a New Question

The idea that non-rational behavior might offer advantages is an important one that has not been systematically investigated in politics and international relations. We might be missing something important. What if it helps in achieving strategic goals? What if cognitive biases are an important component of leadership, strategy, and security? Perhaps they help boost ambitions, identify threats, deter rivals, rally the troops, persuade allies, gain public support, or win elections, as well as help us face daunting challenges. They might also spur us to keep fighting when we'd otherwise give up. Perhaps they simply help us avoid making even more costly mistakes in the other direction— pushing us toward action and away from the dangers of inaction, for example. They will not always succeed, of course, but what is the dividing line between when they work and when they fail? Are they more useful in certain contexts rather than others? And, if they are beneficial, how can we harness or exploit them?

The tools for this novel take on cognitive biases naturally arise from the field of evolutionary biology and, in particular, the subfield of "evolutionary psychology."[5] Evolutionary psychologists are dedicated to understanding precisely the problem at hand: the *adaptive functions* of human psychological and behavioral dispositions.[6] That is, what problems our evolved dispositions were originally "designed" to solve, how they improved reproduction and survival in our evolutionary past, how and when the relevant physiological and cognitive mechanisms are triggered, and the positive and negative effects of these biases today. This approach offers a range of novel insights, predictions, and sources of variation that can be tested with empirical data, as well as a unifying scientific theory to understand the origins, causes, and consequences of human cognitive and behavioral biases. In this book, I draw on evolutionary psychology to make two core arguments:

1. *Cognitive biases are adaptations.* Many cognitive biases widely invoked to explain decision-making failures in politics and international relations are in fact adaptive, functional design features of human brains. They are not mistakes or cognitive limitations but

rather adaptations crafted by natural selection. This may be a surprise to some social scientists, but it is no surprise to evolutionary psychologists.

2. *Cognitive biases are strategic.* Cognitive biases evolved because they helped to solve strategic problems in the past, and they can continue to serve similar adaptive functions today, even among political leaders and even on the stage of international politics. The role of cognitive biases in causing mistakes is widely accepted, but their role in causing success has rarely been studied. I argue that in important decision-making domains, and indeed in some key historical cases, cognitive biases bring significant strategic advantages.

These arguments lead to a counterintuitive worldview. If we could replace our leaders, politicians, and soldiers with perfectly rational robots, who would make every decision based on unbiased information processing, I would argue that we would not want to do so. Our strategic interests are often better served by emotional, psychologically endowed human beings—even if they lead us into disaster from time to time. Decision-making in international politics typically involves the familiar challenge of managing conflict and cooperation in strategic interaction with other actors, a task that the human brain has been explicitly designed to deal with over many millions of years. Of course, there are many things that are different between individuals interacting with each other in small-scale societies (as humans have done for millennia) and states interacting with each other in the international system (which has only occurred for a few hundred years). Yet many fundamental processes of strategic interaction are similar, regardless of the type and scale of the actors involved—indeed, this is why game theory remains relevant and widely used in both evolutionary biology and international relations.[7] Moreover, where there *are* differences, an evolutionary psychological approach is helpful because it allows us to predict—given the level and type of "mismatch" between our evolved propensities and characteristics of the modern environment—when cognitive biases are likely to be triggered and how they affect outcomes.

Every day, all of us are able to navigate a stream of complex social and physical challenges without knowing how, thanks to a suite of evolved heuristics and biases. As Kahneman put it, "Our thoughts and actions are routinely guided by System 1 [our intuitive thinking] and generally are on the mark."[8] They often work well precisely *because* they are not slowed or sullied by conscious mental effort. They are our "adaptive unconscious," steering us to make good decisions—often in the blink of an eye—as they have done throughout our evolutionary history.[9] Today, these heuristics and biases continue to aid our individual interests—and even, perhaps, national interests. Instead of finding ways to avoid or suppress cognitive biases, we should look for ways to channel them so they can better work their magic.

A Growing Trend in Adaptive Thinking

The argument of this book dovetails with a growing trend in "adaptive thinking" in the social and natural sciences. Researchers in a variety of disciplines have stressed that strict rational choice, even if attained, is not always the best strategy for achieving goals. Instead, systematic biases inherent to human nature are either more readily available or actually outperform rationality. This has been most clearly explored in the case of cognitive biases which, as discussed, help us navigate various challenges of everyday life.[10] Such biases have been shown, for example, to promote performance in competition, perseverance in difficult tasks, and even mental and physical health.[11] But adaptive thinking is found in many other domains, a sample of which is outlined here:

- *Cognitive heuristics* are critical to many common tasks and activities in which rational choice alternatives are not even possible. For example, the "gaze heuristic" allows us to perform the complex task, in milliseconds, of catching (or avoiding) an object thrown at us, such as a baseball or a spear.[12] We do not gather data and solve the relevant quadratic equations. If we had to do that we'd be off the team (or dead).
- *Error management theory* (EMT) suggests that decision-making biases are adaptive because they help us to avoid the most costly types of errors, even if this means increasing the frequency of (less costly) errors in the other direction. For example, fire alarms are set to be highly sensitive, thus detecting all real fires even though this comes at the expense of many false alarms.[13] That's the bias we want it to have. This general principle is particularly important for cognitive biases so I return to it in more detail later.
- *Emotions* and "emotional intelligence" lend strategic advantages in interactions with others—especially face-to-face ones—helping to craft effective relationships, signal credible reputations, and deter cheats or foes. For example, anger can reliably reveal our preferences to others, improving payoffs over rational approaches alone.[14]
- *Positive psychology* has emerged as a reaction against the focus in psychology and psychiatry on disorders and abnormalities. Rather than focusing on what goes wrong (as typically described in the *Diagnostic and Statistical Manual of Mental Disorders* [DSM], for example), some psychologists have argued for reframing psychological disorders not as the presence of something bad but as excessive levels of "character strengths."[15] In other words, there is a shift in focus to what is good about human pathologies (in moderation) rather than what is bad about them (in extremis).

- *Affective computing* in artificial intelligence aims to simulate or exploit human emotional processes to improve human-computer interactions. For example, many artificial intelligence companies expend significant time and energy making robots look, act, and react like humans, even though it would be far easier and cheaper not to bother.[16]

- *Memory distortion* has surprisingly been suggested to be "better" than accurate recall. Rather than dwelling on precise details of the past, memory is viewed as a mechanism that allows us to generate and test new scenarios based on previous experience. Counterintuitively, distorting the past may help improve our ability to hypothesize, predict, or think about the future, since future events may be similar to but not the same as the past.[17]

- *Superstitions* have even been shown to have adaptive utility. For example, controlled studies find that activating superstitious beliefs in cause-and-effect reasoning improved performance in sports, motor dexterity, memory, and mental games, improving focus and confidence.[18] Mathematical models also suggest that "superstitious" beliefs about the possible presence of another agent in the environment may have been a valuable method of predator avoidance that evolved in animals as well as humans—making us err on the side of caution.[19]

- *Religions* contain beliefs that may be apparently false (a standard that David Sloan Wilson terms "factual realism"), but even false beliefs can be adaptive if the belief itself serves to motivate behaviors that are adaptive in the real world (what he terms "practical realism").[20] For example, among indigenous small-scale societies (and some modern ones), the anticipation of supernatural punishment for violating social norms can help increase cooperation and solve collective action problems.[21]

- *Adaptive markets* are what emerge from reconciling the long-standing "efficient market hypothesis" of economics with the realities of behavioral science, and the bubbles and crashes that result from human sentiment. For example, while irrationality may create volatility and inefficiencies in markets, hedge funds have become "the Galapagos Islands of finance," where strategies built around human biases, not human rationality, are evolving new ways to reap returns.[22]

- Finally, *strategic theory* has long recognized that purely rational behavior is not always the most effective approach *when interacting with another agent*. A rational, calculated strategy may look good on paper but may fail to outwit the other player for several reasons. First, behaving rationally makes one highly predictable. Second, if the *other* actor is not rational, then one's own rational behavior may fail to achieve results even if it is a good idea. Third, if the other actor *is* rational, signaling or performing a non-rational strategy can exploit their rational behavior (now one is on the other side of the asymmetry). As luminary of strategic theory Thomas Schelling wrote, "It is not a universal advantage in situations of conflict to be inalienably and manifestly rational in decision and motivation."[23] Indeed, he suggested that "many of the attributes of rationality . . . are strategic disabilities in certain conflict situations."[24] Instead, there can be a "rationality of irrationality," in which non-rational strategies prevail.[25]

Other more general findings point to an important functional role of human dispositions. For example, human emotions are generally thought of as irrational and undermining of effective decision-making. However, considerable evidence now shows that rational decision-making actually *requires* emotion to function properly.[26] Without emotions, many decisions cannot be made at all because the brain needs some valence (does it *feel* good, or right?) attached to options in order to trigger a preference. Specific emotions may even improve decision-making processes. For example, one experiment found that anger made subjects more likely to focus on information that contradicted their own views (in part because they were motivated to attack it), but as a consequence of this process they were more likely to update their beliefs. Less angry subjects focused on information that supported their preexisting beliefs.[27]

Given all of these potential advantages of non-rational behavior, we might at least begin to question the dominance of rational choice theory. Long ago, Schelling pointed out that "our sophistication sometimes suppresses sound intuitions," and rethinking this omission would help to "restore some intuitive notions that were only superficially 'irrational.'"[28] As a model, within many areas of social science, rational choice remains central. However, it clearly has both theoretical and empirical challenges. Theoretically, there appear to be many domains in which, and mechanisms by which, rational choice may be outperformed by alternative strategies (or itself even undergirded by non-rational processes). Empirically, as a description of human behavior, it is fatally flawed. Thankfully, economics has started to adopt the insights of empirical behavioral science, in the guise of "behavioral economics" (with public policies now being designed around them), and political science and international relations are beginning to follow. The idol of *Homo economicus* that has dominated economics and other areas of social science for decades is a useful baseline for comparison but a poor model of human behavior. Moreover, in many settings it would lead to poor performance even if humans could approximate it. Gerd Gigerenzer and Henry Brighton propose that, instead of *Homo economicus*, we should conceive of ourselves as "*Homo heuristicus*," who "has a biased mind and ignores part of the available information, yet a biased mind can handle uncertainty more efficiently and robustly than an unbiased mind relying on more resource-intensive and general-purpose processing strategies."[29] This might seem radical, but evolution has had millions of years of trial and error to craft effective methods of making decisions under uncertainty with limited time and information. The solution it has come up with is not a cold, calculating machine but a Swiss Army knife of multiple cognitive biases—handy tools for commonly encountered jobs. It should be no surprise if this aspect of human nature is, in the words of Leda Cosmides and John Tooby, "better than rational."[30]

Feet to the Fire: When Are Biases Most Important?

Evolutionary psychologists and behavioral economists stress that cognitive biases are common and important in everyday life. However, there are reasons to believe that they become even more important in the high-stakes and fast-moving situations of crisis and conflict in international politics.

It is an old idea that rationality becomes challenged in times of war, which is "famed for its tendency to irrationality and the imperfection of available information."[31] In such circumstances, intuition becomes vital, over and above any rationality achieved. Carl von Clausewitz stressed the immense complexity of war, not only in the interactions of the people, the military, and the government, on both sides, but also in the chaos of the battlefield itself: "To assess these things in all their ramifications and diversity is plainly a colossal task. Rapid and correct appraisal of them clearly calls for the intuition of a genius; to master all this complex mass by sheer methodological examination is obviously impossible. Bonaparte was quite right when he said that Newton himself would quail before the algebraic problems it could pose."[32] The problem was so great, he believed, that it demanded individuals of "genius" to succeed within it—people, for example, like Napoleon (Figure 1.1).[33]

The observation remains true today. While in academia social scientists seek rational solutions to problems, such solutions often fail when tested against the fire of the real world. In comparing the academic and policy worlds in strategy, Lawrence Freedman warned that "when matters are finely balanced but a decision has still to be taken, a feeling about the problem may be as good a guide as any," especially as in any case, "time often precludes extensive deliberation."[34] The practice of strategy, as opposed to the theory, "provides opportunity for chance and irrationality to hold sway" and in which there are "great contributions made by intuition and hunch."[35] In the fast-moving setting of war, therefore, even well-intentioned rational thought can be overwhelmed or outpaced by psychological dispositions. That is when heuristics and biases come to the fore and their adaptive advantages—as well as their liabilities—can shine through. For these reasons, in this book I focus on conflict and war as it is here that we might expect cognitive biases to be especially important and influential.

FIGURE 1.1. Napoleon crossing the Alps. According to Clausewitz, Napoleon was "the personification of military genius," whose strategic instincts made him one of the most successful and revered military leaders of all time. *Source:* Jacques-Louis David, *Napoleon at the Saint-Bernhard Pass*, 1801, Belvedere, Wien, Inv.-Nr. 2089 © Belvedere, Wien.

Error Management Theory: Making the Right Mistakes

One can see that biases sometimes steer us in a favorable direction, but why is a bias better than accuracy—seeing the situation for what it is and letting Dr. Spock act accordingly? One important answer has come to be known as error management theory (EMT). EMT suggests that wherever the costs of false positive and false negative errors are asymmetric (that is, one is more harmful than the other), the best decision-making strategy is a bias to avoid whichever is the more costly error—literally pushing the decision-making mechanism or organism away from that outcome, even if doing so causes it to make more (of the less costly) errors in the other direction. Applied to the case of *human* decision-making, the argument is that if false positive and false negative errors in a given domain have been asymmetric over evolutionary history, we should expect natural selection to have favored a cognitive bias that avoids the more costly error.[36] For example, we often think a stick is a snake (which is harmless), but we do not tend to think snakes are sticks (which is potentially deadly)—a highly adaptive bias. The underlying logic of EMT has in fact been identified in several different fields (including signal detection theory, engineering, and medicine), applies across a range of decision-making contexts, and can explain a number of cognitive biases.[37] The reason it works so well as a simple but powerful phenomenon comes down to the balancing of false positive and false negative errors in conditions of decision-making under uncertainty. Let's unpack the logic below.

Good decision-making does not have to be perfect. Indeed, it cannot be. A person or device that attempted to make perfect decisions in every instance would require too much information and be too slow to be useful for most practical purposes—in fact, it might never reach a decision at all. Moreover, under conditions of uncertainty, even a "perfect" decision-making process would still sometimes make mistakes, because even a good decision can be caught out by a change in the environment or the intervention of some other factor that remains unaccounted for. Rather, in order to perform well on average, over time, a decision-making mechanism just has to make sure that mistakes, which will inevitably be made (whether few or numerous), are not too costly. Now here's the interesting bit.

If costs are *asymmetric*—that is, mistakes in one direction (e.g., underestimation) tend to be more costly than mistakes in the other direction (e.g., overestimation)—then avoiding the most costly error is much more important than simply avoiding any errors at all. Since mistakes will be made, the challenge is to minimize the *costs* of those mistakes overall, regardless of their number. The solution, as human engineers and natural selection have independently hit upon, is to *build in biases* that steer us away from making the worst possible errors—even if that requires shifting our perceived target above or below its true position. This fundamental logic can be demonstrated with simple mathematics and explains why a biased decision-making mechanism can outperform an unbiased one.[38]

A classic example is fire alarms. When we set the sensitivity of a fire alarm, it is better to err on the side of caution because the costs of a false alarm are negligible (however annoying it may seem at the time), whereas the costs of being burned to death in a real fire are great indeed. One should thus bias the fire alarm to go off a bit "too often." Whenever the true probability of some event—such as the detection of a fire or a threat—is uncertain (and thus cannot be precisely predicted), a biased decision rule can be better than an unbiased one if we are to avoid the more dangerous error. An *unbiased* decision rule targeting the true probability of the event will make both false positive and false negative errors—it will have some false alarms, and it will fail to go off in some real fires. This is far more costly than a *biased* decision rule that generates more false positive errors and fewer false negative errors—this rule will lead to more false alarms, but more importantly it will rarely fail to go off in real fires.[39]

However, this argument is not sufficient on its own. While the biased individual or machine may enjoy an advantage, why would unbiased, rational actors *carry on* being unbiased if they self-evidently keep making costly mistakes? Given their experience, would they not adjust their calculations and change their strategy accordingly to reduce the danger? In nature, organisms that made such mistakes would be selected against and those that made fewer costly errors would evolve and spread. Similarly, over time, rational actors in a modern setting can learn from information and experience and update their decision-making strategies to match, building uncertainty and asymmetric costs into their calculations and, with those empirical measures to hand, work out the right balance of false positive and false negative errors to maximize net benefits on average. Psychologist Ryan McKay and philosopher Daniel Dennett called this having "cautious action policies."[40] For example, we are "biased" to look before crossing the street not because we have an irrational fear of cars but because the costs of failing to check if one is coming are evidently severe. We understand this intuitively and adjust our behavior accordingly—often taking considerable time to look even when no cars are remotely close. One could call this a "bias," but it is perfectly rational.[41]

To understand why we need a *cognitive bias*—a *distortion* of objective reality that shifts our assessments away from rational calculation—we need to look to the constraints of the human brain as a decision-making machine. Decision-making depends on an array of complex inputs and processes, and human brains are not able to keep track of the whole barrage of data on the probabilities, benefits, and costs of numerous false positive and false negative errors over time (we may not even perceive that there are errors, or the cause and effect of those errors, when they occur). This means that humans are not always able to achieve so-called Bayesian updating about the likelihood and outcomes of different events in the real world, as the rational choice argument requires. Even if we were able to take in and integrate all this information, we would still have to learn and accumulate these data through experience, which itself is a long and costly process of trial and error—and in some situations, a single mistake in a novel situation would be dangerous or even lethal. Learning what to do would be too late. In short, perfect rational decision-making is a good idea but an impossible feat for real humans. This is why we are born with biases already built in. Nobel Laureates Daniel Kahneman and Amos Tversky concluded, from their many years of empirical experiments, that humans are "not Bayesian at all."[42]

Instead, therefore, biological organisms adopted cognitive biases rather than relying on conscious calculation.[43] The reasons can be summarized as follows: (1) *speed*—cognitive biases lead to more rapid responses than the grinding demands of "expected utility" calculations central to rational choice; (2) *efficiency*—cognitive biases are likely to have been biologically cheaper to produce, as well as more effective; (3) *evolvability*—cognitive biases are likely to have been more readily available due to preexisting cognitive machinery; and (4) the "*adaptive landscape*"—cognitive biases may have been a small step up the slope of a local optimum in biological fitness (a "fitness peak," in the parlance of evolutionary biology), even if a better solution lay across a "valley" that natural selection could not cross.

Natural selection, in other words, seems to have favored cognitive *biases* as an efficient and effective solution to decision-making problems, circumventing the complex calculations needed for optimal decisions based on expected utility. In many cases, these heuristics are just as good, and indeed sometimes better or faster.[44] In effect, natural selection was "doing" the expected utility calculations, favoring whatever strategies best promoted survival and reproduction over many generations (amid all the other various constraints and opportunities). Over evolutionary time, natural selection gave rise to biases that, on average, helped solve various categories of decision-making problems without humans having to try to do so on the spot each time, with limited information, processing power, and time. We'd program a robot to do the same thing—just as we do, for example, with fire alarms.

An example in the realm of cognition is that humans—and monkeys, in fact—have a bias to overestimate the speed of approaching objects.[45] This makes good sense because it means we take evasive action well *before* an object or predator reaches us, which is of course an adaptive bias: the costs of avoidance too soon are small, but the costs of avoidance too late can be lethal. This is why, although cognitive biases violate modern *economic* conceptions of rationality, such heuristics are *evolutionarily* rational.[46] As Doug Kenrick and Vlad Griskevicius put it, "Being accurate is not always smart."[47]

To summarize, cognitive biases can outperform rational choice because in real life there are significant informational, computational, and biological constraints on decision-making: namely error management, speed, efficiency, evolvability, and the availability of options in the adaptive landscape. This is why humans (and indeed other animals) have evolved heuristics and biases. They were favored by natural selection because they work well—not perfectly, but well enough and often better than the alternatives, helping us avoid the worst possible errors that arise in decision-making under uncertainty. This gives us a very different perspective on biases from the standpoint of evolutionary biology as compared to that of social science. Biases are not decision-making "problems." Far from it. They are elegant *solutions* to decision-making problems.

How Biased Should We Be? Crazy Leaders and Crazy States

An extreme version of the idea that human quirks can be functional is the notion that utility can come not just from emotions or biases characteristic of all human beings but from mental *disorders*. These represent much more radical departures from rational choice. For example, psychiatrist Nassir Ghaemi argues that among political leaders, mental illness is not only common but actually can be advantageous—particularly in times of crisis. When leaders are in unusual environments and facing difficult challenges (compared to politics in ordinary times), specific disorders may help them reach effective decisions. For example, people suffering from depression tend to ruminate more on complex problems, and those who experience mania may find it helps them push through difficult times. He goes so far as to say that, in times of crisis, "we are better off being led by mentally ill leaders than by mentally normal ones."[48] Whether psychological disorders could actually help us is obviously a controversial claim. But from an empirical standpoint, other authors have found that mental illness itself certainly seems to be overrepresented among political leaders compared to the population at large, which begs an explanation.[49] It is hard to tell whether this is because those with mental illness are more likely to seek, win, or survive in office or because office itself generates mental illness.[50] It may be a combination of all of these things. But whatever the reason, it seems to be no coincidence. Psychiatrist Arnold Ludwig also suggested that "certain kinds of 'mental disorders', under certain circumstances, actually may be adaptive," pointing out that if this is the case, the moniker "disorders" may be mistaken.[51] The triumph or tragedy of mentally ill leaders is likely to depend on the form of government, of course, and their unusual and often charismatic traits might merely serve to attract support or votes (or crush opposition) and increase the likelihood of political survival rather than genuine success for the nation. But even there, Ludwig notes, "in the field of politics, if your criteria for adaptive behavior is doing what keeps you alive, then the proof is in the pudding."[52] He suggests that even the delusional paranoia of Joseph Stalin, Mao Zedong, and Saddam Hussein probably helped them stay alive, whereas one could say that Abraham Lincoln, Mahatma Gandhi, and John F. Kennedy "were not 'paranoid' enough."[53]

Of course, there are other factors—besides psychology—that may make otherwise rational states act in a non-rational manner, such as a lack of (or bad) information, organizational pathologies, multiple actors generating conflicting policy goals, or rapidly shifting situations that mean policies are out of sync with what is required.[54] But sometimes states appear to be irrational by design rather than by accident. Yehezkel Dror's book *Crazy States* begins with the observation that it is "a source of surprise and amazement that the possibilities of crazy states are nearly completely neglected in contemporary strategic thinking."[55] The field, he points out, has tended to focus exclusively on how one should deal with *rational* states. But what if other states and their leaders are not rational? He offers a classification scheme for states to be considered "crazy" if they score highly on dimensions of ambition, commitment, risk seeking, lack of means-end logic, inflexibility, and deviation from norms of behavior.[56] Even if rare, he stresses, when "crazy states" arise—like Nazi Germany—they can be exceptionally important.

The problem at issue is not just the difficulty of predicting the behavior of such states but designing strategies to deal with them. Dror suggests that since crazy states will not be influenced by the usual methods of diplomacy and deterrence, unusual measures are required instead, such as interference with their internal government, political assassination, or military intervention. Of course, "normal" states may have many good reasons to be unwilling or unable to adopt such measures. So much so, indeed, that concessions to crazy states may be necessary if confronting them with conventional means is costly and unlikely to be successful anyway. And that means the crazy state wins.

I would go further to suggest that international relations needs to explore not only *other* "crazy" states but also non-rational aspects of our *own*, Western democratic governments. While it is typically dictatorships, rogue states, or violent non-state groups that are seen as irrational and dangerous, we might not be as rational as we like to think either. We have little reason to expect human beings—irrespective of nation—to act as rational actors. In fact, we have copious evidence to the contrary. But we have almost no evidence on whether this is a good thing or a bad thing (we have only looked at instances of the latter). Like other scholarship in the field, Dror sees non-rationality as a detrimental aspect of international politics. Yet his own conclusions suggest that there are significant benefits for crazy nations. If they are crazy enough, there are situations in which other states may have little choice than to bend to their demands. Craziness may thus lend terrific strategic advantages, extending a state's power beyond its mere military or economic capabilities and allowing it to punch significantly above its weight. Perhaps, therefore, we *should* be a little crazy. As Dr. Seuss once observed, "To live on Earth you don't have to be crazy, but it helps." Natural selection seems to have discovered this long ago in the evolution of one mild form of craziness: cognitive biases.

We may remain skeptical that mental *disorders* are useful, or that crazy states are a good model to follow, but what this chapter shows is that there are many theoretical reasons and empirical examples to suggest that non-rational factors can be useful in decision-making and performance—even significant irrationality. In the context of this growing trend in adaptive thinking, this book is therefore not as bizarre as it may seem. All I am arguing is that the fairly subtle dispositions of cognitive biases *that all mentally healthy people tend to have as human beings* may be useful rather than detrimental. After all, having evolved amid the rigors of natural selection, they are likely to be there for a reason.[57]

The Adaptive Advantages of Cognitive Biases

Although cognitive biases have become widely invoked variables for understanding international politics, we do not have a solid theoretical foundation for their origins, causes, or sources of variation.[58] They are just there—empirical facts without good explanation. Most surprising of all, we do not even know when they are good or bad in today's world, and few have even asked the question. This is where evolutionary psychology can help. While evolutionary psychology offers many possible insights for politics and international relations, this book focuses on just one, but perhaps one of the most important, and certainly one that has been significantly overlooked: the possibility that there are adaptive, strategic *advantages* of cognitive biases.

Cognitive biases—such as overconfidence, the fundamental attribution error, and in-group/out-group bias—are well-established psychological phenomena that apply to all mentally healthy adults. However, different disciplines see them very differently. Cognitive biases are generally seen by political scientists as cognitive *limitations* or *mistakes* that undermine national interests, produce inefficiency or waste, prevent rational negotiation, inflame prejudice, and cause policy failures, disasters, and wars. By contrast, evolutionary psychologists see exactly the same biases as *adaptive solutions* to specific challenges in our evolutionary history. They are therefore far from "mistakes" but rather *context-specific problem-solving strategies* that promote effective behavior. In short, they are there to help us.

It is hardly surprising that they often *look* like mistakes when they lead us astray in the modern world—human physiological and psychological traits evolved to deal with the adaptive problems of our evolutionary past, not with the often very different kinds and scale of problems that we experience today, especially in international politics.[59] The human lineage spent 99 percent of its history in a Pleistocene environment of small groups of hunter-gatherers and only 1 percent in the post-agricultural environment of large, urbanized societies with sophisticated technologies. As a result, we should not necessarily expect evolved cognitive mechanisms to trigger in appropriate circumstances or to cause their intended effects. Even when they *are* triggered by an appropriate stimulus (that is, an evolutionarily relevant one), in modern settings this may nevertheless cause inappropriate or costly outcomes. Our penchant for sugar, salt, and fat is one prominent example—an evolved disposition that

FIGURE 1.2. A "caveman" with fast food captures the idea of "evolutionary mismatch," in which evolved dispositions lead us into detrimental behavior in novel environments. *Source:* Courtesy of Simon Woodcock / Alamy Stock Photo and Pest Control Office, Banksy, Los Angeles, 2008.

was highly adaptive when these commodities were rare in our evolutionary past, but in today's world of plentiful junk food the same disposition contributes to heart disease and diabetes, which kill half a million Americans a year (see Figure 1.2 for a striking image that drives home the point).[60]

The crux of the matter is this: *whether our Pleistocene brains generate positive or negative outcomes depends on the context.* Sometimes our evolved dispositions will lead us into disaster (usually because of some *novel* situation encountered in the modern world), and sometimes they will help us (often because of some *similar* situation encountered in the modern world). If a modern scenario resembles one that was common in the past (e.g., cooperation or conflict between people), then our evolved cognitive mechanisms should work just as well. If a modern scenario differs from those of the past (e.g., stock market trading using complex algorithms or fighting wars with drones), then our evolved cognitive mechanisms are more likely to suffer from mismatch and cause problems. So what *are* the conditions conducive to our evolved decision-making mechanisms having *positive* outcomes? An evolutionary psychological approach offers a systematic scientific framework to address this problem and generates a set of empirical questions that can be explored for any particular bias of interest:

- What was the original adaptive problem the cognitive bias was "designed" by evolution to solve?
- What are its biological causes (i.e., what are the social and physical stimuli, biochemistry, and neurological processes that elicit it)?
- What are the conditions under which it becomes more or less likely to be triggered or strong (i.e., what are its sources of variation)?
- When does this mechanism "misfire" in modern circumstances and cause mistakes and detrimental behavior?
- When does this mechanism correctly "fire" in modern circumstances and bring utility and strategic advantages?

At minimum, an evolutionary perspective will challenge existing approaches, question our assumptions, and ask new questions. At best, an evolutionary approach offers a theoretical foundation for understanding cognitive biases and their positive and negative effects, generates novel predictions, and ultimately suggests practical new interventions to help resolve conflicts, increase security, and improve strategic decision-making. Many significant problems in international relations may best be solved not by suppressing our cognitive biases but rather by channeling their adaptive features to useful ends— whether among leaders, diplomats, bureaucrats, soldiers, or citizens. Soon we will begin to explore exactly what those adaptive features of cognitive biases are, starting with the pervasive bias of overconfidence. But first, in chapter 2, let us take a step back to ask why and how international relations would benefit from an evolutionary approach at all.

CHAPTER TWO

The Evolution of an Idea

POLITICS IN THE AGE OF BIOLOGY

*The social scientist's wager is that socially produced meaning—be that
in the form of culturally specific interest maximisation, republicanism,
apotheosis or whatever—is so strong among humans as to be the decisive
force in human life. In that, we are unique until further notice.*

—IVER NEUMANN

*We are not here concerned with hopes or fears, only with the truth as far as
our reason permits us to discover it.*

—CHARLES DARWIN

ACCORDING TO MANY COMMENTATORS, we have now entered an "Age
of Biology."[1] By virtue of major breakthroughs in evolutionary biology, genetics, medicine, biotechnology, neuroscience, and numerous other fields, we
are witnessing a dramatic flourishing of the biological sciences. With the
human genome mapped, DNA fingerprinting and brain imaging becoming
ever easier, powerful new experimental and computational techniques, and
rising mountains of data, the future holds huge promise not only for understanding and exploiting biological phenomena themselves but also for applying these methods and insights to examine problems in the *social* as well as
the natural sciences. A biological approach is also powerful because it is unified under a single theoretical framework—evolution—which explains the origins, diversity, and adaptations of all life on Earth, including of course human
adaptations.

Investment, jobs, grants, and students are pouring into life science departments and the biotech industry like never before, while the humanities and
social sciences often find themselves under threat compared to STEM subjects (science, technology, engineering, and mathematics).[2] The upside new

challenge is the enormous potential for cross-disciplinary research that E. O. Wilson called "consilience."[3] Social scientists can seize the opportunity to ride the wave of scientific advances in understanding and methodology, looking at old questions from a new perspective. Interdisciplinary, rather than competing, fields of expertise promise to yield magnificent advances in understanding.[4]

The range of biological insights for social sciences in general and political science in particular is vast. For example, recent work finds that the genes we carry influence our ideology and voting behavior,[5] that our physiological reactions to events reflect our ideological leanings,[6] that psychological differences underlie moral intuitions,[7] and that neurological activity in different parts of the brain alters our judgment and decision-making.[8] Such findings challenge the view that humans are "blank slates," affected only by nurture and not by nature and, moreover, demonstrate that biology not only provides novel *insights* into political phenomena but also improves our ability to *predict* them empirically.[9]

This might seem like uncharted territory for political science and international relations, but it should not. The theory and practice of domestic and international politics are at root largely *about* human nature—the characteristics and behavior of the actors under study. Human nature has played a central role in the development of political theory and international relations theory. This was true for Plato and all the great political theorists since, from Thomas Hobbes and Jean-Jacques Rousseau to Immanuel Kant and Hans Morgenthau. Political scientists have always really been studying human beings, as well as the ideas and institutions that humans create. Are humans fundamentally self-interested or moralistic? Are they rational or emotional? Cooperative or conflictual? Or what mixture of these traits makes up human nature? And how do humans interact with each other as individuals and groups? In recent decades, such fundamental questions about human nature have faded in the everyday study of international politics, in favor of theories of rational choice, social norms, international institutions, and the structure of the international system. But any major new theory that comes along has to tackle the question of human nature, just as Kenneth Waltz, Robert Keohane, and Alexander Wendt had to do in developing their theories of international politics—even if they ultimately reject it as being that important.[10] The message of this book is that, whether we like it or not, mounting scientific evidence forces us to rethink our assumptions about human nature that underlie theories of international relations.

These developments go well beyond mere speculation on the *origins* of human behavior. Political science aspires to *explain and predict political events*. Explanation and prediction in the social sciences have already been hugely advanced by scientific *methods*—in the form of statistics, modeling, computational techniques, experimental methods, data collection technologies, and so on. But they have also been advanced by insights from scientific *studies* of human beings—experimental psychology and behavioral economics in particular. Typically, political psychologists draw from the psychology literature to generate hypotheses about how established psychological phenomena play out in the political domain. Political psychology has been very successful at coming up with plausible explanations for why and when decision-makers, citizens, and voters did certain things and not others, filling important lacunae in our understanding that rational choice fails to explain. Despite this success, psychological approaches struggle to compete with mainstream theories of international relations. Indeed, major theories of international relations generally ignore and often explicitly reject the role of psychology (or even the influence of individuals at all), despite making implicit if not explicit assumptions about human nature, avoiding the vagaries of the human mind in favor of the more tangible role of power, economics, or institutions.[11] Political psychology occupies the margins, building a literature of powerful but often disregarded ideas that merely serve to address gaps in more dominant theories such as neorealism or neoliberalism.[12] Even if the role of psychology in political science is gradually gaining acceptance for its empirical insights, however, it lacks a cohesive theoretical framework for *why* people behave the way they do. If things stay this way, psychological approaches will never be mainstream—they will never generate their own theory of international relations. For many scholars and approaches, the quirks of *Homo sapiens* will remain an awkward puzzle to be glossed over in favor of parsimony.

Bringing Psychology into the Core of the Discipline

This book suggests that such a state of affairs has arisen because political psychology lacks a scientific grounding or overarching scientific framework.[13] Although it rests on the impressive scaffolding of mainstream psychology, with its numerous theories, rigorous experiments, and insights, psychology itself does not explain where human dispositions come from in the first place or what they were originally for.[14] Similarly, most work in political psychology derives explanations and predictions from information on *how* people behave empirically, without too much attention paid to *why*. Without a scientific grounding for the long list of quirks of human nature, why should we take them too seriously? Perhaps they are just a jumble of empirical findings without any systematic rhyme or reason.

To understand the origins and functions of cognitive biases, and to understand the selective pressures that shaped the brain in the first place, we must turn to evolutionary biology. Psychologists often explain the existence of dispositions as being "psychologically adaptive," in the sense that they offer people a sense of control, cognitive mastery, or comfort.[15] But this is no explanation for why a given trait would have emerged, survived, or spread under the rigors of natural selection. It also leaves open the question of whether psychological phenomena originate from nature or nurture. Without any theory of their origins, cognitive biases often seem to remain random idiosyncrasies of the human mind—a mix of instinct, experience, and culture, which are interesting but hard to fathom.[16] As long as we lack a holistic explanation of human dispositions grounded in some scientific logic, political psychology rarely can, or rarely even attempts to, challenge core theories of international relations. Empirical regularities on their own are not enough to build a comprehensive theory of human nature, let alone of politics and international relations. Yet, since assumptions about human nature underlie numerous theories of politics and international relations, it is time that these theories were challenged from the perspective of the life sciences.

Evolutionary biology offers a powerful alternative approach here, because as well as explaining and predicting human behavior (like psychology and political psychology), it *does* have a holistic theory for the origins and functions of psychological phenomena. An evolutionary perspective generates hypotheses for why and how a given psychological trait—just as with physiological traits—increased survival and reproduction in the course of human evolutionary history. It also offers an account of what the biological and social triggers were for a given trait, the contexts in which that trait is adaptive, and the sources of variation that increase or decrease the levels of the trait expressed. In short, the argument is that psychological dispositions evolved as features of the human brain because they increased survival and reproductive success over the course of human evolutionary history and were therefore favored by natural selection. Not all psychological (or even physiological) traits are necessarily adaptive, but the evolutionary approach suggests that most are, and this is a good starting assumption that can then be tested.[17] It is this evolutionary perspective, I argue, that is essential to understanding and predicting the influence of human psychology on politics and international relations. Only with an evolutionary lens can we gain a full understanding of the origins, functions, and design features of human psychological traits. Without it, they are hard to make sense of at all. As Jim Sidanius and Rob Kurzban prompted political psychologists, "Trying to understand humans and their interactions with other humans without the benefits of adaptationist thinking is an unnecessary handicap."[18]

Evolutionary psychology is already revealing huge implications for domestic and international politics.[19] A growing body of research has demonstrated the significance of evolved dispositions for a range of political phenomena, including the causes and consequences of cooperation,[20] democracy,[21] ideology,[22] voting preferences,[23] public opinion,[24] revolutions,[25] ethnic conflict,[26] terrorism,[27] decision-making,[28] strategy,[29] leadership,[30] causes of war,[31] territoriality,[32] military effectiveness,[33] and war termination.[34] Despite the range and importance of these insights—and in such central phenomena for the field—the human brain rarely attracts much attention in political science and international relations, and even less attention is given to the all-important perspective of the brain's evolutionary legacy.

This situation is odd. As evolutionary anthropologist David Sloan Wilson observed, "Economic or social policy that ignores the way we are as a species and how cooperation evolves in all species is no more likely to succeed than an architect who ignores the laws of physics."[35] In a similar way, political scientists typically try to understand international relations, crises, and war without any understanding of the mechanics of the human brain. Of course, complex phenomena can sometimes be usefully modeled without needing to understand all the details of the component parts (leaving them as "black boxes"),[36] but our theories and empirical tests are far better when we *do* understand such details (leaving no, or fewer, black boxes). Political science and international relations are well poised to explore and consider what new work on human cognition in the Age of Biology means for the many cherished theories that currently ignore it.[37] At least this way we can identify which assumptions in the field remain solid and which are empirically or theoretically challenged. Given the fantastic recent advances in evolutionary biology, genetics, neuroscience, and psychology, treating the human brain as a black box is no longer necessary, justified, or defensible. On the contrary, major new insights await.

Do Individuals Matter? Resistance to Psychological Approaches in Explaining State Behavior

One immediate challenge is whether biases developed among individuals in our evolutionary past extrapolate to the behavior of states in the modern world. There are two embedded questions here: (1) Do biases at the *individual* level apply to decision-making at the *state* level, which is made in the context of groups and bureaucracies? (2) Do adaptations that evolved in the *past* continue to affect modern judgment and decision-making *today*? Let us deal with the former first and move on to the question of evolutionary legacy in the next section.

Any theory of international relations that invokes individuals as causal actors raises the question of whether *individual* behavior can tell us anything about *state* behavior. Therefore, this first question is not a criticism of an evolutionary approach per se but a criticism of *any* theory that argues that individuals play a role in how states behave (whether from the perspective of public opinion, electoral politics, political leaders' decision-making, leadership style, personality, psychological characteristics, neuroscience, or whatever). All such theories have to consider how individual-level variables affect the decision-making and behavior of the larger state apparatus.

The notion that individuals *can* matter—at least in theory—is strongly supported by the presence of government itself. After all, the whole point of government is to control or encourage the input of multiple voices and to establish checks and balances so that considered and collective decisions can prevail *despite* individual preferences and biases that can be so strong. When power is concentrated in a dictator, subject to the will and whim of an individual, states can easily be led into disaster and ruin, as the Greeks and Romans discovered long ago. In modern democracies today, no individual is allowed such power. Decisions take time, and are made by groups. So even where psychology is an important explanation of a given individual's preferences and behavior, it is not necessarily an important explanation of the grinding machinery of the state in which those individuals have become but a small cog. What room is there, therefore, for individuals and psychology to affect political outcomes? There are several well-trodden answers to this.

First, in democracies the preferences and biases of individual citizens are, at least to a degree, represented in the political manifestos and political leaders elected to office—and the extent to which they are tolerated or supported within it. Those underlying citizens' preferences and biases may thus also percolate through into the goals of the state, if slowly and imperfectly.[38]

Second, bureaucracies, organizations, and governments themselves are designed, run, and led by human beings, whose own dispositions influence how they function. To the extent that those institutions dampen leaders' own policy preferences, therefore, they do so via the manifestation of a complex of other individuals' preferences and biases.[39]

Third, state leaders are still the actors who make important strategic decisions from among a set of policy options—albeit in consultation with a group of advisors. Those actors, where the buck stops and with whom the responsibility for making decisions ultimately resides, are potentially affected by their own dispositions (as indeed are their advisors and the advice given, of course), which in turn influence which options are considered and presented, and which decisions are taken and which are not.[40]

Fourth, while group decision-making is widely lauded as more inclusive and reasoned, research has shown that group processes can, in themselves, introduce or amplify the influence of cognitive biases (a phenomenon sometimes referred to as "groupthink"). Group decision-making can therefore increase the influence of individual cognitive biases rather than decrease them.[41]

Fifth, since cognitive biases are contextually dependent, they are often shared by multiple individuals at once (for the same externally or environmentally induced reason that affects all actors in a similar way). This would sustain or reinforce the bias, even if there is variation among individuals and even if decision-making is done collectively by a group.[42]

Sixth, even in democracies, if individual leaders have a special or direct influence on state decision-making (such as strong or authoritarian leaders whose personal judgments and decision-making are made independently or against broader advice or opinion), then their cognitive biases will have special influence on state behavior as well. These biases may even gradually become built into the institutions and personnel of government—leaders firing detractors and surrounding themselves with "yes men," for example.[43]

Seventh, although we might expect the apparatus of the state to make careful and reasoned decisions over such important matters as foreign policy, in crises and war there is often little time for careful information gathering, deliberation, and exhaustively exploring options. It is precisely in high-stakes, fast-moving situations demanding prompt action that our intuitive thinking comes to the fore. Leaders in crises and war can, therefore, be *more* prone to cognitive biases than the average person or the average situation and thus a greater influence on state behavior.[44]

Eighth, it may be the case that biases are actually accentuated among leaders, not due to the situation but due to the office itself. Given the strong selection pressures on positions of leadership—filtering out only those who try hard to attain office in the first place, manage to succeed in winning it, and then are able to survive in high-pressure positions of power—biases that help leaders survive the ruthless profession of politics itself may be *overrepresented* among such individuals, compared to the public, and perhaps especially in wartime. The British public embraced Winston Churchill during the dark days of World War II, but despite his success they voted him out once peace had returned—possibly precisely because of psychological dispositions that made him suited to wartime rather than politics as usual.[45] Experiments suggest the effect may be quite a general one. In scenarios of hardship or struggle, people prefer stronger, more hawkish leaders.[46] Even if leaders are not particularly biased when they seek or reach office, the attainment of power itself appears to increase leaders' tendency to rely on their own judgment and their belief in their own efficacy.[47] Once leaders are in power, therefore, their biases can become magnified and increasingly influential.

In combination, these factors make any cognitive bias acting at the individual level an important ingredient of state behavior. Beyond political leaders at the top of the hierarchy, we can expect similar effects among the "middle managers" who actually conduct the day-to-day business of politics, diplomacy, and war. In fast-moving, high-stakes interactions in competition with rivals, we are similarly at the mercy of the individual traits of civil servants, negotiators, commanders, and soldiers.

Clearly, numerous factors affect the behavior of states, including bureaucracies, organizational processes, types of government, parliaments, culture, international institutions, and the international system itself. Even so, as theories of international politics have recognized from the time of Thucydides, humans affect state behavior as well.[48] Psychological variables are not mutually exclusive of other important influences on state behavior, such as power or domestic politics. Rather, they add additional explanatory leverage over and above that provided by other levels of analysis. While the debate about the importance of individuals will no doubt continue at the theoretical level, there is an enormous literature in international relations demonstrating that, empirically, individuals do matter a great deal in making and shaping international politics.[49] And this is not even to mention the central importance of individuals that is already well recognized in other fields such as history, sociology, psychiatry, psychology, and military history.

Does Biology Matter? Resistance to Evolutionary Approaches in Explaining State Behavior

As we have seen, the application of psychology to international relations has had its own obstacles and critics. But the application of *evolutionary* psychology raises even greater hackles, because on top of the mere "levels of analysis" concern about whether psychological variables are a causal factor in state behavior, the idea that biology underlies these psychological variables directly challenges deeply held theoretical assumptions and approaches in the field. Biology has not failed to break into political science purely because of ignorance, although that is one factor. It has also failed to break in because of active resistance—not only do many people not *know* about it, but many don't *like* it.

At one end of the theoretical spectrum, part of the resistance to biological accounts of human behavior in international politics stems from the focus on the *structure* of the international system, rather than its component parts (whether governments or individuals). In some forms of realist international relations theory, for example, states can be likened to billiard balls that shift only in reaction to the movements of other states in the international system. Consequently, any characteristics of particular states themselves, let alone the individual human beings within them (as discussed in the previous section), are ignored.[50] The originator of this influential theory, Kenneth Waltz, explicitly considered individual-level explanations for international politics. Arguing that all states will ultimately "socialize" to respond in a similar way to the universal pressures of the international system, and that the behavioral traits of human nature are "fixed" (which any biologist will tell you is patently false), he concluded that individual behavior cannot satisfactorily explain variation in political outcomes, such as peace and war.[51] In so doing, this "first image" explanation of international relations became tainted, or at least subordinated, for generations of international relations scholars to come.

Another part of the resistance to biological accounts of political behavior stems from the dominance of rational choice theory—the idea that humans accurately weigh up the expected costs and benefits of available options and their probabilities of success, and then select the one that is expected to produce the highest utility.[52] Under such an assumption, even theories that do consider individual decision-making merely assume that the decisions these individuals take are mechanical calculations, with consistent and predictable outcomes. Decades of work in psychology has, of course, shown the rational

choice paradigm to be a poor descriptor of human behavior. Yet, both economics and political science have been loath to discard the clean rational choice
paradigm for the messier and more complex reality of human nature.[53]

At the opposite end of the theoretical spectrum, other political scientists
are resistant to the role of evolution in human behavior not because they see
it as irrelevant but because evolutionary psychology challenges a deeply held
"blank slate" view of human nature.[54] This is the idea that humans are born
with no predetermined preferences or dispositions, and thus that it is purely
culture that shapes people's thinking and behavior (100 percent nurture and
no nature). As Iver Neumann put it in the quote that opens this chapter,
"socially produced meaning" is seen as "the decisive force in human life."[55]
Consequently, so the argument goes, culture underlies all variation in political
phenomena. This view of human nature is simply wrong, given our knowledge of genetics, physiology, cognitive psychology, and neuroscience. It has
nevertheless continued to be taught to generations of social science students,
who are then in danger of being brainwashed to reject scientific approaches
out of hand. Over the years I have been repeatedly surprised by the numerous
faculty and graduate and undergraduate students who are clearly *ideologi-
cally* opposed to evolutionary approaches to human behavior, irrespective of
facts or evidence. They assume that the application of evolutionary ideas to
human affairs—and especially politics—is misguided and leads to dangerous
or immoral "justifications" for behavior. The social sciences were evidently
scarred by the experience of the "sociobiology" debate of the 1970s and have
tended to reject evolutionary approaches to human behavior ever since, even
though half a century later the theoretical and empirical science has advanced
almost unrecognizably.[56] Such a mind-set renders people not only unwilling
but often unable to even entertain such an approach, let alone study it and
compare its merits with rival theories. Their training has burned into them
the idea that evolutionary explanations of human behavior are fundamentally
flawed, hopelessly deterministic, or morally reproachable. Such views may
come to represent a lost generation of social science—scholarship left behind
because it fought science as an enemy rather than engaging with it as an interdisciplinary endeavor and pursuing the consilience of knowledge.

This situation is changing, however. Across the social sciences, many
researchers *are* seeing the utility of, or at least the need for, new approaches
to social phenomena. Political science is perhaps particularly primed to benefit. Since the end of the Cold War, the rise of non-state actors, transnational
movements, ethnic conflict, civil wars, terrorism, rogue states, populist politics, and influential leaders has led to dissatisfaction with many social science
models that previously held sway in political science.[57] In their place, there are
signs of a resurgence of interest in the role of behavioral sciences and human
nature.[58] Modern scientific methods combined with the explanatory power of
evolutionary theory promise to shed new light on many puzzles and problems

in politics and international relations.[59] They clearly offer something new and important to understand and explore. So what *does* evolution tell us about human behavior?

An Evolutionary Approach: New Insights for Old Questions

Evolutionary psychology is based on the premise that the human brain was fashioned by natural selection over many millennia among small-scale foraging societies.[60] As a result, intuitive judgment and decision-making mechanisms are the result of selection pressures we experienced in our evolutionary *past*, not in recent times. In today's environment, many of these mechanisms look *biased* by the standards of rational choice or other models of good decision-making.[61] However, since they were designed to deal with a very different social and physical environment, it is no surprise that they may sometimes lead to counterproductive beliefs and behavior in contemporary situations.[62] Not only does evolutionary psychology help account for why these biases occur in the first place, it also helps identify the conditions under which these biases will arise, when and where they will go wrong, and, as I argue in this book, when and where they will "go right."[63]

It is important to emphasize that mistakes are to be expected (even in the environment in which the trait evolved), because as we saw in chapter 1 it is rarely possible to design a decision-making algorithm that makes exactly the right decision in every instance, especially for complex choices made under uncertainty and with limited information and time. But we might expect *more* mistakes in the modern world than in the environment of our past, because today's world is so different from that in which our behavioral strategies evolved. Social scales, technology, and complex institutional structures mean it is far more common today for judgment and decision-making mechanisms to be triggered in inappropriate contexts and cause suboptimal outcomes.

Even so, we must remember that the apparent ubiquity of mistakes can be overplayed. First, biases may bring *net gains* over the long term, even if they cause mistakes along the way, which are often more conspicuous (so we need to look at their overall effects across a large sample of instances).[64] Second, they may bring benefits in the *real world*, even if they look foolish in the laboratory (so we need to look at them in their naturalistic context).[65] Third, they may in fact be important to *achieving* success when successes occur, in addition to any role they may play in detrimental outcomes (so we need to look at both positive and negative impacts). The problem is that biases are often studied in isolation, in the lab, and in making mistakes. Even when successes are studied, people rarely search for cognitive *biases* to explain them, since there was no "error" or failure to explain. They look instead for the careful, rational decisions that are assumed to generate such good outcomes. If we did look

Table 2.1. Physiological or psychological traits of any organism can be "adaptive," "maladaptive," "exaptive," or "side effects," given their past and present effects on biological fitness (as measured by survival and reproductive success)

		Fitness Benefits Today?	
		Yes	No
Fitness Benefits in the Evolutionary Past?	Yes	Adaptive (*e.g., hunger*)	Maladaptive (*e.g., sweet tooth*)
	No	Exaptive (*e.g., wings*)	Side effect (*e.g., white bones*)

over a longer period of time, in the field, and at all outcomes—as evolutionary biologists and evolutionary anthropologists do in their research paradigms—we might find the intuitive dispositions of human nature at work in our many successes as well as in our failures.[66] It therefore remains an empirical question whether, in today's world, cognitive biases remain "adaptive" or have become "maladaptive"—crucial terms of distinction that I outline in the next section.

ADAPTIVE VERSUS MALADAPTIVE BEHAVIOR

To avoid confusion in the application of evolutionary theory, it is essential to distinguish between "adaptive" and "maladaptive" behavior (see Table 2.1). For evolutionary biologists, the costs and benefits of a given "trait" (a physiological or psychological feature of an organism) are measured in "Darwinian fitness," which is the genetic contribution an individual makes to the next generation. Fitness is increased by any trait that promotes survival and reproductive success (on average, over an individual's lifetime). Adaptive traits are those that confer a net fitness *benefit*. Maladaptive traits are those that confer a net fitness *cost*. However, whether a trait appears to be adaptive or maladaptive today tells us nothing about whether or not it has an evolutionary *origin*. As Table 2.1 illustrates, a trait that confers no fitness benefit today, and is therefore classed as maladaptive, may nevertheless have evolved because it was adaptive at some previous point in our evolutionary past. In that case, it remains an evolutionary "adaptation" (a result of natural selection), even if it is no longer "adaptive" (an example is our sweet tooth, once vital for seeking out scarce sugars).[67] "Side effects" are incidental traits that do *not* confer fitness benefits either now or in the past (for example, bones being white rather than some other color). "Exaptive" traits are those that provide fitness benefits today but were co-opted to do so after having evolved to serve some other function in the past (the classic example is wings, which are thought to have originated as cooling devices, not flying devices).[68] The key point of this explanation is to clarify a very important concept for the book: cognitive biases such as overconfidence are usually considered *maladaptive* (that is, dysfunctional for the organism). However, an evolutionary perspective suggests that we need to consider an alternative: (1) they are *adaptations*, whether or not they are useful today; and (2) they may in fact still be *adaptive* today, if they continue to bring net benefits to their bearers—on average, over time.[69]

WHAT DOES "ADAPTIVE" MEAN FOR STATE BEHAVIOR IN INTERNATIONAL RELATIONS?

A crucial question might arise at this point: What constitutes "adaptive" behavior for states in international politics? "Adaptive" and "maladaptive" in the biological literature refer to the benefits of a trait or behavior conferred to *individuals* (measured by survival and reproduction). However, from an international relations perspective, we are interested in the benefits of a behavior conferred to *states* (measured by material characteristics—such as security, power, and prosperity). This could be divided further into benefits to *state interests* versus benefits to *state leaders* (which often overlap in their goals but are not always the same). In this book I focus on the latter—benefits to the goals of state leaders—because I want to evaluate whether cognitive biases help leaders achieve their strategic goals. I do not make judgments about whether decisions served the national interest overall, because such an evaluation would be subject to policy preferences and ideological commitments (e.g., is fighting a war against state X worth it or not, and is it right or wrong?). That is orthogonal to the point of the book. I am interested in whether cognitive biases help state leaders achieve their goals in strategic interactions with other states, whatever those goals are and whether we agree with them or not. This means that I equate "adaptive" (that is, a trait still useful today) with behaviors conferring "strategic advantages," and "maladaptive" (that is, a trait no longer useful today) with behaviors conferring "strategic disadvantages." Finally, there is no claim that strategic instincts also bring survival or reproductive benefits to state leaders *personally*; that may or may not be true but is a question for another time.[70]

PROXIMATE VERSUS ULTIMATE EXPLANATIONS OF BEHAVIOR

Having established the criteria for determining adaptive and maladaptive behavior in both individuals and states, it is now vital to distinguish between different possible *causes* of cognitive biases. To understand any trait or behavior in biology it is important to differentiate its "proximate" cause (the physiological mechanisms that generate the behavior) and its "ultimate" cause (the evolutionary problem that the behavior is designed to solve).[71] Focusing only on one cause without consideration for the other can generate confusion in trying to understand behavior—whether in humans or other animals. The *ultimate* explanation of bird song, for example, is that it helps in asserting territories and attracting mates, but the *proximate* explanation is that as day length increases, hormones are released that stimulate birds to sing.[72] Both explanations are correct, but each one captures only part of the story. If we want a complete understanding of behavior, for animals as well as for humans, then we have to consider both proximate and ultimate causes of that behavior. As we shall see below, one does not necessarily correlate with the other.

EVOLUTIONARY MISMATCH: EXPECTING MISTAKES

Now here's the crucial part: differences between ancestral environments (the ones in which we evolved) and modern environments (the ones we experience today) mean that proximate mechanisms may be activated even if the ultimate goal is not achieved. For example, if you put a bird in a laboratory and artificially increase day length with electric lights (triggering the proximate mechanism), it will start to sing even though there are no rivals to deter or mates to attract (so the ultimate goal fails). Similarly, many human behaviors that are puzzling in today's world can be explained as strategies that were perfectly adaptive for dealing with the problems of our ancestral environment but look peculiar in novel contemporary contexts where their proximate mechanisms are triggered but do not, or cannot, lead to the original ultimate goal. For example, addiction of various kinds is a widespread problem because of powerful neurological pathways that evolved to lead us to repeat behaviors that result in dopamine secretion. In the past, dopamine was stimulated by adaptive behaviors, but today it is also triggered by artificial stimulants such as drugs and junk food (triggering the proximate mechanism), even when adaptive benefits are no longer attained (so the ultimate goal fails).[73]

Because of the rapid pace of societal transformation and the slow-changing legacy of our evolutionary makeup ("phylogenetic" constraints), our behavioral mechanisms are not in equilibrium with our modern environment. As the caricature goes, we are living a modern life but still have "Stone Age brains." Hence, we should in fact *expect* to see people carrying out bizarre or costly behaviors when proximate stimuli are triggered—just as evolution intended— even when they occur in inappropriate or hopeless modern situations where the ultimate function is no longer attained. And indeed we do see this all the time.

This is not only a human peculiarity. The behavior of animals is also often led astray in unusual situations—even in their natural environment—and serves to illustrate the point. A famous example in the animal world, first noted by Aristotle, is the cuckoo. Female cuckoos are "parasitic" in that they lay their eggs in the nests of *other* bird species, and the "host" parents do all the work of incubating the egg and feeding and raising the cuckoo chick.

Remarkably, this happens even though the cuckoo egg is bigger than the host species' own eggs, the cuckoo chick throws the other chicks out of the nest, and then even massively outgrows the host parents! Yet the parents continue to look after the enormous cuckoo chick regardless. It looks idiotic, but the explanation is simple. The hosts' evolved *proximate* mechanisms for parenting are triggered by the presence of chicks and their begging calls in the nest, irrespective of their exact appearance, even when they are investing energy in the genes of someone else's chick—indeed a chick of a completely different species. The proximate mechanism is fooled by an unusual situation. This raises an obvious question: Why have the hosts not evolved to detect and eject cuckoo eggs or chicks out of the nest? In fact, some species have, but it is an ongoing arms race, in which the cuckoo stays far enough ahead to thrive. Because it is a relatively rare event for a host—most birds do not find cuckoos in their nest— there is not a strong enough selection pressure to develop a sophisticated discrimination of eggs or chicks, especially because doing so would come with a cost. If hosts evolve a tendency to eject possible cuckoos, then they run the risk of accidentally ejecting their own eggs or offspring as well. Observing a giant cuckoo chick in the nest of a graceful warbler can make it seem as though the host has been miserably failed by evolution (Figure 2.1). But in fact its arduous parental behavior is a highly adaptive trait that only looks like a mistake in unusual circumstances. For most potential hosts, there are no cuckoo eggs, and a disposition to feed the occupants of one's nest works well.[74]

Animals—including humans—evolved behaviors that worked well on average *in our natural environment*, but these behaviors can easily be fooled when we encounter novel circumstances (or manipulative competitors). In the modern world, we often behave like cuckoo hosts, allowing proximate causes of our behavior to feed all sorts of misguided interests—instances of "evolutionary mismatch." We should expect such mistakes. But not always. Like most hosts, those same proximate mechanisms usually help us to survive and thrive.

EVOLUTIONARY MATCHES: EXPECTING SUCCESS

Political scientists often study unusual events that can make human nature look flawed. The defeat brought on by overconfidence is like the bird that is cuckooed—both seem idiotic *when viewed in isolation*. Evolutionary psychologists, by contrast, look at the causes and consequences of behaviors over lifetimes and across generations—which are generally adaptive *when viewed on average, over time*. A single event would tell us nothing about whether a given behavioral trait is adaptive or not. Examining isolated cases is common in social science and the humanities, where the focus is often specifically on what makes an individual, period, object, or place unique and different from its surroundings. That is fine as long as general patterns are not deduced from unique events. Often in political science and international relations, however,

FIGURE 2.1. Marsh warbler working hard to feed the enormous chick of another
species: a cuckoo. The mother cuckoo laid her egg in the warbler's nest, and after
hatching the cuckoo chick pushed all of the host's own offspring out of the nest.
An example of "evolutionary mismatch"—the warbler's instinct to provide parental
care to chicks in its nest is perfectly adaptive behavior, but it is misled by an
unusual situation (most warblers' nests contain their own warbler chicks).
Source: iStockPhoto / hstiver.

general patterns *are* deduced from one or a few individual cases—hence the
"case study" method as a test of a bigger theory.[75]

If decision rules have evolved to deal with complex choices made under
uncertainty, with limited information and time, then we should not expect
them to be perfect. Instead, we should *expect* them to make mistakes from
time to time. But, critically, we should also expect intuitive decision-making
mechanisms to be sometimes or even usually successful. Evolution is highly
economic. It generates adaptations that are good enough to perform some task
successfully on average, over time.[76] The occasional mistake, unless it is catastrophic, will not undermine the overall advantages of a given decision rule.

Many traits that evolved in our past are still just as useful today, even in a
very changed environment—thus remaining "adaptive"—because the causes
and consequences of the trait remain similar. Hunger, sex, and the fight or
flight response, for example, are still just as essential to humans today as they

FIGURE 2.2. Peregrine falcon at home in Toronto, Canada. Peregrines evolved to live on cliffs and eat other birds, and have thus found a perfect habitat in modern cities with plentiful skyscrapers and pigeons. An example of an "evolutionary match"—adaptive behavior that *remains* adaptive even in a novel environment. *Source:* iStockPhoto/hstiver.

ever were. But many less obvious examples can be found among animals as well as humans. Peregrine falcons evolved to nest on cliffs and hunt other birds (they are the fastest species in the animal kingdom), and they have turned out to be beautifully adapted to life on man-made skyscrapers in cities full of pigeons (Figure 2.2). This book asks where we can find the peregrines of international relations—the strategic instincts that continue to serve us well.

Objections

The social sciences, and political science in particular, have long-standing concerns about the moral, ethical, and prescriptive implications of biological explanations of behavior. Arguments about human evolution have been associated with conservatism, racism, eugenics, and the supposed acceptance of immoral behavior (such as violence or war) because it is "natural."[77] Although biological theory has indeed been abused in the past, such arguments fall prey to the "naturalistic fallacy": just because something is natural does not mean it is right—one cannot derive an "ought" from an "is."[78] While we may not like everything we find out about human nature, we should like to understand it. We have a far better chance of solving the perennial problems of security, cooperation, and justice by comprehending human nature than by ignoring or denying it. In the future we will increasingly need to incorporate science and human biology into the way we theorize and practice politics, especially given technological change, severe threats to global ecosystems, and advancing scientific knowledge and methods. If one wishes to mold mankind, or the institutions we create to organize it, one needs to understand the clay one is working with.

Other questions arise over the causal validity and predictive capacity of biological theory. Here, scholars have raised a variety of concerns, for example: (1) the ease with which one can conjure up "just so" stories about the possible benefits of certain behaviors in our ancestral environment, without definitive proof or obvious ways to falsify them (Richard Lewontin and Stephen Jay Gould called this "adaptationism");[79] (2) difficulties in translating findings from non-political domains (e.g., laboratories, primates, computer simulations) to the political domain; (3) the danger of simplistic biological determinism (and the worry that evolved human traits are "fixed"); and (4) the problem of using biology to categorize types of people (based on genotype, neurological responses, hormonal profiles, etc.). Based on these and other doubts, Duncan Bell and Paul MacDonald offer a sweeping dismissal: "sociobiological microfoundations provide no additional analytical leverage in explaining and understanding international politics."[80] What these and many other scholars fail to realize, however, is how far evolutionary theory and human biology have advanced since the "sociobiology" debate of the 1970s. As one example, we now have strong evidence that genetics are a powerful predictor of people's voting behavior, explaining more of the variation in the data than do classic social science theories of voting.[81] The science has moved on, and so must we.

Contrary to another common criticism, biological theories can be rigorously tested. Their predictions can be held to the fire of empirical data, using hypothesis testing against alternative theories in experiments under controlled laboratory conditions, quantitative analyses of real-world data, and qualitative analyses of historical case studies of political leaders and their decisions and behavior.[82] Their plausibility and domains of importance can also be examined with mathematical models and computer simulations.[83] Much more such work remains to be done, however.

A final but crucial common critique is that the "constant" of human nature cannot explain *variation* in political outcomes, such as war and peace—stemming in no small part from Waltz's misguided rejection of "first image" explanations of international relations long ago because he argued human nature was fixed.[84] The notion of behaviors being "hard-wired" is widely misunderstood. No biologist thinks human nature is a constant. To the contrary, human behavioral traits are well known to be subject to enormous variation contingent on a range of factors including the environment, gene-environment interactions, upbringing, personality, gender, age, biochemistry, stress, and social and physical context.[85] Indeed, work in epigenetics explicitly recognizes that whatever our inherited genetic complement, individual genes can be differentially activated by external factors and environmental contingency (as has always been known in the differentiation of cells into different types during development, for example).[86] Humans are not deterministic automata: inherited predispositions coexist with influences from the environment and conscious decision-making, all of which interact to contribute to variable outcomes. Social experiences can even activate or deactivate genes. Such phenomena do not make genes less important; rather it makes them *all the more* important in explaining behavior. Genetics increases our knowledge of the sources of biological variation and our ability to predict its role and effects.

Importantly for this book, humans have evolved to adapt flexibly and strategically to their local environment, such that different environmental contexts lead to different behavioral responses depending on the situation and one's status within it. That flexibility in itself is highly adaptive (contingent strategies that are activated when useful are better than blanket strategies that are activated all the time regardless of circumstances). For example, a relationship has been found between the presence of a particular form of monoamine oxidase (MAOA) promoter gene and aggression,[87] and such effects have been shown to be mediated by whether or not people suffered adverse social environments as children.[88] The nature versus nurture debate is dead—at least for biologists. No natural scientist would make the extreme claim that *biology* is the *only* factor of importance in explaining human behavior. But oddly many social scientists continue to claim, against all the available evidence, that *nurture* is the *only* factor of importance! A more nuanced and conciliatory view is clearly needed.

Onward

The science of human behavior will move on with or without us, and this book aims to explore where it can help improve our ability to understand and predict phenomena in political science and international relations. A small but growing number of political scientists have come to recognize the massive potential of the life sciences for advancing the field.[89] But they are few and far between. Within the natural sciences, evolutionarily minded scholars have been on the march for a century and a half, but in political science, they remain on the margins and the insights are only now beginning to be explored. This book aims to advance consilience of the social and life sciences by exploring new questions that might not occur to a social scientist but arise naturally out of an evolutionary approach to international politics: Are cognitive biases *present in successes*, rather than just failures? Do these cognitive biases actually help in achieving these successes, conferring *strategic advantages*? *Under what conditions* do these cognitive biases work for or against us?

Exploring such questions reveals how, far from being unfortunate errors of cognition, psychological traits of human nature can be adaptive. Cognitive biases are *strategic instincts* with an evolutionary origin and strategic logic that helped us survive and prevail in the past and, I contend, continue to help us today.

CHAPTER THREE

Fortune Favors the Bold

THE STRATEGIC ADVANTAGES
OF OVERCONFIDENCE

*Far better it is to dare mighty things, to win glorious triumphs, even
though checkered by failure, than to take rank with those poor spirits who
neither enjoy much nor suffer much, because they live in the gray twilight
that knows neither victory nor defeat.*

—THEODORE ROOSEVELT

In what field of human activity is boldness more at home than in war?

—CARL VON CLAUSEWITZ

INTERNATIONAL RELATIONS SCHOLARS are fond of citing Thucydides'
history of the Peloponnesian War in which Athens fought Sparta for control
of Greece between 431 and 404 BC. Thucydides offers the founding example
of a realist struggle for power and security in his famous observation: "The
growth of the power of Athens, and the alarm which this inspired in Sparta,
made war inevitable."[1]

However, other elements were also at play, and not least significant was a
certain level of overconfidence about war. After the Spartans issued their ultimatum demanding freedom for the Greek states in return for peace (uphold-
ing the prior Thirty Years Peace Treaty), the Athenians held a council to decide
how to respond. They found themselves persuaded by the speech of Pericles,
the leading politician of the day. He highlighted a range of military, political,
economic, and sociological factors, all of which put the Spartans at a disadvantage. Athens, therefore, should fight. Strikingly, Pericles explicitly considered
the Spartans' perceptions as well as his own but judged that, if anything, it
was *they* who were overconfident, arguing that the war was likely to "last longer than they expect."[2] Having listed all their inferiorities, he noted haughtily,

"Athens is free from the defects that I have criticized in them, and has other advantages of its own, which they can show nothing to equal."[3] In particular, he stressed the Athenians' maritime superiority, compared to the Spartans' limited naval resources, experience, and skill. Although on land the Peloponnesian soldiers may outnumber their own, the strategy would be to fight the war at sea and defend the city of Athens: "If they march against our country we will sail against theirs."[4] Given the Athenians' purported advantages, he dismissed whatever the Spartans might achieve, to the point that he was "more afraid of our own blunders than of the enemy's devices."[5]

Pericles' overconfidence is not just my own reading of the text. Jack Levy used the Peloponnesian War as a classic example of overconfident misperception, noting that "the rest of Greece believed that Athens could not hold out for more than two or three years, while Athens herself probably expected a relatively short, victorious war—but the Peloponnesian War lasted over a quarter of a century."[6] Donald Kagan's study of the war also noted that all of the statesmen involved "expected a short war" (strongly reminiscent of 1914) and, had they foreseen the impending costs, "would scarcely have risked a war for the relatively minor disputes that brought it on."[7] Instead, anger, fear, and "undue optimism" led them to war.[8]

However, two and a half millennia on, perhaps we can ask a novel question of Thucydides. While undue optimism may have increased the probability of war in 431 BC, did the boldness of Athens also lend strategic advantages at other times? Although Athens lost the war, it had up to that point managed to build an extraordinary empire, had defeated the mighty Persians, and held out for twenty-five years against an expanding alliance in the Peloponnesian War itself—moreover, in the end, Athenian democracy prevailed anyway. Whatever the causes of the war, did their brimming confidence not help them to develop and pursue their grand strategic ambitions in the first place, to fight so effectively for so long, and to create and defend a Greek legacy that is venerated over two millennia later?

Athenian overconfidence may have represented a deeper characteristic of their culture, which contributed to great achievements as well as mistakes along the way. It was not just apparent on the eve of war. Their very success and dominance of the region had been built by decades of ambition, conquest, and a belief in the superiority of their people and culture. At this broader level, the war was a "clash between a cautious, traditional oligarchy" in Sparta and the "ambitious, innovative democracy" in Athens.[9] Athens had developed a remarkable democratic society and a flourishing scientific and artistic culture, which it exported to other city-states around Greece and beyond. But it did so aggressively. The *immediate cause* of the war may have been the Spartan ultimatum, but the *underlying cause* of the war was Athens's subjugation of its former allies into colonies that paid tributes for its own enrichment and glorification. Pericles "famously claimed that Athens was providing a lesson

FIGURE 3.1. Pericles' funeral oration during the Peloponnesian War, honoring the soldiers who had fallen in the first year of fighting with Sparta, yet inspiring men anew to fight for the glory of Athens in a war that would rage on for another quarter of a century. *Source:* After a painting by Phillipp Foltz, Granger Historical Picture Archive/ Alamy Stock Photo.

to the rest of the Greeks through the excellence of her citizens and scale of her achievements."[10] Apparently other Greeks did not agree, and rising Athenian dominance was precisely the grievance that led to the Spartan ultimatum.

Overconfidence may have tempted the Athenians into a costly war, but it also underlay their ambition and rise to power over many preceding decades. It may also have helped them resist the Spartans, their allies, and eventually even Persia as well for a quarter of a century. Although they lost the war of arms, one step too far in an expansion that had hitherto served them well, they won the war of culture that persisted long beyond it. Despite the massive investment in expansion, or indeed by virtue of it given the vast tributes that their sprawling empire had brought over the decades, Pericles had argued that Athens should use "any surpluses that remained after the expenses of war were met to build works that would bring her glory for all time."[11] It is precisely the boldness of the Athenian culture and empire that leaves us discussing it to this day. While overconfidence can get states into trouble, it can also encourage them to set their sights high and achieve remarkable feats. While clearly disadvantageous when too strong, in moderation a tendency to overconfidence can be a powerful strategic instinct.

What Is Overconfidence?

Most normal, mentally healthy people, and especially men, are overconfident. Not all people are overconfident at all times, and not all people are overconfident about all things. Nevertheless, psychologists have long documented a systematic bias toward overconfidence in a wide range of domains. In particular, people tend to: (1) overestimate their capabilities; (2) overestimate their control over events; and (3) underestimate their vulnerability to risk. These three widely replicated phenomena have become collectively known as "positive illusions."[12] Although the term "positive illusions" is common in the psychology literature, in this book I adopt the more colloquial "overconfidence" because it is a much more familiar term in common usage and because it stresses the key idea of a level of confidence *greater than is warranted*. That is the bias at issue.

I define regular "confidence" as the perceived probability that a specified outcome will occur. For example, low confidence may equate with a belief that one has a 25 percent chance of victory, whereas high confidence may equate with a belief that one has a 75 percent chance of victory (whatever the actual probabilities and outcomes are). "*Over*confidence," by contrast, is defined as a level of confidence that exaggerates the true likelihood of an outcome. For example, if a tennis player expects to win 75 percent of their matches but in fact tends to lose 75 percent, this would imply overconfidence.[13]

Studying overconfidence presents empirical challenges because we have to evaluate how confident people "ought" to be, which is not always clear. People may be perfectly justified in taking large risks if the expected net payoff is high enough (or if the alternative outcomes of abstaining are worse), and in so doing they may appear to be overconfident when in fact they are merely accepting a calculated gamble. How do we differentiate overconfidence from risky but rational behavior?[14] This can be difficult, but there are several methodological solutions enabling the empirical evaluation of overconfidence, such as process tracing leaders' beliefs against prevailing information, using third-party evaluations of the probability of a given event, comparing opposing sides' expectations, and so on. In experiments, psychologists have also addressed this problem by evaluating expectations against a concrete baseline (such as actual exam results) that tells us straightforwardly whether or not people expected a better outcome than warranted (and by how much).[15]

But perhaps more interesting than the challenges of defining and measuring "overconfidence" is the effect that the term itself has had on research. The word "overconfidence" leads us to expect it and look for it in events about which people were obviously *too* optimistic or which failed altogether (hence, we deduce they must have been *over*confident). This means we automatically associate a psychological tendency with bad outcomes—bias X seems to lead to outcomes of type Y. But if "overconfidence" is just a psychological disposition, then it might be a good bias to have in other instances or when faced with other types of challenges—bias X might also lead to outcomes of type Z. The existence of failure on its own is not evidence of overconfidence. Similarly, the existence of success is not evidence that overconfidence was absent. "Overconfidence" is a variable that can be found in any event regardless of outcome and may affect those outcomes in different ways. Yet in *calling* it overconfidence, we may have inadvertently narrowed our search template to only ever seek it and find it in the causes of disasters. In this chapter, I look instead at how and when overconfidence can lead to success.

Evidence for Overconfidence

The literature on overconfidence is vast. Much of it comes from experimental psychology and has been extensively summarized in, for example, Shelley Taylor's 1989 book *Positive Illusions*,[16] Christopher Peterson's 2006 *A Primer in Positive Psychology*,[17] and Tali Sharot's 2011 *The Optimism Bias*.[18] These give excellent overviews of a long-standing and wide-ranging research literature. The latest development is extending our understanding of its neuroscientific foundations, with experiments revealing how optimism is maintained by specific areas of the brain blocking disconfirming evidence.[19] Scholars in other disciplines—notably economics—have also identified overconfidence as a recurrent and significant phenomenon in real-world settings. For example, it appears to be a common trait not only among experimental subjects but also among stock market traders, entrepreneurs, and CEOs of Fortune 500 companies.[20] One of the main hypotheses for the collapse of the global financial system in 2008 was the accumulation of years of overconfidence in Wall Street and other financial centers around the world.[21] Overconfidence is also common in a wide range of other areas including politics, law, sports, combat, job performance, and ill-preparedness for natural disasters and climate change.[22]

While the range and prevalence are striking, here I narrow down to focus specifically on experimental studies that have tested overconfidence in settings relevant to politics and international relations. This is important because, although many people take general findings from experimental psychology and apply them to politics, it is not always clear if or how they will apply in explicitly political settings. Experimental war games, in which people make decisions in simulated international crises, is one way in which some of my colleagues and I have started to address this problem in the case of overconfidence.

In collaboration with Rose McDermott and colleagues, we examined laboratory war games run with 200 students at Harvard University.[23] Each person was asked to role-play the leader of a fictitious country, which had just discovered valuable resources along a disputed border. The game was open-ended so players could do whatever they liked, but their behavior in the game was carefully recorded along with a range of personality and demographic data. Before the game, players also forecast their expected ranking—how well they thought they would perform in the game compared to all 200 subjects playing.

We found striking overconfidence. On average, people thought they would do much better than others. However, this result turned out to be mainly due to men. Women actually ranked themselves around average (their mean rank was 93.9; thus tending to rank themselves around the middle of all 200 players), whereas men's self-rankings were significantly higher than average (mean 56.5), with 74 percent (79 of the 107 men) thinking they would come out above average.

This was interesting in itself. The classic overconfidence found in numerous psychological experiments clearly appeared in our setting of international politics too. However, the much more important result was how overconfidence was linked to behavior in the game. What we found was that individuals who were overconfident about winning were also significantly more likely to make unprovoked attacks on their opponent (that is, attacking without any preceding aggression by the other player). The experiment demonstrated that even in politically relevant settings, people are overconfident about success. Moreover, higher levels of overconfidence predicted a greater willingness to fight.

One problem with this study is that, because it was a contest between two opposing players, people may have been taking excessive risks to try to "win the game" regardless of cost rather than pursuing the most appropriate strategy to balance all the various concerns that a real state would have. This may have inflated the attraction of aggressive behavior. We therefore conducted a follow-up study to address this problem.

In this new experiment we studied 130 all-male participants at the University of California, Santa Barbara.[24] This time there was no opponent player to try to beat. Instead, we asked them how they would, in the position of U.S. president, respond to three international crises: (1) a "Hostage Scenario" (in which a commercial airliner was hijacked); (2) a "Central Asian Scenario" (a resurgence of the Taliban in Afghanistan); and (3) a "Latin American Scenario" (a troublesome socialist leader).[25] Each crisis was described in 200–400 words with realistic detail. In each case, subjects could choose from three options: concession, negotiation, or military attack. For example, in resolving the Latin American scenario, subjects could choose to: (a) "cut diplomatic ties and let this leader nationalize American interests"; (b) "attempt to negotiate fair restitution for American companies"; or (c) "allow U.S. special forces to assist the local military leader in staging a coup." The order in which both the scenarios and the policy options were presented was randomized. Along with deciding what to do, subjects were asked about their level of confidence in their chosen policy as follows: "On a scale of 0 to 10, how likely do you think it is that your chosen course of action will succeed?"[26]

What we found was a significant association between people's level of confidence and the aggressiveness of the policies they chose. So, for example, subjects who chose a military attack were more likely to believe that this strategy would succeed compared to those choosing negotiation or concession. We conducted a range of statistical controls and the results remained robust. We also found a significant association with partisanship and real-world policy preferences: those who were more confident and more aggressive in the scenarios were also more likely to identify themselves as conservative or Republican, to favor the 2007 military "surge" in Iraq, and to endorse the possible bombing of Iran.

In sum, there is already overwhelming evidence from experimental psychology and other fields that people display overconfidence in a wide range of domains. Experimental research with my colleagues confirmed that overconfidence emerges in contexts relevant to political decision-making as well. Moreover, people do not just have inflated expectations of success, but this overconfidence predicts the choice of more aggressive policy options. This leads to the all-important question: What are the consequences of such overconfidence in the real world?

Overconfidence as a Cause of Failure

Political scientists and historians have long reported the recurrence and importance of overconfidence in international relations, from ancient times to the present day. Examples abound. We already saw Pericles' overconfidence on the eve of the Peloponnesian War in 431 BC, and the pattern has persisted across the centuries. Even Clausewitz, widely regarded as the greatest strategist of all time, exhibited misplaced overconfidence. In 1806 when Prussia went to war with France, in the words of Sir Hew Strachan, Clausewitz "does what all generals do which is [to] express confidence in the outcome.... You have to believe you're going to win when you go to war, despite Napoleon's reputation. But of course they don't win, they are absolutely smashed in the dual battles of Jena and Auerstedt."[27] Thomas Jefferson opined that the War of 1812 would be "a mere matter of marching."[28] Instead it turned into a costly stalemate with much of Washington, D.C., razed to the ground. On the morning of the battle of Waterloo in 1815, Napoleon declared at a meeting of his senior commanders: "We have ninety chances in our favour . . . and not ten against."[29] Some of his generals cautioned him about the Duke of Wellington's own formidable capability. But Napoleon dismissed their concerns. "Just because you have been beaten by Wellington," he said, "you think he's a good general. But I tell you that Wellington is a bad general and the English are bad troops."[30] Napoleon had never been beaten by anyone. He told them not to worry—it would be a "picnic." Overconfidence can be found in the wars ever since, not least in World War I, World War II, and Vietnam.[31]

The phenomenon persists in contemporary conflicts as well. U.S. Director of National Intelligence James Clapper acknowledged in 2014 that "we underestimated ISIL [the Islamic State] and overestimated the fighting capability of the Iraqi army [the United States' new ally]."[32] France's foreign minister Alain Juppé admitted in July 2011, three months into the long campaign in Libya in which France played a leading military role, "Maybe I underestimated the resistance of Qaddafi, and overestimated the capacity of the [rebel] national transitional council."[33] Matt Waldman found that, in the war against the Taliban in Afghanistan, American civilian and military leaders were guilty of "overestimating the efficacy of military force" and "predisposed to overconfidence and oversimplification."[34] Larry Diamond, senior advisor to the Coalition Provisional Authority in Baghdad in 2004, reported that "administration officials repeatedly deluded themselves into believing that the defeat of the [Iraqi] insurgency was just around the corner."[35] In his article on "hubris and overreach" in the George W. Bush administration, Kevin Phillips noted not the uniqueness but the continuity of the phenomenon. He cited numerous precedents in history for the "cockiness" of the Bush White House, including: "the arrogance of Edwardian Britain, the smugness of Holland's bankers to the world, the military hauteur of the Great Armada and the crack Castilian regiments."[36] Overconfidence, it seems, is not so much a flaw of certain individuals or administrations but a recurring feature of history and human nature.

Overconfidence, or what political scientists sometimes refer to as "false optimism," has been identified by many authors.[37] Historian Geoffrey Blainey's famous study *The Causes of War* (1973) concluded that false optimism is "a potent and pervasive cause of war."[38] Twenty-five years later, political scientist Stephen Van Evera claimed, in his own landmark *Causes of War* (1999), that "at least some false optimism about relative power preceded every major war since 1740, as well as many lesser and ancient wars."[39] "Excessive military optimism," Robert Jervis also found, "is frequently associated with the outbreak of war."[40] Jack Levy's analysis of the causal connections between various types of biases and war concluded that, "of all forms of misperceptions, the one most likely to play a critical role in the processes leading to war is the underestimation of the adversary's capabilities relative to one's own."[41] He found there to be "innumerable examples" of wars begun in the erroneous expectation of victory and, moreover, "numerous—and shocking" examples of states expecting not only to win but that winning would be quick and minimally costly, a phenomenon Levy saw reaching back through all of history from Vietnam, to World War I, to the Peloponnesian War.[42] Even according to the dominant theory of "defensive realism" in international relations, war is seen as costly for both sides and states primarily seek to maintain the status quo (or at least they should do so). War therefore has to be explained as a result of misperceptions, including "excessive faith in the efficacy of military force."[43]

Few scholars deny that overconfidence seems to be a significant contributory factor in the causes of at least some wars. Whenever wars have occurred, overconfidence appears to have been lurking somewhere in the background, if not in the foreground. Indeed, as Robert Jervis points out, even if there were no systematic psychological tendency toward overconfidence in the population as a whole, we are likely to find that wars tend to break out at times when people *are* overconfident (since war will then seem a more attractive option).[44] If overconfidence were merely a random phenomenon, therefore, it would nevertheless be an important cause of war *when it occurs*. Yet in fact, far from being random or rare, it is a systematic and recurrent psychological disposition.

In my book *Overconfidence and War*, I looked in detail at four cases to examine the causal role of overconfidence in decisions for war. In World War I and Vietnam, decision-makers showed evidence of classic positive illusions, and these contributed to the origins and escalation of the war. And this was not just on the losing sides, where most evidence for overconfidence has been amassed. Overconfidence can also arise—and incur costs—for the victors as well. For instance, in 1914 the French "went to war confident of victory," but they could hardly have imagined the crippling costs it would entail—an outcome Robert Doughty argues was a Pyrrhic victory.[45] I then examined the reverse prediction to see whether overconfidence was *absent* in cases of international crises where war was especially likely and yet did not occur. While positive illusions were evident in the causes of the 1938 Munich Crisis and the 1962 Cuban Missile Crisis, other factors conspired to prevent them leading to war. Overconfidence was subdued. Many historians and political scientists have independently identified overconfidence across different regions and periods of history. While the significance of its role relative to other factors may be contested, there is a broad consensus that overconfidence is a cause of war.[46]

Overconfidence continues to be cited as a major problem in international politics. In 2011, prominent international relations theorist Stephen Walt published an article in *Foreign Policy* titled "Wishful Thinking: Top 10 Examples of the Most Unrealistic Expectations in Contemporary U.S. Foreign Policy."[47] What was remarkable in his findings is that so many different domains of international politics appear to be affected by overconfidence. As Walt observed, the United States has been overly optimistic in economic, diplomatic, and military foreign policy issues ranging from progress in the counterinsurgency in Afghanistan, deterring Iran, solving the Israel-Palestine conflict, and the future rivalry with China.

It is notable that so many scholars accept some role of overconfidence in foreign policy decision-making and the causes of war, even when they favor mainstream theories of international relations in which overconfidence plays no part, or even contradicts them. For example, Walt is a realist who believes that international relations is fundamentally about power and states threatening to use that power.[48] But in his argument for the pervasiveness and importance of wishful thinking in contemporary foreign policy, he places overconfidence as a fundamental phenomenon of international relations. Van Evera also dedicates a whole chapter of his book *Causes of War* to false optimism, even though his main arguments are about capabilities and power.[49] Historians do something similar. They focus on major shifts in social and political events (in war and beyond) that form the central themes of history but nevertheless frequently recognize the role of overconfidence as a perplexing yet recurring feature of the landscape. For example, Barbara Tuchman found pervasive overconfidence in World War I and Vietnam but put it down to a somewhat atheoretical "wooden-headedness."[50] What is clearly lacking is a psychological framework and theory to understand overconfidence. Overconfidence can continue to play a role as a kind of "bolt on" to mainstream theories of international relations—a phenomenon that helps explain anomalous events from time to time that other theories cannot. However, if it is so consistently prevalent, perhaps it is time to consider its place at the heart of international relations theory.

Yet the bigger point for the book is that, in all of these examples, overconfidence is argued to have been a *detrimental* influence, one that only serves to increase saber-rattling, brinkmanship, the probability of war, and the likelihood of defeat. The literature therefore leaves a different and important question unanswered. If overconfidence is so bad, why is it so common? This is especially curious on the eve of war when state survival hangs in the balance and level-headedness is seemingly crucial. Perhaps, however, if war is at hand, a boost in confidence is precisely what we need in order to enter the ring in the face of a daunting opponent.

Adaptive Advantages of Overconfidence: An Evolutionary Perspective

For all the talk of overconfidence as a widespread and recurrent mistake, there has been precious little discussion of why we have this bias toward overconfidence in the first place. If overconfidence causes such frequent and costly errors of judgment, why would humans have this bias at all? Wouldn't decision-makers learn from history, or from their own mistakes, and develop the wisdom or experience to resist such biases? Wouldn't overconfident states be eliminated from the international system or socialized toward more accurate judgments? And in the longer perspective of human evolution, shouldn't such a costly decision-making bias have been stamped out by natural selection?

In fact, an evolutionary perspective suggests that overconfidence is a widespread and systematic trait among humans today because, as odd as it may seem, it actually brought adaptive *advantages* in our evolutionary past. Like opposable thumbs and large brains, overconfidence may be an adaptation that arose because it improved survival or reproductive success over the course of human evolutionary history. Most interesting of all, those advantages (also like opposable thumbs and large brains) may continue to bring important advantages *today*—even in international relations.

Seen this way, the empirical prevalence of overconfidence starts to make sense. If CEOs are *too* overconfident, how did they get to be CEOs? If military commanders are *too* overconfident, how did they get promoted? If political decision-makers are *too* overconfident, how did they get elected? Such examples raise the possibility that, counterintuitively, overconfidence is one of the very traits that allow people to perform their role effectively—or for some people to excel within it. Sure, there are always examples or extremes that bring disaster, as with many we have already seen. But what about all the other examples that brought success? As basketball star Michael Jordan pointed out, "You have to expect things of yourself before you can do them."[51] Perhaps we should *want* to be overconfident because on average, over time, it pays dividends, even if the cost of such a trait is that it causes occasional mistakes along the way. But what are the potential advantages it brings?

One might think that, given the typical focus on overconfidence as a detrimental bias, evidence of its advantages would be hard to come by. But in fact, evidence abounds. A cursory examination of overconfidence reveals a number of potential advantages, arising from research in several different disciplines. Note that we are not talking about the advantages of mere *confidence* but the advantages of *overconfidence*—a level of confidence that is greater than warranted given the available evidence or third-party evaluations.

Let's first consider the effects of confidence, before we move on to overconfidence. In general, high levels of *confidence* are known to increase performance in a range of tasks.[52] Confidence helps us focus on our strengths and raises our ambitions, causing us to set more challenging goals and motivating us to achieve them.[53] Also, it can lead to greater persistence in a task once it is underway.[54] Confidence is universally recognized as an advantage and is deliberately cultivated by educational institutions, employers, and individuals. The only question is how high our level of confidence needs to be in any given domain to maximize its advantages and minimize its risks.

Business analysts argue that confidence can be the vital factor that determines whether companies succeed or fail, or ever get off the ground at all.[55] Stock market traders have long understood the roller coaster of financial markets to be tightly linked to investor confidence (or fear)—the famed "bull" or "bear" market.[56] John Maynard Keynes famously drew attention to the importance of "animal spirits" in economic markets, a "characteristic of human nature" that relies on "spontaneous optimism rather than mathematical expectations."[57] Sometimes this can lead to disaster, but among investors themselves, over the long term, it turns out to be the optimists who have triumphed.[58] Sports scientists note that confidence can be the secret weapon that divides champions from the rest. The 1930s Wimbledon champion Fred Perry thrived on his self-confidence, boasting to other players, "I would hate to be playing me today," a bravado that characterizes—and seems to drive— numerous sporting champions from Muhammad Ali to Cristiano Ronaldo.[59] There also appear to be important biological and psychological interactions. One study found that during a judo tournament, men who experienced a rise in testosterone had a higher motivation to win, and this group actually went on to perform better in their fights.[60] Confidence is clearly important in competition, over and above ability or strength. Sports psychologist Jim Taylor goes so far as to argue that "confidence is the single most important mental factor in sports."[61] Finally, poker players will also recognize the crucial role of confidence, which can turn an outrageous bluff into hard cash.

Now let us consider the effects of *over*confidence. Psychologists have argued that *over*confidence, specifically, can be useful because it enables us to take on daunting or even seemingly impossible challenges, boosts resolve, and helps us cope with adversity, even improving physical health by reducing stress (which can otherwise impair the immune system).[62] Shelley Taylor and Jonathon Brown, pioneering researchers in this field, emphasize the fact that people's self-perceptions are not just at high levels but are actually *greater than warranted*: people "view themselves in unrealistically positive terms," they "believe they have greater control over environmental events than is actually the case," and they "hold views of the future that are more rosy than base-rate data can justify."[63] Studies systematically report that a majority of (and sometimes nearly all) subjects rate their own qualities as better than those of their peers, even though of course it is "logically impossible for most people to be better than others," hence the label "positive illusions."[64] Yet, despite these beliefs being wrong, Taylor and Brown find that positive illusions systematically lead to "higher motivation, greater persistence, more effective performance, and ultimately, greater success."[65] Psychologist Suzanne Segerstrom similarly reports that around 80 percent of subjects in her experiments consistently tend to be "somewhat" to "very" optimistic.[66] However, rather than representing a detrimental pathology, such beliefs appeared to generate good outcomes. Optimism led to greater resilience, better relationships, better health, and better performance in attaining goals. Pessimists worry about whether their goals are realistic or attainable, whereas optimists just go ahead and attempt to achieve them. And only those who try will succeed.

Social psychologists have developed theories for how overconfidence works to one's advantage. For example, "status-enhancement theory" holds that *overestimation* (believing we are better than we actually are) and *overplacement* (believing we are better than others) can bring advantages because they help to convince other people that we have high levels of competence—whatever the reality. Meanwhile, "conversational norm theory" suggests that *overprecision* (making statements that are more precise than warranted) can also increase our influence over receivers.[67]

A widely debated article in the prominent journal *Behavioral and Brain Sciences* reviewed the evidence for the adaptive advantages of a number of "false beliefs" (ranging from delusions to supernatural beliefs to positive illusions). While the authors, psychologist Ryan McKay and philosopher Daniel Dennett, remained skeptical of many of them, they saw overconfidence (in the form of positive illusions) as the most compelling case of all, judging the weight of evidence to support the argument that it has genuinely adaptive advantages.[68]

Even in technical areas such as economics and finance where one might imagine unbiased rational decision-making to be paramount, there may be advantages of overconfidence (even if there are also dangers). For example, business studies authors John Beck and Mitchell Wade argue that "CEOs need some insulation from the fear that naturally goes along with risk. If you're obsessed with imagining the costs of failure, it's hard to move boldly toward success. If you can't stop thinking about the damage done by your last mistake, it's tough to avoid the next one."[69] Start-up companies, which are often building from nothing and face extremely high rates of failure, are particularly in need of confident founders, who can sustain and sell a belief in eventual success despite often many years of severe setbacks, competition, and skepticism. Billionaire Facebook founder Mark Zuckerberg was extremely confident, according to former Harvard roommate Joe Green, to the point of being aloof: "You can see that as a bad thing, but you have to have an irrational level of self-confidence to start something like Facebook."[70] Apple's Steve Jobs had similar traits; he was "notorious for being supremely confident in his own ideas—so confident that those closest to him believed his perception of the objective world was permanently warped by a 'reality distortion field.'"[71]

Evolutionary biologists themselves have also suggested that overconfidence can be advantageous: it promotes resolve, strengthens deterrence, and enables us to seize opportunities that otherwise may be passed over.[72] Robert Trivers further argued that the self-deceptive element of cognitive biases (e.g., being overconfident without being aware of it) itself plays a key role in their effectiveness, because this removes the possibility that we will betray weaknesses through our behavior (so-called behavioral leakage). Self-deception can be highly adaptive if it increases our pursuit of beneficial behavior against resistance or increases the credibility of signals it transmits to others.[73] Most pertinent to the book, overconfidence has specifically been proposed to have emerged as an advantageous trait in the origins of human warfare. Anthropologist Richard Wrangham argued that it serves to boost resolve and bluff opponents in the danger and uncertainty of intergroup combat, which can lend a critical competitive edge.[74]

Evolutionary psychologists John Tooby and Leda Cosmides identified the conditions that would need to have been present for warfare to develop in human evolutionary history, key among which was that warriors must believe (a) that they will (or can) win, and (b) that the gains from winning will (or can) exceed the costs of fighting. Only if you believe these things—whether they are true or not—would it make sense to risk life and limb to participate in lethal intergroup conflict.[75] Wherever those perceptions approximate the actual prevailing conditions on the ground, intergroup warfare is more likely to emerge. But overconfidence about success and the potential gains to be made would increase an individual's willingness to participate, and the more willing participants there are to overcome the collective action problem of war, the greater become the odds of success. Overconfidence in the prospects of victory, therefore, can become a self-fulfilling prophecy.

With such a wide range of possible advantages of overconfidence, stemming from several disciplines, it seems naïve to assume that overconfidence is always a mistake. It may in fact be a blessing in disguise. But how can we actually *test* the idea that overconfidence can help us rather than hurt us?

MODELS OF OVERCONFIDENCE:
EVOLUTION IN ACTION

The advantages of overconfidence outlined thus far are compelling but often remain largely theoretical or anecdotal. It is hard to know whether overconfidence in general is really an advantage or not—perhaps one time it was useful by chance but another time it would have been disastrous instead. How can we test whether overconfidence lends a systematic advantage over multiple encounters? Ideally we would repeat a given event hundreds of times, with or without overconfidence, and see whether there is a statistically significant increase in performance when overconfidence was present. Obviously, we cannot do that with real historical events—we cannot "rerun the tape of history." However, one thing we can do is *model* overconfidence in artificial settings, with some simple assumptions, and see how overconfidence fares in competition with alternative strategies. We have done this in two ways: first, as an *agent-based model* (ABM) on a spatial map, and second, as a *mathematical model* using evolutionary game theory. The purpose of this section is to report the results of these studies and to highlight the utility of models in: (a) showing that the hypothesis that a bias can be useful is plausible; (b) identifying specific conditions in which the bias is useful (and other conditions where it is not); and (c) generating novel predictions that can be tested with data.

I did the ABM modeling project in collaboration with political scientist Lars-Erik Cederman and computer scientist turned political scientist Nils

Weidmann at the International Conflict Research group in Zurich, Switzerland. Lars-Erik had pioneered a novel way of exploring international conflict using computer simulations, which allows one to test ideas and processes not possible with empirical data. At his inaugural lecture in Zurich, he addressed the question of why "a nice boy from a small village in Sweden would become so interested in war," and noted that to understand it we "only need to visit the cafeteria in Ikea!"[76] But really it was because he and Nils brought extraordinary interdisciplinary insights and new computational skills to the puzzle of war. We explored the effects of overconfidence using an agent-based model of interstate conflict, which allowed us to evaluate the performance of different "agents" carrying out alternative strategies in competition with each other.[77] Following previous work using this method, the simulation took place on a 30×30 spatial grid (see Figure 3.2), with the cells of the grid constituting "provinces" and agents represented by states of one or more contiguous provinces.[78]

We operationalized overconfidence by assigning each state a "confidence factor" α, such that states with $\alpha > 1$ are overconfident, states with $\alpha = 1$ are unbiased, and states with $0 < \alpha < 1$ are underconfident. Initial α values were randomly drawn from a log-normal distribution, which bounded values at zero but allowed some states to have very high levels of overconfidence (this was to mimic reality: values less than zero are meaningless, while the long positive tail of the distribution allows for a few very overconfident states). With an underlying mean of zero and variance of 1 ($\mu = 0$ and $\sigma = 1$), drawing from this distribution means that simulations begin with a population that is unbiased as a whole, with median $\alpha = 1$.

All states had a certain level of resources, R, which represented their strength in a fight. However, a state's own *perceived* resource level is given by αR (that is, their amount of overconfidence multiplied by their level of resources), such that overconfident states thought they were stronger than they really were, unbiased states saw themselves accurately, and underconfident states thought they were weaker than they really were. Importantly, αR is only used in deciding whether or not to fight. *Actual* R was used in determining war outcomes. Also, while states may distort the perception of their *own* strength (if $\alpha \neq 1$), states are not gullible and always see rivals' true strength. This was important for two reasons. First, the psychological literature on positive illusions shows that people tend to overestimate their *own* capabilities and prospects, but not necessarily the attributes of third parties.[79] Second, if other states were gullible and believed the overconfident claims of aggressors, they would simply back off in the face of a bluff and concede, making overconfidence automatically advantageous; obviously we did not want to prime the model toward this trivial outcome. The model was run over hundreds of time steps, at each of which states assessed their neighbors and interacted according to a series of simple decision rules (consigned here to an endnote for brevity).[80]

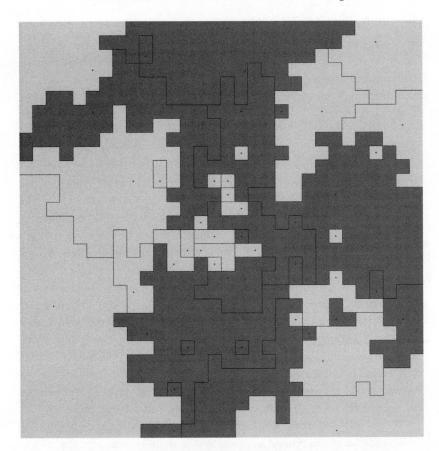

FIGURE 3.2. Screenshot of our agent-based computer simulation of overconfidence in competition with other strategies. Each square constitutes a "province," and agents are represented as states composed of one or more contiguous provinces. Black dots are capitals, and black lines are state borders. Dark gray states are overconfident and light gray states are underconfident (by varying degrees, including not at all, so some states are unbiased). *Source:* From a study by the author and colleagues, originally published in: D. D. P. Johnson, N. B. Weidmann, and L.-E. Cederman, "Fortune Favours the Bold: An Agent-Based Model Reveals Adaptive Advantages of Overconfidence in War," *PLoS ONE* 6, no. 6 (2011): e20851.

Our null hypothesis was that overconfident states should do *worse* than unbiased or underconfident states. Overconfident states should fare poorly because, while otherwise identical to other states, they overestimate their strength (R) and are thus more likely to attack opponents that are stronger than themselves. These are conflicts they are likely to lose. Remarkably, however, over time we found that overconfident states tend to dominate the population at the expense of unbiased or underconfident states, counter to expectation. So why do overconfident states do well?

Overconfident states won for three reasons: (1) they were more likely than other states to accumulate resources from their frequent attempts at conquest (many overconfident states did die, but among those that came to dominate, overconfident states were overrepresented); (2) if wars only occur when the attacking state is unambiguously stronger than its opponent (rather than just closely matched or slightly stronger), unbiased and underconfident states shirk many conflicts they are likely to win (you are likely to win, over time, whenever you are even just a little bit stronger, and overconfident states benefited from this); and (3) overconfident states were more likely to participate in attacks by multiple states on weak neighbors, forcing victims to split their defenses and provide easy pickings. We looked at a wide range of variations in model parameters (including different sizes of the grid, whether it had boundaries or was a continuous surface, the initial number of states, how decisive strength was to the outcomes of conflict, and alternative starting distributions of overconfidence). The superior performance of overconfidence was robust across all these variations. Of course, if the cost of fighting itself is increased enough, at some point the benefits of war are outweighed by its costs and cautious states will do better instead (as we also showed). Nevertheless, the model indicated that whenever the benefits of war are sufficiently large compared to its costs, overconfidence is the winning strategy. This suggests that if wars have historically tended to bring net benefits despite their costs, then overconfidence, via learning or some other selection mechanism, may have spread and become entrenched among modern states, organizations, and decision-makers.

The agent-based model was intriguing but raised the question of whether overconfidence would remain advantageous in more general, non-spatial settings. James Fowler and I built a more general mathematical model of conflict using evolutionary game theory.[81] This model was also important because in the ABM, all change relied on fighting. In the new model, agents could claim resources without necessarily having to fight to secure them. The model again showed that, counterintuitively, overconfidence maximizes individual fitness and populations will tend to become overconfident, as long as—like in the ABM—benefits from the resources at stake sufficiently exceed the cost of competing for them. Why is this?

First, overconfidence was advantageous because it encouraged *weaker* individuals to make a *claim* for resources they might not actually win if it came to a conflict (stronger but more cautious rivals will sometimes fail to contest the claim, leaving it to the weaker actor). Second, overconfidence was also advantageous at the other end of the spectrum, stopping *stronger* actors walking away from conflicts they are likely to win. Over generations, these advantages of overconfidence led to better returns and overconfidence spread at the expense of unbiased or overly cautious actors.

The results of the model may seem counterintuitive, but they concur with related previous findings. For example, systematic overestimates of the probability of winning simple gambling games have been shown to lead to higher payoffs over time—as long as the benefits of the prize at stake exceed the costs of attempting to gain it.[82] In another research paradigm, aggressive strategies (such as "hawk" in the hawk-dove game) have been shown to out-perform other strategies wherever the benefits of winning exceed the costs of injury.[83] In short, all of these results reflect a basic intuition that when there are things worth fighting for, fortune favors the bold.

The mathematical model also revealed the conditions under which over-confidence arises. Perhaps most remarkably, it showed that the conditions under which agents would evolve an *unbiased* view of their own capabili-ties are exceedingly rare (because as long as there is any uncertainty at all in assessments of other actors, then some level of bias is always the best strategy). It also helped to explain why resource-rich environments (rather than scar-city) can paradoxically create more conflict, because increasing the resources at stake increased the optimal level of overconfidence and thus the frequency of fighting. Moreover, we showed that overconfident populations are "evolu-tionarily stable," that is, resistant to invasion by alternative strategies. Over-confidence was therefore not a fluky outcome but a stable equilibrium that would recur time and time again. The mathematical model thus offered a solid theoretical grounding for why (and when) overconfidence can be adaptive, and thus why it may remain prevalent today—and advantageous—in politics, business, finance, and life in general, even if it causes occasional disasters.

Both models were also consistent with the idea that humans evolved in a world in which the value of contestable resources was relatively high and the cost of conflict was relatively low—a situation advanced, among others, by Richard Wrangham's "imbalance of power" hypothesis.[84] The imbalance of power hypothesis suggests that in human evolutionary history (as well as among other social animals), conflict was relatively cheap for the attacker because it tended to be carried out only when one had a numerical advantage, and at a time of one's choosing. Fighting, therefore, often brought large ben-efits to the perpetrators yet carried little risk, contrary to common intuition. Under these conditions, according to the models, overconfidence would be the best strategy to maximize gains. Fear of confronting or fighting rivals would lead to missing out on (sometimes easy) opportunities for gain. Overconfi-dence serves to overcome fear and promote offensive action, especially when one is in a coalition, yielding net benefits over time.[85]

FORTUNE FAVORS THE BOLD: OVERCONFIDENCE AS ERROR MANAGEMENT

In chapter 1, we met error management theory (EMT) as an explanation for why biases can outperform accuracy in decision-making. The logic was that, under uncertainty, attempts at accurate assessments will make both false positive and false negative errors. However, if false positive and false negative errors result in different costs, then a better decision-making strategy over time is a *bias* that steers one away from whichever is the more costly error. The models of overconfidence presented above can be interpreted in precisely this framework: given inherent uncertainty about actors' relative capabilities, and thus the likely outcome of a conflict between them, as long as the prize at stake is sufficiently greater than the cost of competition (such that the false positive error of sometimes fighting but losing is cheaper than the false negative error of sometimes not fighting when one could have won), the best strategy to maximize gains in the long run is a bias toward overconfidence.

One might object that a history of past mistakes—of either kind—should lead decision-makers to update their beliefs and make correct judgments instead. However, as explored in chapter 1, the whole logic of EMT is that even if updating assessments to target the *true* probability of winning were possible (and that in itself can be impossible given a variety of obstacles), uncertainty means mistakes would still be made but now equally in both directions: on average 50 percent of assessments would overestimate the probability of winning (false positives), and 50 percent would underestimate it (false negatives). If false negatives are more costly than false positives (or vice versa), then we want a bias, not attempts at accuracy, because a bias will steer us away from making the more costly error.

Overconfidence is thus "adaptive" in an evolutionary sense because it *evolves* as a solution to decision-making problems in conditions of uncertainty and asymmetric errors. Indeed, this may explain why we observe it empirically as a human cognitive bias—it is an evolved adaptation. However, the bigger question of this book is whether a bias toward overconfidence *remains adaptive* today. Even if the modern world is very different from the world of our past, if the prevailing environment continues to have similar conditions of uncertainty in assessments and asymmetric costs of errors, then the bias may continue to be adaptive today. This begs the question, are uncertainty and asymmetric costs still prevalent in relevant decision-making domains?

In terms of uncertainty, there is no doubt that despite increasing technology and intelligence apparatus, efforts to disguise and discern states' power and intentions remain an immense source of uncertainty in international relations. In times of conflict, uncertainty can become a particular problem. Clausewitz lamented that "many intelligence reports in war are contradictory; even more are false, and most are uncertain," and the task of interpreting them all "becomes infinitely harder in the thick of fighting itself."[86] Indeed, the underlying intuition of error management, and its solution, may have been recognized long ago. As Clausewitz put it, "With uncertainty in one scale, courage and self-confidence must be thrown into the other to correct the balance."[87] Richard Herrmann and Jong Kun Choi stressed that, even in normal international relations, short of war, the problem of assessing other states' intentions "is a notoriously difficult endeavor."[88] And again this seems to lead to a bias as a result. As they go on, while "we might expect the combination of inherent uncertainty and tremendous importance to engender tentativeness and open-minded learning," in fact "this is often not the case. We find, instead, rigidity and excessive confidence, if not cognitive closure."[89] The "inherent uncertainty" and "tremendous importance" of outcomes closely reflect the logic of EMT—high levels of uncertainty and high stakes are, counterintuitively, key ingredients for a bias to become adaptive.

In terms of asymmetric errors, when weighing up whether or not to fight, there are clearly costs to being wrong and fighting a stronger enemy (false positives), as well as costs to being wrong in the other direction and shying away from enemies that can be defeated (false negatives). There is little reason to believe these costs would ever be exactly equal. For overconfidence to be adaptive, the benefits of winning must sufficiently outweigh the cost of fighting over time. This may well have been the case for long periods of history when aggressors could conquer territory and seize resources, and even in many cases of conventional crises and conflict today, despite the increasing scale and destructiveness of modern conflict.[90] But there are limits. With nuclear weapons, for example, the costs of an all-out war would become unacceptable for winners and losers alike, and the benefits insignificant by comparison.

In short, the key conditions for error management theory to apply—uncertainty in assessments and asymmetric costs of false positive and false negative errors—remain significant in many contemporary settings. Overconfidence should thus remain an adaptive bias, even or perhaps especially in the inherently uncertain and high-stakes world of international politics and war.

Strategic Advantages of Overconfidence in International Politics

There are precedents for the idea that high levels of confidence can be advantageous in the realm of politics and international relations. "Far better it is to dare mighty things," Teddy Roosevelt proclaimed in the quote that opened this chapter, "to win glorious triumphs, even though checkered by failure," if one wants to achieve anything significant.[91] Others might point to Alexander, Caesar, and Napoleon as examples of historical leaders whose remarkable confidence and ambition lifted their sights high and carved out empires to match. In particular, confidence plays an important role in combat effectiveness. Military commanders throughout history have noted the importance of boldness in devising one's strategy and making difficult decisions, as well as the essential role of confidence among the fighting troops. World War II general George S. Patton put this in characteristically blunt terms: "The most vital quality a soldier can possess is SELF CONFIDENCE—utter, complete, and bumptious. You can have doubts about your good looks, about your intelligence, about your self control, but to win in war you must have NO doubts about your ability as a soldier."[92] But he was standing on the shoulders of even greater giants. Carl von Clausewitz wrote: "Boldness in war . . . must be granted a certain power over and above successful calculations involving space, time, and magnitude of forces [i.e., over and above material factors], for wherever it is superior, it will take advantage of its opponents' weakness."[93] Modern studies have found that military personnel, especially in elite combat roles such as special forces, fighter pilots, and submarine captains, exude very high levels of confidence; this can make them hard to handle but gives them a vital edge in lethal encounters with their adversaries.[94] Randall Collins's analysis of fighter pilot aces found that they "believed themselves [to be] surrounded by a magic halo that kept them safe and victorious."[95]

Confident leaders can also help to generate confidence among the ranks, as well as instilling fear among the enemy. Wellington said that having Napoleon on the battlefield lent the equivalent of 40,000 extra troops.[96] Andrew Roberts offers some support for this claim, noting that before Waterloo, the French troops' "morale was high owing to their being commanded in person by a general they firmly believed to be the greatest soldier since Alexander."[97] Whatever the hype, the great leader himself clearly recognized the strategic advantages of boldness because, while it was not entirely natural to him, he consciously sought to conjure it up when it was needed. Robert Greene wrote that "even Napoleon had to cultivate the habit on the battlefield, where he knew it was a matter of life and death. In social settings he was awkward and timid, but he overcame this and practiced boldness in every part of his life because he saw its tremendous power."[98]

However intangible the notion of confidence can seem at times, it plays a clear enough role to have drawn the attention of leaders and commentators throughout history. Shakespeare noted it, giving Henry V these lines at the famed English victory at Agincourt: "O God of battles! Steel my soldier's hearts; Possess them not with fear: take from them now The sense of reckoning, if th'opposed numbers Pluck their hearts from them!"[99] Another astute observer of the human condition, Goethe, also recognized the creative advantages of confidence: "Whatever you can do or dream you can, begin it. Boldness has genius, power and magic in it!"[100] Renaissance artist Michelangelo similarly opined, "The greater danger for most of us lies not in setting our aim too high and falling short; but in setting our aim too low, and achieving our mark."[101] The point is intuitively appealing and was perhaps best captured by Virgil's "fortune favors the bold."[102]

Many observers of history have been as impressed by the remarkable feats and victories that great confidence has facilitated as by its prominent mistakes and disasters—Alexander, Caesar, and Napoleon are just as much admired for the audacity that brought them to fame as they are scorned for the hubris that threatened to (or did) undermine them. Even defeats could serve to elevate

Table 3.1. Adaptive advantages of overconfidence in the past and (under the right circumstances) today

Advantage	Past	Today
Ambition	√	√
(Taking on difficult challenges, exploiting opportunities, decisiveness)		
Resolve	√	√
(Coping with adversity, determination, perseverance)		
Deterrence	√	√
(Signaling strength, dissuading rivals, attracting allies)		

their mythical stature. French author Victor Hugo famously claimed that Napoleon was defeated by God, not by the Duke of Wellington.[103] For a variety of reasons, international relations scholars have been anchored on the disaster end of the spectrum—seeing overconfidence as a cause of mistakes—and it seems high time that we look at the problem from a new angle. How and when might overconfidence bring strategic advantages instead?

Table 3.1 summarizes key adaptive advantages of overconfidence derived from the literature in evolutionary psychology and evolutionary biology. In the following, I examine how each of these advantages may translate to offer strategic advantages in the context of international relations.

OVERCONFIDENCE INCREASES AMBITION

Overconfidence can help an individual exploit opportunities that a less confident individual would be too cautious to even attempt. In other words, it may help in *taking on challenges* in the first place, even if it does not necessarily help in carrying out or completing them. Some such opportunities may lead to failure, while others may lead to success. As long as the prize at stake is sufficiently large compared with the costs of competing for it, a bias toward overconfidence can be an effective strategy to maximize gains over time (as we saw in the models).

A related advantage is that overconfidence can help in taking actions that are *decisive*. For example, game theoretical work suggests that there is often a first mover advantage (e.g., in the "leader" or "coordination" game) or an advantage to taking a more assertive stance (e.g., in the "hawk-dove" game, under certain conditions). Such advantages have been shown among animals as well as humans.[104] "Boldness" is often defined as having low levels of fear in novel situations, or in response to isolation, and thus an ability to act independently and lead others. Empirical studies show links between personality traits, including boldness, and leadership.[105] If leaders are bold or risk-seeking, this can give them crucial initiative, even if it also reflects a certain level of overconfidence.[106] Interestingly, bold or even aggressive behavior itself can sometimes determine the outcomes of fights, over and above differences in power. This is reflected theoretically in the hawk-dove game, in which aggressive hawks do well at the expense of doves as long as the benefits of winning exceed the costs of conflict. But the phenomenon is also observed empirically. For example, in biological experiments, animals that escalate first and fastest tend to be the winners of fights, even against larger individuals, while in the field, territorial conflicts tend to be won by territory holders, again even against larger invaders.[107]

How might such effects play out in international relations? *Taking* risk is an important aspect of state behavior in which confidence can help, and choosing one's *moment* to roll the dice is another important aspect in which confidence can be instrumental. Hesitancy in itself can be costly, even if the strategy to be put in action is sound. Decisiveness, by contrast, is widely recognized as an advantage, even if the strategy to be put in action is less sound (action at least is taken). Taking risks and being decisive are both vital, and without them, things can go wrong. While leaders and states may prefer to avoid risk and defer decisions, they cannot shy away from them altogether. They are unlikely to survive or grow in the long term without sometimes taking the plunge on ambitious goals. Overconfidence will encourage states to take bold steps. This may sometimes lead to costly mistakes. However, at other times it may be critical for preserving or increasing power, or indeed for survival. Most major turning points in history revolve around the taking of risk, whether in taking offensive action, fighting back against an intruder, joining a rebellion, or seeking to change the status quo by other means. Examples that spring to mind include the ambition and boldness of Napoleonic France, America's Declaration of Independence, and the defiance of Britain in the face of Nazi Germany.

Nixon's national security advisor Henry Kissinger argued that "a leisurely process of decision-making creates a presumption in favor of eventual inaction," whereas "in a crisis boldness is the safest course. Hesitation encourages the adversary to persevere, maybe even raise the ante."[108] When an American EC-121 aircraft was shot down by North Korea in 1969, Kissinger himself lamented his government's "conduct in the EC-121 crisis as weak, indecisive and disorganized," and wrote that "I believe we paid for it in many intangible ways, in demoralized friends and emboldened adversaries."[109] He noted the same problem in Vietnam: "The bane of our military actions in Vietnam was their hesitancy; we were always trying to calculate with fine precision the absolute minimum of force. . . . Perhaps the most difficult lesson for a national leader to learn is that with respect to the use of military force, his basic choice is to act or to refrain from acting. He will not be able to take away the moral curse of using force by employing it halfheartedly or incompetently. There are no rewards for exhibiting one's doubts in vacillation; statesmen get no prizes for failing with restraint. Once committed they must prevail."[110] Although many would contest Kissinger's approach, and his examples, intuitively we recognize the advantage of boldness and decisiveness—hallmarks of confidence without which defeat can easily be seized from the jaws of victory.

OVERCONFIDENCE INCREASES RESOLVE

Resolve can seem a nebulous concept, meaning different things in different disciplines, yet it is one that is widely regarded as significant in state behavior. Encapsulating a range of related phenomena including willpower, drive, determination, perseverance, and tenacity, it can be, and has been, used to explain a wide range of behavior in international politics and war.[111] In particular, resolve has been argued to underlie effective deterrence, to bolster bargaining positions, and to improve military effectiveness. In his book on resolve in international politics, Joshua Kertzer looked at a variety of situational and dispositional characteristics that underlie resolve (such as the benefits and costs at stake, concerns for honor and reputation, and time and risk preferences) and identified several advantages that resolve can bring to leaders and states. He also recognized that there are likely to be additional factors that generate resolve, and in the final paragraph of his book, he suggested optimism and overconfidence as promising candidates.[112]

There are always other states (both allies and enemies) ready to exploit one's weaknesses and missteps. Major decisions such as going to war or crisis negotiations can be alarming and leaders may approach them with some dread and fear. In the face of such tough decisions, confidence helps decision-makers confront, commit to, and tackle difficult challenges, as well as cope with adversity along the way. Schelling argued that states must stand firm to demonstrate resolve, and doing so with boldness and lack of fear of the consequences increases the chances of the enemy conceding or suing for peace (such as by making binding commitments or burning bridges behind one's line of defense). If the enemy chooses battle, resolve then also helps states fight.[113]

Sometimes, there is no decision to be made. A state is invaded, or has already committed to fight. Now at war, the only thing that matters is fighting effectively, in which determination and resolve again are essential elements.[114] While most of the variation in the outcomes of wars may be explained by military power and other material factors, at the margins differences in the willingness to fight, and to keep fighting, can be extremely important. Overconfidence, along with optimism and morale, has been argued to increase resolve and determination in combat, and if so can help to increase effort and perseverance among decision-makers, soldiers, citizens, and allies.[115] In the context of human evolution, Wrangham suggested that resolve was crucial for engaging in and achieving effective performance in intergroup conflict, and positive illusions offered an adaptive mechanism to achieve it.[116]

Using data on modern war, Dan Reiter and Allan Stam found that levels of morale among the troops do indeed correlate with battlefield success.[117] This echoes Napoleon's famous suggestion that, in war, morale is three times more valuable than physical strength. Even if not that strong, unmotivated or demoralized soldiers will find it harder to fight. Unmotivated or demoralized leaders will find it harder to sustain the effort and stay the course, and will be more likely to negotiate or concede. Unmotivated or demoralized citizens will be more likely to withdraw their support for the government. And allies will be more likely to doubt one's commitment.

Overconfidence also has important *sources of variation* that relate to promoting resolve under certain, conducive conditions. In a study of the "Rubicon theory of war," Dominic Tierney and I explored a phenomenon in which cognitive biases tend to become elevated *after* a decision has been made.[118] This drew on experimental findings that overconfidence becomes particularly significant as people cross a psychological Rubicon in their decision-making— named for Julius Caesar's fateful crossing of the Rubicon River in 49 BC, by which act he broke an ancient law forbidding any general to enter Italy with an army, thus making war with Rome inevitable.[119] Ever since, "crossing the Rubicon" has come to symbolize a point of no return, when the time for deliberation is over and action is at hand. It turns out that such acts have powerful psychological effects. As the prospect of conflict looms nearer, people switch from what psychologists call a "deliberative" mind-set, which is a more rational state of mind, to an "implemental" mind-set, a state of mind that triggers a number of cognitive biases giving rise to overconfidence.[120] The perception that war is imminent, therefore, may be particularly dangerous—pushing people over the brink exactly at the moment that peace hangs in the balance.

On the face of it, this phenomenon may appear to suggest that people become hopelessly biased in trying to implement what, ironically, they have carefully chosen to do. However, the psychological literature suggests that this would be entirely the wrong interpretation. Instead, the different psychological phenomena associated with each mind-set should be seen as adaptive solutions to the particular problems posed by the different phases of action. Psychological traits are selectively engaged depending on the context in which they will be most useful. This permits the *suppression* of overconfidence to allow level-headed decision-making, and then the *engagement* of overconfidence to enhance performance in carrying out those decisions effectively.

In the pre-decisional phase, the deliberative mind-set "requires an accurate view of reality in order to properly weigh the incentives and correctly estimate the probabilities of success and failure."[121] This can aid in effective decision-making, choosing policies that are most likely to lead to success, and avoiding risky or dangerous policies that are more likely to lead to failure (although note that, given error management theory, some level of bias may still help at this stage to encourage taking on the right balance of risks over time).

By contrast, in the post-decisional phase, when enacting the decisions made, cognitive biases kick in to maintain concentration on the task at hand and promote optimism and perseverance (which under normal circumstances, it is argued, allows for more effective action). As Shelley Taylor and Peter Gollwitzer write, when "people attempt to implement the chosen goals (intended projects) as efficiently as possible . . . the vacillation of the predecisional phase is replaced by determination."[122] Thus the "implementation of a course of action appears to be a time when positive illusions are mustered, even exaggerated, in service of an explicit goal."[123] Applied to international relations, this suggests that overconfidence not only becomes more *apparent* as the probability of conflict increases, but actually becomes more *useful* as an aid to effectively implementing dangerous and difficult actions in crises or war. This focus on the contingent role of different mind-sets to tackle different tasks means that, rather than merely constituting an "error," overconfidence is advantageous—engaged to foster resolve when it matters most.

OVERCONFIDENCE INCREASES DETERRENCE

Whether or not overconfident acts, or beliefs, improve one's own performance, if they *signal* strength or willingness to fight to the enemy, then overconfidence may also bring strategic advantages as a bluff. Potential enemies may be deterred or concede because they (falsely) believe that our high level of confidence must be warranted—that we are more formidable than we really are. There is a large literature on signaling and bluffing, and a common argument is that bluffing is merely "cheap talk" and adversaries will learn to ignore it. Indeed, in evolutionary game theory, bluffing can be evolutionarily unstable because there will be strong selection for discriminating strategies— individuals that call the bluffers' bluff. However, under certain conditions, bluffing can work.[124]

First, bluffs can work if they represent hard-to-fake *signals of commitment* to fight (I act stronger than I really am because I am willing to fight harder than the adversary). An example from nature is male elephants in the state of musth, when they develop visible and odorous signs of being in a frenzied reproductive state due to gland secretions.[125] What is not visible is that they have levels of testosterone circulating in their body that are fifty times higher than normal, which makes them willing to fight long and hard against any challenger. And indeed, when in this state, small males often defeat larger males. Musth is a way of advertising the fact that the elephant, however small, is for the time being willing to sustain great losses of time, energy, and even injury in pursuit of its goals. Like elephants in musth, overconfident individuals don't necessarily pretend to *be* stronger; they *act* as if they were stronger by actually attacking opponents—a hard-to-fake signal, especially when they attack opponents stronger than themselves. In the human world, we are alert to bluffs and are often skeptical of the bluffer. Yet, signalers are constantly bluffing and receivers are sometimes fooled. Often, at a minimum, we cannot be sure whether an adversary is as dangerous as they appear to be, and a blustering display can stop a cautious foe in its tracks or even extract concessions from them without having to fight.

Second, therefore, bluffs can work when there is *uncertainty about outcomes*. Although in ideal conditions bluffing might be expected to be selected out by discriminating strategies, bluffing can survive if there is sufficient ambiguity in one's own or others' strengths and thus who is likely to win. If so, bluffs and reality cannot always be reliably distinguished (meaning, information on rivals' capabilities is not a reliable predictor of success), and bluffing can remain advantageous, at least up to some limit of "believability." Interestingly, bluffing can also succeed (even when it is detectable) in conditions and among animals in which serious injury is possible, because in those circumstances the costs of calling a bluff can be high or even lethal.[126]

Whatever the theory, at the empirical level, natural selection has favored numerous adaptations for bluffing across the animal kingdom. There is an extraordinary diversity of physiological and behavioral adaptations, among many thousands of species, to bluff strength, capabilities, or commitment in order to deter rivals or predators—ranging from elephants advertising their status of musth, to cats raising their hair to appear bigger, to moths with startling eye markings on their wings. Wrangham argued that bluffing opponents was the second of the two key adaptive advantages of positive illusions in intergroup conflict (the first was resolve).[127] In the realm of international politics, the potential for bluffing is also theoretically and empirically significant. Given inherent uncertainty, the turnover of leaders, diverse issues and opponents, and the time that elapses between conflicts, one can never know the true commitment and capabilities of an opponent. Both the stakes and the level of uncertainty are high, and bluffing remains prominent if not routine in international politics. This is no doubt because sometimes, at least, it works.[128]

Finally, overconfidence may signal one's strength or willingness to fight to *allies* as well as enemies. People are more likely to join an alliance and fight alongside partners if they perceive them to be strong and committed. Allies that exude weakness or doubts are—or will seem to be—liabilities. On 15 June 1815, when Napoleon's troops were already advancing on his position, the Duke of Wellington spent the evening at the Duchess of Richmond's ball. According to Roberts, "By attending—if only relatively briefly—he calmed the fears of the Brussels populace, put heart into his assembled colonels, [and] showed that Sir Francis Drake [who famously finished his game of bowls before attending to the Spanish Armada in 1588] was not the only British hero to display insouciance in the face of danger."[129]

To summarize, there are several adaptive advantages of overconfidence that translate into strategic advantages in the realm of international relations.

Overconfidence may not always be strong or important. However, it has consistent effects that can bring a competitive edge over and above material power and resources, potentially tipping the balance between victory and defeat. Consider this thought experiment. Two nations are identical except one is overconfident (the Bold) and the other is not (the Meek). Each nation may be competent and well resourced. But there will be important differences in their behavior. The Meek will be more hesitant, less willing to fight, and more likely to allow opportunities to pass by for fear of failure. When war looms, they will be less likely to deter opponents, attract allies, or reassure their citizens. If war comes, they will find it harder to take risks, maintain resolve, and persist in the face of obstacles. By contrast, the Bold will be more decisive, more willing to fight, more likely to take advantage of opportunities, and in the face of war more likely to deter rivals, attract allies, win support, and, in war itself, take risks, maintain resolve, and fight tenaciously despite setbacks. All else equal, the Bold will prosper at the expense of the Meek. Their overconfidence may seem arrogant and hubristic to other states, and they may be more likely to make mistakes and get themselves into costly fights along the way, but as long as the spoils of victory tend to exceed the costs of fighting, they will do better on average, over time. As a rule, the Bold are less likely to miss opportunities to gain power, and as a result they are more likely to be among the survivors of anarchic competition.

Limits on Overconfidence's Advantages

Overconfidence is only likely to be adaptive at moderate levels.[130] Unrestrained and unlimited overconfidence can lead to: (1) taking on tasks that are too difficult or impossible; (2) incurring such significant costs that they outweigh any potential advantages gained; and (3) undermining any potentially beneficial strategic effects on others (e.g., they will be more likely to call your bluff). Psychologists have noted these limits on the utility of overconfidence and Baumeister suggests that, to be adaptive, there is an "optimal margin of illusion."[131] Too little means the advantages of confidence cannot be brought to bear, while too much leads to unrealistic goals, overreaching, and failure.

Although the general rule seems to be that only *moderate* levels of overconfidence are adaptive, and too little or too much is bad, there may be exceptions. In some situations, the bigger the bias, the better. Extreme confidence may work in the perpetrator's favor if its very implausibility makes it unlikely to be seen as a bluff—as the saying goes, "if you're going to lie, lie big." If someone were lying, why would they tell such a big, unbelievable lie? In 1925, infamous "con artist extraordinaire" Count Victor Lustig, posing as a government official, secretly "sold" the Eiffel Tower to a scrap metal merchant for 250,000 francs. Of course, the Eiffel Tower was not for sale and the French government had no intention of dismantling it. But Lustig was able to convince people otherwise. As Robert Greene observes, had Lustig "tried to sell the Arc de Triomphe, a bridge over the Seine, a statue of Balzac, no one would have believed him. But the Eiffel Tower was just too large, too improbable to be part of a con job."[132] Indeed, it worked so well that Lustig came back to Paris a few months later and sold the Eiffel Tower *again* to another scrap metal merchant—for more!

Sun Tzu and other gurus of military strategy have similarly advocated the strategic advantages of a preposterous bluff in the context of international relations and war. One example comes from the legend of Li Guang and the 100 horsemen. In 144 BC, Han general Li Guang and one hundred of his men stumbled upon several thousand Xiongnu soldiers. If they attacked, they would be annihilated. If they fled, they would be chased down. Li Guang realized, however, that the Xiongnu did not know if he and the 100 horsemen were alone or an advance contingent of thousands about to appear over the horizon (the rest of Li Guang's force was in fact faraway). Guang had his men dismount, shoo their horses away, and prepare themselves as if for combat. Seeing this, the Xiongnu forces retreated, fearing they were being baited into an ambush.[133] As it had for Lustig in Paris, a preposterous bluff worked.

Under normal conditions, evidence suggests that some moderate level of overconfidence is adaptive. But as illustrated here there may be cases—especially those involving signaling to a bargaining partner or an enemy—where even extremes can pay off too. One important difference, however, is that moderate overconfidence appears to be instinctive and natural, whereas feigning invincible strength may be unnatural, demanding the intervention of intelligence, conscious deception, and planning, which could give the game away. Moderate overconfidence may thus be more generally reliable as well as more generally advantageous.

When Does Overconfidence Help or Hurt Us?

Earlier, I promised to look at *when* overconfidence is likely to be advantageous rather than disadvantageous. The theoretical models outlined above explicitly explored the effects of changing conditions on the advantages or otherwise of overconfidence. First, in the evolutionary models, overconfidence paid off across a wide range of parameter settings, as long as the cost-benefit ratios of competition were favorable (and in general, that was when the benefits of the prize at stake exceeded the costs of competing for it).[134] Second, error management theory suggested that overconfidence can be advantageous as long as decisions are made under uncertainty and alternative errors have asymmetric costs. We already looked at the importance of uncertainty and asymmetric costs and concluded that they remain prominent in modern international relations, and war in particular. Here, therefore, I focus on whether the cost-benefit ratios of contemporary conflict are also in the "right" direction to favor overconfidence.

What *are* the prevailing cost-benefit ratios of competition in the real world—are they still conducive to overconfidence today? This will vary across domains, but let's focus on the big one: the costs and benefits of war. Some international relations scholars and historians argue that the benefits of war, at least for the victors, exceed its costs.[135] However, others (perhaps a majority) argue that war brings net costs—to both winners and losers alike.[136] Neither extreme is likely to apply across the board. What is likely is that there is considerable variation from war to war and among actors, and we therefore need to track broad trends over a large sample of wars, as well as pay attention to whether this has changed over time. Empirical analyses of interstate wars show that *initiators* (those that choose to launch the war) have won one-half to three-quarters of wars since 1495, making it a better-than-even bet on average.[137] However, even for much stronger initiators, this has fallen to a minority of wars since 1945.[138] This suggests that war was more likely to bring net benefits in the past but today (for a variety of reasons) is more likely to bring net costs. If so, overconfidence may have been adaptive in our historical past, as well as our evolutionary past, but may now be becoming an increasing liability. However, note that these statistics are for all states in general. For any *given* state, in a given region or environment—especially a powerful state (e.g., a military hegemon like the United States) or a rising challenger (like China)—its own particular cost-benefit ratio of war may be different. Certain states may still find themselves in a position and an environment conducive to bold behavior.

Finally, we must remember that—whatever the reality on the ground—it is the *perceived* costs and benefits of conflict that will trigger proximate mechanisms underlying overconfidence. So whatever the *real* costs and benefits of war, states may act on the *legacy* of costs and benefits in the past or on their hopes for different costs and benefits in the future. Moreover, these perceptions can deviate markedly among actors. For example, political leaders themselves don't personally suffer the consequences of war (so direct costs to them approach zero), whereas soldiers do (their direct costs are high and can be extreme). Therefore, viewing the same war, and from the same country, political leaders may perceive (and in fact may have) a favorable cost-benefit ratio and favor hawkish strategies, whereas military leaders may perceive (and have) an unfavorable cost-benefit ratio and favor peace. Although this contradicts a popular stereotype of a gung-ho military favoring war, it is in fact exactly what empirical and historical studies have found.[139] Overconfidence may thus hurt some actors at one level but help others at another level.

Implications of Adaptive Overconfidence for International Politics

Whatever its positive or negative consequences, overconfidence remains widespread and important in international politics today. Stephen Walt noted, for example, that "since the end of the Cold War, U.S. leaders have repeatedly exaggerated the efficacy of using military power, and tended to assume that a little bit of military power will produce large, predictable, and uniformly beneficial results."[140] Debates over the 2003 invasion of Iraq, in particular, often revolved around whether the U.S. administration was overconfident about the task it had taken on.[141] At the time, Kevin Phillips warned of "overreach" in the projection of U.S. power: "The hubris of the Bush White House and cabinet hardly needs elaboration. Satisfaction with the republic of yesterday is no longer enough, and talk of empire is open in Washington."[142] Yet overconfidence is not limited to the Bush era. Even the apparently very different administration of Barack Obama expressed remarkable overconfidence in different ways and in different domains (and indeed was the administration during which Walt published his article on the top ten forms of wishful thinking in U.S. foreign policy). At the time of writing, the Donald Trump administration's brimming confidence is ever more striking. The phenomenon also extends beyond the United States, and beyond the realm of war.

During the 2008 euro currency crisis, for example, European political leaders convened summit after summit to extend the measures put in place to deal with the situation. Each step was never enough. While part of the reason was an understandable reluctance to commit the vast sums required to bail out the collapsing Greek economy, many observers noted that there was also a tendency to "consistently underestimate what confronts them."[143] Overconfidence has been implicated in momentous decisions around the globe and throughout history, from the Peloponnesian War to World War I, from Vietnam to Iraq, from the financial crisis to climate change and a variety of contemporary political challenges today. But with overconfidence blamed for disaster in so many cases, it's time that we looked for it in instances of success as well as failure, and asked whether and how its effects can sometimes be good as well as bad. I suggest that sometimes, perhaps even often, it brings great dividends.

IMPLICATIONS FOR LEADERS

At the most basic level, knowledge of systematic biases such as overconfidence is critical to effective decision-making, especially in crises where limited information and limited time bring cognitive biases to the fore. Leaders must be aware of the bias—and its potentially dangerous effects—and factor it into their strategies and public pronouncements.

But the evolutionary perspective of this book also suggests some novel insights. Overconfidence can help us. We have long been told that overconfidence is bad and leads to mistakes, disasters, and failure. Yet in an anarchic world of competition and conflict, overconfidence may in fact be an essential ingredient of success—as it appears to have been in our evolutionary past—promoting ambition, resolve, and deterrence. Perhaps it makes us prone to bite off more than we can chew and to sometimes fight opponents that are stronger than we realize. But in so doing, it may help us avoid an even worse error, which is to prevaricate and fail to exploit opportunities or face down aggression where they arise. When war is at hand, the bold seize the initiative and fight hard, while the meek—even the rational—are comparatively hesitant, risk exploitation, and may lack the mettle to fight and persevere. And this, as Clausewitz recognized, gives boldness an edge.

So far, we have only considered how overconfidence might directly aid a state's strategic position vis-à-vis other states. However, political actors may also benefit by exploiting overconfidence *within* the state. History has plentiful examples of leaders pursuing unpopular or expensive wars for which they needed public backing. In drumming up support for costly or controversial policies, leaders may (consciously or unconsciously) play on overconfidence to frame their own nation's skill and strength as superior, the risks of war small, and the benefits large—just as Pericles did to convince his countrymen to launch the Peloponnesian War. Like a boat traveling downstream, such arguments will be swept along by citizens' own natural disposition toward overconfidence, making bold action seem more convincing and compelling.

A powerful example is World War I. Large segments of society on all sides welcomed war, believing their own nations to have a superior culture and military capabilities.[144] Political and military leaders offered bellicose rhetoric about the righteousness of their cause, the promising odds of victory, and the advantages of boldly seizing the initiative. As well as representing genuine beliefs among key decision-makers, this rhetoric powerfully tapped into public sentiment that dovetailed with overconfidence. Thousands of young men signed up to fight, expecting a short and victorious war. Thousands of others enthusiastically supported the decision to fight and the war effort thereafter. The point of this example is not that overconfidence affected policy decisions but simply that overconfidence can be exploited to boost support for whatever one's policy may be (whether exaggerated optimism about war, exaggerated optimism about peace, or some other desired outcome). This would be illustrated again by Chamberlain and the appeasement of Hitler, and later by Bush and the invasion of Iraq.[145]

IMPLICATIONS FOR INTERNATIONAL RELATIONS THEORY

Assessments of capabilities are vital to international relations, in both theory and practice. If states do not accurately perceive their relative power in comparison with other states, then we might expect them to make serious errors in bargaining, deterrence, and defense and, at the extreme, launch wars they are unlikely to win. In international relations theory, whether or not (or the extent to which) states are prone to make such errors of judgment is a key distinction among hypotheses about the international system. According to the dominant theory of defensive realism, for example, because war is so costly to winners and losers alike, its existence—or at least its frequency—can only satisfactorily be explained by states overestimating the threats they face and the efficacy of military force they can muster to meet them.[146]

However, if overconfidence can actually offer strategic advantages, rather than merely representing ill-fated misperceptions, then this changes the landscape of international relations theory as well as what policymakers might do about it. Perhaps states *should* be biased in their judgments, if they are to perform well in a competitive environment of hostile actors. Perhaps states should *expect* to make mistakes, because they are primed to offensive action and, though risky, that is the best strategy to adopt over time. This is more in line with the theory of "offensive realism" in international relations.[147]

All this has arguably changed, however, in a world with nuclear weapons. Kenneth Waltz wrote: "So complex is the fighting of wars with conventional weapons that their outcomes have been extremely difficult to predict. Wars start more easily because the uncertainties of their outcomes make it easier for the leaders of states to entertain illusions of victory at supportable cost."[148] As soon as nuclear weapons appeared on the scene, however, there was little room for rosy assumptions and expectations. Instead, the possibility of the use of nuclear weapons "focuses one's attention not on the probability of victory but on the possibility of annihilation."[149] Overconfidence is only advantageous in a world where there is a favorable cost-benefit ratio to participating in competition and where there is uncertainty in outcomes. This was clear in our models. First, an offensive advantage, in larger benefits and/or smaller costs of war, increased the utility of overconfidence, but nuclear weapons create a world where there is a *defensive* advantage, at least in theory, for nuclear-armed states. Second, greater uncertainty led to a greater optimal level of overconfidence, but, as Waltz argued, nuclear weapons mean a reduction in uncertainty about outcomes and we might thus expect a corresponding reduction in the utility of bravado and brinkmanship. In the nuclear context, overconfidence may lose its advantage. Being bold and playing chicken is OK when opponents have conventional weapons (it can pay off, but if not, mistakes can be recovered from) but risks everything when one or both sides could resort to (or accidentally trigger) the use of nuclear weapons.

IMPLICATIONS FOR DEALING WITH OVERCONFIDENT COMPETITORS

Regardless of the level of overconfidence in one's *own* decision-making, it remains vital to analyze and understand it because of the danger of overconfidence in *other actors*. Overconfidence among our allies or enemies can be extremely costly to us, whatever it does for them. Even if we were perfectly rational, if foreign leaders are overconfident and overestimate themselves or underestimate *us*, this can in itself cause failures in negotiation, bargaining, or deterrence and drag us into expensive arms races, confrontations, and wars. Saddam Hussein's conviction that the United States would not fight to liberate Kuwait in 1990–91 had major consequences for Americans as well as for Iraqis. War occurred again in 2003 largely because Saddam played a similar strategy of brinkmanship, believing that the United States would ultimately back down or, if not, would become bogged down in an urban quagmire that he could eventually win.[150] Saddam was too confident and brought on his own demise, but only after his overconfidence had cost everyone dearly.

This book adds an additional twist. Overconfidence may be *helping* our enemies, even if it sometimes hurts them. If overconfidence increases their own ambitions, resolve, and deterrence, that will help to make *our* strategies fail and theirs succeed. This raises an interesting question. When we are dealing with a threatening state that is overconfident, is the most effective deterrent a cold, calculating, rational one (which relies on them being rational too) or a strategy that counteracts their own biases by being or acting overconfident back? This was essentially the lesson of the game theoretical models of overconfidence discussed earlier. The commonsense assumption is that rational actors should do best of all. But *in competition with other* strategies, they do poorly and are outcompeted by overconfident actors, who take advantage of opportunities more readily than others. It may be counterintuitive, but as Schelling often pointed out, that's the nature of strategic interaction.[151] As any poker player will attest, you cannot win the game against other human beings if you don't confidently assert the hand you are playing, however strong it is.

Conclusions

An adaptive, strategic perspective on overconfidence leads to some novel insights. First, overconfidence is not some sort of unfortunate "error" or design "flaw" in human cognition as so often assumed. On the contrary, evolution has refined it as a design *feature*.

Second, if overconfidence conferred adaptive advantages in our evolutionary past, there is no reason to expect that it would not continue to do so today. It may sometimes cause mistakes but nevertheless confer *net benefits over time*. The contemporary world is very different from that of our past, but despite its vastly greater scale, complexity, and technological sophistication, international politics is still essentially about strategic interactions between individuals and groups, and assessments of one's own and others' capabilities. Overconfidence is a strategic instinct that helps us survive and prosper in such a world.

Third, if overconfidence is an evolved trait, then it is likely to be *contingent*, emerging in contexts where it is useful and taking a back seat where it is not.

Adaptive traits are designed to alter behavior to match specific scenarios (or decision-making domains), not to inflexibly "hard-wire" behavior so that it is the same at all times irrespective of the situation. This variation is important for generating predictions about where and when the bias is likely to be present or absent, strong or weak, and, crucially, positive or negative in its effects.

Even if overconfident *individuals* (or states) are killed, if overconfident *strategies* are more successful than alternative strategies (e.g., than unbiased or cautious ones) then the trait of overconfidence itself will spread even if many of its bearers die. This is a common feature of natural selection in nature, whereby individuals may be eliminated from the population but their successful characteristics live on in the genes that give rise to them (even if those characteristics increase risky behavior, such as fighting itself). It also precisely reflects the logic in the agent-based model presented earlier: judged by the number of states that get wiped out, overconfidence is a dangerous strategy. But so are all the other strategies. Judged by who is left standing on the battlefield, overconfidence is the best route to survival and supremacy. In a land of lethal competition, only the bold can be king.

The prevalence and importance of overconfidence suggest that, rather than a quirk that plugs a few gaps in our understanding of international relations, it should be placed at the heart of international relations theory. A major paradox in the field is the fear that underlies the security dilemma in times of peace but the almost universal false optimism on the eve of war. The fact that states are fearful of each other most of the time but become supremely confident when it comes to conflict can be explained by the Rubicon theory.[152] This theory can account for not only why overconfidence varies but also how this variation represents an adaptive, contingent response. Overconfidence comes to the fore precisely when it becomes most useful: when war is at hand.

The reach of overconfidence is, however, not limited to war. Levels of confidence affect numerous activities in international relations, from diplomacy and deterrence to trade and international cooperation. In all of these domains, its advantages could be important. One example stands out to me, in that overconfidence may have major positive effects in overcoming collective action problems—both within and between states. Here's the logic for why that may be the case.

Within states, collective action is a daily headwind for multiple issues in society and politics, but revolutions and rebellions perhaps represent the epitome of the challenge. They are dangerous struggles by the weak against the strong, and for whom committing sedition against entrenched powers may bring the ultimate price. Weighing up the costs and benefits of participation, a rational actor might well decide to stay at home. But with an optimism that one individual can make a difference, that sufficient others out there agree, and that the power of the people can overcome tyranny, revolutions do sometimes manage to get off the ground—optimism becomes a self-fulfilling prophecy. Timothy Garton Ash called the Polish Solidarity movement in the face of Soviet power in the 1980s "the most infectiously hopeful movement in the history of contemporary Europe."[153] Before and during such struggles, the odds may seem insurmountable, and in the face of hardship, violence, and retribution, it often seems extraordinary that people persevere at all. Yet sometimes revolutions occur and succeed even in the most challenging of circumstances. As Nelson Mandela famously remarked, "It always seems impossible until it's done."[154] If something seems impossible, we might need leaders with great confidence to make them possible.

Between states, we need inspiration for solving the collective action problem at the global level more than ever. Here, current challenges to the planet are especially daunting and difficult, ranging from expanding populations and dwindling resources to species extinction and climate change. Some inspirational confidence in the face of such challenges could make all the difference. As one commentator railed against states' failure to address the United Nations' ambitious Millennium Development Goals to eradicate poverty and hunger: "It is pessimism, scepticism and cynicism that are the three worst enemies of the global anti-poverty agenda. Its three best friends are the space to adapt and tailor global targets, an explicit focus on equity, and a quantum leap in imagination."[155] We don't want to be reckless and set impossible goals, but we may need to have more confidence—maybe even some overconfidence—if we are to attempt to solve massive global challenges. As Teddy Roosevelt recognized, we certainly won't achieve such things if they are not attempted.

I have argued that, in general, a modest amount of overconfidence is adaptive. It evolved to become the norm in the population because it represents an advantageous strategic instinct. It may be that, in the *modern* world, overconfidence leads to failure more often than in the past, and only a few freakish outliers lead to success. For every Mark Zuckerberg, there are a thousand failed start-ups.[156] For every Muhammad Ali, there are a thousand unknown boxing wannabes. For every Napoleon, there are a thousand generals killed on the fields of battle. However, even if that were the case, overconfidence would remain important. If the overconfident are more likely to have grander ambitions, to take bigger risks, to attempt things that others would shy away from, and to have greater resolve to see them through, then they are likely to have an inordinate impact on history.

Although history is littered with the casualties of human overconfidence, it is that same overconfidence that has often made history itself. The great confidence of the Athenians, Caesar, and Napoleon, among others, underlay not just their downfall but also the extraordinary conquests from which their fall was so great. Pericles ended his final speech to the Athenian assembly before the outbreak of the Peloponnesian War by observing that it is "out of the greatest dangers [that] communities and individuals acquire the greatest glory."[157] For other great luminaries of history, of course, such as Alexander the Great, Genghis Khan, and Ulysses S. Grant, there was no downfall, only victory. Without the confidence—often the *over*confidence—needed to allay our fears and enter the fray, the rewards of competition can never be won in the first place. The next chapter asks whether we might witness precisely this effect in one particular insurgency, fought against great odds, that went on to have a tremendous impact on world history—the American Revolution.

CHAPTER FOUR

The Lion and the Mouse

OVERCONFIDENCE AND THE
AMERICAN REVOLUTION

It seems to be a law of nature, inflexible and inexorable, that those who will not risk cannot win.

—JOHN PAUL JONES

The Delaware crossing thus becomes a sudden reversal of fortune, as if an American mouse, chased hither and yon by a British cat, brazenly turns about and declares itself a lion.

—JOSEPH ELLIS

THE UNITED STATES OF America might never have come into being if it had not been for the extraordinary confidence of General George Washington and his dogged determination that carried the American Revolution to victory in 1783. From today's standpoint, with the United States the unrivaled hegemon and leader of global military, economic, and cultural forces, it seems almost predetermined that Washington and the colonials would win the war and thereby give birth to the United States. The histories of the revolution often read like a river leading unstoppably from colonial subjugation and British imperial arrogance to popular uprising, rebellion, the Declaration of Independence, and victory—"like a story," as one historian put it, against a wicked empire with the end "a foregone conclusion."[1] How could it have been any different?

Yet, in the eighteenth century, Great Britain ruled a quarter of the Earth's surface, boasted the world's most powerful navy, and commanded a large and disciplined army that was hardened to war and accustomed to victory—including many times in North America. The American forces were, by contrast, a motley collection of often untrained, poorly equipped, and scattered volunteers. And there was no destiny. As James Morrison stressed, the course of the war was hardly obvious, even after the famous surrender of General Charles Cornwallis that is often heralded as the end of the war: "It is widely assumed that Britain's capitulation became 'inevitable' after the loss at Yorktown in 1781. Students of international politics, however, know better than to blithely accept claims of historical inevitability."[2] The king, George III, wanted to press on regardless, writing "defiantly that the news did not make the smallest change in his views."[3] As the recent Seven Years' War (1756–63) had demonstrated, the European great powers were willing to commit massive effort and military power to sustain their empires, even if it meant incurring debilitating costs in the process. In the end, Britain would invest over £100 million attempting to quash the American uprising (around £15 billion in today's money, but half of GDP in 1783).[4] The battle for North America was not just about putting down rebellious colonial subjects evading tax collection; it was a struggle to preserve global political and economic power at a time of intense competition with lethal enemies, mainly France and Spain, which threatened not only Britain's colonial territories but also the British Isles themselves. Britain had absolutely no intention of losing its valuable assets in America.

Many things could have happened. The American states might have stayed British, become part of a giant Canada, become French or Spanish, or developed into independent countries.[5] The idea that the thirteen colonies would become some kind of United States of America was an outside possibility. The fact that this was achieved, especially when no other colonies anywhere else on the globe had defeated the British military (let alone achieved independence), was, in the view of many historians—and Washington himself—something of "a miracle."[6] The striking question is, therefore, given such daunting circumstances, what on earth led Washington to believe he could win?

A Role for Overconfidence?

My argument is not that Washington or the colonial leaders misunderstood the task before them or made the wrong decision. On the contrary, they knew exactly what they were up against and made the right decision at a big moment, leading to what was perhaps "the most significant political-economic event in the Western Hemisphere since Columbus's arrival."[7] Rather, my argument is that Washington in particular would not have made the decision to fight, and to keep fighting, if it had not been for his remarkable level of confidence—arguably overconfidence—that stood out in stark contrast to the attitudes and beliefs of many of his contemporaries and third-party observers. Where others saw disaster, he believed he could win. Without his indefatigable confidence, he would never have believed victory was possible, and he would not have put his life and livelihood—not to mention those of many tens of thousands of others—on the line. Confidence would help in sustaining resolve and perseverance in the long years ahead but, at the beginning, it was an essential ingredient for the colonists to even attempt to fight at all. America, therefore, may owe its victory not so much to the generalship of George Washington but to his supreme confidence—for daring to believe the impossible.

But how can we go about testing whether this claim is true? It is a common misconception to think that states should only fight if they expect to win. In fact, a state may do so even if it expects to lose. A perfectly rational state might decide to fight even if it only has a 10 percent chance of success, as long as the prize at stake is large enough to warrant the attempt (rational actors are expected to maximize utility, which is the probability of winning *multiplied* by the benefits, minus the costs). This is why people are willing to part with their hard-earned cash to enter lotteries. Even though their chance of winning is several million to one, the prize is so huge as to make it seem worth a shot. This is important, because it means that to demonstrate the existence of overconfidence, it is not enough to show that Washington was merely unlikely to win—perhaps there was only a 1 in 4 chance of victory, and Washington correctly estimated this, but he considered those good odds (and/or better than the consequences of not fighting, which might be considered worse). The prize of independence, after all, was a big one in the eyes of the Founding Fathers. Rather, we have to show that Washington *overestimated* the chance of victory, however large or small it really was.

One way to establish whether Washington—and perhaps many of his compatriots—was overconfident about victory is to look at the expectations of *other* states and actors at the time (third parties), as well as the judgments of historians and political scientists since. Did Washington's expectations simply parallel those of everyone else? Or did he stand out as unusually confident, expecting victory where others expected defeat? Let us first consider some of these third-party views, including contemporary views in Britain and America at the time, and then what scholars have concluded since, with the benefit of hindsight and studying the archives.

It seems fair to say that, in the 1770s, few people expected Britain to lose its North American colonies. It might be hard-pressed to contain emerging rebellious tensions, especially as new tax laws came into effect in the aftermath of the costly Seven Years' War, and indeed it was likely to face sporadic unrest and fighting as there had been in other colonies. The British army and navy became occupied, for example, fighting Hyder Ali of Mysore in India—conflicts they won decisively, despite the intervention of the French and other allies.[8] Given Britain's widely vaunted army, navy, economic might, and technology, it had been, and was expected to continue to be, perfectly capable of putting down insurrection, maintaining control, and preserving its rich and valuable colony in America.[9]

Even when outright war loomed, most people expected the British to win. Indeed, the question of whether they would win or lose was hardly even considered; it was more a question of whether and how much Britain might have to alter its policies to bring the colonials into line. Other issues were given far more attention—certainly by Britain itself. As William Martel put it, "The War of Independence was a sideshow for Britain, whose primary competitor and enemy was France."[10] There was a fundamental expectation that British rule would rumble along—and even continue to expand—as it had always done since the founding of Jamestown in 1607. "While the colonies were considered of vital importance to the prosperity and world status of Britain," Barbara Tuchman wrote, "very little thought or attention was paid to them."[11] Britain did not even have a government department administering the colonies until 1768. British leaders were more concerned about the geopolitics of the European powers and the domestic political wrangling at home—"who's in, who's out."[12]

When the British Parliament officially declared New England to be in rebellion in February 1775, and named the commanding officers for the campaign, "their future . . . recall and surrender was then unimaginable."[13] The king, the cabinet, and a majority of Parliament "could think no further ahead than affirming supremacy and assumed without thinking about it that military victory over the 'rabble' was a matter of course. They never doubted that Americans must succumb to British arms."[14]

Of course, the British might have been biased themselves (toward overconfidence), but this was not just their own hubristic view—other observers also expected Britain to win. This is widely reflected by historians. Joseph Ellis, for example, wrote that before December 1776, the prospects for the revolution "appeared to be certain defeat," and he wrote of "the improbability of American independence."[15] John Ferling called it "almost a miracle" (and indeed used that phrase as the title of his book on the war, echoing Washington's own allusion to the victory as a miracle).[16] Morrison called the British defeat a "shocking loss."[17] And Andrew O'Shaughnessy concurred that "it was a war Britain seemingly should have won."[18] As for contemporaries of the time, Andrew Sinclair wrote that, at least among colonials along the Eastern seaboard cities well aware of British sea power, "few settled families thought that the mighty British Empire could lose the war."[19] Indeed, the large numbers of neutrals and loyalists in itself suggests that a majority did not expect the rebels to prevail. British Secretary for the Colonies Lord George Germain developed his war strategy in 1775 "based upon a variety of American intelligence sources which agreed that the colonists' will to fight was fragile and would never survive a major defeat."[20] All in all, with Britain on the rise as an industrial and military hegemon, "it is little wonder that many contemporaries imagined that the war would be an easy triumph for Britain."[21] With good reason, the British expected to win, and to a significant extent so did everyone else.

The odds were not only against the Americans at the *start* of the war. As the war progressed, if anything there was *increasing* evidence that the odds were against them, which might well have dissuaded the colonials from persisting. After the British withdrew from Boston in March 1776, John Hancock lauded Washington for having faced down a superior army led by experienced generals. But as Ellis notes, "Subsequent events would soon show that this was an overly optimistic appraisal."[22] For one thing, British General William Howe "was unaware" that the army besieging Boston was "at times barely capable of offering resistance" in the face of desertion and recruitment crises.[23] Nathanael Greene despaired as they began "going home in shoals" and argued that Washington was partly to blame for "expecting too much of the army he had inherited."[24] For another, Howe had planned to redeploy to New York anyway—before Washington even arrived. Then, in the fall of 1776, when fighting resumed in the new battlegrounds to the south, Howe won a series of victories around New York which, in Lawrence James's words, "indicated that the British army was unbeatable" and, by the end of November, "he felt strong enough to issue a proclamation which offered an unconditional pardon to all rebels who surrendered and reaffirmed their allegiance to George III. Many Americans, well aware of the pitiful state of Washington's army, were glad to accept Howe's clemency."[25]

In Washington's retreat through New Jersey, noted Ferling, "civilian morale had sagged with each backward step he had taken," and "even one signer of the Declaration of Independence had defected to the British."[26] Arguably, it was at this point that Washington's confidence stood out more than ever. Despite the bleak outlook, with prewar expectations that the deck was stacked against the colonials apparently proving true, from somewhere Washington found the determination to rally his men and keep fighting against all the odds. Indeed, it was not long after this, in December 1776, that Washington staged his daredevil counterattack across the Delaware (Figure 4.1), which led to his first significant successes at Trenton and Princeton.

One might point to American battlefield victories as encouraging signs that they would ultimately win. But in fact they were widely outnumbered by British victories. Figure 4.2 shows that there were 127 British victories, 85 American victories, 18 Franco-American victories (later in the war), and 5 draws or indecisive outcomes. One might further think that masked beneath these *overall* figures, those American victories must have increased over time. However, this is not the case. Figure 4.3 shows that, comparing battlefield successes year by year over the course of the war, British victories (gray bars) outnumbered American victories (black bars) in all years of the war except 1775 and 1780, and the British were still winning more battles in each of the last three years of the war—1781, 1782, and 1783. (Evidently, French allies were starting to have an impact, but even if one adds American and Franco-American [white bars] victories together, Britain still won more battles in every year of the war except 1775, 1779, and 1780—and again won more in the final three years.) While one battle may not be as important as another in the outcome of a war, of course

FIGURE 4.1. Washington's bold crossing of the icy Delaware River on Christmas night, 1776, in what many see as the turning point of the war as well as the lasting iconic symbol of the American Revolution. *Source:* Emanuel Leutze (American, 1816–1868), *Washington Crossing the Delaware*, 1851. Metropolitan Museum of Art, New York, Gift of John Stewart Kennedy, 1897 (97.34).

(some were minor, some were critical), the overall asymmetry is striking and adds to the puzzle of why the Americans persevered given such a persistently negative scorecard. It also amplifies the level of optimism one would need, in the face of these setbacks, in order to carry on believing victory was possible. Rational choice theorists often characterize war as a "bargaining process" in which the fighting itself reveals information about the capabilities and commitment of the other side, enabling actors to update their estimates of the likelihood of victory and its costs and benefits as war goes on. In this case, that assumption appears to be strongly challenged. Washington persisted despite growing negative information.[27]

Even American *victories* might have given pause for concern. When the British suffered significant defeats (embarrassing to the empire and ignoble to its generals), this often led to redoubled effort and *greater* investment in the war. Even in success the Americans might thus have become exasperated at the monumental—and growing—task ahead. The loss of British General John Burgoyne's entire 8,000-man army at Saratoga in 1777, in particular, served as a wake-up call. "In England, the incredible fact of a British Army surrendering to colonials stunned [the] government and public and awoke many who had hardly concerned themselves about the war until then."[28] Despite such disasters, or even because of them, politicians and citizens alike upheld their

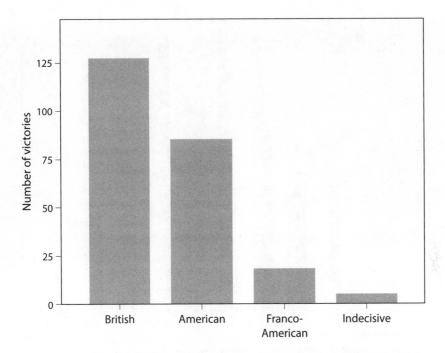

FIGURE 4.2. Number of victories won by each side in the American Revolution (1775–83).
Source: Original figure produced by the author, using data from Wikipedia's "List of
American Revolutionary War Battles," https://en.wikipedia.org/wiki/List_of_American
_Revolutionary_War_battles.

support for the war—and continued to approve the mounting resources necessary to fight it. The king, for his part, remained "convinced of the rectitude
and therefore the necessary triumph of his actions."[29] From Washington's perspective, Saratoga was a coup, but one that might only serve to stir the dragon
to greater anger. Indeed, the Americans would have to continue to face their
stubborn opponent for many years to come.

For the time being, however, Washington had his own problems. Valley
Forge, Washington's winter quarters in 1777–78, has become widely used as
a metaphor for great suffering. Desperately short of food, clothing, and shelter in "brutal winter conditions" that seemed bitterly cold even to the New
Englanders, Washington implored Congress to aid them or the army would, he
warned, imminently "starve—dissolve—or disperse."[30] And starve they did, in
"a squalid environment of low, choking smoke and the stench of death."[31] Over
2,500 men and 700 horses perished from disease, from cold, and from hunger.
If there was a miracle in this war, it was that Washington still found himself
with an army as the winter that year finally receded—especially as Howe, well
aware of the plight of the Continental Army, inexplicably failed to seize the
initiative and send any of his 17,000 troops in nearby Philadelphia (just twenty
miles away) to finish them off.[32]

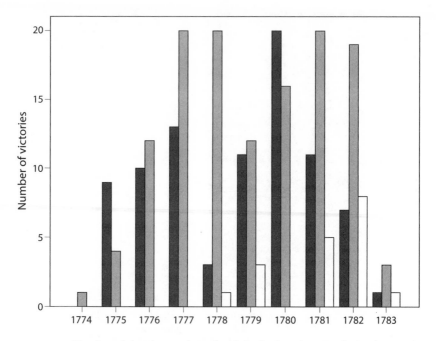

FIGURE 4.3. Number of victories won by each side in the American Revolution (1775–83), broken down by year for the British (gray), Americans (black), and Franco-Americans (white). *Source:* Original figure produced by the author, using data from Wikipedia's "List of American Revolutionary War Battles," https://en.wikipedia.org/wiki/List_of_American_Revolutionary_War_battles.

Even after Washington allied with the French in 1778, and brought in professional European soldiers to help organize his army, there were plenty of reasons to doubt that the British would capitulate. If anything, a Franco-American alliance merely meant that, for Britain, there was added motivation and efficiency in being able to fight both enemies in the same place: they could now kill two birds with one stone. To the king and core British ministers, American independence and British withdrawal "was still unthinkable."[33]

By the summer of 1779, both France and Spain had joined the war, amassing 30,000 troops in preparation for an invasion of Britain itself, which lay vulnerable as much of the Royal Navy was at sea, spread out around the globe. "Even with the homeland threatened, however, Shelburne [to become prime minister, in office 1782–83] refused to accept American independence."[34] With existential threats at home, British politicians were, however, becoming increasingly and vociferously divided. For example, James notes that "Germain favoured an all-out effort while [Prime Minister Lord] North still held out hope for a negotiated settlement."[35] But despite the arguments, the war pressed on. Perhaps most remarkably, even the major British defeat at Yorktown two more years down the road did little to dissuade George III and

Lord Germain, who "wanted to push on and continue the war," although by this point many others—among the British public and in Parliament—were beginning to question how long they could go on.[36] After Yorktown, in many people's minds the battle that won the war, it still took another two years for Britain to throw in the towel, the war only ending with the Treaty of Paris in 1783. Over the many long years of war, Washington could have been forgiven for believing that Britain would never give up, whatever the cost.

Washington's confidence, however, was pervasive and powerful. He was not just confident about the decision to fight in the first place. His confidence persisted even in the face of defeat after defeat, and after plentiful evidence that the British were determined to win the war and willing to pour resources into it year upon year. Even though more battles were being lost than won, Washington continued to believe that he would ultimately succeed. Another general might have bowed out to another commander, sought terms, or surrendered—or, even if they had stayed in command, might have failed to take the many difficult and risky decisions that kept America in the war. As O'Shaughnessy argued, the British "might yet have prevailed against less capable opponents, above all Washington, who was critical to the success of the American Revolution."[37] While I have focused here on evidence from third parties and facts on the ground to explore his levels of confidence, Washington's own statements suggest that he certainly saw himself as uniquely capable of achieving remarkable feats, despite the significant constraints ranged against him. After the British fled Boston, he wrote to his brother: "no Man perhaps since the first Institution of Armys ever commanded under more difficult circumstances."[38] Plenty more were to come.

Foregone Conclusion? Factors in Washington's Favor

One should not overstate the victory as a "miracle." There were, in fact, many factors in Washington's favor. First, and perhaps most widely discussed, as many historians have noted, was the idea that the British were "compromised by halfhearted and often inept leadership."[39] It may not be an exaggeration to say that Washington did not win the war but rather the British lost it. Had Howe pursued Washington more vigorously in New York or through New Jersey, had General John Burgoyne been reinforced as planned by Howe at Saratoga (who advanced on Philadelphia instead), or had Cornwallis been rescued by Clinton's force at Yorktown (who showed up five days late), among many other blunders, the British might well have prevailed. In the end, so this popular argument goes, incompetence in British planning and generalship led to these and other failings that effectively handed victory to the Americans.[40]

Second, Germain, the minister in charge of the war, was directing overall strategy from London. The British war effort was severely hampered by slow communications between the government and its field commanders. It took at least two and sometimes three or four months for a letter to cross the Atlantic in one direction—a reply could take eight.[41] Coordinating activities, strategies, and supplies, and especially making changes in response to a fluid situation, was extremely difficult. Washington still had to send and receive letters by horsemen in the field, but by comparison with Britain, both the commander in chief and the decision-makers in Congress were on the spot.

Third, the war was fought over a vast geographic area: "The North American battlefield encompassed a million square miles," noted James, composed of mountains, forests, rivers, and swamps.[42] British troops were heavily reliant on imported food and equipment and were weighed down having to carry it with them. Where they were able to extract supplies from local sources, it was often heavily resented and further degraded efforts to win over "hearts and minds." By contrast, the colonial army was largely self-sufficient, often supplied and supported by the local population (in Vietnam and Afghanistan the United States would find itself on the other side of this important asymmetry). They did not always manage to gather what they needed to sustain an army in the field, as at Valley Forge, but it was generally easier for Washington's troops to find support from fellow American farmers and citizens in the countryside than it was for the despised British redcoats.

Fourth, while British soldiers and commanders were often experienced and hardy, they were nevertheless in a foreign land, while the colonials were defending home territory, with local knowledge and intelligence. In addition, individual citizens, soldiers, and militiamen were often avenging the widespread acts of brutality by the occupying forces—acts that were proscribed by British commanders who recognized the importance of winning hearts and minds, but that were occurring nevertheless—giving them added motivation.[43]

Fifth, in February 1778 the colonists allied with France, which provided significant loans—critical to sustaining the war effort—and deployed its navy and troops in direct support of military operations and attacked British supply routes to the Americas. In 1779, Spain joined the alliance against Britain as well. The Netherlands, Russia, Sweden, Prussia, Portugal, and Denmark also continued to trade with the colonists, just as the Royal Navy was trying to blockade them. America had many friends in their hour of need.

Although Washington did enjoy these important advantages, at least to some extent, they do not stand up as evidence against overconfidence because they were not known to Washington and others when they initially made the decision to fight (or even during much of the war), or they were counteracted by other factors. First, with regard to the charge of British incompetence, Washington did not anticipate poor British military leadership. He had fought for Britain in the Virginia army and held it in great regard. Indeed, he himself had lobbied for a commission in the British army (unsuccessfully) and later sought to model many aspects of his own army on theirs.[44] He may have fancied his chances against the soldiers and system he had observed at close hand, but he did not know who would be in command, or where, when, and how they would act or interact with his own troops. He certainly harbored a strong respect for his seasoned foes. Moreover, other historians have challenged the "incompetence myth"—a convenient, but overplayed, historical explanation—arguing that British leaders were, in fact, competent and effective under the circumstances but hobbled by the constraints of their wider *world* war as well as the one in America.[45]

Second, while communication with London was poor, Howe and others were perfectly capable of making key strategic decisions on their own (whether good or bad ones). With months-long delays in communications with England, they had to act independently, and had the authority to do so. The British Empire could not have been won and maintained without significant independence from home. So while the information flow certainly did not help matters, the field commanders had enough power and freedom of action to adapt and respond to changing circumstances regardless of what was going on in London.

Third, while the geographic expanse of the conflict did present a problem, with guerrilla tactics making supplying and holding occupied areas difficult, this was not decisive. The British had faced similar, or worse, problems in supplying and sustaining troops in far more remote and foreboding environments in Africa, India, and Canada. In America, Merriman also reminds us, "the most significant battles of the war were fought in the classic European style of confrontations, not as engagements between hit-and-run patriots and British regulars."[46] In these kinds of set-piece conflicts, the British were disciplined, well trained, and much experienced. Judging by recent decades and centuries (and earlier battles in this war), even if the fighting was spread out over large areas, they could be expected to win.

Fourth, it was not obvious at the start how effective local colonial militias or regiments would be, or even if they could be reliably assembled at all or maintained for long. Their ad hoc composition and frequent motivations of vengeance came at the price of independent and sometimes conflicting actions by soldiers and commanders. It did not make for an easily directed army. When Washington took command of the New England army in July 1775, according to Nathaniel Philbrick, rather than "a proper army" of 20,000 "battle-tested soldiers" promised by Congress, he was instead "disgusted" by what he saw as a "mob of puritanical savages."[47] He had to invest significant time over the coming months reorganizing the army and dealing with fractious tensions among them. As for the officers, Washington also thought many of his own commanders were below par, "a motley collection of frenetically ambitious, impetuous, and irascible officers,"[48] and this was not just in Boston but throughout the war. The top level of command was made up of political appointees by Congress, so Washington also had a limited ability to select or fire them. As for local knowledge and intelligence, Washington did benefit from this,[49] but so did the British, who had considerable experience and many sources among the loyalists in the population, as well as among Native American allies.

Finally, the French and their allies certainly were important and possibly critical to the final outcome. But at the start of the war, and well into it, it was not clear that they would help at all; nor was it clear when and where or what kind of help might genuinely materialize. Washington did not decide to fight on the basis of possible future French help (and indeed first had to fight for three long years without it). In fact, he initially hoped to *avoid* any such alliances for fear of simply becoming a vassal of another colonial power. It was not a part of his (or the Continental Congress's) initial calculus.

Overall, there were factors working at least partly in Washington's favor. But these were not unopposed advantages that would have made a rational actor confident of victory, even if they could have been known in advance.

Forlorn Hope? Factors Not in Washington's Favor

Compared to the list of possible advantages on the American side discussed in the last section, the colonial forces faced a longer and more certain list of major obstacles acting against them—all of which add to the remarkable confidence that Washington must have had to enter the ring and to keep picking himself up to fight another round.

First, the colonials had thrown down the gauntlet with the Declaration of Independence, necessitating a major showdown resulting in either victory or defeat. As early as the siege of Boston, Washington "had long since come to the conclusion that a reconciliation with the mother country was a virtual impossibility."[50] Unlike other wars in which states might initiate hostilities to test each other's strength and resolve, with the option of ending the fighting on negotiated terms, the Declaration meant that the United States had to win outright. This was no skirmish but a struggle for absolute victory. William Martel argues that this experience hugely influenced the "theory of victory" that came to define America and its wars for the next two centuries: "The nation's first experience with war was one in which failure was not an option; any outcome other than victory would have foreclosed the possibility of a successful movement toward independence."[51] Washington thus had to create an army capable not merely of harassing the enemy or securing territory before suing for peace but of destroying the fabled British army on the battlefield.

Second, perhaps the single biggest obstacle to the revolution getting off the ground, let alone winning the war, was pulling together disparate leaders and citizens of independent states into a unified army. One might think that this was merely a matter of gathering up able-bodied men from among the masses who were united in hatred of British tyranny and yearning for the opportunity to fight. But this was not the case. Indeed, it presented no mean feat in a region of complex interests, dependencies, and loyalties. Philbrick points out that Washington "was attempting to be something that did not yet exist—an American."[52] As it was, Sinclair describes, "the coming of the revolution caused ugly splits in American society, between the merchant and the frontiersman, between the port city and the back country, between the planter dependent on the London market and the small farmer who hated taxes and tight credit."[53] The British were well aware of these divisions and worked to exploit them, and indeed the campaigns against New York and Philadelphia were designed to drive a wedge between the northern and southern colonies.[54] Britain also encouraged Native American tribes to attack the frontiers, forcing many would-be rebels to remain at home in defense of their families and farms. The Declaration tends to be thought of now as representing universal opinion. However, even at the time John Adams estimated that only "about a third of the colonists were wholeheartedly behind independence and that the rest were either Loyalists or neutral."[55] And this remarkably low figure was likely to move against them. After driving Washington from New York, "to judge by the numbers who took advantage of Howe's amnesty, the balance was in danger of swinging [even further] against supporters of independence."[56] Confirmation of the extent of support for Britain (or at least bets on them winning) is revealed by a striking fact: it is estimated that, after the revolution, around 60,000–80,000 loyalists among the American population fled to Britain, Canada, or the West Indies.[57]

Third, even once an army was formed, basic resources were thin on the ground. Not only did Washington lack funds to pay soldiers or buy military equipment (he repeatedly had to ask benevolent donors for financial support), there was a constant want for fundamental necessities such as clothes and boots. At times, they lacked sufficient shelter and food to feed their army, as at Valley Forge, to the extent that thousands died of disease, exposure, and malnutrition. Even when the army was in fighting condition, they often did not have the gunpowder necessary to shoot at the enemy. Washington fretted over the lack of ammunition, and in December 1775 grieved that "our want of powder is inconceivable."[58] Indeed, had he foreseen the lack of material available for the war, he fumed, "no consideration on earth should have induced me to accept this command."[59] At one point, American ships had to sail out to the Bahamas to seize British ammunition stores held on New Providence. The Continental Army had an "authorized strength" of 75,000 troops, but this was "never attained," only ever stretching to 18,000 (in October 1778).[60] Moreover, to fund the war effort, Congress resorted to printing paper money, and borrowing heavily from France, debts that left the American economy "in ruins" already by 1778 and took the new country decades to pay off.[61]

The colonial army itself presented its own challenges. As well as the constant problems of leadership, pay, and supplies, there were difficulties of coordination among and between militias, states, and commanders. Significant desertions and mutinies persisted throughout the war.[62] Given the litany of problems that beset the armies of even long-established nations at war, the colonial army might have appeared doomed—as it often did to Washington even when far from the enemy. This was an unending concern for Washington, and much of his time was spent recruiting, re-recruiting, and retaining his army over the course of the war (let alone training, equipping, and deploying them).

Even after the victories at Trenton and Princeton, the obstacles continued or arguably worsened. Barbara Tuchman captured Washington's tribulations at the end of 1778: "Without central funds, Congress could not keep the armies in pay or supplies, which meant deserting soldiers and another winter of deprivation worse than Valley Forge, with rations at one-eighth normal and mutinies on more than one occasion. Washington was harassed by political cabals, betrayed by Benedict Arnold, disobeyed by General Charles Lee, subjected to scattered but savage warfare by Loyalist and Indian groups, disappointed by the failure of the attempt in combination with the French fleet to regain Newport and by British success in the Carolinas including the capture of Charleston."[63] Things would frequently look bleak even to the end. Ferling wrote, "Virtually everyone on the allied side believed that campaign 1781 [sic] was their last hope."[64] Part of Washington's fame, of course, was his very skill at holding the army together, and this in itself was in no small part aided by his brimming confidence—a trait soaked up by his men.

It would have been hard enough for Washington to win with a regular, fully paid, and well-equipped army (after all, the British had defeated the French in North America only recently and would defeat none other than Napoleon a few years hence).[65] As it was he had to conjure up an army out of nothing and keep them fighting—for several years—despite dire conditions, poor pay, and woeful provisions. Washington's army was a sword that sometimes seemed as if it had to be drawn out of stone.

Chance: The War That Britain Should Have Won

So far I have argued, first, that Washington saw victory where others predicted defeat. Second, although Washington enjoyed some potential advantages, these were equivocal or not even known at the time of the decision to fight and thus could not have served as evidence he was likely to win. They did not, therefore, vindicate great optimism. Third, I outlined several significant obstacles for the revolution that should have suppressed or eliminated optimism rather than encourage it. But above all of these factors, another element lends credence to the argument that Britain was likely to win (and thus that Washington was overconfident): chance.

Chance events can be argued to have conspired to steal a British defeat from the jaws of victory, in a war they "should" have won from the standpoint of military power, logistics, resources, and historical experience. Indeed, given the asymmetry between the sides, and Washington's obstacles, if we were to rerun the tape of history many times, the British might have won on many or most occasions. Of course, engaging in hypothetical what-if scenarios treads on dangerous ground, but the point is simply to establish that—from the history we know—the war might reasonably have been expected to go much worse for the revolution than it did. If so, Washington's confidence becomes more remarkable still.

Critical stages of the war were very much determined by the particular path of events—things that, had they gone as expected, should have led to British victory. Numerous chance events significantly buffeted the course of the war, including the weather, inadvertent moves on the opposing sides, unpredictable allies, events in other parts of the world, and dumb luck. But prime among these are the examples of Saratoga and Yorktown.

In 1777 Burgoyne returned to Britain to join Germain in devising a "knockout campaign" to divide the colonies "and end the war before the next Christmas."[66] The plan was a giant pincer movement that, with Howe's forces advancing up the Hudson from New York and Burgoyne marching down from Quebec, would meet in the middle and cut off the rebellious northern states from the south (in addition to splitting the enemy, it would also prevent crucial supplies for the Continental Army coming from New England). This could have divided and destroyed the revolution. However, events would conspire against this grand plan.

Howe made a unilateral decision not to march to meet Burgoyne after all, as he needed forces for a campaign against Philadelphia. This left New York woefully inadequately defended. General Henry Clinton attempted to link up with Burgoyne with the remaining troops in New York, but it was too little too late and they never reached them, "leaving Burgoyne's troops stranded and outnumbered two to one."[67] The result was a disaster, born not of military weakness or poor strategy but of an unanticipated failure to carry out what had been planned. Burgoyne became trapped and, facing a superior force, surrendered at Saratoga on 16 October, "shattering British prestige the world over."[68] Sitting as a prisoner in Albany, Burgoyne fumed that, above all, he had been "totally unassisted by Sir William Howe."[69] Meanwhile, although Howe succeeded in capturing Philadelphia—potentially a major triumph—he was not able to hold onto it because he had failed to gain control of the Delaware River. These well-known follies serve to demonstrate, apart from what many historians regard as remarkable incompetence among the British commanders, that the war was hardly a foregone conclusion. Under better (or at least consistent) leadership, this campaign, and the war as a whole, might well have been successful. With hindsight, many of Washington's expectations and decisions seem perfectly rational, *given these failures on the British side*, but at the time they represented great confidence, since the fateful decisions of Howe and others could not have been predicted in advance.

Similar failures occurred later on. The British turned their attention to the south, achieving several victories, including at Savannah and Charleston, until the sudden and unexpected defeat at Yorktown on 19 October 1781—"an incident that few foresaw might be the last major engagement of the war."[70] Washington himself had long been "in a frenzy to attack New York" instead.[71] However, when the French fleet arrived, breaking Cornwallis's lines of communication with the north that were vital for providing reinforcements (or at least escape), Washington was able to rush his and a French army south, surrounding the stranded Cornwallis with superior numbers.[72] Once again it was, like 1777, largely down to chance events rather than an inevitable result of the military balance. Reinforcements from New York did get through, but five days *after* Cornwallis had surrendered. Had they arrived earlier, it might have been a very different story. Washington's quick reactions to these opportunities were as remarkably good as the British failures were remarkably bad. With Washington in charge and always poised to act, his British opponents had no room for error. But it was a close-run thing. Washington himself had written in a letter a few months before Yorktown (and intercepted by the British) that "if the war did not end with the next campaign, the cause would die of poverty and exhaustion."[73] A British victory had been close at hand.

The point here is that Washington could not have foreseen an easy military victory over the British. Rather, it was rightly expected, by many observers if not Washington himself, that winning would be extremely hard, and in some people's eyes impossible. Given British military power, resources, and experience, along with significant obstacles for the revolutionary side, victory seemed rather unlikely. Had the British operated effectively, or even normally, they might have—perhaps would have—won. As Tuchman put it: "The American Revolution, given its own errors and failures, cabals and disgruntlements, succeeded by virtue of British mishandling."[74] In a game of chance, Washington seems to have been better disposed to seize the advantage.

Washington fought an extraordinarily difficult, costly, and prolonged campaign against a superior and hardened British army (and navy). Few bookkeepers would have given favorable odds on an American victory at the time of the signing of the Declaration of Independence, after the battles in 1776, or perhaps even after Saratoga in 1777 or Yorktown in 1781. Of course, Washington and the United States won handsome dividends on his investment in the long odds of American victory. But it remains a puzzle how he was (and was able to remain) so confident of victory through the long and hard years of the war. Whatever the cause, confidence was certainly a striking, and fortuitous, aspect of his personality.

The View from George Washington:
Personality and Disposition

So far we have largely tried to deduce any overconfidence on the part of Washington by looking at the pieces on the chessboard as he played. But what about the man himself? One may wonder whether Washington was really so personally confident. He does not seem to match the characteristics of more infamous examples of super confident historical figures like Caesar or Napoleon, with delusions of grandeur that helped lead to their demise. Certainly, according to his numerous biographers, Washington was a complex figure.[75] Yet he stood apart from contemporaries, which was arguably vital to the revolution's success—the "indispensible man," as James Flexner called him.[76] Rick Shenkman's study of all American presidents in the country's history found Washington to be unusual in many respects. In particular, Shenkman singled him out as "alone among the presidents" for achieving political power without sacrificing principles.[77] Indeed, he established "the bedrock principle . . . that the office should seek the man, not the man the office."[78] General histories tend to offer broad recognition of "his powers of leadership, his stoicism, and his integrity."[79]

However, there are curious features about Washington suggesting that— as an individual—he did have a remarkably confident, perhaps overconfident, personality. His early life appears to foreshadow both his ambition and his confidence. Some of his later traits were evident in his service with the Virginia Regiment during the French and Indian War, where he was "a tough disciplinarian, whipping malcontents and hanging deserters at a rate that equalled, if not exceeded, what prevailed in the British Army."[80] His forthright approach was also applied to the enemy. In 1754, for example, he held out with 400 men at Fort Necessity against a superior force of 900 French troops, only surrendering after half his men were dead or incapacitated.[81] After six eventful but not always victorious years of soldiering, he turned his attention to his estate. Although born wealthy, Washington "was very much a man on the make" and spent his early years striving to enrich himself through land. "Land was everything in Washington's youth, the symbol of wealth and prestige, and he had set out to acquire as much of it as he could."[82] Of course, this was a common aspiration among men of the colonies. But in Washington's case it came with a certain zeal. Despite inheriting Mount Vernon and its 2,000 acres, "that hadn't come nearly close to satisfying his appetite. He didn't want just a lot of land. He wanted more land than anybody else."[83] This continued to drive his ambitions and decisions—even in affairs of the heart. His decision to marry a woman described as "neither particularly pretty nor particularly social adept" was not an obvious choice, especially given that he was in fact in love with someone else (the neighboring Sally Fairfax). But Martha owned land and money, and on marriage, it became his, comprising 6,000 acres and the means to buy much more. But his quest did not end there. "Not even all that was enough to satisfy him," wrote Shenkman.[84] He later seized land set aside for the Indians, binding his surveyor to secrecy, and after that another 20,000 acres he engineered from Britain in return for his military services in Virginia (the land was originally earmarked for his soldiers).

These material ambitions only appeared to fall away (or perhaps to have been fulfilled) once the revolution came. However, while the interests changed, the man did not. Washington's characteristic ambition simply identified new targets: "Acquiring land was no longer enough. Being rich was no longer enough. Believing himself to be in a position to affect history, Washington lifted his sights and became something no one had any right to expect he would. Now, instead of acquiring land, he would seek to acquire what people in the eighteenth century called fame."[85] As the storm clouds gathered in Boston, Washington put himself forward for the role of commander in chief, on the strength of his service in the French and Indian War, to fight the yoke of imperial Britain. He leapt eagerly into the war, "as fired by ambition as ever . . . inspiring his fellow Americans as no one else did."[86] There were other compelling candidates to lead the Continental Army against the British, but by the day of decision, Washington staged a fait accompli by arriving at the Continental Congress in full military uniform.[87]

If a high level of confidence was a genuine character trait and not just an epiphenomenon or appearance of the time, we should expect it to have persisted. And it did. His confidence remained in strong view throughout and even beyond the war. Shenkman notes that he was "personally fearless" and "never traveled with a guard" even during his many journeys later as president—something unthinkable today.[88] Ellis also made the interesting observation that, "based on his bravery during several battles," Washington "apparently believed he could not be killed."[89] David Hackett Fischer wrote, "The only fear that George Washington ever acknowledged in his life was a fear that his actions would 'reflect eternal dishonour upon me.'"[90] His portraitist Gilbert Stuart, having studied Washington's demeanor in prodigious detail, felt that his calm appearance hid "the strongest and most ungovernable passions," and "had he been born in the forest, he would have been the fiercest man among the savage tribes."[91]

Edward Lengel's biography noted not only Washington's high levels of confidence but also the fact that it carried advantages. Washington had developed a firm belief that well-trained troops could match British regulars, and this "conviction would sometimes lead to overconfidence during the Revolutionary War, when General Washington denigrated the British regulars and overestimated the ability of his Continentals." However, Lengel recognized that, while this represented overconfidence, it also served to "inoculate him against the defeatism that crept among some of his generals in the dark days of 1776, and again in 1780."[92]

After the revolution had been won, his new country faced enormous challenges, not least building trust between individuals, the disparate states, and the brand-new institutions of government that would watch over people and their business. Yet even in this challenging public domain his confidence shone through, and successfully so. As Rosabeth Moss Kanter suggested in her study of confidence, "Washington conveyed the optimistic idea that there was no limit to the improvement of human abilities and circumstances."[93] Even if an exaggeration, Washington's optimism seems to have been instrumental in pulling Americans further forward, and closer together, than they might otherwise have ventured.

Of course, much is made of Washington's humility after the war was over. Following the victory, he simply went home, and was famously reluctant to accept the presidency at all. Does this not belie the image of Washington as an ambitious and overconfident power-seeker, and cast him as a humble public servant instead? I would suggest, in fact, that it reinforces it. Part of the reason for his reluctance is that his fame was already assured, as victor of the revolution and Father of the nation. There was no greater summit to conquer. If anything, the presidency only presented a new risk that his hard-won reputation might be tarnished by political wrangling and necessary but unpopular decisions. Washington was humble in his political ambitions, especially in comparison to all other presidential candidates who have fought tooth and nail to win it ever since, but only in grudgingly accepting the position of first president of a country that he himself had more or less created. His humbleness only served to protect and elevate his fame.

Washington the man, ever since his younger years, was profoundly ambitious and confident in his abilities. There is little doubt that this great confidence—a confidence which exceeded that of many of his contemporaries—helped to lift the scattering of poorly prepared volunteers and militiamen, against all odds, to defeat the British Empire. It was a miraculous feat that had never been achieved before by any colony, and Washington had proven to be the one to do it.

Did Overconfidence Lead to Strategic Advantages?

So far we have established that the task Washington faced was immense, and that despite this, he appears to have maintained striking confidence—arguably overconfidence—in his personal demeanor and in the cause at hand. But this still leaves open the most important question of all: If Washington was overconfident, did it help?

From the outset, confidence appeared to be a prominent motivator on the rebel side. Major John Pitcairn, commander of the British marines in the first battle, at Lexington, Massachusetts, "was astounded at the Yankees' confidence," remarking, "The deluded people are made to believe that they are invincible."[94] One journal of the time "even argued that the American armies on their own soil could defeat all the armies of Europe."[95] John Merriman wrote that "some of the colonists fought with an almost evangelical fervor that reflected the fact that many of them saw the struggle as one of good against evil."[96] It is tempting to suggest that such a fighting spirit was only to be expected among the early Americans, who often had to rely only on themselves to carve out a living in their new world. Tuchman wrote that "the colonists were . . . offspring of exceptionally strong-minded and enterprising dissidents of the British breed."[97] They were people of ambitious and adventurous stock who would never have set out for America in the first place, or succeeded there, if they had lacked confidence and willpower. We should therefore perhaps not be surprised to see it in evidence in the decision to fight and in the fighting itself (and perhaps to be greater, on average, than among the British).

But even against this background, Washington himself stands out as remarkably confident in his ability, and in the ability of his Continental Army, to prevail. Perhaps the strongest corroboration of the idea that (a) Washington was overconfident, and (b) this overconfidence helped him to win comes from historian Joseph Ellis's biography, *His Excellency*:

> He [Washington] was not, by any standard, a military genius. He lost more battles than he won; indeed, he lost more battles than any victorious general in modern history. Moreover, his defeats were frequently a function of his own overconfident and aggressive personality, especially during the early stages of the war, when he escaped to fight another day only because the British generals opposing him seemed choked with the kind of caution that, given his resources, Washington should have adopted as his own strategy. But in addition to being fortunate in his adversaries, he was blessed with personal qualities that counted most in a protracted war. He was composed, indefatigable, and able to learn from his mistakes. He was convinced that he was on the side of destiny—or, in more arrogant moments, sure that destiny was on his side.[98]

Ellis's summary contains several important points: Washington lost many battles (so a rational actor might have updated his expectations and quit); defeats were often explicit collateral damage of his overconfidence (so although it may have brought victory in the grand scheme of things, overconfidence clearly incurred costs along the way—precisely the logic of error management theory—and no doubt it would have been seized upon by historians had Washington lost); the British themselves suffered from being *overly cautious* (a bit more confidence might have done wonders for them too); and finally, Washington's personality, beliefs, and behavior suggest that he was strikingly confident and assured, and this influenced his decisions (so a similar general but with less confidence would not have acted the same way).

Other biographers have also stressed a link between Washington's confidence and its effect on the war. Ferling's biography *The First of Men* found that "there was a gambler's audacity to Washington's makeup, a willingness to run great risks by attempting bold strokes rather than waiting for his adversary to seize the initiative."[99] He was not exactly reckless but sometimes had a tendency to go for broke. On many occasions, it was precisely these audacious moves that contributed to victory (rather than to defeat). Who would have expected Washington to send ill-equipped troops across the icy Delaware River in a storm on Christmas night in 1776? Or when they barely made it back, to muster them again a few days later to repeat the entire ordeal? These were extremely risky and daring strokes, but it is precisely their risky and daring nature that gave them a strategic edge and ushered in victory.[100] According to Lengel, "In practice, he [Washington] scrapped policy and acted by instinct . . . he could never resist a chance at fighting the decisive battle."[101]

Washington's victories at Trenton and Princeton following the Delaware crossing may have been instrumental in winning the war. Although they were small in scale, and militarily not particularly significant, they appear to have had a very important psychological effect, raising morale among the colonists and demonstrating that the Hessian army (at Trenton) and the British army (at Princeton) were not unbeatable in open battle.[102] Ellis suggests, no less, that "the actions at Trenton and Princeton were the most consequential in American history, for these stunning victories rescued the American cause *from what appeared to be certain defeat* and thereby transformed the improbability of American independence into a distinct possibility, eventually an inevitability."[103] These daring raids, born of Washington's remarkable confidence, might never have been attempted by more cautious commanders in chief.

Tuchman, so dismissive of arrogant hubris on the British side, nevertheless recognized some advantages accruing to the American side: "For all their disadvantages in shortage of arms and supplies and of trained and disciplined troops and in the short-term enlistments that were their most disabling factor, they had a cause to fight for, a commander of heroic stature and unflinching will and occasional stunning limited victories as at Trenton and Princeton to reinvigorate morale."[104] An "unflinching will" is precisely the kind of strategic advantage of overconfidence that, while it can contribute to mistakes or disasters (such as Washington's long list of defeats), also helps throw the dice when there is an opportunity to clinch historic victories.

One might worry that hindsight makes us pick out dramatic successes and retroactively infer confidence—just in those events. But there is evidence of the same high level of confidence even in events that did *not* come to pass. For example, in the winter of 1775–76, eager to break the siege of Boston, Washington proposed a full frontal assault on the city, with soldiers storming across the frozen Charles River against prepared British positions—a plan historians have judged "suicidal."[105] In a council of war with his officers, they "would not hear of such strategy" and he was overruled.[106] A much more cautious strategy was chosen instead (seizing the unoccupied Dorchester heights to gain a vantage point over the city). Similar schemes arose at other times too. Even later in the war, when historians generally agree that Washington became somewhat less risk prone and more patient, his idea to stage a siege of the British stronghold in New York "seemed to become a fixed idea virtually to the exclusion of every other possibility."[107] While success would have been a dramatic coup, "the odds against success were considerable."[108] The combined American and French armies, and the French navy, would have been barely larger than the British, and European experience taught that such sieges demanded at least a 2-to-1 superiority to have any hope of success. Yet as Ferling notes, "Washington's fascination with besieging New York was in keeping with his proclivity for the grandiose, for the most bold, resolute design."[109] The French would not support such a risky endeavor, and vetoed it. These two examples show that Washington's confidence extended beyond a few freak successes to include plans that were never undertaken. They also show that his confidence was bounded, not limitless—even if it sometimes had to be reined in by others.

Washington's confidence was not only important in pushing for bold strategic decisions. It was also important—perhaps even more important—as an elixir to recruit, retain, and urge on his soldiers. His confidence in himself, in the cause, and in his own soldiers was absolutely vital not only for boosting morale among the troops but literally for keeping them in the field—especially in preparation for the Delaware crossing and the chilling winter at Valley Forge—when they had homes and families to return to. Many did leave, and many more would have done had it not been for Washington's significant effort and skill in providing inspiration as well as pay and provisions. Without it, no war could have been fought, let alone won.

Alternative Explanations: Confidence or Compulsion?

In the previous sections I argued that, compared to peers, against the facts on the ground, and in the view of historians, Washington appeared to be remarkably confident—even overconfident—in the face of the vast resources and capabilities of the reigning superpower of the day. His growing tally of defeats seemed to confirm the asymmetry. There are, however, alternative explanations for Washington's behavior without invoking overconfidence.

First, rather than overconfident, perhaps he was simply happy to wait it out in anticipation that the British would eventually tire of fighting an expensive war far from home (like the Taliban did in Afghanistan). For large parts of the war, the colonial forces' deliberate strategy was indeed a protracted guerrilla war, in which small contingents of militia would surprise and harass the enemy when opportunities arose. This may partly explain Washington's persistence—a long, hard struggle was a strategy of success, not a symptom of failure. However, the sit-and-wait thesis is unconvincing. Despite the attraction of guerrilla tactics, from the time of the bloody battle of Bunker Hill it was clear that the colonials were going to need "a professional Continental-style army" and fight conventional European-style battles if they were to defeat the many thousands of British redcoats in a reasonable time frame, rather than just chase them around the countryside.[110] Furthermore, part of the problem was that Washington was not going to be able to keep *his own* army together and in the field for long. How many more winters like Valley Forge's might the army endure? How many more years could soldiers be recruited, and paid in a collapsing American economy, for what was starting to seem like a never-ending war or even a stalemate? Washington's goal of outright victory therefore required not only the use of local militias but large-scale recruitment and fighting by organized troops, deployed for decisive engagements—precisely what the British army was equipped and trained for, and in which the colonial army lagged far behind. After all, this is what he sought in a French alliance and European military advisors. And such a victory would have to come soon. As late as 1780, Washington lamented that winter as "the most distressing of any we have experienced since the beginning of the War," and even then Ferling notes that the "bleakest" and "in some ways the most dangerous" period was still to come.[111] Rather than waiting out the war, Washington's window of opportunity was closing. If one side was likely to give up from war weariness, it was just as (or more) likely to be the Americans.

Moreover, the bold Declaration of Independence meant that the revolution could not just continue forever or fizzle out. To realize their political goal, they had to win on the battlefield. Britain's military dominance meant this could only be done with a large coordinated campaign. As Martel put it, "Since Great Britain was an eighteenth-century superpower and could draw on resources from around the globe, it was absolutely necessary for the colonies to win decisively."[112] Both of these factors should have sunk expectations of victory even lower. Not only did they have to win, but they had to do so in the British army's own favored style of fighting.

A second alternative argument is that the colonials had *no choice* but to fight, given the draconian legislation imposed by Britain. All options were bad and perhaps war just seemed the least bad outcome, even if waged against a superior opponent. However, this only adds to the puzzle: Why did they believe that an armed struggle, by the weak against the strong, was likely to help rather than worsen their cause? That makes sense if one might win such a conflict, which returns us to the question of why they believed *that*.

A third alternative argument is that they did not expect to win outright but were fighting for a deal—demonstrating their unwillingness to concede and fighting for long enough to force a negotiated deal on favorable terms. In the early days of the rebellion (e.g., in 1774–75), that may have seemed a possibility for some in the newly formed Continental Congress and among colonial officials. However, it was not long before enough bad blood had accumulated that the war could only be resolved militarily. By killing ever greater numbers of British soldiers, let alone allying with Britain's mortal enemy France, Britain was likely to tighten the screw. If the British were drawn into an extended and expensive fight, they would be more likely to impose harsh penalties rather than make concessions. Leaders of the rebellion risked being imprisoned or executed rather than invited to talk. Certainly by the time of the Declaration of Independence on 4 July 1776, the revolution had gone far beyond striking a deal with their imperial masters; it was about seeking victory over them. They did not ask for discussions or an agreement on independence; they declared it. It was not long after, in the fall of 1776, that many rebels accepted General Howe's unconditional pardon for those who surrendered and declared allegiance to George III.[113] After that, the remaining rebels were on their own.

Clearly, there are alternative explanations that could at least partially account for the American decision to fight, and to keep fighting through many years of difficulty and defeats, but none of them take much away from the central fact of an extraordinary level of confidence held by General Washington. If anything, they merely make the puzzle greater. In a David against Goliath confrontation, it is remarkable that he managed to maintain his determination and the belief they could prevail through thick and thin. He had plenty of moments of anxiety and despair, but he never gave up. I am not arguing that an American victory should have seemed impossible. Rather, I am arguing that, as many realized at the time, it was a Herculean task. This was in large part for the simple reason that Congress did not have the power to compel the different states to supply soldiers or money to finance the war—let alone fight or win it. Not only was Washington up against the trials and tribulations of the battlefield, he often barely had an army to fight with. Indeed, the improbability of success against the British Empire was recognized by Washington himself, who in his Farewell Orders to the Continental Army after the long years of war were finally over "expressed 'astonishment' at the American triumph" and declared his victory "little short of a standing miracle."[114]

Aftermath: The Mouse Really Was a Mouse

To reinforce the enormity of the challenge that Washington faced, it is worth considering the aftermath of the war as it starkly exposes the asymmetry of power that had prevailed (and continued). Victory had been won, but at a significant cost. No timid general could have persisted and won such a war. While the absolute number of casualties was low compared to other American wars (only the War of 1812, the Spanish-American War, and the 1991 Gulf War had fewer total numbers of casualties—dead plus wounded), the *proportion* of losses given the size of the population was extremely high.[115] Relative to the American population at the time, the percentage killed in combat was

0.15 percent, which was not quite as high as World War II (0.22 percent) but over seven times higher than Vietnam (0.02 percent).[116] The proportion of losses among the enlisted soldiers themselves was even more dramatic. On the American side, a total of around 200,000 men enrolled in the colonial army and militias over the course of the war. There were a total of 10,623 casualties (4,435 combat deaths, 6,188 wounded, plus an unknown number that died of other causes). Of the 200,000 soldiers, that meant 2.2 percent were killed and 3.1 percent were wounded.[117] This represents the highest attrition rate of any American war (excluding the Civil War), with the percentage of combat deaths higher even than in World War II (1.8 percent) and much higher than in Vietnam (0.5 percent). Such a high proportion of American servicemen would never again be killed fighting a war against another state. It is also worth noting that, compared with other wars, it was also America's longest war until Vietnam two centuries later (and even that was only slightly longer, at ninety months compared to eighty). Washington faced not only enormous obstacles in fighting at all but also one of America's longest and bloodiest conflicts ever.

The military balance *after* the war also brings the disparity of the confrontation into sharp focus. Once Washington took office as president the American army was only around five hundred men, "about the size of the police force needed today to protect Des Moines, Iowa."[118] And there was no navy at all. The new democracy had around 400,000 "free adult men" (a number that excluded the "disenfranchised or enslaved, Indians, Negroes, women, bondservants, children, aliens, and the insane").[119] America was a mouse, and Britain remained a lion, with tens of thousands of troops deployed around the world. A few short years later, Britain would defeat one of the greatest military leaders of all time, Napoleon. Somehow, in North America, it was the mouse that had won.

Perhaps most remarkable of all, it was not that Britain was in decline, such that the Americans faced a master with dwindling resolve or resources and were simply the first ones lucky enough to exploit it. Rather, Britain was on the rise. In colonies from Canada to India, and Africa to Australia, vast overseas territories would remain under direct British rule for two centuries hence. America was incredibly unusual in throwing off the shackles of empire so early. Although many British elites had feared the worst if America was lost, Britain "was to survive the loss well enough and go on to world domination and the apogee of imperial power in the next century."[120] The decades following the revolution—indeed the centuries following—therefore only make it seem all the more remarkable in retrospect that the Americans had won.

The balance of power after the war, as a tiny new nation in the shadow of a still hegemonic older one, drives home the fact that it had been a terrific venture into the unknown—a "leap in the dark," as Ferling called it.[121] Whatever one thought about the apparently slim chances of winning the war itself, there was also the daunting postconflict phase to consider, in which the fledgling nation would face severe obstacles that equaled, and perhaps exceeded, those of the war (bizarrely reminiscent of the challenges the United States faced in nation-building in Afghanistan and Iraq in the 2000s). After the war, "city mobs threatened property, debtor farmers rose in open revolt in Shays's Rebellion. The Articles of Confederation did not work. Congress could not collect its taxes, raise a standing army, honour its debts, or regulate trade either internally or abroad. Local interest in the states effectively managed policy and taxation without any reference to the national interest." [122] The influence of individuals and states has always stayed strong in the United States in part because the collective was so weak. Of course, these were precisely the problems that led to the drafting of the Constitution, which came into force in 1789. However, that, like the Declaration of Independence and the war that followed, is another marvel of history that required considerable skill and the optimism of some remarkable men to succeed. Even then, it was not until 1800 that the United States resolved the severe internal wrangling over the political course it was to take, when Thomas Jefferson and the Democratic-Republican Party took the presidency from John Adams's Federalists. Until then, "many feared that seemingly insoluble political and economic problems doomed the Union." [123] The origins of the United States of America, it seems, was a close-run thing—and indeed would be tested again to the breaking point over the next generation.

Conclusions

I have argued that Washington was remarkably confident, and that this remarkable confidence helped win the American Revolution. In the past, it is *British* overconfidence that has been the focus of attention, and used to explain failure, not success. Indeed, building on a long-established view in the literature,[124] historian Barbara Tuchman popularized the excessive hubris on the British side in her book *The March of Folly*.[125] Her argument is that throughout history, states and their leaders have succumbed to recurrent overconfidence, which has led to self-defeating policies and disaster. In the case of the American Revolution, Britain had "made rebels where there had been none" and ended up engaging in a conflict in which "the cost of the effort, even if successful, was clearly greater than the possible gain."[126] Oddly, however, she did not ask whether this recurrent overconfidence was also evident on the American side, and if so how that could be squared with *winning* the war. This highlights the point that where we see overconfidence, we tend to assume that it must be a cause of failure. And where we see failure, we tend to search for and find overconfidence. Where there is success, we have tended not to look for cognitive biases at all, and perhaps least of all *overconfidence* (if they won the war, why would we think they were overconfident and thus even search for evidence of it?). Yet there is no reason to assume that overconfidence would appear on one side and not the other.

Looking at the British side only, we find the conventional story about over-confidence: arrogance and hubris contributed to unnecessary war and ignoble defeat. In this chapter, more unusually, we instead scrutinized evidence for overconfidence on the *winning* side, rather than on the losing side, and we found significant overconfidence there as well. But it did not bring defeat, and indeed it may have helped bring victory. In the War of Independence, as Blainey put it, "both sides envisaged victory," and this fits into a broader pattern on the eve of wars throughout history.[127] But while overconfidence may have hurt the losing sides, perhaps it helped the winners. In the right context, great confidence—even overconfidence—can bring rich dividends, as it did for Washington. Maybe this is rare. But if overconfidence is common to both sides on the eve of war, as Blainey and others have argued, then it might apply to up to 50 percent of cases—or more, if it helps even losing sides fight better before they are defeated. This raises the question of what the effects of overconfidence were on the British side.

Both before and during the war, Britain appears to have been plagued by overconfidence. Tuchman found that "British contempt for the colonial soldier . . . was the oddest, deepest, most disserviceable misjudgment of the years leading to the conflict."[128] General Thomas Gage declared that "there is not a man amongst [the colonists] capable of taking command or directing the motions of any army."[129] When addressing the House of Commons, Colonel James Grant, who had served in the colonies and knew the Americans well, said they "did not possess any of the qualifications necessary to make a good soldier . . . [and] would never dare face an *English* army."[130] In fact, he boasted, he could "go from one end of America to other [*sic*] and geld all the males."[131] Lord Sandwich told the House of Lords that "they are raw undisciplined cowardly men . . . if they did not run away, they would starve themselves into compliance with our measures."[132] Blainey gives additional examples. Major John Pitcairn ventured that the rum his English troops were drinking was a greater danger than the colonial army, and wrote to Secretary of State Lord Sandwich in 1775, "I am satisfied that one active campaign, a smart action, and burning two or three of their towns, will set everything to rights."[133] The letter was shown to King George III, who endorsed it strongly. Not long after, Pitcairn was dead—killed at the start of the ascent of Bunker Hill by a former slave, Peter Salem, just as he was heard shouting to his men, "The day is ours!"[134] The British won that early battle at Bunker Hill but at a terrible cost; as Nathanael Greene quipped, "I wish [we] could sell them another hill at the same price."[135] The British would have much to learn about their new enemy. Perhaps most remarkable of all, apart from army and navy officers who had been deployed there, not a single member of the British government had ever visited America.[136]

Among countless self-defeating policies and failures, Tuchman found "a sense of superiority so dense as to be impenetrable."[137] Such complacency requires explanation, and Tuchman found it in the patronage and incompetence of the British government. If "Mister" Washington, as the British insisted on calling him, had been aware of all of this, he might have taken heart and been rightly expectant of victory since he was apparently facing a rabble of buffoons. However, at the time, many of these failings were not evident, at least over in America. Many American visitors to Britain were taken by surprise at the extent of British flaws and complacency. Franklin, after visiting Europe, wrote of "the extreme corruption prevalent among all orders of men in this old rotten state."[138] John Adams, following the peace negotiations years later, wrote, "The pride and vanity of that nation is a disease; it is a delirium; it has been flattered and inflamed so long by themselves and others that it perverts everything."[139]

However, other historians have questioned the long-assumed extent of British hubris and errors. While they may have been present, it is argued, they were not decisive, and O'Shaughnessy rejects British blundering as the "incompetence myth."[140] In his view, British leaders were experienced and competent but faced a difficult war raging around the globe against the mortal enemies of France and Spain, among others, and of which the American Revolution was just a part. Incompetence is thus not required to explain the loss of one campaign in a larger war. For our purposes that particular debate does not matter. Whether overconfidence was present on both sides or not, my argument is simply that it was present on Washington's side and it helped the Americans win.

But if Washington was overconfident and it helped, why did Britain's overconfidence—to the extent that it was there—not help them? There seem to be two key reasons, located in the manifestation of overconfidence and to whom it applied.

First, British overconfidence tended to be manifested as being dismissive *of their foe* and complacency about their lack of mettle—they would inevitably crush the ant somehow or other and prevail. But Washington's confidence tended to be manifested in confidence *about his own abilities* and in the boldness of his decision-making, to face and take risks at critical junctures. The latter form of confidence was much more useful.

Second, although overconfidence appeared to be rife among the British aristocracy as a whole, it was lacking in the individuals that mattered (and among whom it could help): the commanders in the field. A critical difference in the effects of overconfidence between Britain and America, therefore, may be that American overconfidence primarily affected leaders on the battlefield, whereas British overconfidence primarily affected the institutions and strategic planning at home. The British commanders in the field were, if anything, the opposite—far too cautious and hesitant.

Lawrence James, while acknowledging the obstacles of the vastness of the theater, the problem that the towns did not contain "economic resources" and were thus not worth defending, and the problem that the British never knew where the enemy was, suggests that "bold and imaginative generals might have overcome these difficulties, but the thinking of the British high command was uninventive and often timid."[141] General Howe in particular appears to have suffered from a *lack* of confidence. For example, though successful, the battle of New York might have been a much bigger victory for the British: "Howe proceeded cautiously and in doing so missed the opportunity to fight a decisive engagement. For a time, Washington had been prepared to risk the bulk of the rebel army to save the city, but Howe did not offer battle. Instead he attacked the enemy's earthworks piecemeal and, when it was clear that New York would fall, shrank from a pursuit of the badly mauled and demoralized American Army."[142] Later, he similarly failed to snatch Washington as he made his escape southward across the Delaware, pursue him after the British victory at Brandywine (where, according to a French officer, "if the English had followed up their advantage that day, Washington's Army would have been spoken of no more"), and again to pounce on him while the Continental Army huddled freezing and emaciated at Valley Forge.[143] All of these instances are widely regarded as forgone opportunities to pursue and destroy the revolutionary army. Washington himself was repeatedly "perplexed" by Howe's failure to seize these opportunities.[144]

Other British commanders appear to have suffered from a similar lack of confidence. Clinton, in charge of the troops in New York during the disaster at Saratoga, was "given to fits of paralysis of will."[145] With too small a force to defend New York, let alone reinforce Burgoyne as well, he vacillated, marched up the Hudson toward Burgoyne, then changed his mind and turned back again.

The timidity of Howe and Clinton provides a striking counterpoint to Washington. Washington showed many times that, in order to achieve victory, he was able and willing to seize the initiative, even at great risk to himself and his own forces. This is illustrated in numerous examples but in particular in the dash from New York to cut off Cornwallis at Yorktown in 1781 and in the earlier feat that began to reverse the tide: the daring raid across the Delaware in 1776. There is a compelling case that Washington was unusual in the extent of his confidence and daring, and that without this quality in their commander in chief, the American cause might well have failed.

Lengel suggests that the bloody British victory at Bunker Hill seems to have undermined Howe's confidence at the same time as inflating Washington's to greater heights. He wrote that "much of the excessive caution that characterized Howe's later conduct can be attributed to his Bunker Hill trauma. The same event boosted Washington's confidence, but also made him reckless. 'Winning' another Bunker Hill and thereby bringing a quick end to the war became for him a kind of obsession."[146] He was always searching for the decisive blow. Eventually, he would get it, first in turning the tide in spite of "desperate risk," in Trenton—where "Washington himself led the attack in the center"—and then in Princeton, where again he led his soldiers into the battle. These coups flooded hope into the American cause, and Washington would persevere to seal the victory, even though it would only come several grueling years later, and ironically far away in his home state of Virginia.[147]

Britain was the world's leading military and economic power before *and after* the war. It was by no means yet in decline and was the odds-on favorite to win the war, or at least to end it on favorable terms.[148] I suggest that Washington, in no small part by virtue of his great confidence, was able to turn the tables and seize victory from the jaws of defeat, an achievement epitomized by his daring raid across the Delaware. Joseph Ellis wrote that "the British Commander, William Howe, could probably have won the war and ended the American Revolution in November of 1776 with more aggressive tactics. The Delaware crossing thus becomes a sudden reversal of fortune, as if an American mouse, chased hither and yon by a British cat, brazenly turns about and declares itself a lion."[149] And lions, not mice, win wars.

CHAPTER FIVE

Hedging Bets

THE STRATEGIC ADVANTAGES
OF ATTRIBUTION ERROR

Motives are the most elusive of psychological data, distorted as they are, frequently beyond recognition, by the interests and emotions of actor and observer alike. Do we really know what our own motives are? And what do we know of the motives of others?

—HANS MORGENTHAU

If it is disastrous to mistake an enemy for a friend but not so costly to take a friend for an enemy, then decision-makers are well-advised to suffer the latter misperception rather than run a high risk of the former.

—ROBERT JERVIS

THE FALL OF Troy in the twelfth century BC offers a stark lesson in the pitfalls of trying to predict an enemy's motives. After a ten-year siege of the city, the Greeks packed up and sailed away, leaving behind them an enormous wooden horse. The Trojans, seeing the Greeks disappear over the horizon, wheeled the horse into the city as a trophy. That night, Odysseus and his soldiers, who had been hiding inside the hollow horse, slipped out and opened the gates, with the rest of the Greek army returning under cover of darkness to storm into the city. Troy was sacked.

Tragically, the Trojans had been warned of their impending doom by the king's daughter, Cassandra. She had been granted the gift of prophecy by Apollo, so taken was he with her beauty. But when his love was not returned, he added a curse, such that no one would ever believe her prophecies. The night the Greeks had apparently given up and gone home, Cassandra pleaded her warnings in vain and, according to Smyrnaeus Quintus's *Fall of Troy*, "snatched a brand of blazing pine-wood from the hearth and ran in fury: in the

FIGURE 5.1. Cassandra imploring the citizens of Troy to heed her warnings of impending danger, but no one would listen. *Source:* Designed by Kenny Meadows (1790–1874) and engraved by William Henry Mote (1803–1871), Cassandra, mythological prophetess from Troy, daughter of King Priam and Queen Hecuba, from Henrietta Lee Palmer, *The Stratford Gallery; or, The Shakespeare Sisterhood, Comprising Forty-Five Ideal Portraits* (New York: D. Appleton, 1859), Classic Image/Alamy Stock Photo.

other hand she bare a two-edged halberd: on that Horse of Doom she rushed, to cause the Trojans to behold with their own eyes the ambush hidden there."[1] But the Trojans held the crazed Cassandra back. No one believed that Troy was any longer in danger, a complacency that enabled its destruction.

Unlike Cassandra, we cannot predict the future. However, precisely because we cannot, sometimes we need a Cassandra-like doomster looking over our shoulder, warning us of dangers we might not appreciate or even be looking out for. Especially in the face of lethal threats to our security or survival, we might do well to err on the side of caution and maintain a healthy suspicion of others' motives and designs, even—or especially—if the evidence is ambiguous. The problem has haunted us from Troy to the twenty-first century. As the 9/11 Commission found, for example, what was lacking in the years before Al Qaeda's attack on the American homeland was not adequate information but a "failure of imagination" about new and emerging threats, as well as what they might be capable of achieving. Similar allegations surround the failure to avert Egypt and Syria's surprise attack on Israel in 1973, the Cuban Missile Crisis in 1962, the Japanese attack on Pearl Harbor in 1941, and the rise of Hitler in the 1930s. A Cassandra mentality can verge on paranoia and costly overreaction, but in good measure it can be helpful in keeping us vigilant of new dangers ahead.

Experimental psychologists have revealed that we all have a version of Cassandra in our heads. The fundamental attribution error (FAE) is the human propensity to be suspicious of others' motives. We tend to see the behavior of others as driven by their character traits but to see similar behavior of our own as dictated by circumstances. The result is that people "infer stable personality characteristics from the behavior of others, even when the presence of external factors severely constrains the range of others' possible behaviors."[2] This does not mean that we always perceive others' behavior as threatening but rather that we will perceive threatening behavior as *intentional*. The bias is significant for international politics because in a world of rival states jockeying for power, we must allocate finite resources to genuine threats and avoid wasting resources on false ones. This is easier said than done. Indeed, international relations is pervaded by the "security dilemma," whereby states are compelled to arm *themselves* in defense but must assume that *other* states are arming in pursuit of power. The result is that both end up less secure rather than more secure, and arm further.[3]

While to some extent this may be considered a rational response to the problem of survival in anarchy (an actor that fails to arm leaves itself extremely vulnerable), the FAE suggests that we systematically *overestimate* the threat that others represent. We tend to assume—whatever the reality—that other states' behavior represents their intentions rather than merely a reaction to circumstances, exacerbating the security dilemma. At first glance, therefore, the FAE implies that we will make too many mistakes in the positive direction—overestimating the threatening motives of other states and wasting precious resources to confront them (and more of them in number, as well as each to a greater extent). However, the point of this chapter is to explore a novel possibility: that this is, over time, a *good* strategy. While the literature has lamented the FAE and the inflation of threats it leads to in international relations,[4] I argue that the costs of these mistakes are worth paying if it helps to avoid even greater costs of errors in the opposite direction—*underestimating* the danger of other states when some of them do in fact turn out to pose a mortal threat.

What Is the Fundamental Attribution Error (FAE)?

We are challenged almost daily to work out the causes of our own and others' behavior. Although it might seem obvious, understanding how we do this is a major area of research in psychology called "attribution theory" (because the question is, to what cause do we attribute behavior?).[5] Although attributions can be influenced by a range of psychological factors, such as self-esteem, impression management, just world beliefs, and the availability heuristic, there is one particular bias that has come to dominate attribution research: the fundamental attribution error (FAE).[6] The FAE describes the phenomenon by which people tend to attribute the behavior of *others* to "dispositional" causes (their characteristics, personality, or motives), while one's *own* behavior—even if identical—is attributed to "situational" causes (constraints of the environment or time, competing commitments, or being forced into a corner).[7] For example, we might explain a period of our own poor performance at work as a result of immense pressure from competing demands on our time, whereas we might explain a period of poor performance by others as a result of their laziness, disorganization, or insufficient commitment to the job. People thus tend to see their own behavior as being constrained by or responding to *external* situational factors but to see others' behavior as a result of their *internal* disposition or character.[8]

The original insight behind the FAE can be traced to Austrian psychologist Fritz Heider, who captured the gist of the phenomenon with his famous phrase: "behavior engulfs the field."[9] By this he meant that the originator of an act, being so salient, dominates the perception of all other possible causes. The American psychologist Edward Jones, who pioneered much of the experimental work in interpersonal perceptions, later reflected on the power of Heider's insight: "What is more reasonable, after all, than the brute, palpable fact that there can be no action without an actor? The notion that situations can cause action is abstract and derivative, almost metaphoric in its implications."[10]

The term "fundamental attribution error" was coined much later by another eminent psychologist, Lee Ross. He gave it this ambitious label because, he argued, the phenomenon represents such a pervasive force that it provides the scaffolding for the whole of social psychology—the FAE itself underlies or gives rise to, and thus explains, a huge range of other phenomena.[11] In a detailed review of research on the bias many years later, psychologists Daniel Gilbert and Patrick Malone concurred, calling it still "one of the most fundamental phenomena in social psychology" that, in itself, may help explain a host of other effects.[12] For example, the FAE has been suggested to be the engine behind other famous findings such as people's rapid obedience to authority (cf. Stanley Milgram's experiments in which people follow orders to harm others)[13] and the bystander effect (where people fail to intervene to help others)—both products of assuming that a victim's plight is due to their own disposition rather than unfortunate circumstances beyond their control.[14]

The FAE also underlies a variety of other tendencies. We tend to admire actors and performers much more than the directors, writers, and others slaving away in the background (attributing the quality of the overall performance to the cast rather than the many contextual factors contributing to their success or the production as a whole). We are also easily captivated by ventriloquists speaking through a dummy even though we realize it is fake (intuitively accepting the idea that the dummy has its own dispositions and downplaying the "situational" influence of the puppeteer).[15] We often experience the FAE in everyday life in the form of the closely related "sinister attribution error."[16] Here, we are led to assume that even trivial behavior by others is the result of negative intentions toward us. Why didn't X return my call? Is it because she is annoyed with me? What did I say? We rapidly begin to entertain such thoughts even though the much more likely explanation is that X was too busy, forgot, or hasn't gotten around to it yet.[17]

An important additional finding is the interaction of the FAE with behavior deemed good rather than bad. Although we tend to attribute others' behavior to their disposition and our own behavior to the situation, we finesse this belief depending on its consequences. We tend to see *our own negative* behavior (e.g., missing meetings) as a result of situational constraints (I'm constantly struggling for time) but *our own positive* behavior (e.g., a major achievement) as a result of disposition (I'm a hard worker). Conversely, we tend to see *others' negative* behavior as dispositional (they are selfish) but *others' positive* behavior as a result of external factors (they are trying to impress the boss). Interestingly, when others help us (rather than threaten us) or do what we want them to do, we also tend to attribute their behavior to our own implicit or explicit influence.[18] The influence of good and bad outcomes extends to perceptions of in-groups and out-groups. For example, a study in India found that Hindus attributed undesirable behaviors carried out by fellow Hindus to situational constraints but similar behaviors by Muslims as dispositional.[19] This good versus bad twist on the FAE makes it especially malicious in social interactions: our behavior is always heroic; others' behavior is often contemptible.[20]

Whatever the extent of its reach across psychology as a whole, the FAE is a pervasive and powerful phenomenon.

Evidence for the FAE

Before the FAE was recognized, attribution theory posited that people would—much as we might expect of a rational actor—see the causes of behavior as a mixture of both internal (dispositional) and external (situational) factors and be able to distinguish the relative role of each depending on the constraints that the agents in question are operating under.[21] However, in early tests of this hypothesis, such an expectation was found to be wrong. People were in fact heavily biased in their perception of the roles that internal and external factors played, paving the way for a major rethink of attribution that culminated in the FAE literature.

The classic experiment was conducted by psychologists Ned Jones and Victor Harris in 1967.[22] They gave subjects copies of essays that either supported or opposed Cuban president Fidel Castro, along with one of two cover stories: either (a) that the essayist had freely chosen the point of view expressed; or (b) that the essayist had been assigned to defend that particular point of view by a debating coach. Jones and Harris had designed the experiment to demonstrate the basic predictions of attribution theory—that people would attribute dispositional traits (in supporting or opposing Castro) only to those who had *chosen* the point of view themselves. If it had been assigned, the substance of the argument could hardly be pinned on the author. However, the surprise was that subjects tended to believe that even authors that had the essay *assigned* to them actually supported that viewpoint as well. This unexpected finding stimulated intensive further scrutiny of the phenomenon and, in Gilbert and Malone's words, "fueled an active cottage industry that produced dozens of careful replications and extensions."[23] This succession of experiments uncovered the same phenomenon in a variety of settings, with subjects tending to conclude "that an actor was predisposed to certain behaviors when, in fact, those behaviors were demanded by the situations in which they occurred."[24] Importantly, these controlled, experimental studies were able to rule out alternative explanations, alter the rationale given for the "no-choice" condition (that is, the story behind the situational constraint), and demonstrate the bias across a range of different issue areas, experimental designs, and subjects.

The reason that the FAE is so important to social psychology and everyday life is that it skews our basic understanding of others' behavior—a task that is hard enough as it is. As Gilbert and Malone noted, "Character, motive, belief, desire, and intention play leading roles in people's construal of others, and yet none of these constructs can actually be observed. As such, people are forced into the difficult business of inferring these intangibles from that which is, in fact, observable: other people's words and deeds."[25] Jones had argued many years before that "making inferences from behavior about personality, is a ubiquitous activity of paramount significance for all of us . . . [and] one of the most fundamental problems in social and clinical psychology."[26] We do it all the time in everyday life. We have to. But it's really hard to get right.

Why does this matter for international relations? Because, as suggested by the quote from Morgenthau that opened this chapter, assessing other *states'* intentions is similarly one of the hardest problems in international politics—"futile and deceptive" as he put it, foreshadowing the psychologists to come, "because motives are the most elusive of psychological data, distorted as they are, frequently beyond recognition, by the interests and emotions of actor and observer alike."[27] The difficulties identified by Jones and Morgenthau remain as challenging as ever. Intentions may be notoriously difficult to ascertain, but at the same time it is essential to ascertain something if one is to decide what course of action to take. In one of the most recent studies focusing on the "extremely difficult" task of discerning intentions in international relations, Keren Yarhi-Milo reiterated that "how policy makers gauge their adversaries' intentions remains fundamental to international relations theory and world affairs."[28] In a multiyear study of how experts made predictions and learned from experience in their assessments of security on the Korean peninsula, Richard Herrmann and Jong Kun Choi also found that a persistent problem was the assessment of intentions. "Morgenthau was right," they concluded, that "estimates of another country's motives were the most fundamental judgments experts made, and that they determined the fate of nations."[29]

Assessments of intentions are important, in particular, because they have enormous consequences for war and peace. James Richardson, who studied seven Great Power crises since the mid-nineteenth century, concluded that misperceptions of military *capability* were responsible for only one of these (Russia opting for war with Japan in 1903) but that misperception of *intentions* was a factor exacerbating all of them, and a very significant factor in three.[30] With the assessment of motives and intentions clearly of such critical importance for the theory and practice of international relations, so is our understanding of the FAE.[31]

The FAE as a Cause of Failure

Yarhi-Milo's study of how leaders assess intentions concluded that a rational choice approach, though eminently sensible in theory, offers a poor model for what happens in reality. Instead, "the process of gauging intentions is influenced by an actor's prior theories and expectations, which in turn guide the selection of information and process of updating."[32] "In most cases," Yarhi-Milo found, leaders do not evaluate and update information in an evenhanded manner, and thus "a decision maker's learning process diverges from that described in a rational Bayesian formula."[33] There are many theories about why assessments of intentions "go wrong." However, whatever the particular theory, both psychologists and political psychologists have tended to focus on consequences of attribution error that are *detrimental*. Early on in this research, Jones warned that the fundamental attribution error "is purchased at the high cost of premature closure both about the actors we observe and about the reality that they mediate. . . . [and] may create havoc in the courts, the schoolroom, and the family, to say nothing of the special arenas of counseling and diagnosis."[34] Gilbert and Malone's review agreed about its dangers, although they put it in more poetic terms: "Juries misjudge defendants, voters misjudge candidates, lovers misjudge each other, and, as a consequence, the innocent are executed, the incompetent are elected, and the ignoble are embraced."[35]

The FAE has also tended to be invoked as a cause of mistakes and disasters in international relations. Evaluating other states' intentions is critical to diplomacy, strategy, and deterrence, so the FAE is likely to be especially important in this domain.[36] Since talk is cheap, and gullibility costly, decision-makers are typically thought to rely on other states' *actual actions and behavior* as the only sure guide to their true intentions—otherwise they might simply say one thing and do another.[37] The FAE means that leaders and citizens are likely to perceive the actions of foreign states—for example, military deployments, territorial claims, alliances, or defense spending—as representing hostility or deliberate belligerence, while one's own military deployments, territorial claims, alliances, or defense spending is perceived as being defensive or a necessary response to circumstances.[38] The problem is exacerbated because, as well as being oblivious to the FAE in our own attributions, we do not realize that *others* suffer from it too, so we tend to assume that our own defensive motivations will be obvious to the adversary and they should not, therefore, see *us* as hostile.[39] Ironically, we end up believing that other parties *ought* to know and understand our own position, even as we ignore theirs. Of course, the adversary sees the situation with the same set of biases from the other side. When we see that they are outrageously interpreting our merely "defensive" moves as hostile, this raises suspicions that they may be deliberately using our innocent behavior as an excuse to escalate. A vicious cycle ensues, and the FAE thus accelerates a slide toward mutual suspicion, deterrence failure, crisis, and war. Such misperceptions may be frequent, and have significant consequences. In *Causes of War*, Jack Levy and William Thompson find that "exaggeration of the hostility of the adversary's intentions is a particularly common pattern in the processes leading to war."[40]

Let us consider some specific examples. Jervis suggested that one reason the 1962 Cuban Missile Crisis was so dangerous was because the installation of missiles on Cuba was seen as an act reflecting dispositional Soviet aggression. Situational causes, such as the Soviet concern to protect Castro, were downplayed. Exactly in line with the FAE working to fit observed behavior into a model of longer-term dispositions, the argument was that if the USSR was this aggressive over Cuba, they were likely to continue to be aggressive in other parts of the world in the future—and possibly more important ones like Berlin. Given such an assumption, facing them down in Cuba despite the risks seemed absolutely imperative and may have helped bring the world unnecessarily close to nuclear war.[41]

The 1975 *Mayaguez* incident offers another example of the FAE leading to detrimental outcomes. The seizure of the American cargo vessel USS *Mayaguez* off the coast of Cambodia seemed to the U.S. government to be a deliberate attack on U.S. interests. However, a lack of knowledge about the context and background of the incident contributed to a perception of the crisis as a military confrontation requiring a forceful response.[42] More attention to regional politics (the situational factors) might have revised this view. The *Mayaguez* was captured not just anywhere but close to Puolo Wai Island, the focus of an increasingly hostile territorial dispute between Cambodia and Vietnam at the time.[43] There was oil in the area, and both countries were mobilizing soldiers to stake their claims. "By early May," wrote Elizabeth Becker, "the Khmer Rouge were so concerned with Vietnamese designs on sacred Khmer soil that they began stopping all foreign ships cruising in the area."[44] A Panamanian and a Swedish ship had recently been challenged already. Even more important, it was only on the early morning of 12 May—the very day of the *Mayaguez* seizure—that the Khmer Rouge had sent soldiers to Puolo Wai itself "and assert[ed] Cambodian claims to the island."[45] Later that morning, the *Mayaguez* appeared on the scene and "sailed so close to Puolo Wai that the Khmer Rouge navy, under orders to protect the island from foreign invasion, stopped and seized the ship. The operation was carried out by patrol boats from the Southwestern Zone with no direct contact to Phnom Penh. Officials in Washington learned about the seizure before the party did in Phnom Penh [who later claimed they heard of it on Voice of America radio]."[46]

What the United States perceived as a deliberate attack on its shipping in international waters designed to test its resolve and credibility—sensitive as it was following the recent defeat in Vietnam—was in reality a mistake. It was a preexisting policy applying to all nations' ships and enforced by local authorities, not state decision-makers. Had it been treated that way in Washington, the *Mayaguez* incident might have been resolved much more quickly, easily, and successfully. In the event, forty-one U.S. soldiers were killed and dozens wounded in a rushed military operation to attempt to rescue the crew. Although the problem was exacerbated by a lack of information about a fast-moving situation, there was a strong assumption that the seizure represented the deliberate behavior of a hostile actor—a perception promoted by President Ford and his advisors committing the fundamental attribution error.

The FAE has been invoked in many other examples of failure. Daniel Heradstveit argued that the FAE contributes to damaging misperceptions in Arab and Israeli views of the Middle East conflict.[47] Deborah Larson suggested that the FAE, among other factors, drove the U.S. containment policy of the Cold War to such an extent that it undermined mutual opportunities for deescalation and disarmament.[48] Alexander Thalis described how NATO's "hubristic expansion" eastward in the post–Cold War world constitutes a genuine threat from a Russian perspective, while NATO itself claims it is purely an extension of democratic norms and shared values among former members of the Soviet Union.[49] And Scott Atran argued that the FAE underlies a common reaction to terrorism, which is to assume that it is the result of the behavior of psychopathic maniacs who are fundamentally evil and intent on indiscriminately killing as many people as possible. Atran's point is that the FAE tends to make us discount the situational causes, which clearly contribute—at least to some extent—to terrorist organizations and campaigns.[50]

Finally, the FAE has also been argued to be important in other domains of international relations, beyond conflict and war. For example, the FAE appears to act as an important obstacle to action on climate change, at both national and international levels.[51] At the *national* level, citizens often perceive the behavior of governments, industry, and other groups in society as deliberately acting in their own interests (via raising taxes, imposing carbon limits, free-riding on the efforts of others, etc.) while reducing ordinary individuals' hard-won freedoms or prosperity in the process, especially in tough times. This is another example of assuming dispositional causes of behavior and discounting situational causes. At the *international level*, citizens and leaders alike tend to perceive their own country's efforts to curb climate change as working against numerous difficult constraints, whereas they perceive other nations as shirking their share of the burden in order to get ahead, oblivious or dismissive of those other countries' own (unique or similar) constraints. In these settings, the FAE is a severe obstacle to international cooperation because in collective action problems such as this, the mere *perception* of free-riding or exploitation by others—whether it is true or not—becomes a strong incentive for people to withdraw their own cooperation.[52]

In all of these examples, the fundamental attribution error is argued to have been a malicious force, which inflated threats, generated or exacerbated conflict, or reduced the scope for peaceful conflict resolution. Whatever the reality, the FAE predicts that people will be biased in a systematically conspiratorial direction, seeing the worst in others' behavior, while the counterfactual of people jumping to the conclusion that others are trying to help them is rare. Such a bias seems to undermine our own interests. In Walt's rebuke of wishful thinking in contemporary U.S. foreign policy, he noted that "'worst-casing' can be just as serious an error as excessive optimism."[53] But what about Cassandra? Is assuming dispositional causes of behavior in a competitive world always a bad thing?

Adaptive Advantages of the FAE:
An Evolutionary Perspective

Although the fundamental attribution error offers a compelling explanation for some important errors of judgment in history, there is no reason to believe that it should always lead to disaster. Psychologists themselves recognize many potential benefits of the FAE, although as is quite common in their field they tend to focus on "psychological benefits," meaning benefits to one's sense of well-being or comfort rather than material advantages. Heider and others saw the FAE as a way of distilling data into something manageable—a theory of what causes behavior that works well as a good approximation, even if imperfect.[54] This way, a large range of possible attributional influences can be reduced to a general assumption that actors' behavior is a result of their disposition. Making dispositional inferences allows the decision-maker to gain a "sense of control," which may yield psychological benefits. The problem with this explanation is that if such inferences are not always correct, it merely represents a kind of wishful thinking that "gratifies the individual who wishes to predict the behavior of others."[55] That might be comforting but it does not necessarily bring any systematic material advantages along with it. Here, therefore, we may benefit from developing evolutionary as well as psychological perspectives on the possible adaptive advantages of the FAE.

PSYCHOLOGICALLY ADAPTIVE AND EVOLUTIONARILY ADAPTIVE

Although psychological benefits of the FAE may be genuine, Gilbert and Malone noted that they may stand on some other cause, because "this sense of control [being able to understand the causes of behavior] may be illusory, but even illusory control can have sanguine effects, and thus the mechanisms that produce it may have an advantage."[56] Gilbert and Malone's own view was, however, that this was not good enough, because why would such a data reduction technique necessarily assume that disposition rather than situation is the default mode of causation? It could just as well be the other way around. One possible explanation derives from the characteristics of Western culture, in which religious, philosophical, democratic, and capitalist ideas strongly emphasize the causal role of human agency, rather than the environment (and the opposite may be true in Eastern cultures).[57]

But while cultural factors could account for the overweighting of dispositional attributions among Western subjects, it fails to explain why the trait is widespread around the globe (even if stronger in the West) or why such a universal bias would have arisen in our evolutionary history (before we were "capitalist," etc., or otherwise). So pressing on for a deeper explanation, Gilbert and Malone also recognized that "most modern psychologists are functionalists in that they define the ultimate cause of a behavior in terms of its beneficial consequences for the organism. It is said that a particular phenomenon occurs because it (or the more basic process in which it is grounded) fills a need of the individual and is thus selected (or, at least, not selected against) at the ontogenetic or phylogenetic level."[58] This aligns with the evolutionary psychological approach. Gilbert and Malone stress the fact that, even if it sometimes leads to errors, the detrimental consequences of the FAE are probably not very large (as they put it, "errors on the plane of pure reason do not always count as disasters on earth").[59] Indeed, the FAE may be useful if, despite a few errors, it saves time and energy overall and sometimes leads to fair attributions anyway. Gilbert and Malone thus suggest that the FAE might be advantageous because it offers a useful "rule of thumb" that works well amid the barrage of information and complexity in real-life judgment and decision-making.[60] Dispositional inferences are easy to make, quick, and often correct.

Social scientists are often wary of claiming (let alone gathering) "objective" measures, but in the natural sciences there are many, and the beauty of evolutionary biology is that there is a widely accepted one for adaptive behavior: Darwinian fitness. If a bias serves merely psychological benefits, such as comfort or gratification, then that is all very well but it tells us nothing about why the bias arose in the first place or how it is maintained in competition with accurate assessments. A different way of addressing the problem can therefore be to use the *evolutionary* concept of "adaptive," in which biases and dispositions are evaluated by their material effect on the organism's brute survival and reproductive success.

If the FAE led humans to make systematically poor decisions, then it would incur net costs and should have been eliminated by natural selection. Occam's razor therefore suggests that the FAE provided some adaptive utility in our evolutionary past, and we have it for a good reason. Indeed, this is precisely what the literature suggests. Weighing up the intentions of other social agents and responding appropriately is thought to have been vital for Darwinian fitness.[61] It underlies a whole gamut of social behavior and strategic interaction important to fitness, including cooperation and reciprocity, coordination and collective action, deterrence and coercion, and fighting and mating behavior. It is likely to have been under significant selection pressure and, as a result, we can expect (and indeed we observe) our judgment and decision-making to feature well-honed adaptations to monitor and make assessments of others' intentions, and where necessary, to assume the worst.[62] These include, for example, strong dispositions for detecting cheats, a well-developed theory of mind, and a powerful coalitionary psychology.[63] Obviously, international politics is very different from the social and physical environment of our ancestral past. But important features of strategic interaction remain similar since time immemorial—not least deducing the intentions of potentially lethal adversaries, echoing the original problem that our cognitive mechanisms were designed to solve.[64] Where this is the case, the FAE may still bring adaptive advantages.

From this perspective, we might expect the FAE to offer tangible material benefits in helping to avoid succumbing to dangers and threats, even if it means missing out on a few potential deals or friendships along the way.[65] "If it is disastrous to mistake an enemy for a friend but not so costly to take a friend for an enemy," as Jervis put it, then that's the right mistake to make.[66] In a tough world where security and survival are never guaranteed, perhaps we want to be more like Cassandra than Chamberlain.

ERRING ON THE SIDE OF CAUTION: FAE AS ERROR MANAGEMENT

Historian Ernest May told the story of a twentieth-century British Foreign Office retiree who claimed that "for fifty years, year in and year out, he had assured foreign Secretaries that there would be no major European war. In all that time, he boasted, he had been wrong only twice." Those two occasions, of course, were mistakes of monumental proportions.[67] May contrasted him with Field Marshall Lord Kitchener, who made the opposite error. Kitchener got things wrong a lot and yet was one of the few to accurately foresee a "long and bloody" war in 1914. So, putting it in baseball terms, while the Foreign Office retiree "would have had a 0.960 batting average, he would not necessarily have deserved a higher grade than Kitchener." Evidently, as May points out, "accuracy is not enough."[68] By this he meant that what was critical was getting the big decisions right, not just most decisions right. This is classic error management theory (EMT) logic.

The FAE serves to increase attention, preparedness, and preemptive action against potential threats, prepare for worst-case scenarios, and avoid risking dangerous mistakes. Even if such behaviors incur some costs (assuming ill intent when there is none), it may still be adaptive if it serves to avoid even greater costs in the opposite direction (assuming predatory actors are benign). Though they were writing before EMT was developed, Gilbert and Malone intuitively saw its logic in understanding why people express the FAE: "To the extent that a surfeit of positive and a lack of negative consequences can be said to explain why a psychological phenomenon exists, the ultimate causes of correspondence bias seems tractable."[69] Evolutionary psychologists Martie Haselton and Daniel Nettle explicitly used EMT to argue that the closely allied "sinister attribution error" is advantageous in interpersonal interactions, precisely because the costs of not detecting a threat or exploitation are generally greater than the costs of being overly cautious.[70]

The same error management logic has been identified in international relations by Philip Tetlock: "Deterrence theorists might note that setting a low threshold for making dispositional attributions can be adaptive. One may make more Type I errors (false alarms of malevolent intent) but fewer Type II errors (missing the threats posed by predatory powers such as Hitler's Germany)."[71]

EMT offers exactly this kind of explanation, understanding decision-making biases as a balancing act between the mistakes they generate *and* the successes they generate. If you cannot eliminate mistakes altogether (given inherent uncertainty in decision-making), you have to find a way of steering your behavior to at least minimize the worst sorts of errors. Interestingly, even Jones's early work hinted at the FAE as an error management mechanism. He speculated that "the mistake of overindividuating [*sic*] the social environment is less costly than assuming that people are typical until they clearly demonstrate otherwise."[72] He also suggested that the "error" of the FAE in generating mistakes may be an example of "cognitive inertia," in which the FAE is "the misapplication of a heuristic that is normally useful."[73] In other words, out in the real world, we generally correctly associate people's motives and behaviors (on average and over time), but in the laboratories of social psychologists this usually useful rule of thumb can easily be made to look like a mistake in contrived one-off scenarios. This now raises an important question: Do the critical ingredients of EMT—uncertainty and asymmetric costs—obtain today, such that the FAE is likely to remain adaptive?

In terms of uncertainty, as we have seen, Morgenthau, Jervis, Herrmann and Choi, and Yarhi-Milo, among others, have repeatedly stressed the severe difficulty of assessing other states' intentions in international relations. While states have a hard enough time evaluating each other's *capabilities*, these are at least in principle observable and measurable. By contrast, the evaluation of other states' *intentions* raises uncertainty to a whole new level—variables that are not readily observable or measurable at all. Indeed, states frequently get it badly wrong. The fact that we are dealing with *international* politics can exacerbate this uncertainty. In domestic politics, issues and interaction partners are at least somewhat familiar, usually speak the same language, and have a shared history and cultural context. By contrast, in international politics, states are by definition dealing with foreign countries and cultures that for myriad reasons they are likely to misunderstand and whose actions they often find it hard to anticipate or explain.

In terms of asymmetric errors, I have already emphasized that perceptions of another state's intentions can be tremendously important for security and survival. So the stakes are high. But are they asymmetric? While excessive vigilance and armament can be costly, as often argued in the "threat inflation" literature, it can also be argued that this is the right mistake to make—especially in the context of the "anarchy" of international relations.[74] While the costs of false alarms may be persistent and significant, they pale in comparison to the occasional but catastrophic mistake in which a dangerous adversary was given the benefit of the doubt—as in the Yom Kippur War in 1973, the Cuban Missile Crisis of 1962, the Japanese attack on Pearl Harbor in 1941, and the Munich Crisis of 1938.

In short, the key conditions for error management theory to apply—uncertainty in assessments and asymmetric costs of false positive and false negative errors—are significant for a range of contemporary challenges in assessing other actors' intentions. The FAE should thus remain an adaptive bias, even or perhaps especially in the inherently uncertain and high-stakes world of international politics.

Strategic Advantages of the FAE in International Politics

We have explored examples where the presence of the FAE may have had detrimental outcomes—exacerbating the Cuban Missile Crisis and the *Mayaguez* incident, fueling the Arab-Israeli conflict and the Cold War, muddying our understanding of terrorism, and undermining cooperation on climate change. Yet, a tendency to assume that other actors and states are driven by dispositional motives might sometimes—perhaps even most of the time—be a *good* bias to have, if it helps steer us toward decisions that better guard our security, prosperity, or power.

Let us rethink what the FAE actually does. The FAE is a tendency to assume dispositional causes behind the behavior of other actors and to discount situational factors. This biases our decision-making in a systematic direction, erring on the side of caution in assuming that others' behavior represents their intentions rather than being an accident of their situation. In international relations, this means we are likely to attribute the behavior of other states to deliberate underlying motives, not to whatever constraints they might be under. Obviously, that can sometimes lead to erroneous conclusions. But in an anarchic and often hostile world in which states must look after themselves, such a bias may in fact be generally useful even if it sometimes causes mistakes. It might help us lean in the right direction to survive and thrive in the face of significant headwinds. Most notably, it: (a) increases the *likelihood* of making the safest decision to avoid exploitation (e.g., to arm in response to other states' arming, rather than taking the risk of not arming); and/or (b) increases the *magnitude* of the response (e.g., to arm a lot, rather than taking the risk of arming too little). In both senses, the FAE could offer strategic advantages. On average, therefore, the FAE might be useful rather than detrimental.

While the FAE could help, this may not be obvious because practitioners and scholars are less likely to notice when that is the case. As with other biases, the FAE may only seem prominent (or worth looking for at all) when it is associated with disaster, even if it is also present (but invisible or unsought) when

Table 5.1. Adaptive advantages of the fundamental attribution error (FAE) in the past and (under the right circumstances) today

Advantage	Past	Today
Threat detection *(Identification of enemies, discernment of intentions, erring on the side of caution)*	√	√
Preparation for war *(Allocating, organizing, and increasing resources for deterrence or possible conflict)*	√	√
Alliance formation *(Seeking, persuading, and maintaining partners to help deter or defeat threats)*	√	√

things go well. The consequences of underestimating threats are usually all too clear, whereas exaggerating threats in the other direction may be hard to recognize as mistakes at all. As Richard Betts noted, "A surprise attack or defeat make the costs of *under*estimates obvious and dramatic; the unnecessary defense costs due to *over*estimates can only be surmised, since the minimum needed for deterrence is uncertain."[75] So how can we know whether a bias to overattribute dispositions is useful or not? Let me work up to an answer.

Amid the constant noise of potential new security threats around the globe, states have a tough job sifting the wheat from the chaff. They must avoid expending resources on threats that turn out to be harmless but also avoid being caught off guard and failing to react when a genuine threat arises.[76] This balance has historically led to mistakes in both directions.

First, let us look at a case where a state was overly suspicious but it may have helped. During the 1980s, argues former U.S. secretary of defense Robert Gates, the United States "made the right mistakes" in assuming that the Soviet Union had aggressive intentions.[77] Although Gorbachev turned out to be a genuine cause for peace, the United States had to work on the assumption that the USSR remained a tangible threat. Exaggerated concern over Soviet intentions was the right strategy in order to prepare for the worst-case scenario, at least in Gates's view. If he is right, then the FAE—which Larson found to have aggravated the Western view of the USSR as an incorrigible and aggressive foe—may in fact have been advantageous, a disposition that gave a strategic edge (or hedge) given difficult decisions under uncertainty.[78] Even if it was a false perception, it helped ensure that the United States and its allies remained vigilant, sufficiently armed, and maintained an effective deterrent. That way, they were sure to avoid exploitation. It may have ultimately even contributed to "winning" the arms race that bankrupted the USSR and handed global hegemony to the United States.

However, as foreshadowed by Betts's quote above, it may not be convincing that the FAE was advantageous in examples where deterrence worked and nothing happened (because how do we know if the threat was genuine and deterred—with or without the help of the FAE—or bogus and there was nothing to deter?). More compelling may be cases where a state was not suspicious *enough*, because then one can argue that a *stronger* FAE bias would have been useful—regardless of precisely how much more suspicion was needed (this is why I chose a reverse case for chapter 6). One example is Hitler's invasion of the Soviet Union in June 1941, which shocked the world. But perhaps the most shocked of all was Stalin himself. Having signed the famous Ribbentrop-Molotov pact of non-aggression with Germany in 1939, the USSR thought it had sealed itself from danger for the time being at least and diverted resources from western defenses. Even if Stalin anticipated that Hitler would turn against him eventually, he did not expect a strike from the blue at this time, especially without first knocking Britain out of the war or issuing some kind of ultimatum. Indeed, Stalin's initial reaction was one of disbelief, and it took some time for the reality and scale of the invasion to sink in.[79] Stalin is widely thought to have suffered from paranoia, but despite this making him a prime candidate for FAE-like thinking, there was little evidence of it in his perceptions of German intentions in 1941. Had it been present or stronger, it would have encouraged greater suspicion of the dispositional character of Hitler's expansive aggression and prepared the Soviet Union much more effectively for the possibility of a surprise attack (after all, Hitler had unexpectedly struck other countries many times). In this case, the FAE seemed absent, or too weak, precisely when it would have helped to avoid or mitigate a major disaster.

The FAE might also have been useful in other cases where states were not suspicious enough of rivals. In 1973 Israel was caught completely unawares by a two-front invasion from Egypt and Syria.[80] Previous wars with its Arab neighbors made Israel no stranger to hostility. Yet somehow Israel's sophisticated political, military, and intelligence apparatus failed to see it coming. Perhaps the most commonly cited cause of this failure was complacency arising from their spectacularly successful war of 1967, in which they defeated Egypt and Syria in six days and vastly expanded Israeli territory. After that dramatic demonstration of Israeli military prowess, many assumed that the Arab states would not dare to attempt to challenge Israel again, or certainly not so soon afterward. In the face of such insouciance, one can imagine that the FAE should have helped Israel avoid such a massive intelligence failure. There were several signs that a war was imminent, ranging from numerous Egyptian military exercises to King Hussein of Jordan issuing a direct personal warning to Israeli prime minister Golda Meir. Yet Israeli decision-makers failed to attribute the behavior of their neighbors to any imminent hostile intent. The FAE was evidently not powerful enough.

These examples serve to illustrate that there are important cases in which the FAE, in principle, would have helped states reach the right assessment rather than the wrong one. Even though states appear to commonly overestimate threats (hence the "threat inflation" literature), history is nevertheless replete with examples of nations falling prey to surprise attacks and failing to foresee emerging threats.[81] Given the danger, as the USSR found in 1941 and Israel found in 1973, the FAE may more typically help to harden attitudes toward potential enemies, avoid exploitation, and deter or defeat rivals (as with the United States in the Cold War). While the FAE may cause costly threat inflation in some or even many cases, by doing so it increases the probability of making the safest assumption under uncertainty and minimizing the danger of potential threats—promoting vigilance, preparations, and alliances.

The FAE is especially interesting for international relations because it sharpens the security dilemma. As Tetlock sees it, "The fundamental attribution error exacerbates matters by lowering the perceptual threshold for attributing hostile intentions to other states. This tendency—in conjunction with the security dilemma—can lead to an inordinate number of 'Type I errors,' in which decisionmakers exaggerate the hostile intentions of defensively motivated powers. The security dilemma compels even peaceful states to arm; the fundamental attribution error then leads observers to draw incorrect dispositional inferences."[82] Thus, even if arming is a consequence of rational actors making an unfortunate but understandable decision, the FAE makes the problem worse by elevating the assumption that others are doing so for malevolent ends.

However, Tetlock also pointed out that the FAE could be advantageous for states in the international system, precisely because of the logic of error management theory. Making dispositional attributions "can be adaptive," he realized, because "false alarms of malevolent intent" may be less costly than "missing the threats posed by predatory powers."[83] Given the asymmetry in the consequences of these alternative errors, the FAE can be a good bias to have. Whether and when that is the case in international relations remains an empirical question. States fear for their security in part because the FAE encourages the assumption that other states have nefarious intentions— whether they really do or not. According to some theories of international relations such as offensive realism, this is the assumption that states *should* make if they are to maximize their chances of survival. One could make the same observation about nature in general.[84]

The FAE may not always be strong or important. However, it has consistent effects that can bring a competitive edge. Consider this thought experiment. Two nations are identical except one has the FAE (Suspicious Land) and the other does not (Impartial Land). Each nation may be competent, well resourced, and well defended. But all else equal there will be important differences. Impartial Land will be more empathetic to the other side's situation, more aware of the constraints and pressures upon them, and less likely to perceive hostile intentions. They will find it *easier* to accept that other states must arm themselves for their own self-defense, that they have other rivals to contend with, and that they are doing what they must given their predicament. Impartial Land will also find it *harder* to perceive any aggressive motivations, the agents responsible for other states' behavior, and any threat to themselves. Both countries might excel in wealth and power but, all else equal, Suspicious Land is more likely to expect, detect, and be prepared for situations in which other nations pose a threat. Their suspicion may seem exaggerated to other states and may demand larger defense budgets and alliance commitments, but that may be a price worth paying. In an anarchic international system, fear of the capabilities and intentions of other states can be a good cautionary stance to have. Suspicious Land is less likely to be exploited or taken by surprise and, consequently, more likely to live long and prosper. It may cost more, but survival is worth it.

Limits on the FAE's Advantages

As with other cognitive biases, the FAE is only likely to lend advantages at moderate levels. Too little will not raise our attention to threats enough. But too much can be counterproductive. This is not merely a binary decision-problem (i.e., *is* state X a threat or not?) but a continuous one (*how much* of a threat is state X?). So while one wants to get the *classification* of threat/no threat correct, one also wants to factor in the *severity* of the threat in deciding how and how much to respond. Extreme under- or overestimates of the severity of the threat may therefore become detrimental. For example, even when the FAE successfully helps identify a state representing a genuine threat, if the extent of that threat is exaggerated too far, extreme measures may drain budgets, sow panic, and undermine appropriate preparation. There is therefore a narrow path to be trodden, where the FAE is advantageous as long as it pushes decision-making in a direction—*and* to an extent—that minimizes the costs of both possible mistakes (under- and overestimates of threat). I therefore predict an inverted U-curve, where a certain amount of bias is useful and adaptive, but either too little or too much will lead to maladaptive behavior.

Of course, the calibration of the "right" amount of bias (where the peak of the inverted U-curve lies) will depend on prevailing conditions—how dangerous the external environment *actually* is over time. In a given context or period, a greater or lesser amount of bias may lead to better outcomes. It is interesting to consider, for example, how far these limits might stretch under extreme conditions. Individuals who believe that everyone in the world is hellbent on attacking and destroying them quickly cross a boundary into a psychological *disorder*: paranoia. Usually, paranoia is debilitating and leads to poor judgment and decision-making.[85] Yet one can imagine that in an extremely hostile and life-threatening environment, extreme levels of suspicion—perhaps even clinical paranoia—could be an advantage. Fittingly, paranoia seems to become particularly common among political leaders in dangerous times and places, especially when they have many potential enemies (as did Stalin, for example).[86]

Psychiatrist Arnold Ludwig reviewed the biographies of a large sample of twentieth-century political leaders and concluded that paranoia—at the level of a psychological disorder—afflicted a large proportion of them, well above the population average, and even among democratically elected leaders.[87] His data suggested that 4 percent of political leaders in the twentieth century "definitely" suffered from paranoia and another 9 percent "probably" did.[88] He notes that while in some cases this was dysfunctional and contributed to these leaders' own demise, in other cases it may actually have been helpful because it led to hypervigilance and extensive protection that reduced the chances of assassination, opposition, or overthrow. For them, paranoia may have been necessary for survival. But for most people, and for most states in international politics, a little bit of Cassandra is likely to be better than a large dose of Stalin.

When Does the FAE Help Us or Hurt Us?

When is the FAE likely to have positive or negative effects? Psychologists have explored some of these conditions and point out that the FAE will, in fact, lead to perfectly reasonable assessments if dispositional and situational causes are *correlated* across cases. If they both predict roughly the same behavior, then focusing on either cause can be a good heuristic for attributing cause and effect. The conditions in which dispositional and situational causes can become correlated include: (a) if dispositions are themselves a *cause* of the situation (e.g., all states in a region seek expansion and thus create an environment of extreme insecurity); (b) the situation is a *cause* of the disposition (e.g., the anarchy of the international system socializes all states into similar self-help behavior); or (c) the situation is the *same* as the one for which the decision-maker is trying to predict future behavior (e.g., in wartime a given state is always compelled to take certain actions).[89] In all these cases, situations and dispositions are not independent (the influence of one depends on the other), and thus assuming either dispositional causes or situational causes can be an equally good predictor of behavior. However, making *dispositional* attributions can be best of all because they are simpler and faster to make. In such circumstances, the FAE will be adaptive.[90]

In more general terms, an evolutionary perspective suggests that we should expect the FAE to play to our advantage in conditions of interpersonal and strategic interaction between individual actors, reflecting a challenge that was prominent in the small-scale societies in which we evolved. The FAE is especially important in maintaining reciprocal relationships, for example. As experimental psychologists have found, monitoring intentions is crucial for the success of ongoing interactions and for individuals to maximize the spoils of cooperation while avoiding exploitation. Evolutionary models show that suckers who assume others will act generously toward them will be quickly selected out of the population.[91] The much more reliable strategy is one that is cooperative but immediately punishes or shuns defectors.[92] In fact, "cheater detection" is perhaps the single most clearly articulated and well-demonstrated cognitive adaptation in evolutionary psychology.[93] There is good experimental and other empirical evidence that the avoidance of exploit-ative individuals and cheats has been very important in human evolution, and we have highly sensitized mechanisms for identifying them.[94] There is also strong evidence that adaptations for cheater detection are universal across all cultures, both modern and indigenous.[95] Identifying reliable and unreliable interaction partners has vital importance for fitness-critical behaviors ranging from reproduction and coalitions to intergroup conflict and trade. The FAE keeps our eye on the dispositional causes of people's behavior, over and above whatever situational factors they may claim are forcing their hand.

In short, there is a powerful adaptive logic to being cautious about the intentions of others given the costs and potentially harmful threat of cheats, deceivers, and manipulators—especially in our past but also often today.[96] The FAE helps solve this problem because it puts us on high alert for exploitation, even making us suspicious of others' intentions when there is no evidence that we should be—the very situation in which we are most vulnerable.[97] Indeed, human brains feature a so-called Hyperactive Agency Detection Device (HADD), coined by psychologist Justin Barrett, which appears to be specifi-cally for detecting *agency* in the cause of events. It is "hyperactive" because it overdoes it, perceiving agency even where there is none. Such a bias is thought, however, to have evolved as a defensive and anti-predator device in both ani-mals and humans.[98] Furthermore, our attribution of agency as the cause of events has been found to be *stronger* for negative rather than positive events.[99] Our instinctive bias to be watchful, especially in perceiving agency behind *negative* events, is highly adaptive precisely because we are not always able to reliably detect exploitation until it is too late—like the Trojans.

On the negative side, having explored conditions under which the FAE might help, we should note that the bias could be *more* likely to lead to mistakes in the modern world than in the ancestral environment in which it evolved. This is simply because our social and physical environment has changed so much that the FAE is increasingly likely to be triggered in evo-lutionarily novel circumstances. If the FAE is an evolved heuristic that was designed to deal with the cost-benefit ratios of adaptive challenges that we faced in our evolutionary past, then it may be somewhat impermeable to dif-fering cost-benefit ratios encountered today. In other words, we might not be able to help it biasing our assessments even when it generates negative consequences. The FAE might therefore influence our judgment and decision-making in inappropriate settings and lead to inappropriate responses ("evolutionary mismatch"), especially in situations of great scale or technological novelty—such as, for example, a nuclear standoff or cyber warfare. However, this need not be the case in important domains of modern life. Many aspects of politics and international relations operate at larger scales and via technological marvels but remain essentially forms of interpersonal and strategic interaction—as with reciprocity and cheating—and where this is the case the FAE may do its job just as effectively today as it did in the past ("evolutionary match"). But while it is a strategic instinct that can work well on average, over time, whether it helps or hurts in any specific case remains an empirical question—and one to be explored in the following chapter.

Implications of Adaptive FAE for International Politics

The problem of assessing other states' *intentions*—as opposed to their *capabilities*—is severely understudied in international politics. The focus has for a long time been on actual power differences and the assumption that greater power implies offensive intentions, or at least a greater threat (now or in the future).[100] Such assumptions have become important in international relations theory and practice, but we clearly need to better understand how they arise. In the field of economics and behavioral sciences, Herrmann and Choi noted, "More than twenty years ago, Herbert Simon argued that assumptions about an actor's intentions, values, and perceptions did far more explanatory work than the theoretical frameworks they were typically inputs to [such as rational choice]; and more important, they were empirical questions that should not be left to deduction and armchair conjecture."[101] Jervis similarly highlighted the importance of assessing others' intentions in the context of international relations: "If he is to decide intelligently how to act, a person must predict how others will behave. If he seeks to influence them, he needs to estimate how they will react to the alternative policies he can adopt. Even if his actions do not affect theirs, he needs to know how they will act in order to tailor his actions accordingly."[102]

Although it is famously difficult to assess an actor's real intentions—especially in the smoke and mirrors of international politics—an *evolutionary* perspective on the FAE sheds new light on this problem. It suggests (a) that there is an underlying adaptive logic for why we will tend to overestimate threat, and (b) that this can be strategically advantageous. Evolution has been dealing with the problem of how to allocate resources in the face of threats to survival for many millions of years, and it appears to have come up with a simple heuristic solution for humans: a cognitive bias to err on the side of caution in attributing the causes of others' behavior.

While cooperation is prevalent in nature, interactions are cagey and organisms never assume friendly interactions or help where it is not demonstrated. In dangerous environments, the FAE can be a good strategy because even if it causes many errors (assuming a threat when there is none), it avoids the possibility of even worse errors (assuming no threat when there is one). By this error management logic, the FAE can be beneficial even if it leads to mistakes nearly *all* of the time, as long as it helps in making the right judgments and decisions in rare but critical cases where survival is at stake (we watched the sea for French and Spanish ships for decades even though they hardly ever came, but on the occasions they did it was crucial that we were in the habit of doing so). This is why the FAE evolved in the first place. It was evolution's way of protecting us from potential harm, especially remaining vigilant against the most dangerous predator of all: other human beings.[103] There is every reason to believe that this bias serves us just as well in the anarchic world of international politics as it did in our equally anarchic ancestral past.

IMPLICATIONS FOR INTERNATIONAL RELATIONS THEORY

In international relations, the FAE means we are likely to assume the behavior of other states represents their core motives, not their constraints. This flies in the face of neorealist theory, because structural realism is premised on the fact that states only (or mainly) act as a response to their environment, and thus that any type of government or leader would act the same way in the same circumstances (for a given size of state relative to others). In the extreme version of the argument, Stalin and FDR, for example, would have acted the same way if either had been swapped into the other's particular country and era, so powerful are situational constraints. By contrast, the FAE suggests, whatever the true balance of situational versus dispositional causes of state behavior, empirically, as human beings, we don't think like that. Instead, we tend to attribute the causes of behavior not to state *power* and *position* (situational causes) but to state *leaders* and *intentions* (dispositional causes). This raises interesting questions not only about how the FAE impacts the *practice* of international relations in the real world but also about how it is theorized.

The behavior of states in the international system depends to a large degree on the distribution of power.[104] But since states do not always use their power for offensive purposes (e.g., Canada), what can matter most in terms of explaining and predicting states' behavior is their *perception of threats*—whether real or imagined.[105] As Stephen Walt argued, much of international relations can be accounted for by beliefs about potential threats, over and above actual power differences.[106] Even empty threats are important for explaining state behavior if decision-makers believe the threat is real and act upon it. If Walt is right, then any cognitive biases affecting the assessment of and response to threat (such as the FAE) would play a major role at the heart of international relations theory.

To summarize, the FAE has different implications depending on one's favored theory of international relations. If Waltz is right and states behave as a reaction to their environment, then international relations is all situational and the FAE is a real hindrance to statesmen and scholars alike—dispositional attributions are generally wrong. On the other hand, if neoclassical realists and constructivists are right and states behave as a result of leader-led, normative, and cultural patterns, then the FAE may offer a helping hand—dispositional attributions really are key drivers of international relations and don't just seem that way. Neoliberals fall somewhere in between, resting on the same assumptions as realists about the structural problem of anarchy but optimistic about the promise of rational interventions and institutions that can offer dispositional solutions to situational problems. Certainly, the FAE, and its positive as well as negative effects, has significant new things to say about how we theorize international politics as well as how it happens.

IMPLICATIONS FOR THE HISTORY OF INTERNATIONAL POLITICAL THOUGHT

There are broader implications for international relations theory in the way that the FAE shapes theorizing itself. Psychologist Kurt Lewin argued that the transition from an Aristotelian to Galilean worldview (rejecting the belief that the Earth was the center of the universe) "was a transition common to the evolution of all scientific thinking."[107] Scholars start by assuming dispositional causes of phenomena, but as research progresses they gradually come to appreciate the role of situational factors. In psychology in the early 1900s, for example, there was a tendency to overestimate the role of individuals in explaining behavior, at the expense of important situational factors. Gradually the role of context and social environment rose to greater prominence, however, in part precisely because of the realization of the phenomenon of the FAE: "only when social psychology had itself recognized the significance of situational forces would it be prepared to ask whether ordinary people recognized the same."[108]

There appears to have been a similar bias in the history of international relations theory. Initially, there was a tendency to focus on the role of individuals or leaders, building on the central role of kings and statesmen in the "great men" theory of history. The focus on individual agency was key. This would help explain the development of classical realism, for example, as the product of a focus on actors' dispositions as the driver of international relations, such as Morgenthau's *animus dominandi* or Neibuhr's notion of man as evil.[109] However, this changed as the field developed. Just as Lewin argued that Aristotelian physics gave way to Galilean physics in our understanding of the universe, and just as psychologists increasingly discarded individual explanations of behavior for situational ones, so international relations theory began to focus on the characteristics of the environment to explain the behavior of states instead of the individuals that led them. Hence, it may be somewhat predictable not only that Kenneth Waltz came up with structural realism to explain the behavior of states as a result of their position within the world system but also that there was an increasing salience of the idea for other scholars at the time.[110] The young field of international relations was fertile ground for the emergence of a situational explanation of state behavior.

Ironically, therefore, the FAE offers an explanation not only for many features of international politics but also for the history of the field itself. It is not clear where the intellectual progression would lead next, but it seems likely that there will be a rebalancing (as there arguably is already) such that we rediscover the role of individuals and come to appreciate the importance of *both* dispositional and situational factors. This would accord with the gradual melding of cognitive psychology with neorealism, for example, in "neoclassical realism," and the rise of behavioral science approaches to international relations.[111] Both causes are clearly important to explaining international politics, and we can only reach a full understanding by taking account of human nature *and* context. Either extreme is likely to be too exclusive of real-world complexity. One might point to behavioral economics as another example of a discipline bringing the role of individual dispositions back into the explanation of behavior that had for many decades been entirely focused on situational causes.[112] These trends also parallel the development of life sciences and genetics, in which it is the *interaction* between organisms and their environment that has come to underlie biological understanding and prediction.[113]

Perhaps even more striking about the sociological influence of the FAE is the argument that it may itself have contributed to world history, especially in the interwar period. Gustav Ichheiser, for example, argued that "many things which happened between the two world wars would not have happened if social blindness had not prevented the privileged from understanding the predicament of those who were living in an invisible jail."[114] In other words, a general FAE among European elites and decision-makers may have helped permit Hitler's rise to power in the first place, since they discounted the situational factors underlying German discontent. Similar such patterns emerge in other historical upheavals, from the Peloponnesian War to the French and American revolutions.

IMPLICATIONS FOR LEADERSHIP

Assessing the intentions of other states may be the most important judgment that political decision-makers have to make, as Morgenthau warned. Economic and military power can be measured (however imprecisely), but it is how these resources might be *used* that matters, and how other states intend to use them is not measurable. Since we can make a reasonable estimate of other countries' material *capabilities*, but can never be sure of their *intentions*, a degree of wariness is a good precautionary principle (hence the security dilemma). Historically, evaluations of intentions have represented a lethal pitfall for states trying to establish their strategies and alliances, and on which wars have been fought and lost. And those critical judgments ultimately rest in the hands of individual leaders. Despite the Herculean efforts that intelligence organizations go to in gathering information and producing analysis, Yarhi-Milo found that "decision makers' inclination to rely on their own judgments to infer political intentions is pervasive and universal."[115] The intuitions and instincts of our leaders, therefore, may be more important—and potentially more dangerous—than we think.

But the evolutionary perspective of this chapter also suggests some novel insights. The FAE can help us. In an anarchic world of unpredictable and often hostile actors, the FAE may act as a useful safeguard. Perhaps it makes us a little too suspicious and wary of cooperation. But in so doing, it helps us avoid an even worse error—which is to assume that other actors are merely reacting to circumstances when in fact they may be disposed to deceive, exploit, or attack us. Uncommon as this may be, when it does occur, such as in 1938, 1941, 1973, and 9/11, the consequences are serious indeed.

Leaders would be well advised to consider the effects of the FAE on their own and other states' actions, as well as how they are perceived. Political leaders might in fact be particularly susceptible to the FAE, compared to the average individual in the population at large. With the eyes of their citizens, their party, the opposition, and the world upon them, political leaders are likely to be much more concerned than anyone else about not being fooled on their watch by the intentions of other actors, especially other states.

This affords opportunities as well as dangers. The FAE offers the prospect of gaining significant credit at little expense, if policy and propaganda are pursued in such a way that exploits the FAE bias among observers to attribute good outcomes to the dispositional qualities of the leader. By contrast, if leaders do not adequately signal or explain situational causes of their behavior, then arms races may ensue, deterrence may fail, or they may lose elections. This is especially important precisely because the public is prone to attribute causation to political leaders, as evidenced by the fact that elections often penalize politicians for presiding over events that were beyond their control. One controversial study found that "voters punish incumbent politicians for changes in their welfare that are clearly acts of God or nature," including even droughts, floods, and shark attacks, where "leaders are clearly *not* responsible for good or bad outcomes."[116] While the generalizability or strength of those particular findings might be questioned, the FAE is evidently powerful enough to lead people to blame leaders for actions and events that they could not possibly have been involved in (let alone caused) and to downplay the constraints under which they have to act. Ronald Riggio and Heidi Riggio suggest this may be especially the case in the West: "The strong focus on the leader common in Western cultures often leads to overattributing a group's successful (or failed) outcome to the leader and is an example of the well-known social psychological construct of the fundamental attribution error. . . . Leaders, who are the focal point of attention, particularly in a society that has a romance of leadership, are more likely to be viewed as primary agents or causes of the group's success or failure."[117] The FAE thus becomes a lightning rod for a leader's perceived heroism or humiliation. Riggio and Riggio give the example of Reagan to illustrate the point: "Reagan was elected at a time in U.S. history when morale was low due to poor economic conditions and a decline in U.S. influence abroad. . . . At the same time, blame for a stalled economy and the failed attempt to rescue U.S. hostages being held in Iran was attributed to [incumbent Jimmy] Carter (who is often mentioned as a 'noncharismatic' leader). Reagan, on the other hand, has been attributed by many with reviving the economy (via 'Reaganomics') and causing the collapse of the Soviet Union and the tearing down of the Berlin wall—consistent with the fundamental attribution error, which downplays the situational and other factors that impacted these outcomes."[118]

Turning the tables, rather than leaders being the hapless victims or accidental beneficiaries of the FAE among voters, they can exploit it. History has plentiful examples of leaders pursuing unpopular or expensive wars for which they needed public consent. In drumming up support for such costly or controversial foreign policies, leaders may (consciously or unconsciously) play on the FAE to frame the actions of other states as deliberately aggressive or uncooperative, part of an incorrigible dispositional character that necessitates coercion or aggression. They can similarly dismiss the situational causes that may be contributing to the behavior. Like sailing on a favorable tide, such arguments will be swept along by the FAE, making them seem more convincing and concordant with events.

One obvious example is the selling of the 2003 Iraq War. President George W. Bush and others argued that Saddam Hussein not only had weapons of mass destruction (WMD) but was also disposed to deliberately use them against the West or supply them to terrorists. Neither of these possibilities turned out to have been very likely and there was precious little evidence of any WMD at all. Nevertheless, looking at Iraq in 2003 through our FAE-tinted spectacles, many people could believe it. The United States and its allies had fought Saddam Hussein before, following his overt invasion of Kuwait in 1991, and indeed Western states had since imposed further sanctions and bombing campaigns, after continued violations of international agreements. The WMD narrative in 2003 just seemed like more of the same dispositional character in action. Situational factors were played down, and extraordinary powers were handed to Bush and British prime minister Tony Blair to launch a preemptive war against a nonexistent threat.[119] Whatever one thinks of the wisdom or otherwise of the foreign policy goals of George W. Bush and Tony Blair, the FAE certainly helped them sell it.[120]

Other examples abound, from Bush's sweeping declaration of an "Axis of Evil" in 2001, identifying Iraq, Iran, and North Korea as dispositionally bent on threatening the United States and Western ideals, to Reagan's "Evil Empire" in the Cold War, casting the Soviet Union as a nation of intractably hostile foes, to Presidents John F. Kennedy and Lyndon B. Johnson's fear of the monolithic threat of communism pushing states over like dominos in the 1960s.[121] The United States gets its own share of dispositional attributions as well, of course, from Iran's "Great Satan," Al Qaeda's "paper tiger," and Hugo Chavez's "big loser" to Fidel Castro's "the Empire."[122] As well as representing genuine beliefs among key decision-makers, this rhetoric powerfully taps into public fears that dovetail with the FAE. The point here is not that the FAE facilitated poor policy decisions but that the FAE can be exploited to help generate support for whatever one's policy may be.

Regardless of the blame game at home, for national security, there may also be advantages. The tendency to attribute success to individual leaders, for example, may actually help deter aggressors if the leaders are more likely to be viewed (by those aggressors) as skilled statesmen, well supported at home, and able to wield power effectively—and thus more able to carry out their dispositional intentions to deploy economic and military power. By contrast, if external actors were to perceive the leader as facing serious situational constraints (e.g., domestic political opposition, tight budgets, or challenges to their power abroad), they are more likely to see weakness and opportunity and to play a brinkmanship strategy or seize the chance to expand.

Leaders must recognize the FAE as a widespread and powerful bias in our thinking, and endeavor to take this into account in bargaining, negotiations, and decision-making. This is especially important in crises where limited information and limited time bring cognitive biases to the fore. Leaders must be aware of the bias—in themselves, in allies and adversaries, and in their audiences—and factor it into their strategies and public pronouncements. And finally, when others are suspicious of *our* motives, we should not be surprised and should reflect on the possibility that it is in their strategic interests to assume we have nefarious intentions too.

Conclusions

An adaptive, strategic perspective on the fundamental attribution error leads to some novel insights. First, the FAE is not some sort of unfortunate "error" or design "flaw" in human cognition as so often assumed. On the contrary, evolution has favored it as a design *feature*.

Second, if the FAE conferred adaptive advantages in our evolutionary past, there is no reason to expect that it would not continue to do so today. It may sometimes be undesirable, causing or contributing to fear, arms races, and conflict, but that does not mean it fails to serve the interests of its bearers. The modern world is very different, of course, but international relations still revolves around strategic interactions between individuals and groups and, as Morgenthau observed, working out other states' intentions is a vital, perhaps *the* most vital, aspect of these interactions.[123] The FAE helps us adopt the right heuristics to deal with such a world. While a rational actor might tell us we look over our shoulder too much, the FAE keeps us doing it.

Third, if the FAE is an evolved trait, then it is likely to have been designed to be sensitive to context. Adaptive traits are designed to alter behavior to match specific scenarios (or decision-making "domains"), not to inflexibly "hard-wire" behavior so that it is the same at all times irrespective of the situation. This variation is important for generating predictions about where and when the bias is likely to be present or absent, its magnitude, and its positive or negative effects.

Polymath Lewis Fry Richardson once examined whether sharing a border with another state was a good predictor of war and noted a curious phenomenon.[124] Neighboring countries tended to give different estimates of the lengths of their common border—the smaller country usually reporting it to be longer than it really was. This suggested an exaggerated concern for the threat posed by the other state, but only by the weaker side. Threatened states overstated their exposure. However, this may have been a good bias to have. Given a strong and potentially dangerous neighbor, the safest strategy would be to overestimate one's apparent vulnerability and plan accordingly. Erring on the side of caution leaves less to chance.

This is one likely function of the FAE. Although we might think that a rational actor would arrive at the best strategy for defending the realm, there are both theoretical and empirical reasons to believe that humans adopt a safer strategy in assuming that other states' behaviors are nefarious and deliberate—*more* nefarious and deliberate than they really are. The theoretical logic is that, especially in the domain of national security, the costs of a false positive error are small (assuming danger and arming unnecessarily), whereas the costs of a false negative error are very large (assuming safety and being exploited or attacked). The empirical record suggests that the latter mistake is not uncommon and has indeed been hugely costly in history—from the Trojans in the twelfth century BC to Pearl Harbor in 1941. This implies that a bias may be helpful in (usually) avoiding such disasters. These examples also highlight the negative side of the ledger, in the all-too-dramatic false negatives that bring failure and fiasco. Yet the many false positives—when we overplay deterrence and security, but they work—go unnoticed and uncounted. They are the unsung heroes of Cassandras believed.

The FAE is often the safest assumption to make, even if it is sometimes wrong. The costs of misperceptions can be outweighed by the benefits they bring to avoiding exploitation, especially at times when it matters most such as international crises—when uncertainty reigns and the stakes are high. One of the times it mattered most was standing up to Hitler in the 1930s. Did the FAE help or hurt us then?

CHAPTER SIX

Know Your Enemy

BRITAIN AND THE APPEASEMENT OF HITLER

Perhaps it can be argued that for most of the 1930s Britain was at peace with Germany precisely because the British did not understand Hitler. When, in September 1939, the penny finally dropped, Britain declared war on Germany.

—JOHN GARNETT

Oh well, if you don't make one mistake, you make another.

—LORD HALIFAX

A STRIKING EXAMPLE OF failing to correctly understand the intentions of an adversary is provided by assessments of Hitler in the 1930s. Eventually, of course, Britain, France, the Soviet Union, and the United States realized the colossal danger that Nazi Germany posed and fought a long and costly war to defeat it. However, it took a remarkable length of time to fully appreciate this threat and react accordingly, rendering them unprepared for war and inducing them to concede significant ground to Hitler in the meantime. Britain, in particular, failed to arm adequately or rapidly enough and was still not ready to fight when war broke out in 1939. Moreover, Prime Minister Neville Chamberlain insisted to the very end that Hitler could be brought to terms, a belief that led to the capitulation of Munich—arguably the worst foreign policy disaster of the century.

Underpinning these failings was a serious underestimation of the "dispositional" character of Hitler's goals and Nazi Germany as an expansionist state—something the fundamental attribution error (FAE) should have not only made salient but exaggerated. Instead, Chamberlain and other key decision-makers in the British government saw Germany's behavior as more "situational," forced by social and economic circumstances to reaffirm itself and its borders following the restrictions of the Treaty of Versailles and the turmoil of the Great Depression. Once dispositional causes *were* attributed to Hitler's behavior (for most people, at least by the invasion of Czechoslovakia in March 1939), the Nazi threat was finally appreciated for what it was and rearmament and strategic planning became much more focused and effective.

In contrast to the appeasers, Winston Churchill's dogged arguments that Hitler's intentions were indeed sinister and expansive eventually helped cajole the country and the military (especially the Royal Air Force) to move onto a war footing, even though it came perilously late. So late, in fact, that Britain might even have been compelled to surrender given the military balance after the fall of France in 1940. In the 1930s, the FAE should have helped steer Britain toward a better course of action, not a worse one, and yet among Britain's key decision-makers of the time, the bias—usually so ubiquitous—was strangely, and fatefully, absent.

A Reverse Case: Demonstrating Advantages of the Fundamental Attribution Error

Strategic advantages of the FAE could be demonstrated in two ways: first, by historical cases where the FAE was present (in all or some decision-makers) and contributed to making *good* decisions (helping effectively identify, prepare for, or counter an emerging threat); and second, by historical cases where the FAE was absent or suppressed (in all or some decision-makers) and contributed to *poor* decisions (failing to effectively identify, prepare for, or counter an emerging threat). Both would provide evidence that the bias is advantageous (see Table 6.1).

Examples of poor decisions in the *absence* of a bias offer weaker evidence because: (a) absence of evidence for a bias is not evidence of its absence, only evidence that it was not found (hence it remains possible that it was, in fact, present); and (b) it is hard to show that the absence of something causally influenced policy decisions (since the effects of that absence cannot easily be traced). Stronger evidence would be offered by examples of good decisions in the *presence* of the bias because one can, in principle, demonstrate both: (a) that the bias was present (via the use of appropriate methods and measures); and (b) that the bias causally influenced policy decisions (by tracing the effects of the bias in the judgment and decision-making process leading from assessments to actions). As this chapter will be a reverse case—absence of a bias, poor decision—we might therefore worry that 1930s Britain can at best provide only weak evidence for the FAE being advantageous.

However, the strongest evidence of all would come from *within-case variation*, in which some contemporary actors exhibit the bias (or at least behavior consistent with it) and some do not (or at least behavior inconsistent with it). One can then explore whether those *with* the bias favored or generated more

Table 6.1. Different types of evidence indicating a bias is advantageous

		Decision	
		Poor	Good
Bias	Present	Counterevidence	Stronger evidence
	Absent	Weaker evidence	Counterevidence

Note: Such evidence can derive from: (1) a bias being *present* in a *success* (implying good decisions); or (2) a bias being *absent* in a *failure* (implying poor decisions). The two remaining combinations (a bias being present and associated with poor decisions and a bias being absent and associated with good decisions) represent counterevidence and are the standard argument in the politics and international relations literature for biases being detrimental.

effective policies, and those *without* the bias favored or generated less effective policies (thus offering evidence for both upper-right and lower-left cells in Table 6.1). This is the approach used in this chapter to bolster what might otherwise be weak evidence from a reverse case.

But do we have the necessary within-case variation? Yes, and in two important dimensions. During the 1930s, Britain radically altered its assessment of German intentions *over time*. In addition, at any given point within that period, decision-makers' perceptions varied from *each other*. Some actors' assessments were in accordance with the expectations of the FAE, while other actors' assessments stood in stark contradiction to it. This provides the required within-case variation—over time and across decision-makers—on our proposed explanatory variable: whether Hitler's actions were seen as deliberate, intentional expansion (the telltale "dispositional" causes amplified by the FAE) or innocuous, defensive actions driven by circumstances ("situational" causes suppressed by the FAE). We can then assess whether these changing levels of FAE: (a) influenced assessments and actions; and (b) led to better or worse decisions. My argument is that when the FAE is present, it can lend strategic advantages. When the FAE is absent, it can contribute to strategic disasters. In order to assess this claim, I test the following hypotheses:

1. When the FAE was *strong* (or among those in which it was strong), it helped steer Britain in the right direction of perceiving Germany for what it really was: an expansionist state posing a direct threat to Britain's security.
2. When the FAE was *weak* (or among those in which it was weak), it allowed Britain to drift on a dangerous course that contributed to the policy of appeasement and left it badly unprepared for war.

Demonstrating the utility of the FAE in Britain's perceptions of Germany in the 1930s remains a tricky task. The argument is that the FAE *would have been advantageous* if it had been present, or stronger, in more people (especially the prime minister and his close advisors), but apparently it was not—or at least not strongly enough to influence British policy up until Chamberlain's infamous capitulation at Munich. It is thus an inevitably somewhat hypothetical and counterfactual argument. However, for several reasons this nevertheless makes it a good case to complement the others in this book.

First, as discussed above, I do not focus solely on Chamberlain's perceptions but also on how and to what extent they differed from those of others in the cabinet, the wider government, and other states (third-party observers looking from the outside). It is the *variation* among decision-makers that is important, not whatever Chamberlain's own beliefs were in isolation.

Second, it allows us to look at the problem of biases from a different perspective. One might accept that the FAE could be marginally useful by raising our attention to possible threats, but would it *really* matter if the bias was absent? The road to Munich suggests that it may in fact matter a lot—indeed, the FAE may be a critical tool of survival when we are facing major potential threats under conditions of uncertainty.

Third, the appeasement of Munich is exactly the kind of "worst possible error" that I have argued biases should help to avoid (even if the same bias often causes minor errors in the other direction—overestimating nefarious intentions rather than underestimating them). It is a case of a major strategic disaster occurring precisely because our usually healthy suspicion of other states let us down. Where was the FAE when we needed it?

Hitler's Rise and Britain's Bubble

Early on in the 1930s, the military threat from Germany had been rightly perceived as minimal. Following its defeat in World War I, the restrictions of the Versailles peace treaty, the Great Depression, and domestic political turmoil, Germany had few organized resources let alone a unified foreign policy or threatening military. In the words of historian Wesley Wark, who researched British intelligence on Germany in great detail, "At the start of the Nazi era, the German armed forces posed no threat to anyone."[1]

The problem arose once Hitler came to power in 1933. He did not waste time laying the groundwork for German expansion and the redevelopment of its military. In October, he pulled Germany out of the League of Nations and the World Disarmament Conference, two significant post–World War I initiatives that were of great importance to Western powers. However, in Britain, Hitler's new goals and trajectory did not fully register, and war with Germany seemed to remain out of the question. As Wark found, "In the early phases of intelligence reporting [the early 1930s] there was a general lack of conviction about the danger of an Anglo-German conflict."[2] Even clear-cut indicators of wider aspirations were played down, such as Germany's expansion of its military in contravention of the Versailles treaty. Many in Britain had come to see the treaty as overly harsh, not least because it prevented Germany from having the capabilities necessary to defend itself, which might eventually contribute to instability in the continental balance of power. Perhaps, some argued, Germany's violations of the treaty were therefore justified— and limited. Wark wrote that "the general expectation was that the German armed forces would be rearmed well above Versailles treaty levels but only to a strength sufficient to satisfy the demands of national security. Thus no aggressive intent was assumed from the evidence of Versailles infractions."[3] In some cases, Britain agreed to the infractions themselves. For example, the Naval Agreement of 1935 released Germany from the full maritime restrictions of Versailles which, in itself, John Keegan called an "ill-calculated act of appeasement."[4] As time went on, however, British assumptions about Germany "proved to be a set of grievous underestimates of future German military strength."[5] Here, and especially interesting in the light of the FAE, it was precisely *situational* constraints on Germany—its need for defense and economic recovery—that dominated explanations of German behavior. It is these very situational constraints that the FAE usually leads us to discount, not emphasize.

As well as downplaying the threat, Britain, France, and the Soviet Union also shirked responsibility for dealing with it. They showed little willingness to form a coalition like the Triple Entente of World War I. Instead, they engaged in many years of "buck-passing," increasing their own military strength somewhat, but inconsistently and without coordination, and leaving what they could for others to deal with. For example, in December 1937, a decision was made in Britain *not* to build a large army capable of fighting alongside France on the continent and instead to build up the Royal Air Force to protect the British Isles. The Air Force would of course prove vital in the Battle of Britain, but the focus on aerial assets meant that Britain was prioritizing its own homeland defense against bombardment rather than any serious effort to thwart an advancing German army on the continent. Such a strategy reflected an underestimation of the full ambition of Hitler's intentions. Britain's overall strategy was also influenced by events beyond Europe, where several other threats to Britain's sprawling empire loomed on the horizon. Hitler was just one threat, not yet recognized as the worst or most urgent. Italy and Japan posed more immediate problems for Britain's global interests. All this helped to distract attention away from the growing threat that Hitler posed to continental Europe and Britain itself.

So far, we have seen some evidence that the threat posed by Nazi Germany was not taken as seriously as it should have been in Britain, and its attribution to Hitler's disposition was certainly not elevated or exaggerated as the FAE would predict. However, there was significant variation in perceptions of the German threat over time, and among different parts of government, and this variation was Wark's key finding. At times during the decade, perceptions veered in the other direction and people became overly fearful of Germany. For example, Prime Minister Stanley Baldwin's famous remark in 1932 that, whatever Britain did in trying to strengthen air defenses, "the bomber would always get through" reflected and encouraged a great fear of the likely effects of German air power (this speech to Parliament was titled "A Fear for the Future").[6] Aerial bombing was a new phenomenon of war, dreaded by politicians and citizens alike. Some intelligence reports were also pessimistic, worrying that aerial bombing could deliver a "knockout blow" to London at the outset of a war.[7] As time went on, the methods of intelligence assessment themselves often seemed to favor negativity, in the "proliferation of worst-case assumptions in the middle-years of the 1930s."[8] Wark found that "worst-case analysis, which came to prevail after 1936, not only inflated particular threats but resulted in a cumulative escalation of the overall menace. The costs of such an analysis became apparent in retrospect. It could easily lead to pessimism and yet only once was the method questioned."[9] Note that this newfound fear was in part due to the uncertainties of new technology and the role of aircraft in war rather than any revelations about German intentions per se.

Clearly, therefore, it is not that British intelligence agencies or decision-makers *never* recognized the German threat—they did—but that in the mix of pessimistic and optimistic factors the top echelons of government appreciated its significance far too late. This delay seriously impeded the speed and magnitude of preparations for war, not to mention the persistence of a disastrous foreign policy that led to the appeasement of Munich. As we shall see, it was one thing for the intelligence services to begin worrying about a threat, and quite another as to whether their political masters would take heed. Britain fell behind in an arms race in which they could never catch up. According to Wark, the "acceleration of British rearmament programs occurred from 1936 [in line with assessments becoming more pessimistic], but valuable time had been lost. Grave troubles arose in virtually every sphere of the British rearmament effort—supply, production, and finances. The German armed forces quickly achieved and held on to a quantitative lead, especially in the air."[10]

Chamberlain only came to power in 1937, and into this dire state of affairs brought his own brand of misperceptions (to which we will come). However, the belated concern for the German threat and the increased motivation for rearmament still did not solve the problem in either government or intelligence circles. Wark called the period of 1937–38 the "phase of blindness," in which despite the extent of the Nazi menace gradually being understood, Britain was now panicking after leaving preparations so late. Having been so dismissive of the threat, the pendulum had now swung in the other direction and Britain became alarmed by its own mistake—a double whammy, in which poor recognition of the threat led first to ill-preparedness and then, feeling unprepared, to a fear of acting at all. When Hitler seized Austria in March 1938, "Britain and France protested but did no more. Their inactivity

FIGURE 6.1. Chamberlain's return from Munich in September 1938, where he read out to the crowd the famous piece of white paper, signed by Hitler, stating "the desire of our two peoples never to go to war with one another again." Later that day, in a speech outside 10 Downing Street, he declared "peace for our time." *Source:* Trinity Mirror/Mirrorpix/ Alamy Stock Photo.

was the confirmation Hitler needed that he could safely proceed to his diplomatic offensive against Czechoslovakia."[11]

In the debates of this period, even the armed forces' own *"leitmotif* was Britain's unreadiness and the folly of a war over Czechoslovakia."[12] Britain, as well as France, believed they were wholly inadequately prepared to fight Hitler in 1938, a belief resulting from the shift to a pessimistic British evaluation of the military balance. Indeed, this belief was exacerbated by Hitler's vast program of deception, first to hide German rearmament and later to hugely exaggerate it.[13] Whatever the source, given such a belief, it appeared that the only alternative was political negotiation or appeasement. In perception, if not in reality, British decision-makers were trapped into conceding to a threat that they had not taken seriously enough to prepare for. The British armed services chiefs of staff warned Chamberlain just before Munich that "to take offensive action" before the country had a chance to organize "would be to place ourselves in the position of a man who attacks a tiger before he has loaded his gun."[14] In spring 1939, Hitler marched into Prague, violating the terms of the

Munich agreement. Chamberlain had paid the price for ceding ground to Hitler so many times. When Britain declared its guarantee of Polish independence on 31 March 1939, "Hitler had by now formed the impression that Britain was essentially weak and vacillating, and would not stand by its guarantee."[15] In the light of British behavior during the 1930s, and certainly throughout Chamberlain's time in office, that was a reasonable expectation. Indeed, even when Britain declared war, it didn't do anything to save Poland.

Chamberlain and Churchill: Variation in Perceptions among British Leaders

Key British decision-makers, and Chamberlain in particular, appeared to *lack* the FAE (or at least to have had other proclivities suppressing it or even pushing it into reverse). They downplayed dispositional causes of German behavior and elevated situational ones, so the absence of FAE can only have contributed to appeasement. However, further corroboration would come from establishing whether other decision-makers, ones that *opposed* appeasement, *did* appear to exhibit the FAE.

Certainly, not everyone held the same views, nor did so at the same time. For example, at the start of the Nazi era Britain's Industrial Intelligence Centre (IIC) was "a dissenting voice amidst the general optimism" and argued as early as 1934 that Germany would become a "formidable military factor."[16] The Defence Requirements Committee (DRC) also strikingly concluded in 1934 that Germany would become Britain's "ultimate potential enemy" and, presciently, "that military preparations might make war possible within five years."[17] Evidently there were official bodies less reassured by the mere situational constraints that Germany was under.

There were also notable individuals who had long argued that Hitler posed a significant threat, and one demanding urgent action. Sir Robert Vansittart in particular, from 1931 to 1937 permanent undersecretary at the Foreign Office (the senior civil servant in that department), was concerned about complacency regarding the German threat and worried that the "Service Departments" did not have enough "imagination."[18] He saw Germany's past behavior as a "continuum" of Prussian military values and traditions—a classic dispositional attribution of behavior in line with the FAE (whether true or not).[19] Indeed, Vansittart would later publish a book titled *Black Record: Germans Past and Present*, detailing what he saw as a recurrent aggressive streak in Germany that had persisted throughout history ever since the Roman Empire.[20] After Hitler's reoccupation of the Rhineland in 1936, Vansittart argued that Germany's actions should "teach Britain that German assurances could not be taken at face value" and that "a change of heart in Germany would be nothing less than a 'miracle.'"[21] While Britain's "Cassandra" (as Wark dubbed him) sustained a consistent, unrelenting view throughout his tenure, Vansittart's seasoned alarm bells were discounted by Chamberlain and others, and indeed he was pushed out of office by 1938.[22]

Foreign Secretary Anthony Eden and First Lord of the Admiralty Duff Cooper were also sufficiently opposed to Chamberlain's appeasement policy to resign over it, if rather late, in 1938 (Eden resigned in February, several months prior to Munich; Cooper resigned the day after it). While Eden had initially been open-minded about the extent of German intentions, he could not sustain his support for Chamberlain's appeasement of Mussolini's increasingly aggressive actions in the Mediterranean.

But best known of the detractors was Churchill, not yet prime minister but a constant thorn in Chamberlain's side who would later call Munich a "total and unmitigated defeat."[23] In Peter Neville's words, "Chamberlain was the high priest of appeasement just as Winston Churchill was the focus of opposition to it."[24] In the 1930s Churchill had become "increasingly angry at the National government's supineness in the face of the arming dictators" (referring to Mussolini as well as Hitler).[25] He quickly became the figurehead for contrary views, as "one of the few members of the House of Commons who had been convinced since 1936 that Britain would have to go to war against Hitler."[26] Beyond government circles, the public broadly supported Chamberlain's efforts to engage with Hitler; few wanted another war so soon after the last great cataclysm. However, there were a number of high-profile detractors in the public sphere, and Donald Cameron Watt includes the popular press as one of the "allies" of Churchill and Vansittart in helping to warn of the danger of Germany's military buildup.[27]

With hindsight, Churchill looks clairvoyant. But at the time, with a significant tide of opinion running in the other direction, his fears about Germany's political intentions and military power were, though more accurate than Chamberlain's, arguably exaggerated in the other direction—in line with the FAE. Like Vansittart, he saw Germany as a dispositional actor and rejected the situational arguments that it was being driven by circumstances. As far back as 1934 Churchill spoke earnestly about the need to begin a major rearmament program, create a unified Ministry of Defence, and build up the Royal Air Force. He was insistent about the impending danger and devoted unusual energies to the cause. He helped set up The Focus Group in 1935, a political organization whose explicit goal was opposition to Nazi Germany and the "defense of freedom." But, despite allies, he stood out among the wider crowd. Many people believed that World War I had been caused by too many arms, not too few, and thus actively discouraged a new round of rearmament, a policy further bolstered by the economic constraints of the Great Depression. Indeed, Western powers were committed to the popular World Disarmament Conference under the auspices of the new League of Nations, initiatives that were popular in Britain. As Churchill lamented, "The virtues of disarmament were extolled in the House of Commons by all parties."[28]

For the time being, this overall unwillingness to rearm held sway over dissenting voices, and Churchill represented a contrarian position in comparison with most others in Parliament. For example, "Churchill's lonely, acerbic attack" in the House of Commons on Prime Minister Ramsay MacDonald's suggestion that France abolish its large army (hardly a good idea, of course) "was almost shouted down," and when he finished "members of all three parties jumped to their feet to denounce Churchill as 'a disappointed office seeker' who was trying to 'poison' the spirit of amity and conciliation that MacDonald had worked so hard to forge at Geneva [at the World Disarmament Conference]."[29] Such a strong wave of opinion on disarmament had vital causal influence in our case, because *having failed to arm*, Britain's weakness vis-à-vis Germany (both real and perceived) subsequently constrained the options even available to decision-makers. As Wark describes it, "In the years between 1936 and the Munich crisis . . . exaggeration of the immediate capability of the German armed forces to fight a decisive land and air war led the government to acquiesce in the exercise of German *force majeure* against Czechoslovakia. Once again, the military intelligence contribution to policy was negative. It served to eliminate serious consideration of alternatives to appeasement of the kind advocated outside the cabinet by Sir Robert Vansittart and inside (though more tentatively) by ministers such as Duff Cooper and Oliver Stanley"—both senior cabinet ministers.[30] Thus the failure to recognize the threat not only led to ill preparedness but foreclosed options once the threat *was* realized.

What accounts for the evident variation in perceptions among key actors? Apart from individual variation in worldviews and my hypothesized difference in propensities toward the FAE, a straightforward reason is likely to have been variation in information. There is an argument that Vansittart and Churchill sometimes had better—or at least different—information than anyone else. Vansittart, as the long-serving senior official in the Foreign Office, was privy to a wide range of intelligence sources, embassy reports, secret intelligence, and personal contacts, "to the point of building his own private intelligence service."[31] Churchill had his sources too, and sometimes received leaks of information from Vansittart and others, but key in his case was being in a better position to force the issue publicly. For example, when Parliament discussed the proposal to expand the Royal Air Force in July 1934, Churchill gave a typical warning of the threat of air power and cautioned that Britain's weakness "threatened the very stability of Europe."[32] But, unlike other detractors, "he revealed what he had learned through the network of confidential sources he had assiduously recruited in the Air Ministry and Foreign Office: Germany's aerial rearmament had been going on in secret for years, in violation of the Versailles Treaty."[33] With access to such sources of information, the threat looked worse.

Yet different sources of information do not explain the full extent of people's differences of opinion. Most of Churchill's political peers and the public at large remained antiwar, even once such facts were revealed, and he stood out as a lonely voice in the wind—an image he cultivated himself in his memoirs and public speeches. As he later declared in his famous "iron curtain" speech in Fulton, Missouri, in 1946: "There never was a war in all history easier to prevent by timely action than the one which has just desolated such great areas of the globe. It could have been prevented in my belief without the firing of a single shot, and Germany might be powerful, prosperous and honoured today; but no one would listen and one by one we were all sucked into the awful whirlpool."[34] The fact that his view, back "when no one would listen," was so different from that of the majority (even if perhaps partly due to his particular sources of information), suggests that Churchill was—at least compared to everyone else—somewhat biased. Biographer Peter Neville notes that although Churchill was proven broadly right in his fears of Hitler's ultimate intentions, his claims along the way, for example about Germany's relative air strengths, had at times been "exaggerated" and "seemed wildly erratic."[35] It would be difficult to demonstrate conclusively that Churchill was exhibiting the precise characteristics of FAE (although it seems clearer in Vansittart's case). However, his views were both (a) highly consistent with it, and (b) very strongly held, especially in comparison to those of his contemporaries. Where others saw little or less direct threat from Germany, putting Hitler's actions down to the *situation* (the injustice of the Versailles treaty, the need for Germany to rearm to defend itself, and the desire to unite the German-speaking peoples), Churchill saw a significant and enduring threat arising from Hitler's *disposition* (an ideologue bent on expansion and war). Whether Churchill and Vansittart were overvaluing dispositional causes or not (and to whatever extent), the broader point here is that the FAE would have pushed decision-making in the right direction—promoting the perception that Germany *did* pose a genuine threat and encouraging preparations for war, in contrast to Chamberlain's appeasement.

While Churchill may have been swimming against the tide, he did at least have greater influence than other skeptics of appeasement. Widely regarded among all sides for his force of argument, people paid attention to what he said even if they did not like it. Chamberlain said that debating with Churchill was "like arguing with a brass band."[36] One wonders how much worse Britain's poor preparations would have been if Churchill had not constantly hounded them forward during the many years of resistance.

Where Was the Fundamental Attribution Error When We Needed It?

While there were clearly differences of opinion, the appeasers held sway, as well as holding the keys of government. Britain had lost critical time in failing to recognize the German threat, and from Wark's analysis it is quite clear that this originated specifically from the failure to give enough weight to dispositional attributions of Hitler's behavior—and not just by Chamberlain but by military intelligence as well:

> Despite the early forecasts and the effort spent on drawing up strategic appreciations, the fact was that the prospect of Britain's being drawn into a European war by 1939 was not treated as real until the year arrived. The military in Britain were not prophets of the inevitability of conflict. Admirable as such an outlook was in theory, it had its costs in the delays in rearmament and in the diplomatic defeats suffered by Britain throughout the decade. There can be *no doubt that Britain suffered through a classic intelligence failure stemming, not from an inability to identify one's enemy, but from an inability to understand the real nature of the threat that enemy posed.*[37]

This conclusion is important because it was not that Britain was looking at the wrong opponent, but rather that they were looking at the right opponent and inferring the wrong intentions. Hitler's actions were attributed too heavily to situational factors in Germany, while their dispositional causes were downplayed—exactly the opposite of what we would predict if people were exhibiting the FAE bias. So where was the FAE when we needed it?

The irony is that certain actors *had* made dire and dispositional forecasts about German intentions, and the FAE should have encouraged others to follow suit. But instead Churchill, Vansittart, and others consistently ran up against entrenched opposition. By the time the scope and extent of Hitler's ambitions were eventually acknowledged, it was far too late. Remarkably, it took a disaster on the scale of Munich to wake the rest of Britain up to the reality of Hitler's intentions. By the following March, German troops had entered Prague and seized the rest of Czechoslovakia. Only one question remained: Who was next? Hitler turned east, and Britain and France were powerless to stop him. Lamentably, "the outbreak of war in September 1939, following the German attack on Poland, offered grim proof of the validity of the original forecast set down by the DRC [Defence Requirements Committee] in 1934— that Germany would be Britain's ultimate potential enemy and that military preparations might make war possible within five years."[38] Such views were remarkably prophetic. Yet, unfortunately, they did not permeate the upper echelons of British government.

There is plentiful evidence that, despite varying intelligence reports, which waxed and waned but if anything tended to be overly pessimistic, British policymakers themselves—and Chamberlain in particular—unreasonably dismissed the overall German threat, especially at critical early stages in Hitler's expansionist behavior. Even when they were doubtful about being able to avoid war or being able to fight it, appeasement was nevertheless the wrong strategy to take, because it led to delays in rearmament and undermined deterrence, making stopping Hitler ever harder as time went on. Wark wrote that British intelligence "failed to provide challenges to a narrowly conceived and increasingly dogmatic appeasement policy, and were instrumental in delaying the exercise of deterrence until it was too late to be effective."[39] The FAE should have biased judgments to make British leaders assume the worst of Germany, and this would have favored a different strategy of standing up to Hitler earlier on, which most scholars agree could have prevented a wider war (and if war had come in 1938, against a Germany that was weaker than it would become by 1939).

Even without concrete evidence of the FAE's presence or absence among specific individuals, it is hard to argue that a stronger FAE bias would not have been useful for Britain in the 1930s—wherever it occurred. A greater tendency to assume Hitler had hostile intentions would have helped Britain make the right decisions, meet the threat, and avoid Munich. In such circumstances, the FAE would have been advantageous—increasing the likelihood of adopting an effective strategy in the face of grave danger. The only puzzle is why the FAE seems to be so ubiquitous in the psychologists' labs but was so conspicuously absent when we needed it most.

Were Conditions Right (or Wrong) for the Fundamental Attribution Error?

The puzzle we face is why the FAE, so common and powerful in the way humans tend to think under normal conditions, was apparently absent or suppressed in key decision-makers' perceptions of Hitler in the 1930s. In an almost perfect illustration of the FAE logic, a British Foreign Office memorandum of 1936 offered two alternative perspectives: first, that German behavior reflected "the lust for power of an essentially domineering and rapacious people" (a dispositional attribution); or second, that "Nazism was merely a 'symptom' of Germany's aspirations, whereas the cause was its economic distress" (a situational attribution).[40] Both perspectives were, in fact, present in British government debates throughout the 1930s. But why did Chamberlain and the appeasers cling so strongly to the latter view, against the expectations of the FAE?

The first possibility is that there are reasons why *dispositional* attributions of Hitler's behavior were, in this case, *reduced* (perhaps because of overwhelming contrary evidence, or opposing biases, that counteracted the effects of the FAE). The second possibility is that there are reasons why *situational* attributions of Hitler's behavior were, in this case, *enhanced* (again, because of evidence or biases that might have counteracted the effects of the FAE in this other dimension). Let us look first at why dispositional attributions might have lost out.

DISPOSITIONAL CAUSES: HITLER'S
ULTIMATE AMBITIONS

Hitler's intentions should not have been a surprise. He had "laid down a pro-gramme for his foreign policy" in the 1920s, much of it explicitly spelled out in *Mein Kampf*: "revising the Treaty of Versailles, incorporating Austria and trans-forming Czechoslovakia and Poland into satellite states, confronting France before turning to conquer Russia, and finally achieving world domination" (one other plan that did not come to fruition was a possible alliance with Brit-ain).[41] Evidence suggests that Chamberlain had read *Mein Kampf*, in English excerpts as well as in the original German, and had even annotated it, includ-ing exclamation marks by some sections.[42] With hindsight it is remarkable that anyone—even, or especially, in the 1930s—could have seen Hitler's actions, once in power, as simply a consequence of the situation he found himself in ("situ-ational" factors alone). Hitler was following his own playbook almost exactly. Yet in December 1937, Chamberlain reassured the French prime minister that "the Chancellor had completely changed his view on this subject [of pursuing war] since *Mein Kampf* was written."[43]

As soon as Hitler became chancellor in 1933 he had set to work, although much of it in secrecy. For example, the "agricultural tractor program" made tanks from July 1933, as well as ships and explosives by 1934, "all against the provisions of the Treaty of Versailles."[44] But, as early as March 1935, Germany actually *announced* the German air force, its rearmament program, and con-scription to the world. In 1936, Hitler even declared that Germany "must be ready for war within four years."[45] By February 1938 Hitler had also purged the army leadership, so that it was "more specifically Nazi" and no longer con-strained by dissenting voices.[46] One can point to some reassuring gestures by Hitler, as well as belligerent actions, such as the non-aggression pact with Poland. However, after 1936, "the majority of Germany's actions were hos-tile."[47] Whatever people's views before 1936, by then the FAE should only have encouraged people to (correctly) see Hitler's aggression as dispositional, if they did not already. In the light of Hitler's own stated aims, and events themselves, Chamberlain's failure to recognize German ambitions and antici-pate war looks astonishing. Chamberlain was clearly downplaying disposi-tional causes and focusing on situational causes instead. He "viewed German ambitions . . . as in keeping with the principle of nationalism, believing that Germany had been treated too harshly by the Treaty of Versailles."[48]

An additional factor affecting British perceptions was the widespread "myth" that Hitler's cabinet contained a number of moderates who had influ-ence over Hitler and would keep Germany on a rational course. Unfortunately, any such moderates were few and declining, and held little sway. Donald Cam-eron Watt wrote that this myth of the moderates was merely "evidence of com-plete misunderstanding of Hitler's character and the internal power structure of his Reich," and in reality there was little or no "curb upon his authority."[49] British elites who subscribed to such a view were again downplaying the dispositional nature of Hitler and its effects on German policy.

Employing the logic of game theory, Arthur Stein suggests that by the end of the Munich Crisis, Chamberlain "clearly knew Hitler's intentions regarding Czechoslovakia, but Chamberlain's decision about what to do was contingent on his expectations of Hitler's *future* behavior."[50] This of course, in terms of FAE, is crucial. Was Munich an end point in Hitler's aggression? A final piece of Germany's situational jigsaw puzzle righting the imbalance of the Treaty of Versailles? Or was it just another domino in Hitler's dispositional expansion seeking? The FAE means we tend to see *current* behavior as indicative of *future* behavior, yet Chamberlain seems to have explicitly lacked this tendency, or even to have suffered the bias in reverse (giving far too much weight to situational factors underlying Hitler's actions and far too little weight to his dispositional nature). Accordingly, as Stein notes, his "misperception was to believe Hitler's assurances that these were his last demands. Chamberlain did not extrapolate from Hitler's past and current behavior."[51] And the prime minister genuinely seemed to believe it. When German troops invaded Czechoslovakia in March 1939, Chamberlain was apparently "stunned."[52]

During the Munich Crisis itself, Chamberlain told the cabinet on return from his first meeting with Hitler in Berchtesgaden, on 14 September 1938, that he believed Hitler's objectives "were strictly limited" and that he was "telling the truth."[53] He added triumphantly, but naively, that he had even won "some degree of personal influence over Herr Hitler."[54] At their second meeting at Bad Godesburg on 22–24 September, Hitler upped the ante, telling Chamberlain that he was determined to address the Sudetenland issue, and "I do not care whether there is a world war or not."[55] He now demanded more if any deal was to succeed. Chamberlain, so strongly affected by World War I and, like others, fearful of the unprecedented potential devastation of bombing if war were to break out, saw the offer of peace—even one with major concessions—as an attractive alternative. Hitler pressed the idea that resolving the Sudetenland would settle their differences. During the crisis, wrote Richard Ned Lebow, "on several occasions he assured Chamberlain that the Sudetenland was his last territorial demand in Europe. Poor Chamberlain believed this twaddle and told the House of Commons that Hitler had made these statements 'with great earnestness.'"[56] The essence of the problem was a failure, perhaps even a resistance, to see Hitler in dispositional terms— something the FAE should have amplified. As John Garnett suggested in the quote that opened this chapter, "Perhaps it can be argued that for most of the 1930s Britain was at peace with Germany precisely because the British [and Chamberlain in particular] did not understand Hitler."[57]

Interestingly, Chamberlain's later radio announcement declaring war against Germany "harped on about the personal slights he had suffered from the man he had trusted."⁵⁸ Evidently, he was keen to deflect blame for conceding so much, especially against the advice of ardent critics like Churchill. But in fact his catastrophic error had been to "trust" Hitler in the first place, and apparently far more than anyone else. This is precisely what the FAE usually makes us unlikely or unwilling to do.

To sum up this section, Hitler's dispositional attributes should not have been obscure or a surprise—far from it. They were quite pronounced. It seems that Britain's failure to recognize and confront the threat of Hitler's Germany rested largely on Chamberlain's and other elites' desperate wish to find some way—any way—of preserving peace. An important special condition, not least for Chamberlain, was the recent tragedy and losses of World War I, making even dispositionally driven enemies seem worth placating at all costs. However, even that was a forlorn hope. As Peter Neville put it, "Hitler was not appeased because in the end he was not appeasable."⁵⁹

SITUATIONAL CAUSES: HITLER'S IMMEDIATE CHALLENGES

What about situational factors affecting Germany? Were they so strong and obvious to all as to temper the normal effect of the FAE? Yarhi-Milo finds that the extraordinary, and unusual, policy of appeasement in the 1930s followed from three dominant British perceptions at the time: that Hitler had "limited objectives"; that there was "uncertainty" about the level of Hitler's determination to pursue his goals; and that "Germany's expansionism stemmed largely from economic need."⁶⁰ In other words, while key decision-makers were unsure about Hitler's willingness to follow through with his plans, they assumed that his behavior pursued an isolated set of claims with causes that were situational.

In 1932 German demands to be released from the Versailles treaty obligations were greeted with support by the London *Times*, noting "the timely redress of inequality."⁶¹ At the same time, Britain and other states were seeking mutual *disarmament* agreements via the World Disarmament Conference at the League of Nations in Geneva. Notably, this all began *before* Hitler came to power. "But," notes Stephen Budiansky, "even the coming of the Nazi regime did little to make the supporters of disarmament question the rightness of their cause."⁶² There was a widespread opinion that Hitler was simply reinstating basic German needs and reaffirming national standing. That manifesto was after all partly why he had succeeded in coming to power. Lord Lothian, a strong advocate of appeasement and ambassador to the United States (until his death in December 1940), went so far as to remark that it was "unpatriotic" for people to "refuse to believe in the sincerity of Germany."⁶³ Germany's domestic challenges also led many people to believe that Hitler's actions must have been dictated by circumstances and that he "was being impelled into quicker action to achieve his aims by the economic crisis inside Germany."[64]

Still, Germany was soon not just arming. It was expanding. Yet even military actions failed to prompt significant concern. While alarming to many, the militarization of the Rhineland unfolded "to much popular acclaim at home [in Germany] and little serious criticism abroad."[65] The Rhine region was supposed to remain a demilitarized zone in accordance with the Versailles treaty. France, which had formerly controlled this area, could be fully expected, and was within its rights, to push the Germans out militarily. Hitler himself later recalled that the reoccupation of the Rhineland had been "the most nerve-racking forty-eight hours of my life" because "the military resources at our disposal would have been wholly inadequate for even a moderate resistance."[66] Given how weak Germany was at the time, if France had put up any opposition the German military would have collapsed.

Hitler used the idea of self-determination to great effect in selling a situational-constraints story, in part giving France an excuse to avoid obligations over the Rhineland—as well as in Austria and the Sudetenland. According to Lebow, "Hitler's claim to be acting in accord with the principle of self-determination found an even more receptive audience in Great Britain where revisionist sentiment against the Treaty of Versailles was in vogue among the intelligentsia. Hitler played upon these feelings with commensurate skill."[67] Indeed, he "was successful in arousing considerable sympathy for Germany in Britain, which facilitated Chamberlain's capitulation to Hitler's demands."[68] The government was being persuaded too. In May 1937, British ambassador to Germany Nevile Henderson wrote a comforting memo reporting that German goals were "guided by circumstances and opportunity" and not a systematic policy of expansion.[69] In September, Hermann Göring even managed to dupe him into believing that "the stronger Germany got, the more restraint it would show," and, according to Yarhi-Milo, "Henderson took Göring's statements at face value."[70] The ambassador would continue to argue over the following months that Germany's goals were limited and defensive in nature and that Hitler was not an extremist—rather he was influenced by those around him who were![71] In November, Foreign Secretary Lord Halifax went to Berlin himself and reassured the cabinet on his return that "Germany wanted friendly relations with Britain" and that Hitler had no intention of changing the status quo in Europe as they were "too busy building up their country, which was still in a state of a revolution."[72] In the eyes of key decision-makers in Britain, and via their official eyes abroad, the causes of Germany's behavior appeared to be firmly situational.

Clearly, there were some extraordinary circumstances (or at least permissive conditions) that are likely to have tempered the effect of the FAE by elevating apparent situational causes. Chamberlain and others were led to believe that Hitler was acting to relieve severe constraints—not least, the "harsh" terms of the Treaty of Versailles, the Great Depression, and the demand for "self-determination" of German-speaking peoples. Furthermore, the recent experience of World War I, still at the forefront of people's minds, was supposed to signify "never again." Whether or not Hitler could be appeased, people wanted to believe it. Surely Hitler did not intend to start another European war? Under more typical conditions, the FAE might have warned us otherwise.

Was Chamberlain More Misguided than Other Actors and States?

It is remarkable that Britain, or at least Chamberlain, could have got it so wrong. However, various sources suggest that Chamberlain's perceptions represented a significant deviation from those of other actors in the British government—even from other initial appeasers—as well as those of other states. Let us deal with each in turn, and their implications for the FAE.

INDIVIDUAL DIFFERENCES: CHAMBERLAIN AND OTHER BRITISH DECISION-MAKERS

Remarkable insight is provided by Yarhi-Milo's 2014 study *Knowing the Adversary*. From a detailed reading of primary documents, she argues that Britain's assessments of Hitler's intentions in the 1930s were significantly influenced by psychological factors.[73] Decision-makers did not track changes in plausible indicators such as German capabilities, actions, or military doctrine. Rather, Chamberlain, Halifax, Henderson, and others exhibited "selective attention" in their assessments of German intentions. First, "vivid" personal interactions with Hitler and other Nazi officials, and the insights they derived from these meetings and associated German assurances, weighed on their assessments. As Yarhi-Milo put it, "British decision makers throughout this period relied heavily on cheap talk."[74] Second, the "credibility" of German actions was interpreted through the prism of prior beliefs, which varied among decision-makers. Those who already believed Germany to be an aggressive state (such as Vansittart and Churchill) were quicker to assess new actions as indicative of aggressive intentions. Chamberlain and other appeasers, who believed Germany to be less hostile, were reluctant to infer aggressive intentions—even from aggressive behavior.

The effect was particularly strong in Chamberlain, who remained remarkably equivocal even *after* the invasion of Czechoslovakia proper in 1939 (undermining Hitler's long-heralded claim to be only interested in uniting the German-speaking peoples). Hitler had now "explicitly reneged on his personal assurances to Chamberlain, and in doing so humiliated the prime minister and gave others reason to doubt his [Chamberlain's] judgment."[75] Still, while Chamberlain by this point had to begin to acknowledge Hitler's expansionist goals, it "did not mean that he had ceased to believe he could dissuade Hitler from acting on his plans."[76] Indeed, getting him to change policy "required significant persuasion."[77] Yarhi-Milo stresses that civilian decision-makers relied on very different indicators of German intentions (namely speeches, statements, and assurances) than British intelligence organizations, which focused on the military balance. Not surprisingly, the latter drew an increasingly alarming picture of the German threat—as we saw earlier with Wark's analysis. For the individuals at the top of government, however, the ones deciding on policy, Yarhi-Milo argues that the "overwhelming" impact of personal interactions and the discounting of Hitler's actual behavior together provide a "powerful explanation" for Chamberlain's faulty assessments of Hitler's intentions, as well as why they differed from those of other decision-makers.[78]

The significance of Yarhi-Milo's work for this study is that, in the 1930s, there were clearly powerful factors *counteracting* any possible fundamental attribution error in the key decision-makers that mattered in the making of British policy. Chamberlain was surrounded by plenty of people expounding the dispositional nature of Hitler, but he and his close advisors were led to see a very different picture. The effect was worsened during the 1930s by the composition of those in government. It was not until May 1937 that Chamberlain replaced Stanley Baldwin as prime minister (until then he had been Chancellor of the Exchequer), and as Peter Neville observed, Chamberlain "is open to the accusation that he promoted nonentities who would not oppose his own highly personal view of how British foreign policy should be run."[79] With Chamberlain's ascent to office, appeaser Halifax replaced the skeptical Eden as foreign secretary (whom Chamberlain had come to regard "as an obstacle to an agreement with Germany and Italy"),[80] Alexander Cadogan replaced the seer Vansittart as permanent undersecretary at the Foreign Office, and the wayward Henderson (who exhibited "pro-Nazi overtones") replaced Sir Eric Phipps as ambassador to Germany.[81] Chamberlain was suspicious of the Foreign Office and once characterized it as full of "poets and dreamers."[82] Now, he "had a Foreign Office more in line with his approach."[83] All this, of course, was a recipe for disaster.

The evidence for Hitler's aggressive intentions was mounting, but Chamberlain was in a bubble of illusions, sustained by those around him. Henderson in particular had strikingly conciliatory views of Hitler's Germany, becoming "Chamberlain's confidant," even though he was "a target of ridicule and criticism" at the Foreign Office.[84] Even Cadogan charged that Henderson was "completely bewitched by his German friends."[85] Yet, as Yarhi-Milo found, Chamberlain exhibited an "excessive reliance on Henderson's reports."[86] Even after Munich, when the Foreign Office began to include explicit observations about Hitler's sanity in its reports ("a streak of madness," "barely sane"), Chamberlain "was still skeptical" of the Foreign Office's conclusions about the broader threat.[87] He "questioned" intelligence reports pointing to an attack on the West and "clearly preferred the reassuring reports from Henderson."[88] At this point, "even Halifax and Cadogan were surprised by Chamberlain's willingness to believe Hitler's assurances."[89] By March 1939, Halifax was breaking from the appeasement mold, with Chamberlain's unrelenting optimism and selective use of evidence leading to a "growing split" between them, continuing as he was to depend "heavily on Henderson's reassuring reports."[90] Halifax was angry when, without consulting him, Chamberlain gave an upbeat press conference on 9 March 1939—just six days before Hitler invaded Czechoslovakia.[91] Such optimism among almost anyone else had run dry.

It is interesting to note that not only was Chamberlain misguided, and apparently the most extreme of nearly everyone in his misperceptions, but he also remained confident that he was right.[92] Yarhi-Milo notes Chamberlain's "strong belief in his ability to read Hitler's intentions," even though he was getting it so badly wrong.[93] My previous book *Overconfidence and War* included a case study of the Munich Crisis. The argument there was that Chamberlain harbored significant positive illusions about his own personal ability to craft a deal and win peace.[94] As much of a pessimist as Chamberlain may have been about war, he was a supreme optimist about his ability to avoid it.

If assessments were so heavily (and gravely) influenced by leaders' direct meetings with and assurances from Hitler and other Nazi officials, as Yarhi-Milo stressed, personal meetings themselves to discern intentions seem to represent a liability. Indeed, meeting a potential rival, and exposing oneself to their charms and persuasions, may be worse than relying on our strategic instincts by virtue of which—at least in this case—we would have been more likely to correctly see their fundamental dispositional nature from afar. Although a meeting of leaders seems such an obvious and commonsense way of reconciling differences, it risks a loss of objectivity. Certainly, in the 1930s, Chamberlain and Halifax were hugely influenced—and deceived—by Hitler.

We will never know for sure precisely which biases were present in which decision-makers, to what extent, or how they may have interacted. However, one thing does stand out in the case of 1930s British appeasement fairly clearly: whatever illusions people had about Hitler, they were stronger in Chamberlain than anyone else in government (and as prime minister, these illusions had an inordinate influence on British policy). If the FAE was pushing decision-makers in Britain to worry about the dispositional nature of Hitler's behavior, Chamberlain seemed to have been the least likely to be swayed.

Chamberlain's stance could be partly due to his unique position: there can be only one prime minister, and the buck stopped with him. It was ultimately Chamberlain, therefore, who had to rationalize and justify Britain's fateful policy decisions. If an unnecessary war came, it would be Chamberlain's fault—others could afford to criticize from the sidelines. But this alone cannot explain the degree and consistency with which Chamberlain diverged from others in the cabinet and beyond, even ultimately other appeasers such as Halifax. Rather, Chamberlain seemed to genuinely *believe* Hitler's assurances and gave him the benefit of the doubt—as revealed in private as well as in public pronouncements. After Munich, Lord Lothian singled out Chamberlain applaudingly as *"the only person* who steadfastly refused to accept the view that Hitler and the Nazis were incorrigible and would understand nothing but the thick stick."[95] Chamberlain was clearly unusual. Yarhi-Milo suggests that multiple reinforcing factors supported his favorable perceptions: "The egocentric bias, the salience-vividness bias, and Chamberlain's motivated defensive avoidance all pushed him to adhere to his existing assessment of Hitler's intentions even during late 1938."[96] This perfect storm of factors led Chamberlain to exhibit the strongest resistance of anyone to attributing dispositional causes to Hitler's behavior, and thus he was the least likely person of all to hear the alarm bells of the FAE. Against these headwinds, the voice of Cassandra was lost.

INTERNATIONAL DIFFERENCES:
CHAMBERLAIN AND OTHER STATE LEADERS

What about the perceptions of other states? Was Chamberlain unusual at home but more in line with other national leaders abroad, or was he the odd man out there too? British policy as a whole was certainly divergent compared to that of some other actors at the time. British spokesman Bruce Lockhart was asked by an American audience in the winter of 1938–39, "Will you explain why for six years your country did nothing to avert a danger which . . . was obvious to the rest of the world?"[97] John F. Kennedy later wrote a book about the 1930s titled *Why England Slept* (echoing Churchill's own 1938 book, *While England Slept*).[98]

European states also appeared more visibly concerned by Hitler. France, sitting nervously behind its massive Maginot Line defenses, was under fewer illusions about the threat. They did have their own problems in acknowledging the adversary's formidability. For example, although French intelligence "was able to ascertain German intentions well in advance" and "little about German war planning was left undetected," this knowledge was downplayed by many in the upper echelons of the French military and government who continued to boast of their superior power and deterrence.[99] They were also severely distracted by internal political and economic turmoil.[100] However, whatever the military balance, the top decision-makers do not seem to have been as deluded as Chamberlain about Hitler's intentions. They saw the threat all too well. At a meeting in April 1938, French prime minister Eduoard Daladier himself warned the British in no uncertain terms that Hitler's ultimate aim was "a domination of the Continent in comparison with which the ambitions of Napoleon were feeble."[101] Returning from the Munich agreement to cheering crowds in Paris, and in stark contrast to the famous images of a smiling Chamberlain greeting his own homecoming crowd, Daladier simply commented to his aide: "Ah, les cons" (morons).[102]

Like France, the Soviet Union had profound reasons for concern, having long land borders close to Germany, recent memory of the previous invasion and defeat by Germany during World War I, and in Nazism an implacably ideological foe to the communist cause. Stalin saw 1930s Europe as a "poker game" with three players, Britain, France, and Russia, all trying to get the other two to destroy each other. Although he was ambivalent about whom he might side with, he was by far most concerned about the threat of Germany, especially given a fear that Britain tacitly supported its anti-communist leanings. The Soviet ambassador in London slammed Chamberlain's policy as "one unbroken madness, fermented in the yeast of class hatred, stupidity, and illiteracy."[103] Even Hitler's main European ally, Italy, recognized Hitler's dispositional ambitions and unbending commitment to his goals. Mussolini once described Hitler as "a gramophone that plays only seven tunes."[104] Against these other key players in Europe, under no illusions about the German threat to the continental balance of power, Chamberlain stood out.

One important feature of British policy in the 1930s was the "rejection of alliance diplomacy."[105] Chamberlain believed that the tangle of alliances had been partly responsible for World War I and explicitly sought to avoid becoming involved in them again. Britain would not commit to alliances, would make its own assessments of the German threat, and build up its own forces accordingly ("internal" rather than "external" balancing). Chamberlain's "abandonment of alliance diplomacy," however, frustrated many at the Foreign Office who explicitly called for a coalition with France and Russia. France was always likely to become a strong ally as it had done before. It was Stalin's Soviet Union that posed the enigma for Britain, and the biggest prize.

Eventually, alliances were sought. There remained, however, grave concerns about communism, sometimes to the extent that people have framed Munich as a conspiracy designed to allow Hitler to destroy it in an eastern war.[106] Nevertheless, Churchill and others urged an alliance with the Soviet Union and while Chamberlain acquiesced, he "moved slowly, at least partially because he did not trust Stalin."[107] On this issue as well, Chamberlain differed starkly from most of the cabinet, and only belatedly was convinced to act. In August 1939 Britain and France sent a "hapless and ludicrously low-level delegation to Moscow by slow steamship to offer an alliance."[108] Meetings began on 12 August. Stalin did not take seriously the overtures of the emissaries, General Joseph Doumenc and—stand by for this name—Admiral Sir Reginald Aylmer Ranfurly Plunkett-Ernle-Erle-Drax. A key Soviet demand was allowing troops onto Polish or Romanian soil to form an effective deployment against Germany, which both refused to contemplate. The negotiations were, however, more urgent than they realized: the Germans were in town as well, as Hitler made efforts to come to terms with Stalin.

When Chamberlain heard about these German-Soviet negotiations, he "laughed them off" and said, "I cannot bring myself to believe that a real alliance between Russia and Germany is possible."[109] Simon Sebag Montefiore wrote that it was "turning into an auction for Stalin's favours but with only one serious bidder," Germany.[110] By 14 August German foreign minister Joachim von Ribbentrop himself was on his way to Moscow. An alliance either with Britain and France or with Germany remained possible right up until the last minute. On 17 August, Soviet minister of defense Kliment Voroshilov suggested "a treaty of mutual military assistance to the British and French."[111] It was a real opportunity, and Drax awaited instructions from London. Nikita Khrushchev, then a recently appointed member of the Politburo, had dinner with Stalin, who informed him that Ribbentrop was on his way. "Dumbfounded," Khrushchev exclaimed, "Why should Ribbentrop want to see us? Is he defecting?"[112] But on 23 August 1939, in a remarkable historical coup, Hitler announced the shattering news that he had secured the Molotov-Ribbentrop Pact of non-aggression between Germany and the Soviet Union. Britain and France were out.[113]

Why were other states so concerned about the prospect of a wider great power war with Germany while Britain believed that Hitler could be placated over bits and pieces of German-speaking territory? I hypothesize that among other factors, certain conditions again contributed to the suppression of the FAE among British decision-makers in particular.

First, as argued earlier in the book, biases can be useful heuristics for dealing with recurring phenomena. Threats from other states may be recurring, but the threat from Hitler was in many ways unique, especially for Britain. Other rivals and enemies had arguably acted with greater rationality and restraint in past historical experience, and in the 1930s statesmen had to make sense of an altogether novel kind of leader and his Nazi ideology—both new to the world stage—and it took considerable time to believe and understand their full implications. Keegan described the German transformation as "one of the most remarkable and complete economic, political and military revolutions ever carried through by one man in a comparable space of time."[114] Yarhi-Milo also suggests that, in general, leaders can be good at gauging intentions (or at least believe they are), but when "facing another leader who is manipulative and even charismatic, like Hitler, [they are] . . . more likely to err in their inferences."[115] Even if the FAE was present, therefore, under such unusual circumstances it may not have been strong *enough*. Other European states were arguably less affected by the novelty of Hitler because they had always been threatened by Germany, having shared contiguous borders on the continent, regardless of who was at the helm—whether Frederick the Great, Bismarck, or Hitler. Britain only ever became mortally threatened by a Germany that was led by Hitler.

Second, while the Entente allies had suffered terribly in World War I, they had ultimately prevailed (with U.S. and Commonwealth help), and there may have been a residual confidence that Germany was a state that could be deterred, or if necessary defeated, again by an alliance of strong states. This may have played down the dispositional threat of Hitler's goals and played up the idea that a weakened Germany was merely responding to situational factors at home and in Europe, which included—not least—a formidable ring of foes in Britain, France, and the USSR. Let them build their army, one might argue, as a nation penned in by giant neighbors. Again, this sentiment may have had a uniquely powerful effect on Britain relative to other states. While Britain had suffered in World War I, France and Russia had suffered far more in sheer numbers of dead and wounded, as well as in the destruction of property and resources on their own home territory. Moreover, Britain was an island with natural protection from the sea and could afford to let other states on the continent take the brunt of having to balance against Germany. Britain could also rely on help from its empire and from the United States. The threat to Britain was serious, but it was hardly as serious as it was for France or the Soviet Union. Besides, Hitler himself did not drop his plans for an *alliance* with Britain until 1937![116]

Third, it is hard to rule out the influence of Chamberlain's personal characteristics that set him apart both from political colleagues at home and perhaps especially from his peers abroad. He was unusual in several respects. One of the oldest British prime ministers, at sixty-eight (in 1938, Stalin was sixty, Daladier was fifty-eight), he rose partly by accident, after the fall of Lloyd George's coalition in 1922 changed the political landscape and allowed the rise of "a number of figures from the ranks of obscurity."[117] Unlike many other senior British politicians, Chamberlain had come from provincial political life in Birmingham, where he had served as mayor. He appeared to lack the ambitious drive of many other political figures, writing in 1919 that he was "not looking forward to parliamentary life."[118] Chamberlain sometimes even seemed overwhelmed by the position. Surprised by the crowds on his first trip back to Birmingham as prime minister, he assumed that "there must be a cricket match going on."[119] He also wrote of the significant impact of his responsibilities on his mental health. The combination of age, chance elevation to power, and lack of ambition set him apart from many contemporaries, especially personality opposites like Churchill and Stalin. This is not evidence that Chamberlain should necessarily have been less susceptible to the FAE, per se, but it may help explain why he diverged so strongly in his perceptions of the Nazi threat. Certainly, he appears to have been heavily affected by his personal interactions with Hitler, the level of "trust" he assigned to their relationship, and the perceived personal betrayal by Hitler's subsequent actions. Chamberlain wrote that the Anschluss with Austria, for example, was "most distressing and shocking," representing "a typical illustration of power politics."[120] Yet by this point one wonders why he was so shocked by such events and had such rosy perceptions of the realities of international politics. Perhaps he just wasn't cut out for the job. As Duff Cooper jibed in an article in November 1939, Chamberlain "had never met anyone in Birmingham who in the least resembled Adolf Hitler."[121]

By 1939, Britain's leading economist, John Maynard Keynes, lamented that Chamberlain was "blind to what seems to others the most obvious aspects of the contemporary world."[122] Yet Chamberlain remained single-mindedly focused on his personal objective: to prevent Europe from descending into another conflict. Leo Amery, an ardent critic of appeasement in the House of Commons, described Chamberlain in his memoirs as "inflexibly dedicated to his self-imposed mission at all costs to avert the risk of a world war."[123] If he was to cling to the hope of peace against all the odds, and against all the evidence, Chamberlain would have to overcome the more typical dispositional attributions that others were making about Hitler—especially after the seizure of the Rhineland, Austria, and Czechoslovakia. And, unfortunately, overcome the FAE he did.

An Alternative Explanation: Playing for Time?

Before concluding, let us briefly consider a widely cited alternative explanation. Perhaps British elites and Chamberlain himself were not mistaken about the reality and danger of Hitler's ambitions—perhaps they saw it clearly enough—but had to play down their severity in public and Parliament *in order to buy time to arm*. This revisionist argument gained prominence in the 1970s with the emergence of new documents supporting such a view and has recently enjoyed a revival in work by Christopher Layne, Norrin Ripsman, and Jack Levy. While the argument has its critics, it also has some compelling features.[124] Even John Mearsheimer, perhaps the least likely scholar to see advantages to states in pursuing appeasement strategies, saw no cases at all in the historical record of a state conceding power to an adversary as a short-term strategy to build up resources, except one: Munich.[125] He argues that Czechoslovakia was sacrificed "in part because British policymakers believed that the balance of power favored the Third Reich but that it would shift in favor of the United Kingdom and France over time."[126] If so, conceding to Hitler in the meantime may have been a reasonable strategy.

However, the argument remains unconvincing for several reasons. First, while buying time to arm may be compelling in some respects, such an argument "was not one used by Chamberlain at the time."[127] Had it been an important component of his strategy, we would expect him to have advanced it prominently to colleagues, and perhaps especially to his vociferous critics, as a reason to justify his actions, but there is no record of that ever happening. While Chamberlain did recognize the *opportunity* to rearm as appeasement dragged on, it was not a strategy.

Second, the idea that Chamberlain recognized the threat posed by Hitler but played it down to buy time to arm is challenged by evidence about his own objectives and beliefs.[128] Rather than a ruse to buy time, "Chamberlain was convinced that an understanding with Germany *was* possible."[129] Importantly, it was not just in public pronouncements that Chamberlain downplayed the danger of Hitler (which on its own might indicate mere political expediency). He did the same in a wide variety of private conservations and writings in his diaries, letters to family, and confidences with colleagues.[130] This evidence indicates that Chamberlain genuinely believed that Hitler's goals were limited and that he remained committed to negotiation and, if necessary, making concessions to Hitler.[131] As we have seen, Yarhi-Milo finds evidence for significant misperceptions among Chamberlain and other key decision-makers, which led them to believe that Hitler could be trusted and appeasement would work.

Third, and perhaps even more striking, new work by Brian Rathbun accepts the "rational appeasement" argument, concurring with the idea that Chamberlain was not under great illusions about Hitler and, given Britain's global constraints and limited military power, simply chose the only realistic course of action. However, his own argument is that Chamberlain approximated a rational actor—*lacking* cognitive biases such as the FAE—and yet this rational approach ultimately led to failure. By contrast, he argues that Churchill distinctly did *not* conform to the rational actor model—and indeed strongly emphasized the role of agency in his view of the world in line with a strong FAE bias—and yet this non-rational approach led to the *right* judgments and decisions. Rathbun suggests that, in normal times, we might have preferred the more rational Chamberlain at the top. But the 1930s were extraordinary times. With the appeasers "paralyzed" from acting while Churchill was hellbent on challenging Hitler come what may, "there was a fortuitous meeting of the man and the moment."[132] Churchill was soon to be at the helm, and it was the biased, non-rational leader that found success.

Finally, even if Chamberlain or other British leaders believed that Munich would buy them time to arm, it was the wrong decision to take because in reality the balance of military power went the other way. Germany became stronger relative to the soon to be allies *after* Munich (not least because of the materials and resources gained from the seizure of Czechoslovakia itself). A number of studies show that, had they fought in 1938, the allies could have defeated Germany relatively easily, compared to the struggle after 1939 once Germany had successfully rearmed, expanded, and consolidated its position.[133] Buying time to arm was not the British strategy, and would not have helped anyway.

While there is debate as to how biased or rational Chamberlain was, and whatever he was trying to achieve, all sides can agree that it ended badly and, in retrospect, either his gullibility in the face of Hitler (à la Yarhi-Milo) or his rationality in the face of constraints (à la Rathbun) led to the wrong decisions.

Whoever is right, my argument is simply that, under the circumstances, the cognitive bias of the FAE would have been an advantageous strategic instinct—as it seems to have been for Churchill and Vansittart.

Conclusions

The case of Britain in the 1930s shows that while the security dilemma compels and the FAE encourages states to assume the worst of each other, sometimes even these powerful defense mechanisms fail. And when this occurs, the consequences can be disastrous. States may be exploited or surprised by a rival deemed not to be an imminent threat—like Israel in 1973, the United States and the Soviet Union in 1941, and Britain and France in the 1930s.

Psychologists have found that all of us tend to exaggerate the dispositional nature of other agents and downplay situational causes, such that we assume their behavior is deliberate and likely to be repeated in the future—the fundamental attribution error. My argument is that, far from being a mistake, this bias is highly adaptive in life in general and international relations in particular. Amid the noise of numerous possible threats, the FAE helps us guard against genuine dangers. Indeed, if the FAE is absent, we run the risk of failing to recognize, prepare for, and deal with threats before it is too late. When the FAE was absent, or at least suppressed, among British leaders in the 1930s, they committed what was perhaps the worst foreign policy disaster in history.

On Chamberlain's arrival home from Munich, *The Times* wrote, "No conqueror returning from victory on the battlefield has come home adorned with nobler laurels than Mr. Chamberlain from Munich."[134] For a while, at least to some, it looked like a great coup in seizing peace from the jaws of war. The perceived success in Britain might also seem to be reinforced by the perceived loss on the other side; as Hitler complained to a group of SS officers after Munich, "That fellow Chamberlain has spoiled my entry into Prague."[135] Watt wrote that Hitler "came bitterly to resent the British and Italian intervention which, at the Munich Conference, graciously conferred on him only a part of what he had been about to take by conquest."[136] In 1945, Hitler "looked back on the Munich settlement as a defeat for Germany because it had prevented him from starting a war in 1938, when German military advantage had been, he thought, at its greatest."[137] If true, that would strongly boost my argument here: Hitler must have felt he had demanded so much from Britain and France that it would not be possible for them to accept it, since that's precisely what he hoped would happen. But remarkably they did accept, in itself reflecting Chamberlain's significant underestimation of Hitler's goals and his acrobatic bending over backward to appease him.[138]

There was only one event that convinced Chamberlain that Hitler could no longer be placated: his declaration of war against Britain and France. It is astonishing that this acceptance came so late—long after even other appeasers had dispelled their illusions that Hitler was only seeking limited goals. Once the war was underway, no one was in any doubt about the dispositional nature of Hitler or the Nazi ideology. Churchill had no interest in any further negotiations whatsoever, even those that surfaced in late September 1941, when the rest of Europe had fallen and the United States had still not entered the war. As he made crystal clear, "I am absolutely opposed to the slightest contact."[139] Given Yarhi-Milo's finding that personal interactions can severely mislead assessments of intentions, that might have been an especially good decision. Even the heavy bombing of London did not change Churchill's position one iota, and he "became, if anything, more resolute."[140] Many believed that it was only a matter of time until there was a Nazi victory over Britain as well as France. Across the Atlantic at least, the outlook seemed very bleak: "The fall of France, the entry of Italy into the war, and the blitz of London led to a change in American opinion and policy. Britain was left as the last defender of democracy and surrender seemed likely; Joseph Kennedy, the American ambassador in London, forecast this defeat."[141]

With the benefit of hindsight, Hitler was clearly dispositionally bent on expansion and war—Germany was a state with dangerous intentions for all European powers. The question is why this was not obvious to decision-makers in Britain. Time after time during the 1930s, Hitler took more, and Britain and France allowed him to do so. Even *without* good information on Hitler's capabilities and goals (and there was plenty), the FAE should have made leaders wary of other states' intentions as judged by their behavior, err on the side of caution, and not give them the benefit of the doubt. Unfortunately, it took war itself for Chamberlain to recognize Germany for the mortal enemy it had become. This is all the more ironic given that other bodies within British intelligence circles had correctly identified Germany as Britain's "ultimate potential enemy" as early as 1934, in the famous Defence Requirements Committee report. That fear had continued to be voiced by Vansittart, Churchill, and others throughout the 1930s, and it ever so gradually took root. Toward the end, Chamberlain had to shuffle several key officials to keep his appeasement policy alive.

The absence or suppression of the normally prominent FAE in key decision-makers appears to go some way toward explaining why Britain made the catastrophic error of failing to read Hitler's intentions, downplayed what was arguably the most prominent threat of the twentieth century, and allowed the capitulation of Munich. In life, and in international relations especially, we usually err in the *other* direction—being overly cautious, an empirical phenomenon of such regularity that it is recognized by its own term: "threat inflation."[142] Special conditions appear to have obtained in the case of 1930s Britain—not least the recent calamity of World War I, the efforts to promote disarmament, and the desperate desire to preserve peace—which served to downplay the role of Hitler's dispositional character and play up the role of situational factors in Germany and Europe. Lacking the usual FAE, Chamberlain and his closest advisors made poor judgments and decisions and pursued a dangerous policy of appeasement. Those with views more in line with the expectations of the FAE, like Churchill and Vansittart, eventually were rewarded for their good strategic instincts—recognizing the nature of the enemy and what to do about it, when others were at a loss as to how to proceed. But like Cassandra at Troy, people suspicious of Hitler were not listened to until it was too late. Sir Robert Vansittart wrote at the beginning of the saga in 1934, "Prophecy is largely a matter of insight. I do not think the Service Departments have enough. On the other hand they might say that I have too much. The answer is that I know the Germans better."[143]

In retrospect, it is always easy to look back and see who was right and who was wrong. At the time, it is fantastically difficult to make good predictions, let alone know if they are good or not—especially in assessments of foreign states' intentions, invisible and intangible as they are. But this is precisely why the FAE bias may help us. Amid the chaos of crisis and conflicting information, biases can help steer our judgment and decision-making in the right direction, the direction that leads us away from making the most costly type of error. That's what they are for. As Halifax lamented after Munich, in this chapter's opening quote, "Oh well, if you don't make one mistake, you make another." The trick is to make sure you stay well clear of the big ones.

CHAPTER SEVEN

United We Stand

THE STRATEGIC ADVANTAGES OF GROUP BIAS

Then join hand in hand, brave Americans all,
By uniting we stand, by dividing we fall.

—JOHN DICKINSON

War does not determine who is right, only who is left.

—BERTRAND RUSSELL

IN 46 BC, VERCINGETORIX, erstwhile chief of the Arverni and leader of the Gallic tribes, was paraded through the streets of Rome in Julius Caesar's triumphant procession. The spectacle marked the conquest of all Gaul and the extension of the Roman Empire as far north as the natural border of the Rhine. In the course of the Gallic Wars, 300 tribes had been pacified, 800 cities had been destroyed, and an estimated one million Gauls had been killed (the entire population of 40,000 in Avaricum put to the sword). Another million were enslaved. Gaul was no more. Its inhabitants became Roman citizens, adopted the Latin language, and were absorbed into Roman culture. Gaul would be Roman territory for the next two and a half centuries.[1]

Caesar's triumph was remarkable because the outcome had been far from certain. Only a few years before, Vercingetorix had formed alliances with tribes from across Gaul, joining forces to throw back the mighty Caesar and his legions at the Battle of Gergovia in 52 BC. Thousands of Roman legionaries and dozens of senior officers had been slaughtered. Caesar was forced to break his siege of the city and withdraw from the region. "This brilliant young general," wrote John Julius Norwich, "represented the most serious threat that he [Caesar] had so far faced."[2]

They would soon meet again, at the Battle of Alesia later that year. Vercingetorix had taken his army into the well-defended fortress of Alesia, perched on a hilltop and protected on two sides by rivers. In a remarkable demonstration of Roman engineering, Caesar built a circumvallation—a fortification stretching over ten miles around the entire city—to lock them in. However, Vercingetorix had called on his Gallic allies once more, and a vast army of tribes began to descend on the battlefield. The threat of becoming surrounded was great enough that Caesar felt compelled to cap his engineering efforts thus far to build yet another fortification *behind* his own besieging legions, creating a remarkable dual-ring donut fortification (known as a contravallation—this time even longer than the inner lines). Surely, sandwiched and stretched thinly between two formidable armies, Caesar was doomed again. Forces on both the inside and outside attacked the Roman fortifications—Vercingetorix's 80,000 warriors from Alesia, and what Caesar claimed was another quarter of a million warriors streaming in from the outside, against Caesar's 60,000–75,000 troops. Later historians have suggested that the Gallic relief force was probably no more than 100,000, but even so, Caesar was outnumbered at least two or three to one (even four to one, according to some sources). Hemmed in by a superior force and attacked from two directions, the Romans' fate seemed sealed. Yet after several rounds of fighting with many thousands killed on both sides, when Caesar saw that his troops were on the verge of breaking, he personally led his reserves into the battle to clinch one of the most dramatic military victories in history. In an immense effort against the odds, Caesar managed to emerge victorious, sowing the seeds for the Roman Empire and securing his place in history.

The tribes of Gaul were numerous and powerful and widely thought to be a match for the Roman legions. They had defeated Caesar at Gergovia and surrounded him en masse at Alesia. So how did the many and fearsome Gaulish tribes conspire to find defeat and fail to repel these invaders who were so far from home and on foreign soil? Vercingetorix is remembered not only for his bravery and defiance but also for his skill at uniting the Gallic tribes. But while he did unite many, he failed to unite them all. Many tribes remained on the sidelines, safe in their own regions. Others were half-hearted, failing to commit sufficient support or warriors. Some bluntly sided with the Roman enemy. Caesar's triumph came not only from his military prowess but also from his guile in forging alliances with potential foes and exploiting divisions among his enemies. At Alesia, while the tribes came, they came in too little number. A stronger commitment could have crushed the Roman legions once more; they might even have killed Caesar. But the hundred thousand Gallic warriors were not enough to guarantee victory. The fall of Gaul was, despite the efforts of Vercingetorix, due in no small part to internal divisions among the Gaulish tribes as well as to the strength of the Roman army and Caesar's leadership. While some former Roman allies like the Aedui switched sides to join Vercingetorix's stand, others, notably the Lingones, and the Remi with their vaunted cavalry, remained loyal to Caesar and helped destroy their fellow Gauls. The

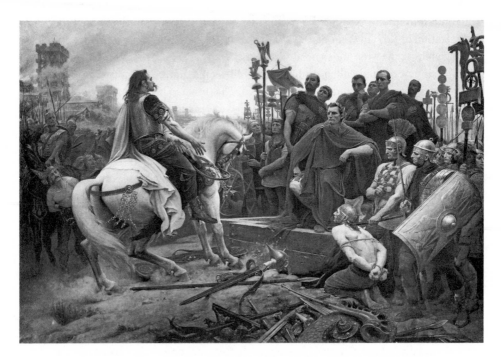

FIGURE 7.1. Vercingetorix surrenders to Caesar after the siege of Alesia in 52 BC. Many tribes answered the call to arms and came from across Gaul to help, but it was not enough. *Source:* Lionel-Noël Royer (1852–1926), *Vercingetorix Throws Down His Arms at the Feet of Julius Caesar*, 1899, Musée Crozatier, Le Puy-en-Velay, France/Bridgeman Images.

Remi even supplied Germani allies from the north with their own fine horses. The Gallic tribes may have been numerous and strong, but when it mattered most, they failed to sufficiently cohere into an effective unified force against the Roman invaders.

Today, on the site of Alesia in France, stands a statue of Vercingetorix built by Napoleon III in 1865. The inscription reads:

Gaul United
Forming a single nation
Animated by a common spirit,
Can defy the Universe.[3]

Vercingetorix was probably right in believing that, by uniting Gaul, he could halt Caesar's conquest. But Gaul was not united. It had not formed a "single nation." The Gaulish chieftain's efforts to prevent the splintering of their lands through rivalries and alliances with the enemy came too late, and the commitment among the Gallic tribes who did join him was too weak. Had they unified earlier and more strongly, Gaul might well have resisted invasion. And perhaps Julius would never have become emperor of Rome; who knows? But one remarkable testimony stands out in the claim that a united Gaul could have won the war for their freedom: it was not the lament of the Gauls, or Napoleon, on that inscription in Alesia; they are the words of Caesar himself.

Experimental psychologists have revealed that we all have a little bit of Vercingetorix in our heads. We are inherently groupish, exhibiting what psychologists call the "in-group/out-group bias." We have favorable dispositions toward our in-group and unfavorable dispositions toward out-groups. This makes us cherish our fellow group members and want to stick together, in distinction to out-groups, which we tend to distrust and disparage. But with so many possible groups with conflicting as well as overlapping interests— kith and kin, partners and coalitions, acquaintances and allies, tribes and nations—it is not always possible to bring people together at the right scale to solve the collective action problems that face us. Vercingetorix made it into the history books because he was successful in uniting many Gaulish tribes to make a remarkable stand against a formidable enemy in Caesar. But he was not successful *enough*. He did not win enough friends to survive the onslaught of the Roman legions. Evidently, Gaul was not a salient enough in-group for the Lingones and Remi tribes, who struck a deal with the devil to fight with the Roman out-group at the expense of their Gallic brothers. If groups, nations, and states are to survive in competition, often lethal competition, with rivals, they must firmly unite and make sacrifices for the common good, even or especially in tough times. Collective action can swing the balance between victory and defeat—as John Dickinson wrote, "by uniting we stand, by dividing we fall."[4] While sometimes we fail dramatically, our groupish nature helps us strive for the former and avoid the latter.

What Is the In-Group/Out-Group Bias?

Among the long list of biases in human judgment and decision-making documented in psychology, perhaps the best known is the "in-group/out-group bias" (sometimes shortened to "intergroup bias" or "group bias").[5] This bias describes our inclination to favor and elevate the in-group and its members and disfavor and deride out-groups and their members. To put it bluntly, humans have an underlying tendency to be nepotistic and prejudiced. It is a pervasive feature of human dispositions and forms the backbone of a now dominant paradigm of social psychology known as social identity theory (SIT), stemming from the seminal work of psychologists Henri Tajfel and John Turner.[6]

Readers may think that this bias describes *other* people that, judging by plentiful examples in the news, are old-fashioned, bigoted, or extremists. But it is a deep-seated cognitive bias among humans to which none of us are immune. As psychologist Susan Fiske cautions, according to some studies,

"80% of Western democratic populations intend benign intergroup relations but display subtle biases."[7] Many others, of course, are openly prejudiced. The bias itself is hard to eliminate, and experiments show that in order to reduce its pernicious effects one has to introduce explicit counterevidence, or shift the bias onto alternative targets.[8]

Evidence for the In-Group/Out-Group Bias

Empirical evidence demonstrates that people: (1) rapidly identify with their in-groups (even when composed of strangers assigned into arbitrary groups); (2) systematically overvalue their own group's performance and qualities; and (3) systematically devalue the performance and qualities of other groups.[9] Experiments have also revealed a number of related effects, for example that people overestimate the ideological difference between their own and opposing groups and see their opponents' viewpoints as more extreme than they in fact are.[10]

The classic study originates in the famous Robbers Cave experiment, conducted with groups of boys at a summer camp in Oklahoma in 1954. The researchers found that the boys quickly jelled with the groups to which they were assigned, even though they did not know each other beforehand. Moreover, when two different groups were brought together to compete in games with valuable prizes, they rapidly developed negative attitudes and behaviors toward the other group. The final stage of the experiment attempted to dissolve the animosity that had prevailed between the groups. However, mere contact was not enough to achieve this, and the researchers found it could only be done by creating greater goals that demanded the direct cooperation of both groups.[11]

Modern studies of the in-group/out-group bias are typically conducted among adults in the laboratory, where treatments can be carefully controlled and confounding factors ruled out. One paradigm is to divide experimental subjects into groups according to their response to some simple task, such as whether their estimate of the number of dots on a picture is too many or too few, or whether they prefer paintings by Klimt or Klee. The grouping process is deliberately arbitrary to eliminate, as far as possible, any material reason to identify with one's own group or against the other. Yet, even in these scenarios, people quickly display a marked favoritism toward their assigned group of random strangers and marked disfavoritism toward the other group.[12]

More recently, new methods have been employed to explore these effects at the neuroscientific level. For example, one study found that when divided into arbitrary groups, subjects perceived their own groupmates' performance to have been better than that of out-group members (even though there was no difference in reality). Brain scans using functional magnetic resonance imaging (fMRI) showed that this arose not from a biased decision-making process when evaluating them (as if exaggerating their groupmates' efforts to make the team look good) but actually during the *perception* of the task itself (their groupmates were literally discerned to have performed better).[13] Remarkably, the bias has also been shown to extend to people with *indirect* markers of in-group identity, even if we don't know those other individuals. For example, we trust people more if they have faces similar to our own, and we are more likely to help strangers with the same last name.[14]

The in-group/out-group bias is strong in laboratory settings even among anonymous strangers. In-groups are not reserved for "friends," and out-groups are not reserved for "enemies." Instead, the effects apply to anyone that happens to fall inside or outside whatever group boundaries are designated by the situation—even in so-called "minimal group paradigms," that is, groups that are created entirely artificially and arbitrarily in experimental labs. This is a testament to the power of the bias. That the phenomenon occurs at all under such conditions is striking in itself. However, if it is easy to look down on a stranger who sees more or less dots, or prefers Klimt rather than Klee, imagine how much the power of the in-group/out-group bias becomes magnified in *real-life* groups in direct, high-stakes competition with each other—Red Sox vs. Yankees, Republican vs. Democrat, Sunni vs. Shia, Redcoats vs. Patriots, Nazi vs. Red Army.[15] In these cases, group differences and group performance really matter, and can escalate over time as a history of idolized victories, defeats, and mutual recriminations accrue and fellow group members strongly reinforce individuals' own prejudices.

A critical feature of the in-group/out-group bias is the tendency for in-groups to perceive themselves as *superior* to out-groups. "Positive illusions" about one's skills and qualities that are widespread among individuals (see chapter 3) are also found among groups, organizations, and societies. People not only overestimate themselves but also overestimate the wider collectives to which they belong.[16] Indeed, the bias is often accentuated at these levels as it becomes mutually reinforced and institutionalized. Daniel Goleman wrote that:

> a well-functioning group is bound together by a kind of group narcissism, one that subscribes to the familiar positive illusions: an unrealistically positive sense of itself, the somewhat grandiose sense of how much the group can make a difference—i.e., control circumstances— and an overly optimistic sense that things will turn out well. These positive illusions support a rosy glow about membership in the group, a sense of specialness that is protected by skews in information gathering quite parallel to those that protect the individual self-schema.[17]

Group positive illusions are important for international conflict for a very simple reason. If people engage in conflict at least partly on the basis of expected costs and benefits and the probability of winning, then anything that increases their expected net gains or the odds of victory will increase the perceived utility of intergroup competition. This makes the group, or nation, more likely to fight—and also more likely to become provoked in the first place, cocooned as they are in a bubble of self-reinforcing superiority. A review of human aggression studies found that "groups whose members demonstrate higher levels of self-esteem also demonstrate higher levels of hostility and violence," and thus "collective violence tends to be linked to explicit beliefs in the superiority of the violent group."[18] This finding concurs with studies on the Mafia and youth gangs, in which lethal violence tends to follow specific insults to a group's status.[19] In fact, experiments have shown that mere membership in a group increases aggression and the willingness to inflict pain on other groups, compared to individual interactions under the same conditions.[20]

Psychologist Irving Janis argued that decision-making within groups is especially likely to exacerbate optimistic biases because "groupthink" creates and reinforces perceptions of superiority, including: a shared illusion of invulnerability; collective attempts to maintain shaky but cherished assumptions; an unquestioned belief in the group's inherent morality; stereotyping the enemy as too evil for negotiation or too weak to be a threat; a collective illusion of unanimity in a majority viewpoint (based on the faulty assumption that silence means consent); and self-appointed mind guards to protect the group from information that might weaken resolve.[21] Groupthink and positive illusions are likely to reinforce each other dramatically. As Daniel Goleman noted, the groupthink bias of invulnerability, "the sense that whatever the group plans is bound to succeed," is "an illusion that is virtually the sum total of the three positive illusions that [psychologist Shelley] Taylor describes for the individual."[22]

In-group/out-group bias can also alter people's perception of blame. It is common to find both sides blaming the other for being the root cause of a conflict or war, whichever side is on the attack or defense.[23] And this goes for a variety of small-scale intergroup contexts as well as states. A study of rivalry between gangs found that while there were many things that distinguished them, the moral logic of all gangs was similar: "Because the enemy was thought of as evil and bad, the fight was conceived of as a fight in self defense, even though the 'enemy' had not made the first move."[24]

The in-group/out-group bias has been demonstrated specifically in the domain of international relations. For example, Richard Ashmore and colleagues gave subjects a Vietnam War peace proposal and asked them to evaluate its likelihood of success and its sincerity. When subjects were told that the proposal came from the United States, or even South Vietnam, subjects rated its efficacy and sincerity as significantly greater than if it was purported to have come from North Vietnam (the "enemy").[25] In all cases, the text was identical. Though the in-group/out-group bias affects all groups, it may be especially amplified at the level of nation-states. Stephen Van Evera argued that states' perceptions of each other are systematically reinforced by "chauvinist mythmaking," which he sees as a "hallmark of nationalism" that includes "self-glorifying, self-whitewashing and other-maligning" via school curricula, popular history, literature, and political propaganda.[26] Psychologist Norman Meier similarly noted long ago that "intensive nationalism, like excessive egotism, is inclined to lead toward attitudes of superiority, with corresponding ratings of inferiority for others."[27]

There is a direct link with perceptions of security in particular. Many authors have argued that a degree of personal security is required in order to permit the tolerance of other groups (so-called existential security). By contrast, existential insecurity can increase the in-group/out-group bias. A study by Ronald Ingelhart and colleagues tested this in Iraq during the violence following the U.S.-led invasion in 2003. At this time, security was extremely poor for civilians, facing direct threats from a variety of armed factions as well as a lack of basic resources. They found that the Iraqi public showed extremely high levels of xenophobia and extremely high levels of solidarity within ethnic groups (and these appeared to *follow* rising insecurity, rather than being a cause). Indeed, these measures in Iraq were at the highest level among all eighty-five societies for which data were available.[28] The in-group/out-group bias, it seems, becomes extreme in times of existential insecurity, when individuals are under severe and imminent threat. Military psychologist Lawrence LeShan stresses this phenomenon at the *state* level too, where in-group/out-group distinctions that glorify the in-group and vilify the other increase dramatically in times of war.[29]

Evidence for the in-group/out-group bias is no longer disputed. It is powerful, has been widely replicated, and occurs across numerous different contexts. The bigger question is *why* we have such a bias, which remains much more open for debate.[30] Tajfel and psychologists following in his tradition argued that the in-group/out-group bias results from people's deep-seated desire to maintain positive self-esteem and that the most reliable way to do so is for people to find "membership in a distinctive group that one views positively on subjectively important dimensions . . . *vis-à-vis* a comparison group."[31] The core idea is that people seek *social identity*, which nurtures their self-esteem as they bask in the reflected glory of their adopted group. Although there are variations on this theme, social identity theory (SIT) has remained a dominant paradigm in psychology for many decades, supported by a vast literature of empirical studies.[32]

In-Group/Out-Group Bias as a Cause of Failure

While it may be central to people's self-esteem, the in-group/out-group bias is widely seen as a malicious force because it causes or exacerbates intergroup prejudice, conflict, violence, and war. Psychologist Susan Fiske called it nothing less than the "problem of the century."[33] Indeed, there are so many negative invocations of in-group/out-group bias in contemporary society and human history that it is hard to know where to start. One can find examples of groups looking down their noses at each other from the earliest histories of human civilization (such as the Athenians and Spartans, or Romans and Carthaginians), to more recent centuries (such as the French and Germans, or Soviets and Americans), to a variety of present-day divisions across tribal, religious, and ideological lines (such as Israelis and their Arab neighbors, Hindus and Muslims in India, Christians and Muslims in Nigeria, or liberals and conservatives and any number of other social and party political divides around the world).[34] One of the most obvious examples of group biases contributing to conflict is competition between different ethnic groups, which often goes beyond material disagreements to out-group resentment and "ancient hatreds."[35] A number of studies have identified ethnic rivalry as an important cause of war in its own right, especially in the many civil wars that have raged around the world in recent decades.[36]

But the effects of group biases on competition and conflict extend powerfully across national borders too. Early studies of global data sets found an empirical association between states' "ethnocultural contrast" and the level of conflict between them.[37] While it is evidently not a necessary or sufficient condition for war, in-group/out-group distinctions are a common contributory factor, sometimes a very powerful one, and they routinely fan the flames whether or not they helped start the conflict. One example is World War I. Although there are a range of contested causes of the war, the in-group/out-group bias was a notable and potent feature among many societies and elites of the time, and this is widely argued to have exacerbated the motivation to fight.[38] Nations on all sides emphasized the quality and superiority of their own culture and soldiers, beliefs that made war look more necessary and more attractive, and made the outcome seem more likely to pan out in their favor.

In Germany, for example, there were widespread beliefs among its citizens in their cultural superiority. This has been explored by a number of authors including Van Evera, who found that "Wilhelmine-era German nationalists proclaimed that Germans were 'the greatest civilized people known to history' and that 'the German should feel himself raised above all the peoples who surround him and whom he sees at an immeasurable depth below him.' Germans were assured that 'the French Army lacks the . . . united spirit which characterizes the German army, the tenacious strength of the German race, and the esprit de corps of the officers.'"[39]

Even intellectuals such as Rainer Maria Rilke and Thomas Mann stirred German superiority and righteousness and, as Stanley Weintraub relates, "viewed the war as an essential defence against hostile forces representing cultures less rich and technologies less advanced."[40] Rilke, Germany's leading poet, "celebrated the resurrection of the god of war rather than a symbol of weak-minded peace."[41] As for Mann, "to be excoriated [by their adversaries] as Hun barbarians when Germans allegedly represented the higher civilization appeared to him an absurd inversion of values, a feeling shared by educated young officers at the front who came out of professional life."[42]

The feeling of superiority was rife among the Entente powers as well. The British, according to Gordon Martel, "rated themselves [even] more highly than the Germans did."[43] Paul Kennedy found that "qualitative assessments by British generals were all too obviously influenced by cultural and political prejudices."[44] To their detriment, "no real effort was made within the CID [Committee of Imperial Defence] or any other body to debate or to challenge statements about the quality of potential enemies', or allies', forces."[45] This perceived superiority was widely held among British citizens and civilian leaders as well.

The French also extolled remarkable beliefs about their people's supremacy over their neighbors, prompting claims that "we, the French, possess a fighter, a soldier, undeniably superior to the one beyond the Vosges in his racial qualities, activity, intelligence, spirit, power of exaltations, devotion, patriotism."[46] Even French schoolbooks noted "one Frenchman is worth ten Germans."[47] As Stephen Van Evera argued, the "wide currency of such nationalist chest-pounding in prewar Europe goes far to explain the rosy optimism that infected both sides as they rode to war in 1914."[48]

Such in-group/out-group biases, though striking in this case, were hardly unique to World War I and have been rife throughout history long before and ever after. Indeed, it became a guiding principle for the rise of the Nazis only a few years later, and thus underlies the causes of World War II as well. The most obvious and horrific outcome was the Holocaust, but it pervaded the beliefs and major decisions made by Hitler regarding out-groups in general. For example, Hitler despised Slavic peoples too, and before long, "the Germans had turned their attack on the Soviet Union into a race war as well as a war between rival nations."[49] Hitler viewed many other nations in out-group terms. He saw the United States, for example, as "a nation corrupted by racial mixing."[50]

But again, group bias was not limited to the extremes of Hitler or the Axis powers. For example, British complacency about enemy capabilities before Japan's invasion of Malaya during World War II contributed to the collapse of Singapore. Defenses were left to the last minute, at least partly because senior commanders held the belief that Japanese soldiers were small, were physically weak, had poor eyesight, suffered from inferior leadership, and could not drive armor through the jungle. Air Chief Marshal Sir Robert Brooke-Popham observed Japanese soldiers across the border wire in Hong Kong and, seeing "various sub-human species dressed in dirty grey uniform," remarked, "I cannot believe that they would form an effective fighting force."[51] It was argued that "terrified Japanese would flee at the first sight of a white solider."[52] In

Malaya, one battalion commander complained to his commanding general: "Don't you think my soldiers are worthier of a better enemy than the Japs?"[53] Within two months, the Japanese army had advanced across the Malay Peninsula and the 130,000-strong British and Commonwealth army in Singapore surrendered.[54]

William Miller observed that the dangers of making assumptions about the qualities of other groups is a phenomenon that can be traced back to Thucydides: "It is an ancient tradition to denigrate the grand martial acts of your enemies as something other than the courage that you claim for your own grand actions. If their courage is conceded, then it is a lesser courage or just plain luck. Pericles thus tried to bolster Athenian self-esteem by arguing that Spartan courage was inferior because it did not come naturally as Athenian courage did. Why would the Spartans need to train so hard if it were not to compensate for their natural shortcomings?"[55] The Athenians would find out on the battlefield.

One can find numerous other cases in which the in-group/out-group bias has been argued to color military assessments and decisions for war. What is striking, however, is that nearly every account sees the in-group/out-group bias as a detrimental factor—an error in judgment and decision-making that undermines rational calculation and promotes false optimism and unnecessary or costly conflict. However, what of its *positive* consequences, such as the cohesion that Vercingetorix so sorely needed in Alesia or the inspiration to rise up against a formidable opponent? In this chapter I argue that, while it carries dangers, the in-group/out-group bias can also bring important advantages, increasing military effectiveness via the promotion of collective cooperation, unit cohesion, and offensive action.

Whatever the role of the in-group/out-group bias in the *causes* of war, this chapter is concerned with the effect of the bias after war breaks out. Even if undesirable in times of peace, does it lend a helping hand in times of war? Many scholars have noted that the in-group/out-group bias becomes particularly prominent and powerful once wars are underway, but few have examined what the strategic *consequences* of this are. My hypothesis is that it may be extremely effective in the fighting itself—increasing the probability of success by bolstering in-group cooperation and out-group competition.

Adaptive Advantages of the In-Group/Out-Group Bias: An Evolutionary Perspective

Perhaps even more than any other psychological disposition, the in-group/out-group bias is seen as a great evil because it causes or contributes to negative outcomes such as stereotyping, discrimination, prejudice, xenophobia, racism, conflict, violence, and war.[56] The in-group/out-group bias can obviously be a serious impediment to cooperation, peace, and equality between different groups, and we must strive to reduce or manage it wherever it has malicious effects. However, we are unlikely to be successful in this task if we do not understand the origins or causes of the bias. Psychologists have documented the empirical characteristics of the bias in great detail, identified the conditions under which it occurs, and argued compellingly that it provides psychological rewards in terms of self-esteem—a *proximate* explanation of its cause. But there is less discussion in the literature of why human brains have the in-group/out-group bias in the first place—what is the *ultimate* explanation of its cause? Its pervasive and universal nature suggests it is not a cultural epiphenomenon but a deep-seated characteristic of the human brain. If so, why did it evolve? What is it for? In other words, what is its evolutionary function in terms of Darwinian fitness?

This section explores the idea that the in-group/out-group bias is evolutionarily *adaptive*, and then the next section builds on this perspective to explore whether it could continue to offer strategic advantages today, even in international politics. The argument is that individuals who favored their in-group (promoting cooperation) and disfavored out-groups (promoting competition) enjoyed greater survival and reproductive success over the course of human evolutionary history, and the in-group/out-group bias was thus favored by natural selection—at the expense of individuals who made no distinction between members of their own and other groups.

Obviously, international politics is very different from the social interactions of our ancestral past. But important features of the international environment reflect core dynamics of social interaction that have remained similar since time immemorial—not least cooperation and conflict with potentially lethal adversaries—resembling the original problems that our cognitive mechanisms were designed to solve. Where this is the case, the in-group/out-group bias may still bring adaptive advantages.

Below, I outline two major ways in which the in-group/out-group bias can bring adaptive advantages: (1) as a method of solving the collective action problem and achieving cohesion among self-interested individuals, so mutual benefits are easier to obtain; and (2) as a method of motivating competition and offensive action against rivals and enemies, so they are easier to face and, if necessary, fight. These are observations on combat effectiveness, not on the ethics of war. As Bertrand Russell noted in the quote that opened this chapter, "War does not determine who is right, only who is left."[57]

IN-GROUP COOPERATION: DEALING
WITH EACH OTHER

Humans are unique in achieving extremely high levels of cooperation among unrelated individuals, and an enormous literature in social science, economics, and biology has been hotly engaged in discovering how this cooperation originates and how it is maintained.[58] However, a question less often asked is what this cooperation is *for*. Collective action problems form an important component of a wide range of tasks in small-scale human societies, from hunting and food sharing to conflict resolution and communal building projects.[59] All of these were undoubtedly important in our evolutionary past. But recent literature stresses that there was another extremely significant collective action problem that plagued the life of our ancestors: warfare. This subsection explores how the in-group/out-group bias may help solve the very important but also very difficult collective action problem of organizing for war—whether in defense or offense.

For a long time, especially in the years following World War II, it was fashionable to think, like Jean-Jacques Rousseau, that early humans lived in peaceful harmony without violence. Violence was seen as a by-product of *modern* society—a consequence of states, dense populations, greed, and modern technologies. Archaeological and ethnographic evidence, however, has increasingly revealed that intergroup violence was a fact of life as far back into our history as we can see.[60] Even conservative estimates suggest that around 13–15 percent of deaths among men in small-scale preindustrial societies can be attributed to warfare.[61] In some indigenous societies around the world it is much higher.[62] This compares to a mere 1 percent killed in Western populations during the so-called bloody twentieth century. Intergroup killing is also common in other primate species, among some social carnivores such as lions and wolves, and among social insects such as ants, so it is not possible to claim that it is a phenomenon unique to humans or to human culture. Rather, it evidently has ancient evolutionary origins.[63] Together, this evidence suggests that intergroup conflict has exerted a strong selection pressure on human adaptations over our evolutionary history. It should therefore be no great surprise that we find evidence of cognitive adaptations for in-group cooperation and intergroup conflict, including a bias that favors the in-group and disfavors out-groups.[64] Both can be critical to survival and prosperity.

Ethnographic studies give plentiful examples of the wariness and suspicion of out-groups that is a recurrent feature of small-scale societies—as well as remarkable illustrations of the high level of *within*-group cooperation that kicks in during times of intergroup conflict.[65] One example comes from English explorer Samuel Hearne's account of a journey with Chipewyan and Yellowknife Dene Indians from Hudson Bay to the Arctic Ocean in the summer of 1771. On reaching the Coppermine River in July, Dene scouts discovered an Inuit camp a few miles ahead. On this news, recounted Hearne, "their whole thoughts were immediately engaged in planning the best method of attack, and how they might steal on the poor Esquimaux the ensuing night, and kill them all while asleep."[66] Hearne took a disparaging view of his fellow travelers' customs and organization, referring to them as an "undisciplined rabble . . . by no means accustomed to war or command." But he was clearly struck by their sudden coordination of action when conflict was at hand. The Dene acted quickly and "with the utmost uniformity of sentiment. There was not among them the least altercation or separate opinion; all were united in the general cause, and as ready to follow where Matonabbee [the group's leader] led. . . . Never was reciprocity of interest more generally regarded among a number of people, than it was on the present occasion by my crew, for not one was a moment in want of any thing that another could spare; and if ever the spirit of disinterested friendship expanded the heart of a Northern Indian, it was here exhibited in the most extensive meaning of the word." Hearne, a distraught bystander to events, described how "the poor unhappy victims were surprised in the midst of their sleep, and had neither time nor power to make any resistance." All of them were killed, with no losses to the Dene.

Even where warfare itself is infrequent, it still has an impact on the way people live. A single war per generation can significantly alter death rates, reproduction, intergroup relationships, settlement patterns, fortifications, technological innovation, leadership, divisions of labor, occupations, and political and social organization. Natural selection and cultural selection are therefore expected to have favored traits that promote survival and success in intergroup competition and conflict—even if war was relatively rare. Archaeologists and anthropologists have detailed many such hallmarks of our violent past.[67] Villages tend to be built for defense against attack. Young men are initiated and maintained as warriors. Weapons are continually made, improved, and carried around. Men practice fighting. Oral histories are replete with stories of war, defeat, revenge, and victory. Ceremonies, meetings, marriages, trade, movements, resource use, and information are intricately designed to manage intergroup politics. Discussion is consumed by the activities and whereabouts of other groups, and religious rituals revolve around solidifying and distinguishing the in-group, often in reference to others, with many if not most cultures around the world having specific gods of war.[68] The outstanding question, however, is how exactly the in-group/out-group bias might help in such a context of ubiquitous competition, conflict, and war.

Biologist Richard Alexander noted that, across the animal kingdom, forming into groups is a common adaptation to defend against predation.[69] Exactly the same problem faced humans as well, he argued, the only difference being that the predators were not saber-toothed tigers or packs of hyenas—they were *other human groups*. Sticking together and within-group cooperation was essential for effective competition and defense. Members of early human groups would have been highly dependent on each other for collective survival. Empirical analyses of 186 historical societies around the globe bear out Alexander's hypothesis: societies with a higher incidence of war tended to grow to larger group sizes and were more likely to have moralizing codes of practice that promoted in-group cooperation.[70] In-group cooperation, and banding together against out-groups, appears to have been a fundamental tool of survival.

The problem only increased as civilizations developed. As soon as human societies adopted agriculture and became settled, this opened up significant opportunities for seizing the resources of others, and indeed it was in precisely this period that fortifications, warrior classes, and social hierarchies became pervasive.[71] Alexander's insight was that settling in ever-larger societies was the best defense against other groups: safety came in numbers.[72] Groups rightly feared other groups, and they rightly favored their own. In-groups represented safety, sustenance, and protection. Out-groups provided opportunities for trade, marriage partners, alliances, and information, but they could also be the harbingers of theft, exploitation, or annihilation. Given such a history, it is perhaps not surprising, therefore, that the in-group/out-group bias is one of the strongest human psychological dispositions.

While the world is very different today, it remains the case that out-groups routinely represent competition and not infrequently pose a direct threat. That aspect of the world is not too dissimilar from the environment in which we evolved. There was no Leviathan to police competition and aggression between different groups then, and there is no such Leviathan in international politics now. In both worlds, therefore, group bias is likely to be an adaptive inclination, helping to stay competitive in times of peace and helping to solve the collective action problem of deterring and preparing for conflict, and fighting effectively, if war comes.

Yet even in the face of competition, cooperation is hard to achieve, especially in large groups. Alexander's argument was that groups must get larger, but cooperation in larger groups is even harder than in small ones. This is why he went on to focus on the necessary emergence of *moral* systems as well— social norms that align the interests of people even in large groups of anonymous strangers in order to reduce self-interest, promote cooperation, and pull together to achieve common goals.[73] But out-group competition and conflict can in itself directly trigger in-group cooperation.

Studies of collective action have long found that cooperation among self-interested agents dwindles over time, unless special conditions are in place.[74] Cooperation can be induced and sustained, for example, by adding some other factor such as punishment or the opportunity to establish rules.[75] Psychologist Mark van Vugt and colleagues found another way to increase cooperation within groups.[76] They conducted an experiment in which one control group played a normal collective action game (in which, as is typical, cooperation declined over time). Another group played exactly the same game with one simple difference: they were told that students from rival universities were also playing the game. There was no reason that this, by itself, should have increased their cooperation because they were not in direct *competition* with the other group—they would not win greater monetary rewards if they did better than the subjects at the other university. However, simply priming them with this in-group/out-group setting significantly increased their levels of cooperation. The mere intergroup context itself raised the motivation to suppress self-interest and work as a group. Remarkably, this experiment demonstrated that a simple in-group/out-group cue can help to overcome the famous and thorny collective action problem. Computer simulations have uncovered similar phenomena. As long as individuals are able to identify in-group members and preferentially interact with this subset of the whole population, when in competition with others, cooperation can flourish where otherwise it cannot.[77]

Evidence also comes from field studies of indigenous societies around the globe.[78] Richard Sosis and colleagues hypothesized that groups with more intense warfare would also be the ones that have more costly rituals—such as warriors' initiation rites. The logic behind this prediction is that costly rituals help to overcome collective action problems, as each member of the group displays hard-to-fake signals that credibly demonstrate their commitment to the group (in deeds rather than words). If they are willing to endure the costs of these rituals, then this is good evidence to other group members that they are genuinely committed to the group and likely to step up to join the fight in any conflict. Sosis's team found that the costliness of a range of cultural signals was indeed significantly related to the frequency of warfare. Groups with more warfare underwent significantly more costly rituals. Moreover, the most costly—and permanent—signals (such as tattoos, scarification, or other painful initiation rites) were more common among groups with more "external" wars against out-groups (usually non-kin and different language groups). By contrast, less costly—and temporary—signals were more common among groups with more "internal" wars *within* the wider community (usually extended kin groups). So once again, out-group competition promoted in-group cooperation.

How far might one's in-group/out-group commitment go? Some evolutionary biologists have suggested that if conflict among groups is intense enough, then subordination of self-interest and the adoption instead of group interests—even to the extent of committing sacrificial behavior—may be adaptive, for two reasons. First, if competition among groups is strong, then natural selection can work at the level of group interest rather than individual self-interest: groups with more altruists are more likely to survive and spread, at the expense of groups with individualists more concerned with self-preservation.[79] This is "group selection," however, which requires special conditions to occur.[80] Second, even if there is no selection at the group level, it may in fact be in the individual's (or, strictly, the genes') interests to risk injury or death in battle if this increases the probability of the survival of kin.[81] This invokes "inclusive fitness," in which natural selection favors behaviors that benefit one's genes *wherever they reside,* most obviously in oneself but also including copies of those genes we share with kin. Thus, as mathematical biologist J. B. S. Haldane quipped, he would jump into a river to save two siblings, four nephews, or eight cousins.[82] In either case, we would expect the evolution of in-group altruism *as a trait* even if it is costly, and even if it is sometimes lethal, to the *individuals* that carry it out. In sum, there are reasons to believe that the in-group/out-group bias may have evolved not only to promote in-group cohesion and wariness of other groups but to cohere precisely in order to fight them more effectively.

OUT-GROUP DEROGATION: DEALING WITH ENEMIES

The in-group/out-group bias has another feature that may increase combat effectiveness: motivating competition and offensive action against rivals and enemies so that they are easier to face and, if necessary, fight. At the extreme, it may also serve to dehumanize the enemy and make it easier to kill.[83] There are many wars that would illustrate the point, but the Spanish conquest of the Americas is perhaps the clearest example. Above all the Spaniards wanted wealth and resources. But they also had a larger mission: conversion. They viewed Native Americans as subhuman inferiors who were destined to burn in hell unless they converted to Christianity. With this perception, the Spaniards felt little need to obtain the blessing of the indigenous population if they got in the way of treasure hunting. Indeed, killing them was sometimes seen as the most expedient solution—that way they could be judged by God. The conquistadors' extraordinary arrogance in the face of a different culture and, importantly, different religions led to a genocide that (with the help of European diseases) wiped out up to 90 percent of Native American populations and handed over the vast resources of south and central America to Spain. Many factors contributed, from European technology and weapons to the help of allies among the often-rival indigenous populations.[84] Nevertheless, there is little doubt that the Spanish would not have achieved so many of their goals if their religion had not sanctioned their draconian actions and helped fill the expeditionary coffers at home in the name of spreading the word of God abroad. The perceived superiority of their own group and its religion increased the conquistadors' success by dehumanizing the enemy and justifying and expediting aggression against them—as it would, of course, for many other colonial powers in the centuries before and after.

In our evolutionary past, intergroup competition was not just about accumulating resources; it was about survival. Competing and fighting with other groups, and sometimes killing, was not necessarily desired but it was commonly practiced, and if a group was to survive or prosper they might have to be prepared to do it—in defense if not in offense. We saw earlier that intergroup warfare was common across indigenous, archaic, and contemporary hunter-gatherer societies. What is notable is that while violence could occur both *within* groups and *between* groups, there is a difference. Brian Ferguson's review of warfare among small-scale indigenous societies found that "everywhere, belief systems mark off killing in war from murder."[85] Within groups, it is the worst possible violation of social norms. But between groups, it is allowed or even encouraged.[86] Dehumanization is argued to be an important switch that allows this reversal of values to take place and facilitates not just killing but cruelty and brutality as well.[87] As Malcolm Potts and Thomas Hayden noted in their history of violence in human evolution, "Once you have dehumanized your enemy, the evidence is that it matters little which way you kill him."[88]

Lab experiments have shown a sharp in-group/out-group distinction in action under controlled conditions. In one study of over a thousand Israeli schoolchildren aged eight to fourteen, they were given an account of the Battle of Jericho (in which God instructs Joshua to kill all those inside, including men, women, children, and animals). However, one group got the original text referring to Joshua, while another group got the identical text except that the names were changed to make it about a foreign-sounding "General Lin." Among those with the original story about Joshua, 66 percent approved of his extreme actions and 26 percent disapproved. However, among those with the same story but carried out by General Lin, only 7 percent approved and 75 percent disapproved—a remarkable reversal of justification for violence.[89] In this instance, one's religious in-group appears to exert a special power in promoting in-group/out-group thinking and generating a hypocritical treatment of the two scenarios.

But in natural settings, killing is not committed randomly for the sake of it. Across social carnivores, primates, and indigenous small-scale societies, the empirical pattern is that it tends to occur when the risks are sufficiently low and when there are benefits to be gained for the perpetrator (when risks are high and benefits low, individuals will withdraw).[90] The in-group/out-group bias may help in taking advantage of such contingent opportunities when they arise. Out-group distinctions have been argued to specifically elevate motivation in lethal intergroup conflict, such that a degree of "xenophobia" against a disliked foe can serve to "increase the probability of heroic sacrifice and, thereby, the probability of a heroic individual's coalition's actually being victorious."[91] While out-group hatred has often been proposed as a contributor to combat motivation in modern contexts as well, its effects remain debated and there is greater clarity and consensus on motivation being driven by the process of in-group cohesion discussed above.[92]

To sum up this and the previous subsection, the in-group/out-group bias helps to solve the age-old problem of collective action, especially amid the great personal risks of war, as well as to promote offensive action against out-groups when this is necessary to ensure or enhance survival and security. While increasing cohesion within the group—at all times, but especially when under threat from rival groups—the in-group/out-group bias also offers powerful advantages in intergroup competition and conflict. It *discourages* behaviors conducive to failure—such as shirking duty, desertion or defection, sympathy for the enemy, and reluctance to fight or kill. Instead, it *encourages* behaviors conducive to success—such as commitment, sacrifice for the group, a sense of purpose, animosity toward the enemy, and a willingness to fight and sometimes kill. These are not all pleasant traits, but evolution only cares about what works.

STAYING SAFE: GROUP BIAS AS ERROR MANAGEMENT

The in-group/out-group bias can, like overconfidence and the fundamental attribution error, be understood within the framework of error management theory (EMT). This suggests a common explanation for why a variety of different judgment and decision-making biases are adaptive, as well as setting out generalized conditions for when we should expect them to be advantageous or disadvantageous today.

Evolutionary psychologists Martie Haselton and Daniel Nettle reviewed the literature on cognitive biases and found that the in-group/out-group assumption that members of one's own group "are more generous and kind, and less hostile and violent than out-group members, is a bias that can be understood from an error management perspective. Inferences about relatively unknown out-group members are uncertain. For ancestral humans, the costly FN [false negative] was to miss aggressive intentions on the part of others, whereas the FP [false positive] of overinferring aggressiveness was low, especially for members of competing coalitions."[93]

Lee Cronk and Beth Leech made a similar error management argument for the advantages of in-group cohesion. They suggest that, in general, the error of contributing to a public good that turns up short is much less than the cost of not contributing to such a good from which there could have been great gains. Thus, they argue that humans are disposed to err on the side of participating in group activities rather than avoiding them. Empirically, this is manifested in the finding that people tend to *overestimate* the degree to which their contributions make a difference—a phenomenon that had lacked an explanation but which is likely to aid cooperation.[94] But to what extent do the key ingredients for EMT—uncertainty and asymmetric costs—obtain today in the context of group behavior, such that a bias may remain adaptive?

In terms of uncertainty, it remains that case that the risks and outcomes of collective action and out-group competition are an inherently uncertain business. The collective action problem is a "problem" precisely because one does not know whether or not others will step up to contribute, and if so, by how much. Uncertainty about possible outcomes can be magnified significantly when the collective action at issue is a risky venture such as whether or not to join a rebellion or fight a war (and how extensively to contribute, or whether to collaborate instead with the enemy). With so many factors contributing to the outcome, the possibility of intervention by third parties, and the role of chance, the fragility of in-group cooperation and the outcomes of intergroup conflict can be highly unpredictable—and arguably increasingly so today.

In terms of asymmetric errors, there are clearly large costs to being wrong about when to engage with in-groups and when to compete against out-groups. In general, Haselton and Nettle argue that assuming benign intent of out-group members is a more costly error than the reverse—because of the possibility of either aggression or exposure to disease pathogens.[95] Both present extreme dangers to be avoided. The idea that groupish behavior evolved to avoid disease transmission is well supported in biology, and occurs in several taxonomic groups. This suggests that, along with many other species, over our evolutionary history we have been subjected to significant disease risks that "select social animals, like humans, for an adaptive xenophobia."[96] On the in-group side, the collective action problem is also a "problem" because, as well as the uncertainty about whether the collective goal will be achieved at all, the decision to participate oneself means that one may end up wasting effort or resources in contributing to a lost cause. Having contributed, one is also left in a worse position compared to others who did not. When the collective action is a rebellion or war, the costs of getting this wrong can become extreme. Participation itself becomes a signal of allegiance that may bring retribution from the other side if the enterprise fails or retribution from one's own side if one fails to participate, or to do so sufficiently. And finally, in the context of intergroup conflict the risks themselves are elevated from mere contributions of time and resources to the prospect of injury or death.

In short, the key conditions for error management theory to apply—uncertainty in assessments and asymmetric costs of false positive and false negative errors—remain significant for a range of challenges in contemporary group behavior. The in-group/out-group bias should thus remain an adaptive bias, even or perhaps especially in the inherently uncertain and high-stakes world of international politics.

Strategic Advantages of In-Group/Out-Group Bias in International Politics

The literature on the in-group/out-group bias in international relations tends to focus on cases where it causes mistakes and disasters. However, are there not cases where it has contributed to success? The argument of this chapter is yes. Many of these examples turn out to be the *same* examples used to demonstrate its detrimental effects. Sometimes this discrepancy is resolved by shifting the focus from the chauvinistic saber-rattling in the *causes* of war to the cohesion and collective action achieved in the *fighting* itself. And sometimes the discrepancy is resolved by shifting the focus from what is good for humanity at large to what is good for the goals of individual leaders and states. Like war itself, a bias such as in-group favoritism and out-group derogation can lead to morally reprehensible outcomes, and this is often greatly amplified in times of existential threat. As Michael Ignatieff asked, "What lesser evils may a society commit when it believes it faces the greater evil of its own destruction?"[97] But this does not detract from the possibility that in-group favoritism and out-group derogation succeed in aiding survival or increase the ability of states, and those who lead them, to achieve political, strategic, or military goals—whatever those goals may be. In this section, I outline key ways in which the in-group/out-group bias can help leaders, states, and soldiers.

IN-GROUP/OUT-GROUP BIAS HELPS
COLLECTIVE ACTION AND UNIT COHESION

Cooperation is central to international politics. It is essential for numerous activities ranging from the provision and protection of public goods, to establishing and sustaining trade, to forming institutions and security alliances. But cooperation is hard to achieve because there is always an incentive for individual actors (whether citizens or states) to free ride on the efforts of others—reaping the benefits of collective action while shirking the costs of contributing anything themselves.[98] Perhaps the most extreme form of the collective action problem arises in mobilizing individuals for war, because while participating may be crucial for the group as a whole, for *individuals*, the possibility of serious injury or death only magnifies the already significant incentives to free ride. Yet, if self-interested individuals had not sometimes risked their personal safety for collective goals, then there would have been no wars, no revolutions, and perhaps no nations. So how was this mother of all collective action problems overcome?

Rational choice has been good at explaining why people often do not cooperate but not so good at explaining the many cases where in fact people *do* cooperate (often precisely against the expectations of rational choice).[99] To understand that, we have had to look harder at human nature, and the in-group/out-group bias turns out to be a powerful promoter of cooperation.

One solution to the collective action problem is to reduce the perceived costs of participation. If people *perceive* low costs of participating, then they are more likely to do so, increasing the probability that collective action will occur—irrespective of what the *real* costs are. This might be critical if, as is often the case, the outcome is uncertain and the fighting is likely to be bloody. Reducing the perceived costs of participation can be achieved in a number of ways, but notably by exaggerating the perceived capabilities of one's own group and/or derogating the perceived capabilities of the opposition. Simply put, it can help to think *we* are better than *they* are, whether true or not. While

Table 7.1. Adaptive advantages of the in-group/out-group bias in the past and (under the right circumstances) today

Advantage	Past	Today
Collective action *(In-group unity, rallying to the cause, contributing to joint efforts)*	√	√
Unit cohesion *(In-group bonding, willingness to fight, combat effectiveness)*	√	√
Offensive action *(Out-group competitiveness, motivation, ruthlessness)*	√	√

we might be fooling ourselves into taking a greater risk than we realize, if many of us are so fooled, we become a stronger army.

I argue that lowering the bar for collective action is powerfully promoted by the in-group/out-group bias. Whether one's goals are benevolent (like Gandhi) or malevolent (like Hitler), the in-group/out-group bias serves a strategic logic that helps to attract followers and thereby achieve successful group action. Indeed, there is a self-fulfilling prophecy in which *overestimates* of group superiority can increase the *actual* probability of success, if it attracts additional participants to an apparently promising cause, unites them more firmly in its pursuit, and increases the determination to confront or fight the enemy "other." Political and rebel leaders can use the in-group/out-group bias to their advantage, and in fact have been doing so for millennia. While it often poses a problem in the modern world, promoting prejudice, distrust, and conflict, on average, or in dire circumstances, the in-group/out-group bias may be an essential element of success.

Studies of modern war similarly emphasize the challenge of overcoming the collective action problem. Paul Collier has argued that civil wars primarily occur only when there are material advantages to individuals because political motives alone are not powerful enough to solve the collective action problem (this is the "greed versus grievance" problem). As he explains it, "Whether the government gets overthrown does not depend upon whether I personally join the rebellion. Individually, my preferred choice might be that others fight the rebellion, while I benefit from the justice that their rebellion achieves. This standard free-rider problem will often be enough to prevent the possibility of grievance-motivated rebellions."[100] The dilemma is compounded because only large rebellions can achieve victory against a strong incumbent government, so why would people join them when, initially, they are small? Somehow they need to leapfrog these initial hurdles into a serious movement (this is the "coordination problem"). A third problem is that the benefits only come *after* victory, so one has to trust that the expected rewards will actually be passed from the revolutionary leaders to the participants at some point in the future, assuming of course that they even win at all (the "time-consistency problem").

Together, these three problems present "formidable obstacles" to rebellion, and Collier argues that "rebellions based purely on grievance face such severe collective action problems that the basic theories of social science would predict that they are unlikely to occur, and the empirical evidence supports this prediction."[101] Indeed, they are relatively rare. And even when they occur, many fail. So how do they get going in the infrequent cases where they arise, and sometimes even go on to succeed? Collier suggests that the "usual" way these problems are overcome—along with direct material benefits that rebels may extort from war—is through "social capital," the trust generated among members of informal but powerful networks of associations and societies. In short, you need *groups*, which, by virtue of the in-group/out-group bias, can help surmount the obstacles to collective action—precisely because the perceived costs of joint action are reduced, the motivation to fight a despised foe is enhanced, and the self-fulfilling prophecy of a united group answers the call to arms.[102]

Our first case study of the American Revolution features some powerful examples of the adaptive workings of group bias. Historian Andrew Sinclair wrote: "A successful revolution demands hatred of an enemy, love of a distinct group or place or faith, and organizers of genius. The American Revolution had all three elements."[103] Sinclair cites Samuel Adams, Thomas Jefferson, and Patrick Henry in particular, "who with their 'committees of correspondence' set up a network of resistance, called meetings of local leaders, and saw to the boycott of British goods."[104] Interestingly, the Declaration of Independence itself highlighted the vital role of the *group* in staging a revolution: "The people *as a whole* were declared to have the right to alter or abolish a tyrannical government; a single rebel had no right of revolt. . . . Its price was to insist on the conformity of the individual American to the sovereignty of the people."[105] As for the British side, their punitive actions in retaliation only served to increase American in-group solidarity and determination to fight further, a phenomenon that has recurred in history: when powerful governments push them around, people rally together.

I focused here on revolutions because, under such dire circumstances, the collective action problem is thrown into sharp relief and the benefits of the in-group/out-group bias become critical—perhaps even the tipping point between success and failure. But the same logic applies to interstate conflicts in general, especially in times of crisis. In his study of the psychology of war, LeShan suggested that although a "mythic evaluation of reality" (amplifying in-group/out-group distinctions) may lead us *into* wars that could have been avoided, it may nevertheless be the most effective way to fight a war once it is underway.[106] This applies not only to policymakers and the public at large but also to the military. Studies of soldiers' behavior on the battlefield find that while men may not always fight for king and country, they consistently identify themselves with and fight for their immediate "primary group"—the soldier's "band of brothers" in their unit. Moreover, such unit cohesion is not merely a by-product of enduring the dangers of war; it is a major predictor of military effectiveness.[107]

But what about the apparently pervasive manipulation of the in-group/out-group bias? Whatever the in-group/out-group bias does for a solider or civilian, it can also be exploited as a tool by the elite to promote nefarious ends.[108] Although most people—political leaders and laypeople alike—may not know the details of psychological phenomena such as the in-group/out-group bias, they do of course have intuitions about human nature and what "pushes people's buttons." The in-group/out-group bias can thus be (and often is) exploited by elites to promote both in-group favoritism and out-group animosity. Together, they can be used to garner domestic support for aggressive policies, allowing them to repress minority groups, spark ethnic violence, launch wars, and even carry out genocide. Hitler would never have been elected to power, let alone been able to conquer Europe or murder six million Jews, without first leveraging ordinary Germans to believe in an inherent in-group superiority (the Aryan race, Germans' right to *Lebensraum*, and so on) and to adopt a virulent out-group animosity (perceiving the Slavic races as subhuman, the Jews as responsible for German economic collapse, etc.).[109] Similarly, Slobodan Milošević would never have been able to carry out wholesale ethnic cleansing in the former Yugoslavia without playing on national jingoism about a "Greater Serbia" or the historical enmity between Serbians and their neighbors.[110] As Jack Snyder noted: "Serbs and Croats never fought each other until the twentieth century."[111] It needed agitators to stoke the flames. The point that both of these regimes were immoral or indeed "evil," or that both were ultimately defeated, does nothing to deny the fact that the in-group/out-group bias helped them pursue their goals—despicable as they were. In this sense, the bias gave them a strategic advantage that helped in achieving their objectives. It also made fighting them harder.[112] Of course, "it would be a mistake," as Hewstone and colleagues point out, "to consider ethnic and religious mass murder as a simple extension of intergroup bias," given the importance of other factors, such as that perpetrators may be coerced into their actions, the large social scales across which these events occur, and the complex motives that also include historical and political legacies.[113] The in-group/out-group bias may *contribute* to ethnic violence or genocide, but it does not *cause* them on its own.

Although the more extreme examples of exhibiting and exploiting the in-group/out-group bias are likely to be found among the despots and tyrants of history, the manipulation of in-group/out-group bias to support foreign policy is in fact a common theme among all states, including Western democracies. Reagan's "Evil Empire" and Bush's "Axis of Evil" both played to citizens' fear and distrust of other nations and cultures, which helped—again, rightly or wrongly—whip up support for Reagan's aggressive Cold War strategy and

Bush's Global War on Terror and the invasion of Iraq. And it is not limited to the United States, of course. In Western Europe in recent years, over and above other factors, an underlying distrust of foreigners has fueled the resurgence of right-wing political parties across the continent that advocate draconian immigration policies to stem the tide of migrants from the Middle East, North Africa, and elsewhere. The same sentiment is argued to have contributed to the United Kingdom's "Brexit" from the European Union. Whether one agrees with such policies or not, we can agree that in-group/out-group sentiment has helped carry these parties to power and associated preferences into politics.

Winning public support is always desirous and advantageous for a political leader. Even where exploiting people's in-group/out-group bias is just cynical manipulation by those in or seeking power, if it increases support for a given policy then this may in turn improve its chances of success. In other words, the bias may bring strategic advantages. It enables policies to be put in action, especially expensive or radical ones, that may otherwise be hard or impossible to sell. Wars can be prosecuted more boldly, with greater resources, and thus ultimately more effectively if citizens, voters, politicians, and soldiers are successfully persuaded of an abhorrent enemy and the righteousness of their own people and cause.

IN-GROUP/OUT-GROUP BIAS
HELPS OFFENSIVE ACTION

As Europe fell in 1940, lonely Britain might have conceded to Hitler had it not been for a somewhat irrational boldness in the nation linking arms to face what Churchill promised would only be "blood, toil, tears, and sweat," refusing to submit to the despised Nazis and their demonical leader. Rallying support for the daunting war effort and calling up soldiers to the front would have proved harder to achieve if people had behaved like dispassionate rational actors—seeing the human beings of other nations identically to their own. Luckily for Britain, they did not. Instead, the British believed they were inherently righteous and the Nazis were inherently evil. Many of them also believed that although Germany was strong and Britain was weak, they would nevertheless win. The in-group/out-group bias may generate a distortion of the quality and capabilities of one's own group over another, but sometimes this can be an essential ingredient of motivation and survival.

Psychologists Ervin Staub and Daniel Bar-Tal identified an "ethos of conflict" that arises among societies in times of war, which "promotes devotion to the society and country, rationalizes harming the enemy, and encourages readiness for personal sacrifice."[114] While it can have nasty effects and "fuels the conflict and violence," they also note that, even or especially in apparently impossible situations, it can facilitate "better adaptation" to conflict.[115] In difficult times, in other words, the in-group/out-group bias can help. This may be especially the case for soldiers on the front line.

A famous study by S. L. A. Marshall, published in 1947, claimed that only 15–25 percent of infantry in World War II ever fired their weapons.[116] This remarkable claim has attracted great scrutiny. Frederic Smoler, for example, argued that the study itself was flawed and the figures are highly misleading.[117] But even if a massive exaggeration, it points to an underlying and widely recognized "problem" that many soldiers—especially civilian conscripts—are unwilling or at least uneager to kill. Indeed, they have to be trained to do it. Military psychologist Dave Grossman's book *On Killing: The Psychological Cost of Learning to Kill in War and Society* details the pressures facing soldiers who are socialized in normal life not to harm or kill and then asked to do exactly this in war.[118] Even for those who overcome these barriers and do manage to kill, they often suffer psychological costs that leave them with nagging guilt, regret, or trauma after the fighting is over. Post-traumatic stress disorder (PTSD), for example, afflicted around 30 percent of Vietnam War veterans and 11–20 percent of veterans of the 2003 Iraq War and the subsequent occupation.[119] Whatever the figures and mechanisms involved, it is widely recognized that it is not easy to harm or kill other human beings. However, it is easier to commit such acts against out-group enemies that you have come to hate rather than in-group members that you have come to value, especially when done as part of a strongly bonded group tasked with the same bloody duty. The in-group/out-group bias may thus help soldiers (and military leaders) overcome the significant psychological barriers to performing their job on the battlefield—ultimately increasing combat effectiveness and thereby also increasing the probability of victory rather than defeat.[120]

To summarize both the in-group and out-group effects discussed in this and the previous subsection, the in-group/out-group bias is an effective way of promoting group action, especially when under threat from rival groups. The bias may therefore continue to be advantageous in the wars of today for exactly the same reasons as it was in the past: promoting in-group solidarity, attracting others to join the cause, generating unit cohesion among warriors, and fighting the enemy more effectively. Historical and contemporary examples abound in which the citizens and soldiers of the home state have been flattered and glorified to promote cooperation and cohesion, while those of rival states have been broadly dehumanized, disparaged, and cast as evil to promote and justify rivalry and aggression.[121] When the state exhibiting such prejudice is some *other* society, we recoil at its malicious intent and effects. When it is our own, we (or at least many) are easily carried along with the crowd and often barely notice its hypocrisy. Yet, however wrong or immoral such perceptions may be, if they serve to increase support and resolve among the public and policymakers at home and motivation among soldiers at the front, they can improve overall combat effectiveness.

The in-group/out-group bias may not always be strong or important. However, it has consistent effects that can bring a competitive edge. Consider this thought experiment. Two nations are identical except one has the in-group/out-group bias (the groupish Xenophobes) and the other does not (the individualistic Xenophiles). In conflict, each nation may fight hard, long, and well. But there will be important differences. The Xenophiles will be more trusting of the other side, more impressed by their strength and resolve, and more vulnerable to exploitation or surprise. They will find it harder to generate moral justification for preserving or fighting for their own way of life rather than accepting that of their rival. And they will find it harder to coalesce around the national flag, their political leaders, or their military commanders. They will have greater costs of generating public support, trying to make war with institutions that resist it, and coercing and enforcing compliance among citizens and soldiers that hesitate to fight and are unwilling to kill. And the Xenophiles will find it harder to justify supporting, supplying, and committing violence and death on the other group who are, after all, just like themselves. Both sides might excel in other areas of life but in war, all else equal, the Xenophobes are more likely to win. By contrast, there are no counteracting reasons why the Xenophobes should—again, all else equal—be *less* likely to win. Their hubris and xenophobia may be condemned by the other side, but their beliefs break no laws and suffer no retribution. They may be more likely to overestimate their prowess and underestimate that of the enemy, but chapter 3 suggested that on average that can be an advantage as well. In a world of lethal competition, Xenophobes are more likely to survive and prosper by virtue of their higher levels of in-group cohesion and mutual purpose and by the vice of their out-group competitiveness and willingness to fight.[122]

Limits on Group Bias's Advantages

Group bias is only likely to be useful at moderate levels. Unrestrained and unlimited in-group favoritism and out-group derogation can lead to: (1) severe overestimation of the qualities and capabilities of one's own group; (2) severe underestimation of other groups' qualities and capabilities; (3) unnecessary and costly conflict; and (4) missing out on opportunities for cooperation and alliances with other groups. Clearly, a tendency as pernicious as the in-group/out-group bias is likely to become detrimental—not to mention potentially immoral—at high levels. The argument of this chapter is simply that some moderate level of in-group favoritism and out-group derogation can bring a competitive edge. It enhances in-group cohesion and cooperation, caution in interaction with other groups, and the motivation to compete with them effectively. When that competition becomes significant or lethal, the in-group/out-group bias may become a critical advantage that can help tip the balance between victory and defeat.

One way to think about what *level* of in-group/out-group bias we should have in order to confer net benefits, rather than net costs, is to frame it within the error management theory perspective discussed earlier.[123] The in-group/out-group bias can be adaptive if it pushes decision-making in a direction that avoids making the most costly kinds of mistakes. Too much in-group/out-group bias is obviously detrimental, since it will lead to complacency, dismissal of threats, disproportionate costs of conflict, and alienation of potential allies. On the other hand, a lack of in-group/out-group bias is clearly detrimental in the other direction, since a lack of group identity, poor group cohesion, and low willingness to compete or fight in the face of rival outgroups will lead to inaction or poor combat effectiveness—arguably the more costly mistake. This predicts an inverted U-curve, where a certain amount of bias (and perhaps more than we think) is useful and adaptive, but either too little or too much can lead to maladaptive behavior. The in-group/out-group bias usually keeps us in the safer middle range of this distribution—ensuring *a degree* of in-group unity and out-group competitiveness, while avoiding the pitfalls of pushing our groupish nature too far.

Although I have argued that moderate levels of group bias are adaptive, and too much is bad, there may be exceptions where a strong bias is even better. Psychologist William Swann and others have suggested that, within groups undergoing significant hardship, the "normal" social identity offered by a group is not strong enough.[124] In situations of extreme threat, danger, or war, individuals do not simply *identify* with their group but actually become *fused* with it. Fusion entails a perceptual overlap between individuals and their group, such that their preferences and interests become aligned almost as one. Harvey Whitehouse, Brian McQuinn, and their colleagues found this phenomenon to be prominent, for example, among rebel fighters in the 2011 Libyan civil war.[125] These were often civilians with little military training but strong mutual interests in overthrowing the long-standing authoritarian regime, and it was the collective experience of battle, rather than ideological discussions, that fused usually peaceful citizens into effective fighting units.

While group interests often conflict with individual interests, in the thick of combat, when soldiers' survival depends on each other working closely and reliably as a team, group and individual interests converge. In these conditions, fusion can be good for the group *and* good for the individual. Fusion does not arise among ordinary, everyday groups.[126] Rather, the cognitive processes underlying fusion appear to be triggered by traumatic or dysphoric events, and thus fusion emerges among groups that face severe mutual experiences. But when those extreme situations occur, the extreme solution of fusing with the group offers an effective way of dramatically enhancing performance within them. Fused groups can prevail where mere identification with a group fails.

Under normal conditions, evidence suggests that some moderate level of group bias is adaptive. But clearly there may be cases—especially for individuals subjected to lethal competition and conflict—where high levels of group bias, or even "fusing" with the group entirely, can pay off too.

When Does the In-Group/Out-Group Bias Help or Hurt Us?

Although the in-group/out-group bias was adaptive in the past, there are features of the contemporary world that can make it misguided or dangerous— that is, *more* likely to lead to mistakes or tragedies in the modern world than in our ancestral environment in which it evolved. Our social and physical world has changed so significantly that group bias can often be triggered in circumstances that are evolutionarily novel, leading to incongruous or harmful responses. For example, the scale and sophistication of modern conflict and war is such that, where extreme group prejudices occur, the number of potential victims can reach horrifying proportions. To the extent that atrocities and genocide are goaded by in-group/out-group biases (as contributing factors, not sole causes), the genocides in Rwanda, the former Yugoslavia, and the Holocaust represent the extreme costs that such dispositions can generate in the modern world.

Such extremes are rarely possible, however, without significant social and cultural amplification, and psychologists agree that intergroup biases cannot explain them on their own, given the complex mix of contributing factors.[127] In more typical cases of intergroup conflict and war, group bias in *moderate* form—promoting group cohesiveness and out-group competition—can be a good bias to have. Many aspects of politics and international relations are competitive or conflictual interactions with other groups. Where this is the case, group bias may do its job just as effectively today as it did in the past. But critically, *it depends*. We know that group bias is more likely to be useful in some settings, such as collective action and combat effectiveness, but malicious and murderous in others.

Implications of Adaptive In-Group/ Out-Group Bias for International Politics

One of the key dynamics in contemporary international politics is globalization. It is argued to be slowly bringing societies together through increased interaction, shared institutions and markets, multinational firms, international travel and jobs, and transnational networks of organizations and people with similar interests irrespective of location.[128] In principle, this process should *reduce* the effects of the in-group/out-group bias over time, as information about different cultures and societies diffuses and nations dissolve into a larger, more homogeneous global community. Such mingling and feedback should help to erase misconceptions and prejudices, and might one day make in-group/out-group biases irrelevant. That is certainly one hypothesis.

However, there is a counterargument that despite (or perhaps precisely because of) these changes, if anything groups and societies are becoming *more* tightly bound as they have to work harder to maintain their cultural distinctiveness, identity, language, practices, and beliefs in the face of global homogenization. In the past, many groups that were not cohesive enough—even whole societies and civilizations—became extinct.[129] Globalization may, therefore, act to cement or increase group identification and exacerbate the in-group/out-group bias, rather than diminish it, because porous borders threaten our instinctive ones. Where this is the case, it may become even easier for political leaders to tap into a sensitized in-group/out-group bias to buy support for internal sacrifices and external competition. But there are also some more specific implications for international relations theory and practice.

IMPLICATIONS FOR INTERNATIONAL RELATIONS THEORY

If the in-group/out-group bias is adaptive, and continues to lend strategic advantages today, this has important implications for mainstream theories in international relations. The egoistic "self-help" behavior of states is accepted by several theories (such as realism and neoliberalism), but its underlying cause remains hotly debated. Does it stem from the characteristics of individual states or leaders, or from the characteristics of the international system in which states find themselves?[130] Kenneth Waltz argued that egoistic states are merely a reaction to the anarchical nature of the international system. Alexander Wendt, by contrast, argued that states are not destined to competition but rather that such behavior is an outcome of social processes, which can change.[131] Jonathan Mercer proposed a third approach, in which social identity theory (SIT) supplies an alternative driving mechanism for egoistic behavior.[132] In this view, in contrast to structural or social influences, it is explicitly human psychological dispositions that generate competition. However, both Wendt's and Mercer's theories beg the question of why humans are subject to socialization or SIT in the first place. *Why* do humans identify themselves with groups?

An evolutionary perspective on the in-group/out-group bias provides an answer. Group cohesion and suspicion of out-groups were critical to Darwinian fitness, and thus an in-group/out-group bias was favored by natural selection because it provided adaptive advantages in intergroup competition and conflict over evolutionary history.[133] The egoistic "self-help" behavior of states may therefore be not a result of structure, socialization, or social identity but a much more straightforward extension of human nature.[134] Whenever human groups find themselves in similar situations of conflict today, the in-group/out-group bias is likely to be triggered or amplified. Sometimes (or for some) this will have negative effects, but at other times (or for others) it will have advantageous effects. In anarchy, the in-group/out-group bias helps states to compete and survive—improving cohesion and collective action at home and, when they need to deter threats or repel invaders, promoting inter-group competition and military effectiveness at the front.

IMPLICATIONS FOR INTERNATIONAL RELATIONS

The in-group/out-group bias is a special problem for politics at the *international* level, because of inherent differences in feedback from in-group versus out-group interactions. *Within* societies, inaccuracies about other people are limited by (at least some) overlapping shared interests and by continuous interaction and corrective information. *Between* societies, however, views of in-group superiority and out-group inferiority receive little feedback (or at least less). Negative views about outsiders' moral worth, physical strength, and bravery often go unchallenged. Evidence is hard to obtain or evaluate. Stereotypes are corroborated by others in the group. Misconceptions are contested or corrected much less frequently and are often worsened by contrasting historical experiences, cultures, languages, and values across societies. This results in systematically poorer assessments of other nations. The risk of conflict is therefore raised, because both sides hold reinforced views of their own society's virtues and the perception that they wield superior morals, goals, ideologies, national aspirations, gods, or soldiers.[135]

At this international level, there is also greater variation in how *different* groups are from each other (or how different they *seem*). Where conflict occurs between culturally or linguistically similar states, the in-group/out-group bias may be somewhat limited in its effects or prove hard for political leaders to elicit—there will always be information flows to counteract or contradict any bias (this helps explain the remarkably strong alliance between the United States and Great Britain). By contrast, when the opposing states are very different, the in-group/out-group bias may be especially potent and exploitable (and this might help explain the remarkably strong antagonism between, say, the United States and the Soviet Union during the Cold War). The extreme end of this spectrum would be an invasion by aliens. We would hardly need propaganda to encourage humans on Earth to stand together, differentiate themselves from "the others," and dehumanize them. In the real world, the "more alien" a people are, the easier it may be to consider one's own group as superior and, if necessary, to compete with or fight them.

This has implications, for example, in future confrontations between the United States and China—two nations with vast cultural and linguistic differences and little common history or ideology. This heralds a perfect storm of factors that could exacerbate the in-group/out-group bias and make competition seem more inevitable and conflict more attractive. Although many people see the other as broadly friendly in an era of relative peace and prosperity between the two nations, the Pew Research Center in 2019 nevertheless found that 60 percent of Americans have an "unfavorable opinion" of China, a figure that has almost doubled since Pew began asking the question in 2005.[136] Even before the trade war that began in 2018, it was above 50 percent. Whatever the public think, there has been no shortage of in-group/out-group emphasis by President Donald Trump, for example, on the superiority of the United States and the shortcomings of China.

Although these biases may be kept in check (or seem excessive) during times of peace, they often come to the fore precisely when it matters most: in times of crisis and war. Psychiatrist Vamik Volkan argues that "anyone trying to deal with interethnic or international conflict must grasp the psychological cogency of man's need to have enemies as well as allies, and his stubborn adherence to identification with a group when undergoing hardship and danger."[137] Threatening situations significantly exacerbate in-group favoritism and out-group derogation. Following confrontation, coercion, or attack, we become unified in rage, and indignant toward the perpetrator, finding their actions unacceptable, especially when they are directed at *us*. Throughout much of the Cold War, the United States saw the Soviet Union as inherently evil, and such a view became especially prominent during the Cuban Missile Crisis.[138] The discovery of Soviet nuclear weapons on America's doorstep was shocking, but for many it was perfectly in keeping with their evil nature.

Such effects reach their zenith when crisis turns to conflict. Numerous psychologists, political scientists, and historians have come to a similar conclusion that, whatever the root causes of war may be, in-group/out-group biases emerge to significantly shape opponents' perceptions of each other once they are engaged in mortal combat. LeShan distinguished "sensory realities," which prevail during peacetime, from "mythic realities," which take over in times of war. The mythic perception of events is buoyed by numerous biased but common perceptions, including: a powerful "us and them" mentality; a belief that "our" allies are virtuous, "theirs" are immoral; that God is on "our" side; that winning becomes crucial and losing unthinkable; that the enemy acts for evil motives whereas "we" are fighting out of self-defense, benevolence, or morality; that identical acts are good when done by "us" but evil when done by "them"; and that the enemy is prone to lying so communication is pointless. In addition, contrary opinions are suppressed and those who question accepted wisdom are branded as unpatriotic or traitors, and concerns for underlying causes fade against the importance of outcomes.[139]

All of the above might read like a list of warnings and reasons to *avoid* the in-group/out-group bias. But the broader point here is that if (or when) in-group cohesion and out-group competitiveness are necessary for survival and security, then the in-group/out-group bias can help achieve it.

IMPLICATIONS FOR POLICY

Today, states and societies make major efforts to eradicate prejudice and xenophobia. We are fighting a battle against a deeply rooted aspect of human nature, and this is why it is hard to expunge and why it keeps raising its head in every new conflict that emerges around the world—whether civil conflicts or international wars. It is not purely the result of socialization or education. It is an evolved characteristic of human brains. Socialization and education may be very good at exacerbating it, but they are able to do this precisely because human cognition is primed to make in-group/out-group distinctions salient. This may be an undesirable state of affairs, but that only makes it more important to understand. If we are to identify new ways of thinking or new organizational arrangements so that an inevitable bias does not inevitably lead to disaster, we must take into account its evolutionary legacy.

People have long thought about ways we can avoid or reduce in-group/out-group bias to prevent it from hurting us or hurting others. Or even ways of widening the boundaries of the perceived group until they *include* what would otherwise be rival groups, thus neutralizing any in-group/out-group distinction at all. However, novel insights may also come from ways in which *positive* aspects of the in-group/out-group bias can be marshaled to help us. For leaders wanting to exploit others, manipulation of such group tendencies will always remain a cynical possibility. Political, revolutionary, military, and religious leaders can find leverage in people's in-group/out-group bias to help win support for the pursuit of nefarious ends.[140] But in other cases it can be beneficial. For example, one experimental study found that subliminal priming with images of a national flag increased unity by making people's preferences and voting behavior less extreme, irrespective of their substance.[141] For international institutions and leaders wanting to bring people together for the common good, they might also aim to essentially replicate the Robbers Cave experiment, triggering people's in-group/out-group bias against a greater common enemy that transcends the highest level of national, ethnic, or civilizational groups—for example, in the service of joining forces to tackle global-level problems such as poverty and climate change.

The in-group/out-group bias may also be useful, and easiest to generate, for state interests as well. In the event of war, it may even be an essential ingredient of success. Of course, wars can be won without perfect in-group unity or a frenzy of out-group hatred. But if the in-group/out-group bias increases commitment to the cause and willingness to fight, then all else equal a state with the bias will do better than a state without it. It may be particularly advantageous for weaker actors in a conflict, who must tap into every resource available if they cannot summon or rely on military power alone to win a conventional victory. Greater commitment can make up for material weakness. It is most important of all for new rebel groups, where there will be a severe collective action problem resisting mobilization in the face of possible defeat and retribution at the hands of a powerful state. After the 2003 invasion of Iraq, Shia Muslims became tightly organized in their life-and-death efforts to overturn years of Sunni dominance and fight back against new extremist groups—in a country where many outsiders had argued that such ethnic differences were unlikely to be of much importance. In Libya in 2011, rebels were motivated by mutual commitment to their tribal affiliations and their hatred of the Gaddafi regime. Similar examples come from other civil conflicts around the world.

The in-group/out-group bias is not always important and not always desirable, but without it history would have been less kind to fledgling rebel groups, including those fighting despised tyrannical regimes in England, France, and the United States, and which gave rise to the democratic states we so prize today. Even strong states can benefit too, of course. Without the in-group/out-group bias, it might also have proved harder to mobilize our own democratic societies to organize for war, when the time came, and ask citizens to down tools and be sent off to fight strangers from foreign lands, such as Nazi Germany or Imperial Japan.

Conclusions

An adaptive, strategic perspective on the in-group/out-group bias leads to some novel insights. First, the in-group/out-group bias is not some sort of unfortunate "error" or design "flaw" in human cognition as is so often assumed. On the contrary, evolution has honed it as a design *feature*.

Second, if the in-group/out-group bias conferred adaptive advantages in our evolutionary past, there is no reason to expect that it would not continue to do so today. It may sometimes be undesirable, causing or contributing to prejudice, conflict, and war. But that does not mean it fails to serve the interests of its perpetrators or to come to the rescue of imperiled states in their hour of need. Evolution did not select behavior according to how "nice" it was: nice traits are generally exploited to extinction. We need to understand human nature as it is, not as we would like it to be, and the in-group/out-group bias is an adaptive feature of human cognition—not by accident but by design— likely to have conferred significant survival and reproductive advantages during human evolution and thus to have been a critical component of Darwinian fitness. The world today is very different from the one in which these dispositions evolved, of course, but we still depend heavily on strategic interactions between individuals and groups, and international relations is fundamentally about how in-groups deal with out-groups. There is good evidence that in-group favoritism and out-group competitiveness increase social cohesion in the face of challenges and threats, improve cooperation during times of competition and conflict, and promote military effectiveness in times of war. The in-group/out-group bias may therefore help us adopt the right heuristic approach to dealing with such a world, or at least surviving within it.

Third, if the in-group/out-group bias is an evolved trait, then it is likely to have been designed to be sensitive to context. Adaptive traits are designed to alter behavior to match specific scenarios (or decision-making "domains"), not to inflexibly "hard-wire" behavior so that it is the same at all times irrespective of the situation. This variation is important for generating predictions about where and when the bias is likely to be present or absent, to be strong or weak, and to have positive or negative effects.

We may not like to concede the idea, given collateral damage from its pernicious effects, but the in-group/out-group bias is adaptive if it increases the probability of success in competition or conflict with rival groups—by promoting in-group cohesion and cooperation and promoting out-group competitiveness. In particular, if people perceive low costs of participation in collective action (because of perceptions of in-group strength and out-group weakness), then it increases the probability that they *will* participate and collective action will occur—*irrespective of the real costs* of participation. This generates a self-fulfilling prophecy in which, having attracted additional participants and heightened everyone's commitment to the cause, the *actual* probability of success is increased. For this reason alone, the in-group/out-group bias seems to offer a powerful strategic advantage.

As discussed elsewhere in this book, many evolved features of human physiology and psychology are ill-suited to modern life and cause harm to self and others.[142] The same liability applies to the in-group/out-group bias. Today, in-group favoritism and out-group competitiveness are often unnecessary and damaging, even if they were adaptive in a past environment of lethal competition among rival groups. However, wherever this situation still occurs—and numerous parts of the world spring to mind, as well as the anarchy of the international system itself—if one wants to survive and prosper in competition with fierce rivals, the in-group/out-group bias may continue to bring material advantages and offer a critical edge over opponents. This may be especially the case when facing a deadly enemy in war, such as the United States' campaign against Japan in World War II.

CHAPTER EIGHT

No Mercy

THE PACIFIC CAMPAIGN OF WORLD WAR II

The Japanese can never hope to defeat a nation that produces soldiers like your Marines.

—MAJOR KIYOSHI YOSHIDA, CAPTURED ON SAIPAN

The object of war is not to die for your country but to make the other bastard die for his.

—GEORGE S. PATTON

OSTENSIBLY A WAR ABOUT global ambitions and military power, the Pacific campaign of World War II had a strong overtone of clashing Western and Eastern cultures, with vastly different worldviews and conceptions of themselves and each other. Historians have emphasized the complex roots and widespread expressions of prejudice and racism on both sides, with the Americans and Japanese seeing their own in-group as inherently superior and the out-group adversary as inferior "subhumans" or "demons." However, "in the final analysis," wrote John Dower, "these favoured idioms denoting superiority and inferiority transcended race and represented formulaic expressions of Self and Other in general."[1] Indeed, he describes how while enemy images rose to become extremely powerful in the Pacific War, when it ended, they were then rapidly transferred to the next enemy—the Soviet Union. In other words, group biases are ever present, but they are directed at whoever becomes the most salient rival of the day. This begs the question of the deeper *effects* of such generalized in-group/out-group biases on war. Why do they emerge and become strong when a threat appears, and what are their consequences?

By definition, wars are conflicts between different *groups* of some kind or another, and those different groups must harbor at least enough in-group cohesion to enable them to coordinate their actions and at least enough out-group animosity to make them willing to kill each other. If not, there is no war. Even, or perhaps especially, in civil wars among the "same" people, such as the American Civil War, each side must bury internal divisions sufficiently to identify a coherent in-group, as well as contrast themselves from the "other" sufficiently to identify an enemy out-group. In the previous chapter, we saw how the Robbers Cave experiment and its many replications since show that even arbitrary groups under no danger develop significant in-group favoritism and out-group animosity. When it comes to real-life competition, let alone the bitter life-and-death struggles of war, in-group and out-group sentiment can become extremely strong.

The focus of this chapter is not whether the in-group/out-group bias affected decisions to *go* to war in the first place (although this was not negligible on the Japanese side, given their belief in the superiority of the Yamato race and its manifest destiny to conquer and control Asia). Rather, it is to explore how in-group/out-group biases affected *the way the war was fought.* Beyond fanning the flames of superior racial theories and ethnic prejudice, what does the in-group/out-group bias do? Does it undermine or unify a nation at war? Does it damage or aid soldiers' combat effectiveness? And does it hinder or help in winning? If the latter effects sometimes occur, then whatever pernicious effects it may have, the in-group/out-group bias can lend strategic advantages too—especially in the merciless battles of all-out wars of annihilation.

In some of the most brutal fighting of the century that characterized the Pacific campaign, I argue that the inclinations toward (a) *in-group* cohesion and (b) *out-group* hostility made the United States a more formidable opponent. While many authors have stressed the negative effects of the in-group/out-group bias, I explore its positive effects. It made American citizens more willing to rally together to support and sustain the war effort against a despised enemy—for years on end. It made American servicemen more committed to their units and to each other and more willing to fight the enemy, and when necessary to kill. And it made political and military leaders more resolved to do whatever it took to win.

Group Bias as Bad: Prejudice and the Path to War

Before the war, in-group/out-group biases may only have played into the hands of the Japanese, lulling the United States into a false sense of security against an apparently inferior foe. This had perhaps its greatest effect in the initial attack itself, on 7 December 1941. Pearl Harbor is widely regarded as a colossal U.S. intelligence failure, spanning the lowest to the highest levels of command.[2] Although U.S. intelligence had no specific information or dates regarding the raid, Japanese diplomatic codes had been broken, and a number of sources indicated the likelihood of some kind of Japanese attack on the

United States at some stage. In January 1941 the United States ambassador in Tokyo had even "warned that the talk about town pointed, if war should occur, to 'a surprise mass attack at Pearl Harbor.'"[3] The problem was that, as with all intelligence, "signals announcing the Pearl Harbor attack were always accompanied by competing or contradictory signals," so filtering genuine threats from the noise was extremely difficult.[4] The failure was not for want of information, it was what to make of it, and this is where prejudices crept in.

The possibility of an attack on Pearl Harbor was dismissed as unlikely due to the challenges of such a logistical feat—so far from Japan—plus the complacent belief that "in the eyes of its defenders [it] was manned by superior men and weapons."[5] In the critical months prior to conflict, U.S. naval intelligence was badly misguided, with tendencies that "merely sustained their complacent prejudices about the enemy."[6] American observers argued that a "Japanese attack upon Hawaii is a strategical impossibility."[7] When precisely such an attack came, it was "to the utter consternation and astonishment of everybody in the United States and the Territory of Hawaii. Surprise was complete."[8]

Yet, still the bias persisted. Even after the war had begun, "U.S. officials underestimated Japanese forces and expected a quick, easy U.S. victory."[9] This complacency was not merely about the Japanese military or state but represented extraordinary prejudices about the Japanese people themselves. Indeed, U.S. officials had identified specific characteristics they thought would undermine successful development of the kind of military expertise and skills that were used at Pearl Harbor to such devastating effect: "American experts agreed that the Japanese as a race suffered from myopia, poor night vision, defects of the inner ear, mechanical ineptitude, and a want of individual spirit that made them poor pilots."[10] It was also thought that "Japanese aircrew could not withstand the rigours of high G-forces."[11] *Time* magazine's military analyst and writer Murray Fletcher-Pratt reported that "every observer concurs in the opinion that the Japanese are daring but incompetent aviators."[12] Even where these prejudices were not universally held, it was at least believed that the Japanese would struggle to compete with their U.S. counterparts. The pattern was not a new one. "The attacks on the enemy fleets at Port Arthur [at the start of the Russo-Japanese War in 1904] and Pearl Harbor owed most of their success to the complacency of the enemy," Geoffrey Blainey found, and since "both Russia and the United States had considered themselves to be militarily superior to Japan, and as they were inclined to underestimate the military prowess of Asians, their feeling of security was enhanced."[13] This false sense of security was "boldly exploited by Japanese tactics," and the Americans would pay dearly for their complacency.[14] Historian of intelligence David Kahn summed it up as follows:

American officials did not think Japan would attack their country. To start war with so superior a power would be to commit national hara-kiri [suicide]. To Western modes of thought, it made no sense. This rationalism was paralleled by a racism that led Americans to underrate Japanese abilities and will. Such views were held not only by common bigots but by opinion-makers as well. These preconceptions blocked out of American minds the possibility that Japan would attack an American possession. . . . An attack on Pearl Harbor was seen as all but excluded. Though senior army and navy officers knew that Japan had often started wars with surprise attacks, and though the naval air defense plan for Hawaii warned of a dawn assault, officials also knew that the base was the nation's best defended and that the fleet had been stationed that far west not to attract, but to deter, Japan.[15]

Disparaging views of the foe were not limited to the American side. As Stephen Van Evera observed, "Both Japan and the United States underestimated the other during their 1940–41 approach to war."[16] The Japanese themselves explicitly and overtly believed themselves to be a superior people. Japanese leaders extolled the virtues of the "Yamato race" and charged that Western foes by contrast were depraved and exploitative.[17] Kenneth Macksey wrote that "a majority among the Japanese people believed, for traditional and historic reasons[,] in their invincibility,"[18] contributing to an "arrogant underestimation of American capacity and determination."[19]

Their beliefs also extended explicitly to military prowess. Foreign Minister Togo observed that the Japanese navy "believed itself invincible."[20] The Japanese army, meanwhile, widely believed that "the American people, because of their liberalism and individualism, would not be able to endure a protracted war."[21] There were in fact good reasons to believe that the Japanese military was strong. Between 1933 and 1938 Japan had spent £1,266 million on its military, more than either the United States or Britain, and this represented a more than five-fold increase in its military spending.[22] Yet, as with the Americans, Japanese perceptions of relative strengths went beyond raw comparisons of material power and focused extensively on the inherent qualities of the two peoples themselves. In the light of their history and culture, Japan held their own soldiers and citizens to be vastly superior in commitment, bravery, and moral standing. When survivors of the Bataan Death March arrived into Camp O'Donnell in the Philippines in 1942, the Japanese camp commander announced that "Americans were dogs" and "they were going to be treated like dogs." Their comrades who had died on Bataan, he added, were "the lucky ones."[23] By the end of the war, the 14,000 American prisoners of war who had died in captivity at the hands of the Japanese bore stark testimony to the sentiments held against them.[24]

In sum, group biases on both sides seem to have merely aggravated conditions for war, generating pernicious and faulty assumptions about the superiority of their own nation and inferiority of the adversary. The most obvious

consequences were misperceptions of relative power, delusions of moral righteousness, and prejudice against the enemy that contributed to instances of
cruelty and senseless slaughter. But is that the whole story?

Group Bias as Good? Cohesion and the Path to Victory

Once again we meet a bias that, at first glance, appears to be a source of
mistakes and errors that lead to gross misperceptions, poor decisions, and
detrimental outcomes. However, did it *always* lead to negative consequences,
and in *all* respects? The in-group/out-group bias obviously has dangers and
excesses. But these were no ordinary times.

In World War II the United States directed a staggering 40 percent of its
gross domestic product (GDP) to the war effort. This was capital diverted from
other important needs, and only shortly after the Great Depression had gutted
American society as well as its economy. While the war provided industrial
demand and jobs in a period of renewed economic expansion, it was nevertheless an exorbitant conflict in a faraway land that the American public would
have to support and, indeed, that many of them would have to fight, for many
years to come. Ultimately, the United States enrolled over sixteen million citizens in the military. Suffering over a million casualties—dead and wounded—
Americans experienced a greater number of combat deaths than in any other
war that the United States had fought (though not the highest *percentage* of
servicemen killed, since the military was so huge). What is especially striking is the *rate* at which they were killed, which was the highest ever, at over
6,600 killed in action per month. The next highest was around 3,800 killed per
month in the American Civil War (and that was on *both* sides). World War II
thus saw the United States suffer by far the greatest attrition of its men, and
women, in its history, and roughly a third of these were in the Pacific theater—
that is, killed by the Japanese.[25]

In order to meet this immense challenge, American citizens had to cohere
and cooperate sufficiently to support the war and the war effort at home,
American politicians had to bury many of their differences and turn the
machinery of government over to war, and American recruits had to jell into
crews and platoons of strangers that would pose an effective fighting force
against a hardened and tenacious foe across the oceans and battlefields of the
Pacific. Moreover, if they were going to defeat them, civilians that had been
plucked from peaceful lives across urban and rural America were going to
have to fight and kill a huge number of Japanese people—soldiers, sailors,
airmen, and civilians alike. In what was a brutal conflict from beginning to
end, in-group favoritism and out-group animosity were inevitable, but they
were also essential ingredients of war if America was going to fight and win.
Indeed, American cohesion and aggression were going to need to be strong in
order just to counter the effects of the in-group/out-group bias *of the Japanese*,

FIGURE 8.1. U.S. Marines taking cover during some of the heaviest fighting of the war on Iwo Jima, February 1945. The battle for the island cost the Marines 19,217 wounded and 5,453 killed, not including additional navy and air force casualties (figures from M. G. Walling, *Bloodstained Sands: U.S. Amphibious Operations in World War II* [Oxford: Osprey Publishing, 2017], 438). *Source*: Photo: akg-images.

who took it to extreme levels in their utter subordination to the emperor and their willingness to fight to the death, while taking as many Americans with them as possible.

The Pacific War took on an unusual character because, on the Japanese side, "surrender was explicitly forbidden."[26] The 1941 Japanese Field Service Code instructed servicemen: "Do not be taken prisoner alive."[27] In deference to the emperor, it was the duty of Japanese servicemen, and ultimately civilians as well, to defend Japan and Japanese honor at all costs, even if that meant death in the attempt. This led to fighting that was to become exceptionally vicious—on land, at sea, and in the air. Rather than fight until their position was militarily untenable and then withdraw or surrender, as generally occurred in the European theater and in other wars, Japanese units would invariably fight to the death. This meant that every inch of ground had to be wrested from fanatical Japanese defenders, at huge cost to both sides. In the defense of Saipan, for example, 41,244 Japanese soldiers were killed out of a total strength of 43,682—a casualty rate unheard of in Western nations' practice of war—not to mention the mass suicides among Japanese *civilians* on

Saipan on top of this.[28] Civilians who refused to do so could often rely on their own Japanese soldiers to shoot them instead.

Even in death, they would aim to kill. Japanese prisoners, casualties, and even corpses would become lethal in themselves, as "early in the war they established a practice of booby-trapping their dead and wounded, and using fake surrenders to ambush unwary foes."[29] In one widely circulated incident on the struggle for Guadalcanal in August 1942, as Americans were just starting to learn what kind of war they were in, twenty Marines were ambushed after accepting a staged surrender and wiped out to a man. In John Dower's words, "The psychology of 'Kill or be killed' ruled the battlefield thereafter."[30] Even once the tide of the war turned against Japan, its government, commanders, and soldiers only became more resolute and aimed to inflict as high a cost as possible on the advancing American forces.

On Okinawa in 1945, for example, the United States incurred the greatest losses ever in an amphibious operation. Around 2,000 kamikaze pilots died in the defense of the island.[31] While kamikazes took to the air on their last flights to hurl themselves into American ships and troop transports, cornered Japanese soldiers on land became *Tokko gunjin*, "special attack soldiers" that operated as kamikazes on foot—mounting suicidal charges in which their last act was designed to kill. Other Japanese soldiers set explosives connected to trip wires, and then simply committed suicide. By the time the Battle of Okinawa had ended, the Americans had suffered a staggering 50,000 casualties, and "piles of bleached human bones could still be seen on the beaches a decade after the war's end."[32] The Japanese themselves had suffered 117,000 casualties, of whom 110,000—that is, nearly all of them—were killed. It was this experience that foreshadowed what might come if the United States had to invade the Japanese homeland.

It was an extraordinary war, and it would take extraordinary measures to win. The initial "treachery" of Pearl Harbor had caused shock waves of anger and defiance among Americans that immediately generated a special hatred for the enemy. But as the war progressed, this animosity and desire to fight back only grew to greater heights. While it is often claimed that America ultimately triumphed through industrial might and force of arms, inanimate objects could not win the war on their own. Victory required millions of men and women to unify as never before in a total war of annihilation, to finance, build, and transport the weapons of war, and hundreds of thousands more to use them to kill Japanese soldiers and civilians, or die trying. Logic and reason no doubt motivated many Americans to support the war or fight. But in no small measure American patriotism and hatred of the Japanese were motivations that proved significant as well. Without them, the United States would have struggled more than it already did to sustain the manpower and political and public support for this gruesome and costly war—for four bloody years—let alone press for an unconditional surrender.

Strategic Advantages of In-Group/ Out-Group Bias in the Pacific War

How does the war against Japan fit with the hypothesized advantages of the in-group/out-group bias set out in the previous chapter? This section explores these potential advantages, as they applied to different segments of the American side—the public, the military, and the government. First, I look at in-group biases, and then turn to out-group biases.

FACING THE CHALLENGE: THE IN-GROUP BIAS AT WORK

In-Group Cohesion and the American Public

The United States faced a monumental challenge in raising the men, material, and finance needed to prosecute the war. Indeed, Congress and the U.S. public had remained steadfastly *against* joining the war already raging in Europe for two years. It was only when the United States itself was attacked by Japan that this changed—and radically so. After Pearl Harbor, "American citizens rallied to the war effort, particularly against the Japanese. 'Remember Pearl Harbor!' struck a chord in the United States that 'Remember Belgium' or 'France' could not have."[33] Still, the fact of the Japanese attack did not solve the collective action problem overnight. Bringing the public, the government, and the military together was going to be challenging, but essential, to launching and sustaining the war—and even more so to winning it.

A recurrent theme among Japanese leaders and the Japanese military was that Americans lacked the will to fight. They were seen not just as inherently inferior to their own Yamato race but lazy, deficient in bravery, and uninterested in prosecuting a long, drawn-out campaign. The architect of the attack on Singapore, Colonel Tsuji Masanobu, wrote that "our candid ideas at the time were that the Americans, being merchants, would not continue for long with an unprofitable war."[34] Even if the war would indeed be materially exorbitant, the Japanese had severely underestimated the American motivation to fight back—especially when rallying together in common cause against a despised foe. On the eve of the Battle of Midway, Admiral Chuichi Nagumo's intelligence report reiterated complacently that "the enemy lacks the will to fight."[35] Within 48 hours all four of his fleet's aircraft carriers had been sunk, with many American pilots lost in the effort. The belief that Americans lacked the will to fight was a fallacy repeated multiple times across the Pacific as Japanese commanders prepared to meet their supposedly inferior enemy.

At home, "polls revealed near unanimous public approval for a ghastly conflict of annihilation against the perpetrators of Pearl Harbor."[36] With this backing, noted historian Victor Davis Hanson, the U.S. government "crafted one of the most radical industrial and cultural revolutions in the history of the Republic in turning the country into a huge arms-producing camp."[37] And as another historian, Andrew Sinclair, put it bluntly, "The American armed forces put an end to unemployment."[38]

While in 1942 the Japanese still enjoyed military superiority, this "could not last once the American government, private industry, and the citizenry at large mobilized for war."[39] There were remarkable domestic changes. From 1939 to 1945, agricultural output increased by 20 percent and industrial production doubled. Americans built 16 warships for each one made by the Japanese, and American aircraft workers were four times more productive, man for man, as well as soon outnumbering their Japanese counterparts.[40] By August 1945 America was manufacturing twice as much war material as Germany, Italy, and Japan put together.[41] It had built a remarkable 300,000 aircraft and almost 88,000 warships.[42]

As well as striking productivity, there was remarkable innovation and engineering. At the end of the war Japan was still using roughly the same equipment and technology as it had all along. By contrast, the Americans "were producing planes, ships, and vehicles scarcely imaginable in 1941."[43] For example, while Japanese military hardware like the Zero fighter and Long Lance torpedo had initially been far superior to their adversaries, they soon seemed obsolete in comparison to entirely new American innovations, such as the P-51 Mustang and B-29 Superfortress, not to mention technologies such as radar, signals communication, code breaking—and, of course, the advent of nuclear weapons.[44] All this had come at a price, however. The cost of the war to the United States, according to Sinclair, was a shocking "double the amount spent in all American history before its outbreak."[45] At its peak, the United States was plowing a massive 40 percent of its entire GDP into the war. National debt increased by six times.[46]

Finally, what of the manpower to fight the war itself? Sixteen million citizens would serve in the United States military during the war, of whom, in all theaters of war, there would be well over a *million* casualties—some 292,000 combat deaths, 115,000 deaths from other causes, and another 671,000 wounded (with around one-third of these figures in the Pacific theater alone).[47] No such investments of materiel or manpower could have been made, or justified, without a remarkable level of American unity and desire to destroy the enemy.

In *How We Fight*, Dominic Tierney argues that America's history of wars falls into two very different traditions.[48] "Nation-building" operations, such as those in Vietnam, Afghanistan, and Iraq, are limited wars of choice. In this kind of war, complex interventions, usually into other states' internal affairs, lead to low-level but long and costly endeavors that seem to become never-ending "quagmires." Not only are these wars often unsuccessful, but they are also poorly supported by the American public.

By contrast, wars of national survival, such as the American Civil War and World War II, are all-out wars of necessity. In these "crusader" kinds of war, the United States fights in a very different manner. Mobilizing the full resources of the nation and its people, it retains a laser-like focus on ultimate victory and does everything in its power to achieve this objective. The Pacific campaign was, Tierney argues, the quintessential crusader war. Internal divisions were subordinated to support a massive and costly effort to defeat the enemy, no matter what. The public, military, and political elite were unified in not just prosecuting the war at full tilt but persisting until they had utterly destroyed the Japanese military and much of Japan itself, as well as extracting an unconditional surrender from perhaps the least likely nation to accept it. Support for crushing Japan—not just defeating them—dominated public opinion and extended across the political spectrum.

Although many people, when picturing World War II, think of the war in Europe and the struggle against Hitler and Nazi Germany, America's war started and ended in the Pacific. It was here that, despite the vast and ongoing death toll, "public support for the war effort barely wavered. Large majorities backed the use of all necessary force to compel unconditional surrender."[49] Indeed, if anything the public tended to advocate *increasing* the pressure, as "public support for expansive war aims swelled up and continued to rise during the war."[50] Rightly or wrongly, American in-group cohesion and collective action helped make fighting the war not just possible but a public demand, which persisted even in the face of severe and rising costs, and yet arguably also increased the prospects for success.

In-Group Cohesion and the American Military

Among the soldiers, sailors, and airmen themselves, cohesion was not just desirable but essential for personal survival and for the combat effectiveness of the military as a whole. In any war, this is perhaps the most obvious advantage of in-group bias—group cohesion has been actively and intensively nurtured by military institutions and powerfully felt by soldiers since time immemorial. As John Lynn cautions, cohesion on its own does not automatically signal increased performance, and units can be cohesive and still lose.[51] However, evidence suggests that, all else equal, unit cohesion is a vital ingredient of military effectiveness. In the fighting to come against the Japanese, it would be more critical than ever.

Such cohesion began to be tapped long before any soldier reached the front, following the centuries-old military traditions that serve to bond new recruits together in training, ritual, and allegiance to each other and their service. Without achieving those minimal levels of group identity and cohesion, they would fail to operate and fight effectively as a unit. It may have made them cocky, but it also made them eager and willing. Gerald Linderman found that, for troops in the Pacific War, "following basic training, they believed themselves ready for battle, were impatient to engage the enemy, minimized their adversaries' capacities to oppose them, and seldom worried about the results either for themselves or for their country. An exuberant aggressiveness infused their words and actions."[52] Such sentiments had been amplified by the events at Pearl Harbor and propaganda at home, as well as now by news from the front, and it seemed to help them face the challenge: "To very few did their opponents appear formidable; indeed, Americans approached their enemies with a nonchalance edging on disdain."[53] Before they had even left the shores of the United States, many American troops were tightly bonded and itching for a fight.

As cohesive as units shipping out for war may have been, of course, "bonds among those approaching battle were weaker than they would become as a result of battle."[54] They would strengthen significantly, and necessarily so, as soldiers quickly learned how to fight effectively or suffer the consequences, and above all this meant operating as a cohesive unit. This applied just as strongly to aircrews and ships' companies as it did to soldiers. American servicemen were soon subject to significant and sustained periods of merciless combat, which would only intensify in the years to come. By 1944–45, American casualties were occurring at a rate three times higher than in Europe.[55] And it was not just combat they had to contend with. With each campaign, they also had to endure weeks or months on end of dugouts, rations, rain, mud, disease, shelling, ambushes, and, if they were unlucky enough to be captured, they faced the prospect of torture, mutilation, and execution. But they were at least facing these adversities together. A study by Samuel Stouffer surveyed American soldiers during the war and found that, in difficult times, 61 percent stated they "kept going because they did not want to let their comrades down."[56] Often, so intense and prolonged was the fighting that the reality of life at home faded from view. One soldier on Guadalcanal explained a widespread sense that "there had never been any life but this one. The rest was a mirage."[57] U.S. Marines in particular became strongly cohesive, both in the field and back home, sharing as they did the brunt of the horrors of frontline combat that few could fully understand.

The bravery of soldiers acted out on remote Pacific Islands that few had ever heard of leaves a striking military legacy. When General Holland "Howlin' Mad" Smith toured Tarawa immediately after its costly capture by his men in 1943, he was shocked by the carnage and the loss of life. As the smoke and stench of battle still drifted across the beaches, he remarked to a fellow officer, "I don't see how they ever took Tarawa. It's the most completely defended island I have ever seen."[58] The answer, of course, was the dedication of American Marines, of whom he later wrote, "Only men with the highest morale and willingness to die rather than be defeated could have captured this well-nigh impregnable chain of fortifications."[59] Of the 4,690 Japanese defenders, only 17 survived, one of whom reported that their officers had boasted their defenses "were so strong that a million men could not take the island."[60] It would be a similar story time and time again for the Marines, enduring over one hundred such brutal amphibious assaults, island after island, as they ground a bloody trail across the Pacific toward the enemy homeland.

In his study of courage, William Miller makes the interesting observation that, given the socialization of Japanese *bushido* culture and values, a Japanese soldier putting his life in direct danger or even certain death is just doing his duty. By contrast, for an American, exactly the same behavior is going *beyond* the call of duty—American soldiers are not generally asked to needlessly put their life in danger or make suicidal assaults. If so, he suggests, "can't a case be made that it is more courageous for an American soldier to charge a Japanese pillbox than for a Japanese soldier to charge an American one?"[61] It is within expectations for Japanese soldiers to do so given their traditions and training, but not necessarily for American soldiers. While the unswerving sacrifice of Japanese soldiers may be remarkable, the sacrifices made by Americans were arguably more remarkable still.

Among naval personnel, group unity and cohesion were no less vital. Indeed, this typifies the entire naval tradition and is essential to its function. Operating the enormous, weapon-laden mini cities of warships and aircraft carriers across vast oceans is a hard enough task in itself and requires an extremely high degree of coordination and divisions of labor among hundreds of crewmen. Doing it under fire and in synchrony with dozens of other ships, as well as aircraft above and troops ashore, is harder still. Navies just don't work unless there is a supreme level of cohesion among the crew. This can be achieved with meticulous training, stringent discipline, and strict hierarchies of authority, but in no small measure it also relies on our in-group proclivities. This was tested to the extreme in the Pacific War, especially when many ships were crewed and commanded by "amateurs" recruited from other walks of life.[62] U.S. sailors were intensely proud and committed to the navy, their ship, and their crew. Captains often lived up to their legendary fate to go down with their ships. When we think of the military costs of the Pacific War, we often conjure up images of the crumpled bodies of dead soldiers strewn across the beaches of incongruously idyllic islands across the Pacific. But there are also many thousands of sailors lying beneath its depths, who went down fighting with their ships.[63]

The American navy as a whole showed no shortage of desire to do what was necessary to win, including a willingness to seize the initiative and take great risks. The Japanese navy had a long-established preference for decoy, diversion, and surprise, including operations at night and at long range, which tended to involve spreading their forces far and wide and seeking opportunities for small incremental gains where and when they arose.[64] The Americans, by contrast, had a very different strategy, in "the Western desire for continual and sustained shock encounters until one side was victorious or annihilated."[65]

The U.S. Navy constantly sought out concentrations of the Japanese fleet and, once found, launched everything they had at them. "Almost all serious strategists in the Japanese military," Hanson notes, "acknowledged their discomfort with a quite novel situation of all-out warfare with the Americans and British that would require continual head-on confrontations with the Anglo-American fleet."[66] Only significant levels of cohesion and coordination within and among Allied ships allowed such shock encounters to succeed.

The United States faced no easy task to press the fight on the seas, while the factories and shipyards were still gearing up at home. The attack on Pearl Harbor, though it had missed the carriers (which had by a stroke of luck been at sea), had knocked back the U.S. Pacific Fleet for some time to come.[67] By the time of the Battle of Midway in June 1942, the Japanese navy still enjoyed "vast numerical superiority in every category of ship and its far more experienced crews."[68] However, the Americans did have an edge in certain areas, and this often came down to human rather than material resources. In his study of Midway, Hanson argued that "at critical stages during the planning, fighting, and aftermath of the battle, American military personnel at all ranks were unusually innovative, even eccentric, and always unpredictable."[69] So while the U.S. Navy was running tight ships of strict discipline and hierarchy, it also had individuals ready to exploit strategic opportunities when they arose. In other words, in-group cohesion and subordination was sufficient but not suffocating. For the Japanese, the latter was often more the case.[70]

Finally, what about American airmen? Much attention is paid to the sacrifice of Japanese kamikaze pilots, yet we should remember that while for them death may have been certain, the death of allied airmen was also often highly probable, if not guaranteed.[71] The role of pilots and aircrews thus demanded a remarkably high level of bravery and commitment to their comrades and squadrons. Many American pilots at the Battle of Midway, to continue that example, flew what they realized were likely to be one-way missions, and indeed became "superhuman exemplars" of heroism after the war.[72] Hanson stresses that such acts were no accident or mistake. These men were "enthusiastic rather than merely willing to fly their decrepit planes into a fiery end above the Japanese fleet."[73] Western pilots were not necessarily ordered to carry out such risky feats, and it was often a voluntary decision to put themselves in harm's way in order to carry the fight. The sacrifices of U.S. airmen—and the quick thinking and coordination among the ships' captains—turned the closely balanced Battle of Midway into one of the first and most remarkable American victories of the war and, noted Admiral King, "the first decisive defeat of the Japanese navy in 350 years."[74]

One might think that such examples of self-sacrifice for the wider group were rare on the Allied side. But in fact they were common throughout the war. Dower notes that the number of British airmen killed in combat was *ten times* the number of all kamikazes that perished in the Pacific.[75] Death rates, as a proportion of all casualties, were also highest for aircrews—if they were shot down or crashed, they were often unlikely to survive. The loss rates were well understood by those at the time, but they flew nevertheless. The Japanese were exceptional in deliberately causing their own death, but not in risking it. American airmen were motivated strongly enough to also risk their lives for the collective cause, and for their comrades in arms, and many thousands paid the ultimate price. Like the soldiers and sailors, without them and their willingness to engage the enemy, the war could not have been fought, let alone won. But what of those leading and directing American forces in where, when, and how to fight?

In-Group Cohesion and American Leaders

Until 1941, the United States had managed to stay out of the war altogether. Foreign powers and internal factions alike clamored for America to join the fray, but it remained aloof. Powerful political and public forces sought to preserve America's isolation and avoid becoming embroiled in the seemingly never-ending bloodshed in Europe. It would take an attack on the U.S. homeland to change that, and awaken the "sleeping dragon." Even then, Hanson notes, "in 1941 no one in the Japanese high command seemed aware that a surprise attack on the Americans would in Western eyes lead to total war, in which the United States would either destroy its adversary or face annihilation in the attempt."[76] Within months of Pearl Harbor, the U.S. government had refocused its entire economy and foreign and domestic policy to engage in an all-out war with both Japan and Germany. It would have to call on its citizenry to make this possible—to pay for it, to supply it, and to fight it. This included the enormous draft of millions of citizens into the services. But they were willing. Roosevelt's approval ratings increased 11 percent after the attack, as the public rallied behind the government, and 97 percent approved of the U.S. declaring war.[77]

America's fighting spirit from the outset of the war is especially remarkable given the circumstances of the time. First, the United States of 1941 was not the superpower it is today. Japan was a formidable military power, with a population almost half that of the United States, and it had been building up, and using, its huge military forces for years. Second, it was some time before the United States began churning out large quantities of war machines and material. With a significant portion of the U.S. Pacific Fleet destroyed at Pearl Harbor, Japan's navy remained numerically superior and dominated control of the Asia-Pacific region. Third, Japan was essentially fighting a single foe (in the unified Anglo-American forces). By contrast, from the start the United States subscribed to the Allied "Germany First" strategy and as a result "was devoting the majority of its equipment and most of its armed forces to defeating the Germans and Italians and supplying the British, Chinese, and Soviets thousands of miles away."[78] Throughout the first years of the war there was significant public pressure in America to direct more or all of its efforts against Japan. Roosevelt had to work hard to counter this popular demand.

To overcome these challenges, the United States had to be brought together in multiple ways. It had to create giant international and domestic coalitions to enable and prosecute the war. It had to coordinate massive industrial production efforts to solve major engineering problems and supply the war. It had to ask citizens to absorb a crippling financial investment, for how long no one knew. Yet, above and beyond all of these material demands, American leaders also had to draw out extraordinary sacrifices from citizens themselves. Rational human beings might be motivated to fight by logic and incentives. But for most this would hardly be enough, and the risk of injury or death—or worse, if they were captured by the enemy—had to be justified by something more than that. Individual Americans were not fighting to advance geopolitical goals but for a range of motives closer to their group identities, such as defending the American homeland and its ideals and, not least, the fellow Americans for whom and with whom they were fighting. Many in the field also found renewed motivation in fighting to avenge those who had fallen.

Roosevelt and political leaders recognized this and indeed drew on in-group/out-group themes to rally the public and justify the call to arms. Some of the in-group rhetoric and out-group hostility toward Japan can thus be put down not to cognitive bias but to *propaganda*: deliberate attempts to manipulate public opinion in order to win support for the war effort, financing, and recruiting.[79] However, to whatever extent this was the case, it suggests that such messages were salient to the American public at large—tapping into conducive patterns of in-group/out-group thinking in the audiences of the propaganda. Whatever its other effects, this helped the United States prosecute the war.

Countless rousing speeches, Roosevelt's "fireside chats," and widespread appeals to the American conscience worked hard to strengthen in-group cohesion around patriotism, duty, pride, and the defense of American liberal values. Such efforts were critical—or at least they were deemed critical—for supporting, sustaining, and fighting the war. If they had failed as empty propaganda, the American public had plenty of opportunities to vote their leaders out of office or to protest and resist the war. Neither ever came close to happening. Yet, as well as a bottom-up willingness to fight among a rallying public, which carried the United States a long way on its own, at times there were also explicit top-down requests for sacrifice even on the Allied side. Dower notes that "in several instances Allied leaders at the highest level, including Winston Churchill and Douglas MacArthur, actually ordered their commanders never to surrender."[80] Churchill, for example, directly informed his military leaders on the ground that Malaya and Singapore must be "defended to the death" and "no surrender can be contemplated."[81] No wonder then that General Arthur Percival's surrender of over 130,000 Commonwealth forces in Singapore passed into infamy—John Keegan called it "the single most catastrophic defeat in British military history."[82] If they were to prevail in the bitter fighting against the Japanese, the Allies were going to have to call on their soldiers and commanders to find greater grit and determination and, ultimately, sacrifice.

FACING THE ENEMY: THE OUT-GROUP BIAS AT WORK

While in-group bias boosted a variety of aspects of American cohesion and collective action in facing the challenge of war, what of the out-group bias in facing the enemy itself? Here, I explore whether animosity toward the Japanese contributed to American military effectiveness, in the fighting spirit and wartime strategies employed against them. Did out-group sentiment increase the willingness to join up, fight, and kill, the desire for battles of annihilation, and the demand for unconditional surrender, as well as influence the decision of unrestricted submarine warfare and strategic bombing, and ultimately even the use of nuclear weapons? All of these had a military or strategic rationale behind their employment, but it was arguably an easier decision to use them against a despised foe.

At home in America, support stayed high throughout the war for whatever methods worked. *Life* magazine published a photograph of an incinerated Japanese solider, killed by a flamethrower that they described as the "most cruel and terrifying weapon ever developed. . . . But so long as the Jap refuses to come out of his holes and keeps killing, this is the only way."[83] In nearly all of what follows, it will remain debatable from an *ethical* point of view whether American beliefs and behavior were good or bad. However, this is not the question under study. Instead, the question under study is whether the in-group/out-group bias increased military effectiveness.

Out-Group Animosity and the American Public

Historian Allan Nevins wrote that in all of American history, "no foe has been so detested as were the Japanese."[84] This assessment, Dower suggests, is something that "no one at the time would have disputed."[85] The hostility and hatred expressed toward the Japanese were not so much due to who they were as a people but at least initially a response to what they had *done*. To a significant extent, the out-group hostility toward Japan originated in the way in which the war began: the surprise attack on the U.S. fleet at Pearl Harbor, which was widely perceived not only as cowardly and wanton destruction but as an act of treachery (after the attack, "the single word favoured above all others by Americans as best characterizing the Japanese people was 'treacherous'").[86] The attack did not just elicit surprise and anger but "provoked a rage bordering on the genocidal among Americans."[87] Having committed the act of attacking the United States, a strong desire emerged for retribution, from the president—who immediately dubbed 7 December the "day of infamy"—all the way down to the public at large. For many Christian Americans, the event also notably took place on a holy day—Sunday. As Van Evera observed, "Japanese leaders thought a display of Japanese military prowess would cow the Americans; in fact it aroused and enraged them."[88]

Whatever the role of errors in intelligence that exacerbated the surprise and severity of the Pearl Harbor attack, they also served to amplify the sense of shock and moral outrage it caused. Sinclair wrote that the Japanese had "inflicted on the United States the most humiliating defeat in its history."[89] As an attack without a declaration of war, it was decried as particularly heinous. Indeed, U.S. policymakers have, ever since, been loath to take advantage of surprise precisely because it tends to be seen as a cowardly act, like Pearl Harbor.[90] The result of striking out of the blue, argued Dominic Tierney, was that "the desire for vengeance may have been more powerful in the Pacific campaign than in any other interstate war in U.S. history."[91] Pearl Harbor itself thus went a long way to seeding an unprecedented hatred of the Japanese foe and a collective will to pull together in a monumental national effort not just to fight back but to destroy Japan. Three-quarters of Americans supported the demand for unconditional surrender.[92]

Even in 1941, after Hitler had invaded much of Europe and almost overrun Britain, less than a third of Americans supported a war against Germany.[93] However, on 7 December, "Pearl Harbor put a stop in an instant to all the bickering and uncertainty that had roiled American public opinion."[94] It was war. Admiral Bill Halsey, soon to be commander of the South Pacific campaign, expressed the sentiment the following day: "When we get through with them, the Japanese language will be spoken only in hell."[95]

The bombing of Japan later in the war raised many questions about the logic of targeting civilians and the necessary extent of destruction. Yet the way the war began continued to play into the way it ended. Many Americans saw the bombing of Japan as "retribution for Pearl Harbor."[96] When Truman announced the final surrender to the American people in 1945, he declared Victory over Japan Day: "a day which we Americans shall always remember as a day of retribution—as we remember that other day, the day of infamy."[97]

The sentiment for vengeance was not limited, however, to Pearl Harbor. After the attack, there were several more months of "unmitigated disaster" for the United States and its allies.[98] It began immediately with the invasion of the Philippines, opened by a devastating Japanese air attack that destroyed a hundred U.S. aircraft on the ground—in many ways "a disaster to rival that at Pearl Harbor."[99] In the ensuing weeks, "Malaya, the Dutch East Indies, Hong Kong and the Philippines all fell to a foe deemed to be no match for the white man and often in humiliating circumstances."[100] Britain's empire in Asia "fell with a swiftness which both astonished and dismayed everyone."[101] The loss of Malaya in particular came to be regarded as "one of the most shameful Allied defeats of the war."[102] As Americans deployed into the Pacific, one expressed an "anger and hate and a hot desire to fight back, to avenge our dead. . . . The war must end without compromise."[103] Such sentiments were common among American soldiers, but this one is all the more striking as it comes not from a frontline infantryman but from a nurse, outraged by a Japanese attack on her hospital in Bataan. By 1942, 28 percent of Americans openly declared that they "hated the Japanese."[104] This was not just an opinion on the street; it reflected a major theme in the media and to a large extent became institutionalized, as well as prominent in popular culture. Red Foley had a hit song called "Smoke on the Water," in which the United States would "make a graveyard of Japan."[105] The U.S. air forces would soon start turning that vision into a reality.

One might think that such beliefs and actions pushed the limit of what most leaders, soldiers, and citizens would be prepared to inflict on an enemy, even when deep in total war and losing thousands of soldiers a week. Extraordinary circumstances meant extraordinary actions that were seen as necessary evils but that were perhaps not widely supported. However, "no sustained protest ever materialized" and the bombing of Japanese cities and civilians was "widely accepted as just retribution as well as sound strategic policy."[106] Polls suggested that, "if anything, the American public believed that the military was too timid in targeting civilians. The occasional critic who questioned the carnage was widely derided as a naïf or fool."[107] Much of the American press called on the United States to give Japan "everything it had."[108] Even an article in the *Christian Century* suggested it was not possible to separate out soldiers and civilians in bombing: "If we fight at all, we fight all out."[109] The sustained and significant public animosity toward the Japanese supported the extreme actions that the United States was taking against them. In a democracy, that was a necessary pact.

Dower noted that "it is understandable that men in battle become obsessed with annihilating the foe. In the case of the Japanese enemy, however, the obsession extended to many men and women far removed from the place of battle, and came to embrace not just the enemy's armed forces but the Japanese as a race and culture."[110] They were, it seemed, an incorrigible foe that had to be not just beaten but destroyed. After the war, a U.S. Navy specialist in Japanese culture and language observed that Americans back home saw Germans as "simply misguided human beings, susceptible of [*sic*] re-education, while the Japanese were animals to whom decent behaviour could not be taught."[111] Rightly or wrongly, out-group animosity put the public firmly behind the American offensive.

Out-Group Animosity and the American Military

Despite the public vitriol at home, in the early stages of the conflict there were concerns that out-group hostility among soldiers heading to the front was *too weak*, and this was a problem. Linderman found that "American commanders complained that their soldiers lacked the animosity that the war required."[112] It was argued that beyond just more and harder training, they needed "something to give American fighters the desire to *kill* their enemies."[113] When Colonel Milton Hill, Inspector General of U.S. Army Forces in the Far East, visited U.S. troops in 1942, he reported, "The Jap hates the American with a downright hate that carries him through in battles to success or death. And we could do with more of a similar individual fighting spirit."[114] He observed that American troops were gradually learning the "usual lesson of battle—that it is a case of kill or be killed"—and that many were dead because this had not been sufficiently impressed upon them. But he argued that even this fell far short of what was needed. Rather, he lobbied for the development of "the spirit that goes beyond it—the belief in the heart of every man that he must kill the enemy, and the feeling that he *wants* to kill him to the extreme of his own fighting ability."[115] Written at a critical time in 1942 when the army was urgently figuring out how to adapt to their enemy and maximize combat effectiveness, Hill ended his essay, "From what I saw on Bataan, there is nothing else so important in winning this war."[116]

The previous chapter noted S. L. A. Marshall's claim that only around 15–25 percent of infantry in World War II *ever* fired their weapons.[117] While doubt was cast on that study, and whatever the precise proportions, it captures a genuine "problem" that many people clearly find it hard to kill, and there are significant psychological obstacles for soldiers who are socialized in normal life not to harm others and then asked to do exactly this in war.[118] This is likely to have been especially the case in World War II, where most American soldiers were conscripted from the civilian population. They were not career soldiers and few had prior combat experience. Hill noted wryly that "it is always news in our wars to great numbers of new soldiers that killing the enemy is the principal work of an army."[119]

Sometimes, in-group cohesion and out-group hostility could interact in important ways, one facilitating the other. One of Marshall's enduring insights was that small *teams*, as opposed to individuals on their own, benefited from a group dynamic that significantly increased offensive action.[120] Group cohesion, it turned out, was important to braving hostile fire and effectively engaging the enemy. While soldiers may have hated the Japanese, they needed to "confront the tiger" together.[121] This could then unlock the effects of their desire to fight the out-group. While there is no simple link between hatred of the enemy and military effectiveness,[122] the combination of in-group cohesion and out-group aggression is a virtual prerequisite of combat. When one is asked to kill someone from another group in service of their own, group biases make it easier, not harder, to do. Despite the variety of personal backgrounds and inclinations among American troops, animosity toward the Japanese enemy was widespread, sustained, and strong, and was going to be especially called upon if they were to persist and prevail in the violent struggle ahead.

Linderman stresses the process by which newcomers to the Pacific theater had to experience and see for themselves the extent of Japanese brutality. While in-group/out-group sentiment was already strong before they left the United States, it often took personal exposure to Japanese atrocities to trigger the bias into full gear. The level of barbarity was hard to believe, or at least hard to imagine back home, and only had full impact when encountered by soldiers in the flesh. As well as countless corpses of dead Japanese soldiers and civilians, many of whom had committed suicide or killed each other, they would also find horrifically mutilated fellow American soldiers. After witnessing repeated acts of cruelty against soldiers, civilians, and POWs alike, American views of the foe became ever more deeply entrenched. It would simultaneously sicken them and harden them with renewed resolve for vengeance. In the context of these systematic and growing atrocities, many Americans began to lose the belief that the enemy were human at all. The Japanese were seen as having "abandoned the value of life," and soldiers came to perceive "an enemy believed to lack fundamental human attributes"—and, consequently, one that they saw as "infinitely killable."[123]

Whatever the particular views Americans had, and the extent of skepticism they may have initially retained about whether or not Japanese atrocities were deliberate and systematic, "by the end of 1942 the uncertainties and ambiguities had disappeared, leaving behind an intense, unmixed antagonism."[124] In the hotly contested Battle of Guadalcanal, wrote John Keegan, they learned "both the professional respect and ethnic hatred they were to feel for the Japanese throughout the Pacific war."[125] On 7 December 1942, artillerymen on the island launched a daylong bombardment of the Japanese in what they called the "First Anniversary Hate Shoot," in memory of Pearl Harbor.[126] As the fighting wore on, from Guadalcanal to Saipan, from the Philippines to Iwo Jima and Okinawa, it became abundantly clear that the Japanese were ready to lay down their lives in battle, and American servicemen began to believe that this was, in fact, what they wanted: "In the minds of American soldiers and Marines, their role was to kill Japanese; the role of the Japanese was to die."[127] Given this desire to sacrifice themselves, as one Marine put it, they would "help [them] die."[128]

As the fighting intensified, the soldiers came to realize that they had to kill not just to survive but also because, with the enemy eschewing surrender, it was the only way they were going to prize Japanese soldiers, one by one, off each island. An army poll in 1943 "already indicated that about half of all GIs believed that it would be necessary to kill all Japanese before peace could be achieved."[129] For many—troops and commanders alike—killing itself became the objective, not a means to an end. Admiral Halsey beseeched Americans to "Kill Japs, Kill Japs, Kill more Japs."[130] By 1945, "one out of four U.S. combatants stated that his primary goal was not to help bring about Japan's surrender, but simply to kill as many Japanese as possible."[131] Linderman wrote that "obliteration of the enemy had become the sole means to the nation's victory over Japan and to the Pacific soldier's personal survival."[132]

Comparing the European and Pacific theaters, it is widely agreed that out-group animosity was significantly stronger toward the Japanese than the Germans, and this seems to have translated into a greater motivation to fight. "Commentator after commentator in the Anglo-American camp," Dower found, "stated flatly that the Japanese were more despised than the Germans."[133] Lynn reviewed the "cold statistical evidence of a burning hatred" among American soldiers.[134] Stouffer's study found that 51 percent of recruits said they would "really like to kill a Japanese soldier," a figure that plummeted to 7 percent wanting to kill a German soldier.[135] They also asked specifically about the effects of such beliefs, and 38 percent of American infantrymen in the Pacific said that, in difficult times, they were "helped by thoughts of hatred of the enemy," a figure that was higher than any other theater of war.[136] A poll in 1944 found that 13 percent of the American *public* expressed a preference to "kill all Japanese" after the war. Among American infantrymen serving in the Pacific, fully 42 percent "wanted the Japanese race 'wiped out' altogether."[137] Among new soldiers still waiting to ship out from America, the figure was even higher—67 percent, compared to "only" 29 percent for Germans.

John Lynn is cautious about the effects of mere in-group cohesion necessarily promoting combat success and, in contrast to Dower and others, he is even more skeptical about hatred of the enemy increasing motivation to fight.[138] However, the brute fact remains that if American soldiers, sailors, and airmen had been unwilling to kill Japanese servicemen—and sometimes civilians—between 1941 and 1945, they would not have won the war. They wouldn't even have been able to fight it. While it may have been hard at the start, it became easier. The more experience of fighting the unyielding Japanese they got, the more atrocities they witnessed, and the more friends they lost to avenge, the more they were willing or even eager to kill—as the statistics starkly showed. The behavior of the Japanese, including the treachery of Pearl Harbor but increasingly the ongoing brutality across the Pacific, soon turned a foreign war into a personal one that made at least many, if not all, Americans determined to fight and destroy their enemy.

On its own terms, free from context, out-group animosity is a terrible thing. Its effects had seemingly run far, for example, with the identification of the Japanese as mere animals to be exterminated. Yet, whether or not it was reproachable from a moral standpoint, the question here has been its impact on military effectiveness. Did the growing out-group animosity help solve the problem of the lack of offensive spirit, and reluctance to kill, that Milton had observed undermining American troops in the Philippines in 1942? Did it help in engaging the formidable Japanese navy at sea, especially when outnumbered and in the face of their favored long-distance torpedo attacks in the darkness of night, or in a hail of screaming kamikaze attacks? Did it help airmen to fly what might be one-way missions to sink the Japanese carriers at Midway, or indeed to carry out their gruesome orders to bomb Japanese cities? America was asking its young men to go thousands of miles from home to face a merciless adversary that would do their best to maim or kill them. If they were going to survive, and overcome their fear and reluctance to kill before being killed themselves, out-group animosity would help them to do it. Indeed, it seems to have greased the cogs of war for everyone making difficult decisions up and down the military hierarchy, from the lowly soldier with his finger on the trigger of a rifle to the highest officials with pens poised over the authorization of military operations. As Dower argued, "The dehumanization of the Other contributed immeasurably to the psychological distancing that facilitates killing, not only on the battlefield but also in the plans adopted by strategists far removed from the actual scene of combat."[139] And this is the focus of the next section.

Out-Group Animosity and American Leaders

So far we have seen that out-group hostility among the public and military was persistent and strong, but that it was likely to lend support for the war and motivation to those who had to fight and kill. But was this merely a phenomenon of the masses? A hatred confined to citizens and soldiers that was cynically nurtured by elites of the state to do their dirty work for them? In fact, the same in-group/out-group bias can be seen alive and well right up the chain of command, to the very top of the military and political hierarchy. It was not just propaganda. Indeed, in many respects, this appears to be where the in-group/out-group bias was strongest, and certainly where it leveraged the strongest strategic effects. Many of the choices made at those levels were excruciatingly difficult decisions, each of which could cost hundreds or thousands of American lives, and thousands or tens of thousands of Japanese ones. The in-group/out-group bias affected American leaders as much as American laypeople, and it may have swung the balance in key decisions over paths taken.

The U.S. government did not wish to merely defeat Japan's armed forces but demanded unconditional surrender—the total defeat of the Japanese nation with no concessions. This carried risks because it gave a reason for the enemy to fight harder and longer. But it was something the United States would not compromise on. Vice President Henry Wallace had declared in 1942, "No compromise with Satan is possible."[140] After the objective was announced in early 1943, "powerful domestic forces prevented the United States from altering its demand of unconditional surrender. Eager to obtain retribution for Japanese atrocities and for the surprise attack against Pearl Harbor, the American polity readily accepted the goal and political leaders were quickly locked in."[141]

The outright submission of Japan was seen as crucial for three major reasons.[142] First, the lesson of World War I had been that partial victory only

fostered a greater enemy that would rise again later. Second, Japan's embedded militaristic nationalism could only be dismantled by a complete purge of
Japanese military, government, and social structures. Third, the United States
had to assume that its fanatical soldiers—and apparently many civilians too in
any final struggle for the home islands—would never give in until destroyed.
With this commitment, the United States could not soften or change its terms
as the Japanese dug in and the costs of fighting mounted; Secretary of State
James Byrnes "warned that a compromise with the emperor would lead to the
crucifixion of the president."[143] Instead, military methods had to be found
to bring Japan to its knees, even though no one knew what this would take.
According to one newspaper of the time, the question became "whether, in
order to win unconditional surrender, the Allies will have to kill Japan's millions to the last man."[144] A vicious circle was created in which "the clarion call
for Japan's 'thoroughgoing defeat' in turn reinforced the Japanese militarists
as they struggled to rally the Japanese people to die en masse for their country."[145] And it was this tenacity that faced American soldiers, sailors, and airmen at the front.

In the war at sea, the U.S. Navy was led by a bureaucracy and individuals
with considerable power and decision-making clout. Far from automatons following orders from above, senior naval officers would argue vociferously with
other parts of government to fight the war in their own way. After all, it was
the navy that had been targeted and humiliated at Pearl Harbor, and it was they
that had to literally carry the fight back to Japan. This gave them significant
agency for their beliefs to influence the fighting. Admiral Halsey in particular became famous for his blunt anti-Japanese rhetoric and his "Kill more
Japs" motto. He famously remarked for publication, "The only good Jap is a
Jap who's been dead six months."[146] But there was no shortage of naval commanders who expressed vehement loathing toward the enemy, a sentiment
that urged them to seize the opportunity to engage the Japanese fleet whenever they could—often at great risk. Hanson wrote that "eccentric, pugnacious,
and independent American admirals like Halsey and [Frank] Fletcher could
at times . . . endanger their fleets through their very aggressiveness."[147] But
overall this was precisely the formula that made the American way of fighting
effective and victory possible.

Immediately after Pearl Harbor, the navy also made the striking decision,
in direct violation of the normal rules of war, "to wage unrestricted submarine warfare and thus to sink Japanese fishing, merchant, and passenger vessels."[148] The idea, rather than attacking only military assets when they could
be found, was to just destroy as much shipping as possible, and faster than
they could be replaced.[149] U.S. submarine captains had also initially used
"excessively cautious tactics based on submerged approach rather than surface attack at night."[150] But in the blockade of Japan, they were instructed
to dispense with normal practice and sink as many Japanese civilian ships as

they could, and any captains who refused or failed to do so were relieved of their command.[151] However, all this meant significant losses of civilian life as well as enemy soldiers and sailors. While such an indiscriminate strategy raises ethical debates, it is widely agreed that the aggressive submarine campaign against Japanese shipping was a critical factor in securing the final surrender.[152] Around 75 percent of Japan's key raw materials, as well as large proportions of food and other imports, were relied on from overseas.[153] With Japan's military forces dispersed across the Pacific and Asia, both the home islands and the military were dependent on regular sea transport. As Stephen Rosen explained, "Without merchant shipping, food, oil, and munitions could not be transported within the Japanese empire. Postwar data suggests that the campaign against the Japanese economy, of which the submarine force was an important part, had come close to breaking the empire, without invasion of the home islands, without Soviet intervention, and without use of the atomic bomb."[154] Robert Pape's study, which focused on the role of airpower, concurs that the naval blockade had "devastating" effects on the economy and "submarines had essentially won the tonnage war before air power could intervene to help."[155] Submarine captains became "bored and disgusted because there were virtually no targets."[156] Japan received no further oil after March 1945.[157] By July it had less than one million barrels remaining, yet needed 35 million per year.[158]

If American leaders and sailors had been reluctant to sink civilian and merchant vessels, it is likely that Japan would have carried on fighting for longer and might never have surrendered—or at least not so quickly—and the United States would have had to carry out its planned invasion of the Japanese home islands, at enormous further cost. While it is commonly believed that it was the bombing of Japan, especially the atomic bombs, that brought about Japanese surrender, the Japanese leadership had in fact paid little heed to the months of deadly firebombings that had already taken place across multiple cities in Japan. They kept fighting as long as they had an army that could do so. Ultimately, that capability was removed, and surrender became possible in large part because of the devastation wrought by American submarines on the lifelines connecting Japan to the outside world.[159] While the Japanese never lost their will to fight, they did ultimately lose the *capacity* to fight, with oil, arms, and food literally running out. For the Americans, however, this information was not fully collated and analyzed until later. During the war, the effects of the blockade took a while to show up because, as well as a lack of data, Japan had stockpiled reserves and was able to draw on those to keep fighting. Therefore, for American leaders *at the time*, the submarine campaign was apparently effective but not obviously effective enough, so bombing, invasion, and atomic weapons were still also seen as vital elements of the overall strategy.

Let us now turn to the war in the air. In the light of the devastating bombing of Japan, it is remarkable to look back at America's earlier attitude to airpower, which was outright indictment of aerial bombing as a strategy at all. When Franco and his fascist allies began bombing cities in the Spanish Civil War, and Japan began bombing Chinese cities in the 1930s, there was uproar in America from the public to the president. The U.S. Senate introduced a resolution in 1938 that condemned the "inhuman bombing of civilian populations" and called it a "crime against humanity."[160] When the war began in Europe in 1939, Roosevelt urged all sides to refrain from bombing each other's cities, a practice he called "inhuman barbarism" that had "shocked the conscience of humanity."[161] Even by 1940 Roosevelt was continuing to advocate against it, pointing out that the "United States consistently has taken the lead in urging that this inhuman practice be prohibited."[162]

If this view had persisted, the United States would never have been able to lay a finger on Japan itself until November 1945 at the earliest, and would almost certainly have had to go through with the planned invasion of the Japanese homeland. The invasion of Kyushu, Operation Olympic, was to begin on 1 November 1945 and the invasion of Honshu, Operational Coronet, on 1 March 1946—although note that even those dates were chosen *after* the United States had already bombed Japan to smithereens, so any invasion would likely have been even later if no bombing had occurred.[163] Something significant must have changed to reverse U.S. preferences from abject horror at aerial bombing to becoming masters of prosecuting the horror itself. And the thing that changed appeared to be simply acquiring an enemy that the United States despised enough to be willing to kill in large numbers. As we saw earlier, the American public were highly supportive of the bombing of Japan and maintained their steadfast support throughout the war.

The goals and impact of the air campaign against Japan is an important topic and one that deserves to be addressed in some detail, especially as it culminated in the unprecedented decision to use nuclear weapons.[164] Air raids on the Japanese home islands began as part of an "interdiction strategy" of precision bombing against military and economic targets, which became feasible with the capture of the Mariana Islands in June 1944. However, it was a slow start. By March the following year, there had been just 20 missions, dropping 5,400 tons of bombs, compared to the 160,800 tons eventually dropped on Japan.[165] These early raids focused almost exclusively on Japanese aircraft production. They proved, however, ineffective. Long flight times meant they could only carry 3 tons of bombs per aircraft, instead of the normal 10, and other obstacles included bad weather, Japanese air cover, ineffective ordinance, and initially few available aircraft.[166] Of 9 factories targeted, only 3 suffered long-term damage, and production was falling in any case because of the shortage of materials, not factories. Thus, the bombing had little additional effect—as Pape put it, "unbombed factories simply sat unused."[167] As the obstacles and inefficiency of the interdiction strategy sunk in—as it did in Europe—planners dispensed with precision bombing and shifted to area bombing of Japanese cities instead. The idea now was to employ the "Douhet strategy," attacking civilian population centers with the goal of breaking the nation's will to fight. Or, as air force commander Curtis LeMay put it, to "bomb and burn them until they quit."[168] Over the course of the ensuing months, the Japanese home islands would be subjected to what Pape called "the most harrowing terror campaign in history."[169]

According to many historians and political scientists, the lesson of World War II was that the Douhet strategy fails miserably. Even when it causes massive death and destruction, this only appears to make the enemy nation *more* resolute and determined to fight, not less (as similarly occurred, for example, in Britain). Responding to the postwar Strategic Bombing Survey, when asked, "How did you feel about the Americans during the war?" 11 percent of Japanese people said they had "no ill feelings," 25 percent gave no answer, but 40 percent "spoke in terms of hatred" (the remaining percentage is unaccounted for in the original report).[170] As Pape notes, these figures probably underestimate "antienemy sentiment" because the interviews were carried out by Americans during the occupation. But whatever the figures, the population was, or became, more anti-American rather than likely to overthrow their own government. It is thus often argued that strategic bombing in both Europe and Japan had little effect on the outcome of the war.[171] At least, it could hardly win the war on its own (although some airpower advocates made that argument). Victory could only be achieved by grinding land operations that wrested control of territory inch by inch from the enemy, and held it. If so, any out-group bias that facilitated or encouraged the large-scale bombing of "enemy" civilians may have promoted a punitive sentiment supporting the air campaigns but did not lend a vital strategic advantage. With the benefit of hindsight, that may be correct in the case of the air campaign.

However, *at the time*, strategic bombing was believed to be essential and effective. First, it was prosecuted consistently by all sides in both the European and Pacific theaters right up until the end of the war—supported not just by people like LeMay but even by erstwhile critics of aerial bombing like Roosevelt and Churchill. Second, while it is generally accepted that neither Germany nor Japan surrendered as a result of strategic bombing alone, among the many pressures upon them, it nevertheless contributed as one factor among several that, in combination, led to the defeat of both nations. Without any aerial bombing, the wars in both theaters would likely have lasted longer and been more costly, at least for the ground troops below. Finally, Hitler was only defeated when vast numbers of Allied troops were advancing on Berlin—and the Russians down the street. By contrast, Japan surrendered before a single American had set foot on the shore. This suggests that, while bombing clearly did not win the war in Europe, in the case of Japan, some combination of the naval blockade, the Soviet declaration of war, and the damage inflicted from the air contributed to Japan's decision to surrender even before they'd had a chance to repel an invasion. Despite the shortcomings of the air campaign, therefore, Pape notes that Japan stands out as "the most successful case of modern military coercion . . . Japan's surrender represents a rare instance in which a great power surrendered its entire national territory to an opponent that had not captured any significant portion of it."[172] It is hard to see Japan having done so without the air campaign having first devastated all of its major cities, on top of everything else.

Finally, we come to the bomb. The question inevitably arises whether in-group/out-group biases might have contributed to the decision to drop atomic weapons on Japan. Most experts argue that a cold, logical rationality can explain it perfectly well. Unless Japan could be compelled to surrender some other way, the alternative was going to be an invasion of the Japanese home islands, with such massive costs, to both sides, that no one was sure that the American public would support it (or would have continued to do so after the war, had they later discovered the government had a secret weapon that could have saved hundreds of thousands of American lives).

The prospect of invading Japan was daunting indeed. On the mainland, Japan still had thousands of aircraft and was continuing to produce more, while the army had fully 2,350,000 soldiers standing ready. In addition, in the famous plan to arm the entire civilian population in defense of the nation, "the army was also estimating a force of sixty million, to fight for every foot of the hallowed ground: old men, women and children who could dive under a truck or a tank with an explosive charge strapped to them, or who could hurl a grenade or prepare a booby trap. There were many ways to fight the enemy without confronting him and the army intended to use them all."[173] For a long time there were claims that the U.S. Army "talked of an eventual million army casualties in the war."[174] Although this is now seen as a gross exaggeration, it was hard to know what would have happened if American troops had landed on Japan proper.[175] At the time, Hasegawa reports that U.S. planners were expecting circa 200,000 casualties, of which around 40,000–60,000 would be combat deaths. Whatever the possible figures, no one wanted to put it to the test, and these "were still huge numbers that must have weighed heavily on the president's mind."[176] Thus, Truman's Potsdam Declaration of 26 July 1945 warned that unless they accepted unconditional surrender, "the alternative for Japan is prompt and utter destruction."[177] No response was forthcoming, and the atomic bombs were readied for deployment.

The huge cost of the Manhattan project, and indeed even the existence of the project itself, was not yet publicly known, and Truman's advisors were concerned that there would be outrage—among the public and government alike—if such a massive investment had never contributed to ending the war.[178] Secretary of State Jimmy Byrnes told Leo Szilard, one of the project scientists, that "we had spent two billions dollars on developing the bomb, and Congress would want to know what we had got for the money."[179] Perhaps more importantly still, as the war in Europe wound up and Stalin looked west, there was an opportunity to send a very important signal to Moscow, as well as to secure Japan's surrender before the Soviet Union could use the war to extend its reach in Asia.[180] Given all these reasons to use it, Secretary of War Henry Stimson told John McCloy, his assistant secretary of war, the bomb was a "royal straight flush."[181] Certainly, it is not possible to attribute the use of nuclear weapons to any one particular cause and rule out the several others. Assuming Japan did not unconditionally surrender over the subsequent days, as Budiansky put it, the bomb "would be used on Japan, simply because it had become impossible for anything else to happen."[182]

However, hindsight makes it easy to see the decision to use the bomb as a foregone conclusion—multiple motives or few. There were many reasons not to use it as well. The bomb "gave Truman the power to play God,"[183] and he still had to give the green light on what was clearly a decision of awesome responsibility that would unleash a new era of war—indeed, a new era of international relations. Moreover, from the perspective of strategic coercion, the bombing of Japan had already laid waste to dozens of Japanese cities, and in terms of the immediate death toll, atomic weapons merely replicated what a night's B-29 raid did already. The Strategic Bombing Survey estimated after the war that the effect of both bombs "could have been matched by 330 B-29 sorties using incendiaries—210 for Hiroshima and 120 for Nagasaki."[184] This was only a quarter of the aircraft sorties that the 21st Bomber Command was flying *every week* over Japan in August 1945. The logic of the atomic bomb was the same as the logic of firebombing, to compel surrender through the Douhet strategy—breaking enemy will by the "threat of horrendous further devastation."[185] The means were different, but the aim was the same, and already by this stage, as Tierney put it, "the line between combatant and noncombatant was completely blurred."[186] Conventional attacks would in fact likely have been more lethal and more numerous. After the war, Stimson claimed, "Had the war continued until the projected invasion [of Japan] date of 1 November 1945, additional fire raids would have been more destructive of life and property than the limited number of atomic raids which we could have executed in the same time period."[187] In short, the nuclear option was not the most destructive option in the U.S. arsenal—at least not in the near future.

There is, therefore, an argument that nuclear weapons only offered a new way of doing the same thing rather than a new strategy, and Truman could have chosen to press on as before. The difference was the technology that could now incinerate a city, and tens of thousands of men, women, and children, in seconds. While firebombing could already do that, given a few hours, a single bomb that could do the same thing in an instant was all the more horrific. So in some sense at least, it was a dramatic escalation of violence. After four years of grueling warfare against a hated and lethal adversary, out-group animosity toward the Japanese is likely to have made it an easier decision than it otherwise would have been for American decision-makers—as well as a decision they knew would be easier to accept among the public. As for Truman himself, he claimed he "never lost a night's sleep over it."[188] Hasegawa points out, however, that Truman repeatedly came back to address the question of alternative options and moral responsibility, and the very fact that "he spoke so often to justify his actions shows how much his decision to use the bomb haunted him."[189]

Could the in-group/out-group bias really have affected such momentous, painstakingly deliberated decisions? Some evidence from the next war suggests it might. When the Chinese intervened in the Korean War in 1950, Truman publicly indicated that the United States remained open to the use of nuclear weapons again, causing alarm around the world—not only for developments on the Korean peninsula and China but also for the delicate nuclear standoff emerging with the Soviet Union. Might this mean that the United States was prepared to use them in Europe too? Seemingly not. In an effort to defuse the situation in a debate at the United Nations, the U.S. representative tried to reassure his counterparts by explaining that "Washington viewed the atomic bomb as a weapon for use against 'Asians but not Europeans.'"[190] The sole use of nuclear weapons—against Japan—could only vindicate that view.

In sum, debate will no doubt never end as to whether, and how much, the nuclear attacks contributed to ending the war. Certainly, "most U.S. servicemen praised the dropping of the atomic bomb for ending the war and possibly saving their lives."[191] Pape has his critics, of course, as well as a widespread common intuition, which struggle to buy the argument that nuclear weapons were irrelevant to winning (or at least ending) the war—in some way large or small. Pape himself notes that, in fact, Hiroshima did at least "convince the Emperor and some civilian leaders to favour immediate surrender" rather than delaying the decision even longer.[192] The problem was that powerful Japanese army leaders in the cabinet disagreed, holding out for two more days, by which time the Soviets had begun their invasion of Manchuria. This conflates the pressures that were weighing upon the Japanese government, so we will never know for sure which event made the army come around, as both sunk in. What we do know is that the use of the most ghastly weapon of all time tipped some decision-makers, if not all, toward surrender.

In the end, by a variety of means, the United States became a formidable military instrument that ground its way across the Pacific, defeating and often annihilating Japanese island garrisons defended to the last man. Above, bombers reached out from these newly captured island bases to rain bombs over Japanese cities for months on end. Below, submarines were wreaking havoc on Japanese shipping, sinking any and all ships and starving Japan's far-flung military as well as its citizens at home. And ultimately, Japan became the target of the first-ever atomic weapons. Tierney wrote that "to Japanese civilians, the U.S. military must have seemed like the Martians in H. G. Wells's

1898 story *The War of the Worlds*: an alien adversary whose machines killed with cool, depersonalized zeal."[193] It was a gruesome business that changed America from an isolationist nation focused inward on its recovery from the Great Depression to a global industrial and military hegemon capable of destroying lethal opponents on two continents at the same time.

But that awesome capability is perhaps less remarkable than the United States' willingness to do so. In their efforts to win the war, American leaders had to make a series of difficult decisions about whether to expend yet more lives prizing suicidal Japanese soldiers off each island across the Pacific, whether to torpedo civilian ships, whether to incinerate Japanese cities, and which they should choose to level with atomic bombs. All of these decisions had a rational logic behind them: they were strategies to try to win the war, and to win it quickly. Whether one agrees with them or not, they found favorable winds in the significant in-group cohesion and out-group animosity among the American public, military, and leaders. Debate will remain over which of these components of the American strategy were essential, or not, to winning the war in the Pacific. But the reality is that probably all of them were, given uncertainty *at the time* about what might or might not work, and it is the combination of these bloody strategies of war—ones that under normal times you wouldn't wish on your worst enemy—that closed the net on Japan.

Conclusions

John Dower reminds us that "as World War Two recedes in time and scholars dig at the formal documents, it is easy to forget the visceral emotions and sheer race hate that gripped virtually all participants in the war, at home and overseas, and influenced many actions and decisions at the time."[194] The detrimental consequences of such prejudice are significant indeed, a negative side of the ledger so important that I explore it in detail in the following chapter. Yet at the same time, in a war that was killing hundreds of thousands of soldiers and civilians alike, at a rate higher than any war in its history, Americans needed unprecedented levels of in-group cohesion if they were to fight back, persevere, and succeed in the long struggle ahead. And not least, they also needed some minimal level of out-group animosity toward the Japanese if they were to kill well over a million of them in forcing unconditional surrender. Perhaps Japan should have been appeased and the United States should not have participated in any killing at all. But for anyone who believes that the war had to be fought, and had to be won, then Americans had to lean forcefully into a fight to the death against Japanese soldiers, sailors, airmen, and sometimes civilians.

I have argued that the in-group/out-group distinction—directed at whoever the enemy of the day may be—can offer strategic advantages. It promotes support for the war at home, military effectiveness at the front, and resolve among decision-makers. Win or lose, it helps states fight. To the extent that the in-group/out-group bias influenced the war, it did not usher in victory where otherwise there would have been defeat. An Allied victory was more or less assured in the long run given the vast industrial power of the United States and the gathering alliance against Japan—eventually to include the Soviet Union. However, it helped the United States toward victory in two ways.

First, the in-group/out-group bias helped the United States push the war forward to reach as rapid a conclusion as possible. The strategies taken to win the war—the island-by-island annihilation of Japanese garrisons, shock sea battles, unrestricted submarine warfare, strategic bombing, and nuclear weapons—are less likely to have been contemplated, employed, or supported without the in-group/out-group bias helping to justify such extreme measures. Against the hated Japanese enemy, compared to Germany, there were more options.

Second, the in-group/out-group bias may have influenced the outcome in another way. Although Japan could never defeat the United States, if the war had dragged on, it could have forced a negotiated settlement by which Japan would lay down its arms in exchange for keeping much of its prized new territory in Asia (this was what the Japanese themselves had originally hoped for).[195] This was always a possibility, and U.S. leaders feared it might happen if they were forced to go through with an invasion of the Japanese home islands. Victory would be far less assured, and unconditional surrender might have become too costly to insist upon. Even if Japan could not expect to win, they hoped that the initial invasion would be so costly to the United States that they would have to seek a compromise—and this is one reason why Japan did not surrender earlier. As long as public support remained strong and unwavering, however, the United States would not let that happen, and it would not have to since it had other means at its disposal. Instead, the objective of destroying Japanese forces and Japan itself could be realized from the sea and air, swept in and sustained on the currents of powerful American in-group cohesion and virulent out-group animosity, supporting whatever it took to win.

In reviewing perceptions on each side, where the propaganda often seemed to say more about themselves than the enemy, Dower observed that portrayals of the enemy revealed "a pattern of stereotyping peculiar to enemies and 'others' *in general*, rather than to the Japanese foe or Western foe in particular. This facilitated the quick abatement of hatred once the war had ended—while also facilitating the transferral of the hateful stereotypes to newly perceived enemies."[196] In other words, while Dower saw racism as an underlying dynamic of the war, he also recognized it as one manifestation of a broader in-group/out-group bias, which moves into high gear whenever a new enemy is at hand—soon to become the Soviet Union rather than Japan. This reflects the idea that there is an adaptive logic to biases that is *contingent*. While in-group/out-group bias may be ever present at a baseline level, it comes to the fore in certain contexts, and in those contexts—despite the dangers of its excesses—it can help promote effectiveness in intergroup competition.

This is precisely what we should expect from the in-group/out-group bias. As psychologist Rob Kurzban and colleagues have shown in laboratory experiments, in-group/out-group distinctions may be readily made, but they can also easily be changed.[197] When put in competition with other groups, people will adopt an allegiance to whatever the salient group is. That makes good sense, and it seems to be how the brain is wired up. As a result, the in-group/out-group bias does not necessarily fixate on a liking or disliking of any particular real-life group. What it does is generate a dislike of whatever out-group one has come into competition with and a favoritism for whoever makes up one's in-group standing in opposition. This is the adaptive nature of the in-group/out-group bias.

I emphasized, however, that the in-group/out-group bias is *only* adaptive at some moderate level. When too weak, it will fail to spur citizens, soldiers, and leaders to cohere and compete with rivals. When extreme, it can give up its advantages and become a liability or counterproductive (see chapter 9 for examples of this in the Pacific War—on both sides but especially for Japan). However, this mix of advantages and disadvantages is entirely to be expected. As discussed at the start of the book, the literature tends to focus on biases leading to detrimental behavior—with the implication that biases are always bad and always lead to poor outcomes. In war, however, there is usually a winner and a loser, and little reason to assume that cognitive biases only appear on the side of the loser. Biases appear in most people and many contexts, and while they may sometimes hinder us, at other times they will help. In the Pacific War, I have argued that the in-group/out-group bias gave a net advantage to the Americans because it altered their behavior to better meet the task at hand—increasing the war effort at home, combat effectiveness at the front, and resolve among leaders at the top.

One reason the United States did not reach the extreme levels of in-group/out-group bias that indoctrinated the Japanese military and civilian population is that American culture in fact had strong currents pushing back the other way, not least individualism itself—a direct countercurrent to group subordination. In Hanson's view, this individualism was a vital ingredient of success.[198] The American war machine had its share of doctrine and discipline, but not so much as to stifle innovation, creativity, and violations of military hierarchy when necessitated by events. The United States as a whole was "a nation-in-arms, drawing on the collective wisdom of thousands of freethinking individuals."[199] Using the Battle of Midway as an illustration, Hanson argued that "the American faith in individuality rather than group consensus, spontaneity rather than rote, and informality rather than hierarchy proved decisive."[200] In these respects, the Americans could hardly have been more different from the Japanese.

Hanson's argument brings the case studies back to where we started, with George Washington's victory for American independence, which cemented the rights of individuals as well as collective authority in a free society. As the Constitution began, "We the people" defined a strong in-group but one of fiercely independent individuals and states, unified nevertheless in opposition to a reviled out-group that had affronted it. Tuchman noticed the comparison: "By uniting the colonies into a whole, the Coercive Acts [which withdrew the right of self-government in Massachusetts in 1774] accomplished the same cohesion in the adversary as the Japanese attack on Pearl Harbor accomplished two centuries later—and with ultimately the same result."[201] In 1941, that sentiment was put to the test in pulling the United States together to fight the toughest war it had ever experienced against a foreign adversary. The machinery of American government was turned over to the prosecution of the war, American citizens rallied to support and supply the war effort, and millions of young Americans shipped off to fight, many never to return.

Although the United States won, its overwhelming industrial might and investment in the war might raise the question of whether victory was really that much of a surprise. How could this industrial, technological, and populous giant lose?[202] Yet, as Hanson sees it, "the astounding fact remains: in less than four years, after being surprised and caught in a state of virtual unpreparedness, the United States—while devoting the majority of its forces to the European theater of operation, and without banzai charges, kamikaze attacks, or ritual suicides—not only defeated an enormous and seasoned Japanese military but destroyed the Japanese nation itself, ending its half-century existence as a formidable military power and indeed a modern industrial state. Japan's navy, army, and air force had not merely lost the Pacific War but ceased to exist in the process."[203] To win, Americans had to come together and focus their energies on destroying their enemy. This would have been all the harder to do—maybe just a bit harder, maybe a whole lot harder, but harder all the same—had they not prized their own country and countrymen and despised the enemy they were being asked to kill.

CHAPTER NINE

Overkill

THE LIMITS OF ADAPTIVE BIASES

The excessive increase of anything often causes a reaction in the opposite direction; and this is the case not only in the seasons and in vegetable and animal life, but above all in forms of government.

—PLATO

The unleashed power of the atom bomb has changed everything except our modes of thinking, and thus we drift toward unparalleled catastrophes.

—ALBERT EINSTEIN

SO FAR IN THE BOOK, I have breezily illustrated a variety of ways that biases can offer advantages and bring a competitive edge in strategic interactions. The primary goal was to point out that, at least sometimes, biases can be good. However, this is not to deny that biases can also be bad. In some instances, biases can be very bad indeed, as the existing literature has long been at pains to demonstrate—for example, overconfidence exacerbating the causes of World War I, the fundamental attribution error undermining trust in the Cold War, or the in-group/out-group bias fanning the flames of ethnic hatred among neighbors in the breakup of Yugoslavia. What is critical to realize is that, like most of our behavioral dispositions, cognitive biases are context dependent. Rather than being fixed traits regardless of the situation, they are flexible traits contingent upon circumstances. The challenge is to understand *when* biases may be good or bad—the conditions under which they bring advantages or disadvantages, the level of bias that may be optimal in a given setting, and the threshold beyond which they become detrimental.

This chapter will explore what one might call the "dark side" of strategic instincts, and generalizes to all three biases: healthy confidence becoming hubris and arrogance, attribution error becoming paranoia and preemption, and in-group/out-group bias fueling prejudice and discrimination. As with many things in nature, there are positive and negative aspects to evolved traits. The lion is a majestic hunter, but to survive it must kill. The cuckoo grows into a beautiful portent of spring, but only after throwing all of the other chicks out of its nest. Humans are the epitome of a cooperative and intelligent species, but have used those very traits to oppress the weak, commit genocide, and design nuclear weapons. Wherever one finds good things, bad things are often lurking too. But that does not invalidate the good. The book as a whole focuses on the positives of cognitive biases—precisely because they have been almost completely overlooked in international relations, while the negatives have been done to death—but this chapter will remind us about the danger of the negatives as well. I illustrate these dangers explicitly by revisiting the Pacific War to explore how a bias, when extreme, can lead both sides awry. This serves two purposes.

First, the chapter explores and emphasizes an all-important theoretical point of the book that while biases can be useful *in moderation*, they can become counterproductive and damaging in extremis. Both Japanese and American military effectiveness and strategy were undermined when biased beliefs about themselves and the enemy became excessive. Here, the point is that excessive biases bring *material* disadvantages.

Second, the chapter introduces a new question. Regardless of whether biases are useful or not in promoting military effectiveness, what are the effects of the bias on *moral* behavior? One could argue that whatever the direct effects of the in-group/out-group bias on material outcomes (whether positive or negative), excessive in-group sacrifice or excessive out-group brutality only serve to undermine strategic success via domestic or international repercussions. Here, the point is that excessive biases again bring *material* disadvantages, but this time via the consequences of immoral behavior—among the public, the adversary, allies, or third parties.

Rethinking the Pacific War: Excessive Biases in a Brutal War

In chapter 8 I argued that in the United States' Pacific campaign of World War II, a measure of in-group cohesion and out-group animosity was fundamental for public support and the war effort at home, for combat effectiveness among soldiers, sailors, and airmen in the field, and for resolve and commitment among U.S. leaders. However, the in-group/out-group bias could be taken to extremes, on both sides, which rendered it no longer useful, counterproductive, or morally suspect.

In this chapter, I first explore excesses on the Japanese side, in which in-group sacrifice and out-group demonization often went far beyond the limits of helping public support or military effectiveness, and show how unfettered group biases—both in-group and out-group—not only failed to offer strategic advantages but actually worked strongly against them. Arguably, it led the Japanese to pursue the war for a whole further year—the most costly of the war for both sides—when it was already clear they could not win. The point of this chapter, therefore, is to emphasize the point that while *in moderation* biases can reap strategic advantages, when they are *excessive* they become liabilities and ultimately can be counterproductive—in both material and moral dimensions.

I then turn to excesses on the American side, in which out-group enmity and demonization sometimes stretched the limits of achieving any increments in public support or military effectiveness and arguably broke it. I focus on excessive *out-group* bias on the American side, because this was much more obviously problematic than any excessive in-group bias.

Japanese Excesses: In-Group Superiority and Extreme Sacrifice

In the previous chapter I suggested that the in-group/out-group bias facilitated thinking and action that helped the United States win the war—or at least to win it more quickly. Given Japan's own strong in-group loyalty and out-group belligerence, one might think that the in-group/out-group bias should have helped *them* as well, perhaps even more than the Americans. It some cases it surely did provide military advantages—for example in their willingness to defend territory to the last man and their unbending readiness to attack enemy soldiers. However, in other cases it plainly did not. Japan took both in-group sacrifice and out-group brutality to extremes that clearly undermined its own strategic and military efficacy.

EXCESSIVE IN-GROUP BIAS IN THE JAPANESE PUBLIC

It is hard to overstate the devotion of Japanese civilians, and especially Japanese soldiers, to their nation and in particular to their emperor. Strong traditions of self-sacrifice for the greater good, and the elevation of the Japanese people above others, stem from the state religion Shinto, which emphasized the "unbroken imperial sovereignty of the living god, the emperor, the divine origin of the Japanese race, and the manifest destiny of Japan."[1] Hirohito, the 124th emperor of Japan, represented the direct line of Japanese emperors since Jimmu, the founding emperor in the seventh century BC and supposed descendant of the sun-goddess Amaterasu. Although human, emperors throughout the centuries retained an almost godlike status and represented both religious and political authority in Japan.[2]

On top of this were the cultural traditions of Japanese society itself, rooted in "the ancestral and feudal samurai code that was reinterpreted and refashioned as Bushido by nineteenth-century militarists—the idea that the warrior values of a medieval elite could be superimposed upon the entire new nation-state of modern Japan."[3] In effect, all Japanese soldiers, sailors, and airmen were supposed to live up to the samurai ideal of unflinching bravery and ultimate sacrifice. If defeated, officers were expected to carry out the ritual suicide of hara-kiri. These ideas were strongly entrenched in Japanese society and had been reinforced by many years of official civilian and military policy and practice.

In-group bias generates the belief that one's own group is inherently superior to others in its qualities and capacities, and this was overt in Japanese society. The Japanese "dwelled at inordinate length on their own racial and cultural superiority."[4] They had long been encouraged to believe in the preeminence of the Yamato race, which was deemed far more important than any of the other Asian peoples and entitled them to territory and control over vast regions of Asia. This led to "a homegrown militarism," which was "built on the Japanese people's belief in their national uniqueness and their heaven-granted mandate to assume leadership in east Asia."[5] In the 1930s, the Japanese government and emperor actively promoted this vision of Japan as a super race capable of uniting together into an unstoppable cultural and military power. Individual self-interest would be subordinated to the greater destiny of the nation. It was in large part this powerful in-group thinking that encouraged Japan to launch the war in the first place, and it was partly this as well that prevented them from ending the war when hundreds of thousands of civilians and soldiers were being killed, and Japan was clearly losing.

Western propaganda depicted Japanese people and their devotion to their nation as like "cattle or robots," yet Japan's own government, broadcasting for home and foreign audiences, "harped incessantly on" about Japan being "100 million hearts beating as one."[6] While Western sources were essentializing the Japanese as automata following a unified purpose, this was actually what they were striving for. As Dower noted, "What the vast majority of Westerners believed the Japanese to be coincided with what the Japanese ruling elites hoped they would become."[7] While in principle this was a powerful and unifying force, the outright subordination of individual identity and freedom to the will of the government and emperor had gone too far for Japan to survive the war.

While such beliefs were widespread and deeply held, there were of course detractors. For example, the Japanese government worried a great deal about a communist revolution like those that had taken place in Russia and China. They evidently could not rely on complete universal deference to national unity, especially once the war began to take its toll on the home islands. This was evidenced by the existence of a formidable military police—"a prime instrument for repression of dissent."[8] In April 1945, four hundred people were arrested for suspicion of advocating ending the war. Whatever checks and balances might exist in a democracy allowing dissent from excessive governmental coercion, such restraints were severely curtailed in Japan. While it made no sense for the Japanese to continue fighting, strong in-group biases prevented them from breaking ranks.

EXCESSIVE IN-GROUP BIAS
IN THE JAPANESE MILITARY

While racial logic was widespread and explicit among the Japanese people as a whole, it was often stronger still in the military. The Japanese army in particular was "infected by the spirit of intense racialist nationalism."[9] With military leaders wielding a powerful influence within the government's decision-making structure, this appears to have contributed to Japan's imperial ambitions in the first place, the decision to attack the United States, and the strategies chosen to continue the war against a foe that was expected to eventually give up in the face of the superior will and fighting spirit of the Japanese.

In chapter 8 I argued that military training in the United States inculcated a strong in-group allegiance and discipline that were vital for success. Of course, Japan's military did the same thing, but by a number of accounts it reached a level of ruthlessness and barbarity that undermined rather than underlay military cohesion. "If such behaviour reflected a psyche common to most armies," Max Hastings wrote, "the Japanese carried it to extremes unknown elsewhere."[10] Hanson details how, in contrast to a balance of discipline and individualism crucial to American military effectiveness, Japan "relied on ironclad obedience."[11]

This obedience led not only to perverse behavior among the troops but to perverse decisions at the top. The warrior code was as or more potent among senior commanders, and they would defer without question to authority. In planning meetings around the Pacific, high command issued orders to their commanders without debate as to alternatives or Japan's overall strategy. While many officers later recounted reservations about deployments, tactics, and strategy, at the time they tended to leave them unspoken in deference to higher authority. Hanson identified this as a recurrent problem in the navy, where there was "an institutional hierarchy within the Japanese imperial command that discouraged initiative and independent thinking."[12] The great personal sacrifices and risks taken by commanders and "the unquestioning acceptance of a tactical blueprint from on high were disciplined and soldierly, but not necessarily militarily efficacious."[13] At the Battle of Midway, for example, several senior Japanese officers had "private reservations" about their strategy but dared not voice them.[14] Similar problems bedeviled the military leadership of ground forces as well, as a battalion commander on Okinawa later reflected: "The gravest weakness of *bushido*, Captain Kouichi Ito believed, was that 'no one was allowed to say what he really thought, so that we could not explore better ways to do things.'"[15] Without alternative options they were left to simply wade into slaughter.

In addition to this broad influence of excessive in-group bias on Japan's ambitions, expectations, and decisions, there are also many specific manifestations of in-group sacrifice that in fact proved counterproductive in the military. For example, honor and bravery were so strongly revered that Japanese soldiers who had allowed themselves to be captured, and then were recaptured or found their way back to their own side, were executed.[16] As another example, wounded soldiers blowing themselves up along with the enemy might seem like exemplars of eking out every last possible contribution to the war effort. But in fact it seemed to have had much more detrimental consequences to their own side, since "this would mean not only the loss of his own life but [also] . . . the lives of future wounded Japanese who might otherwise have been saved."[17] Americans would quickly learn to kill them or leave them to die rather than taking any chances.

Another practice that might seem to be the epitome of in-group solidarity and bravery was the infamous "banzai" charges carried out by Japanese soldiers—suicidal frontal assaults accompanied by fierce yelling and wave after wave of troops pushing forward irrespective of resistance and losses. At first glance a fearsome show of resolve that one can imagine could have a powerful psychological if not military effect, banzai charges were usually ineffective. They certainly came at an inordinate cost. The largest banzai charge of the war, at Saipan on 7 July 1944, not only consisted of a large force of soldiers but was followed by phalanxes of Japanese casualties, hobbling forward, inadequately armed and some with no weapons at all, to die alongside their comrades. On the one hand, it was a remarkable show of determination and bravery, but on the other hand it was a suicidal farce doomed to failure and annihilation. As one observer put it, "As regards its only conceivable object, suicide, General Saito's banzai had been an unqualified success."[18] Some American soldiers said that they came to welcome such banzai attacks because they normally signaled that victory was close at hand and merely allowed them to kill the enemy more effectively, rather than having to winkle them out of bunkers and caves with grenades and flamethrowers. Whether or not they achieved any military goal, one thing for sure was that participants of banzai charges would never be available again for any future part of the war effort.

Finally, there were the kamikaze attacks—perhaps the most infamous symbol of self-sacrifice in war—which first began to be seen in the defense of the Philippines in October 1944. By the end of the war, 4,000 kamikaze pilots had died. By some measures this method of attack was effective. For example, they could be more accurate in hitting ships than by dropping bombs or torpedoes from afar, and they certainly caused significant death and destruction, killing some 5,000 Americans, sinking or crippling dozens of U.S. vessels, and causing damage to many more. However, it is unclear whether their one-off hits were a better strategy than the multiple attacks they might have been able to make over future conventional sorties. In the certain loss of pilots and planes, kamikaze attacks were incredibly costly, if not actually counterproductive, to Japan's military effectiveness.

Up and down the military hierarchy, the Japanese "bushido" code made officers and men supremely devoted to the cause and to their units. But whatever advantages this samurai philosophy may have had for unit cohesion on the battlefield (it was arguably rote compliance to authority rather than genuine cohesion), it ultimately seemed to be outweighed by the decimation it brought to their own ranks over and above American efforts to achieve the same thing. In the face of defeat, soldiers in most wars can withdraw or retreat to fight another day, or at least surrender and survive to help rebuild their country after the war. The bushido code meant that Japanese soldiers and commanders fought to the death as a matter of principle, regardless of the overall benefit of defending their particular piece of turf in the context of the war effort as a whole. Often, it was just a senseless waste of experienced manpower. As Hanson noted, "Brilliant admirals are still needed after their ships blow up. Seasoned pilots are more valuable as instructors than as suicide bombers . . . and the expertise of skilled generals is lost when they disembowel themselves."[19]

As hard as the Americans were trying to kill Japanese soldiers, sailors, and airmen, many were doing their work for them, including senior commanders who led suicidal charges or carried out ritual suicide rather than surrender. Here, any in-group bias toward duty, conformity, and sacrifice had gone too far. In comparing Japanese and American courage, Miller concluded that "certain belief systems may just be too good at getting people to prefer the promise of eternal bliss to present life, or to prefer death to the threat of a life of irredeemable shame."[20] Hastings put it more bluntly: Japanese officers had to show "a willingness to fight heedless of circumstances," which ultimately resulted in an army led by men who "possessed the hearts of lions, but the brains of sheep."[21]

EXCESSIVE IN-GROUP BIAS IN JAPANESE LEADERS

The subordination of the individual to the wider group and nation was a problem just as significant among the elite as it was among citizens and soldiers. The Japanese government hamstrung itself in its elevation of military leaders in governmental decision-making and in its deference to higher authority in the emperor: "Rigid hierarchy and complete submission of the individual to the divinity of the Japanese emperor meant that the wisdom of a small cadre of militarists shaped policy largely without ratification or even knowledge of the Japanese people, who were never envisioned as free persons with unique rights that were natural at birth and protected by the state."[22] Even the prime minister himself, therefore, was at the mercy of the military elite. Hastings contends that "Tojo, a supposed dictator, possessed far less authority in militarist Japan than did Winston Churchill in democratic Britain."[23] Instead, Japanese policy was devised and implemented by military leaders, and there was a strong norm for alternative viewpoints from civilian leaders to be left unspoken or, if they were voiced, derided. The emperor himself rarely ever intervened to question the military leaders' decisions and influence policy but rather was present to signal his seal of approval—and in so doing apparently vindicated their plans.

At the same time, the government had great power to impose their beliefs and whatever policies emerged on the masses. While the United States could engage in propaganda to persuade its citizens to fight, in democracies such efforts are always scrutinized and limited—to some extent. In Japan, by contrast, a government led by the military and a divine emperor had enormous power and control over its citizens' information and perceptions. As Pape observed, "The state could indoctrinate the population, instilling belief in the evil nature of its enemies and the value of sacrifice for national goals."[24] Such power can help a state achieve unity and compliance, but often at the expense of propagating falsehoods, generating support for flawed policies, and missing out on the opportunity for feedback and improvement.

The extent to which Japanese leaders demanded the subordination of individual interests to those of the collective clearly became so extreme as to harm the nation and its war effort. At home, the hardships of war visited upon its citizens, including declining food and resources, let alone devastation, homelessness, injury, and death from the air, were borne with steadfast resolve by a people with faith that Japan and the emperor were taking the right course and would ultimately prevail. In fact, however, citizens were merely absorbing monumental suffering to sustain a war effort that was already doomed from 1944, and which made no impact on government decision-making.[25]

At the front, meanwhile, official policy and often direct orders served to undermine military effectiveness. Instead of living to fight another day, soldiers would follow explicit instructions to carry out suicidal assaults or take their own lives rather than risk capture. Sailors would go down with their ships, even sometimes swimming away from American rescue craft. Airmen would take off on one-way kamikaze missions. Even large numbers of civilians would commit suicide as American forces approached, having been advised by the government of the greater horrors should they fall into the hands of the Americans. Across their sprawling Asia-Pacific empire, "the Japanese were told they were fighting a holy war against a demonic foe, and many died believing they were giving their lives for a noble cause—'mad dogs' to their enemies, but martyrs in their own eyes and heroes in the eyes of their countrymen and countrywomen."[26]

Herbert Bix's Pulitzer Prize–winning biography of Hirohito suggests that the Japanese emperor was more than a passive figure. Despite his silence in cabinet meetings, Bix argues that he exercised significant influence over Japanese policy and the military in other ways.[27] But rather than using this to counteract militarist policies, up until the very end he actually used his power to promote them. As Budiansky wrote, "Far from agonizing over his people's mounting suffering as American forces pressed relentlessly on toward the Japanese homeland, far from advocating surrender once Japan's defeat had become a near certainty in the fall of 1944, the Emperor exhorted his commanders again and again to fight to the death."[28] To him, the willingness of his people to die in thousands and millions only confirmed "imperial destiny," as death for the emperor was "the greatest virtue that his subjects could aspire to."[29] This, surely, was in-group devotion taken too far for the good of anyone.

The excesses of in-group sacrifice would have seen a historic crescendo had the planned American invasion of Japan—Operation Downfall—taken place. Japanese leaders were certainly preparing for it that way. The infamous "Ketsugo" plan, devised by the Japanese government, called on all civilians, men and women, young and old alike, to participate in a suicidal last-ditch defense of the homeland. Japanese propaganda lauded it "The Glorious Death of One Hundred Million."[30] Thankfully for both sides, with anticipated casualties at the time running to hundreds of thousands of Americans and possibly millions of Japanese (if its own government's plan came to fruition), Operation Downfall never took place.

Yet the sheer intensity of commitment to in-group sacrifice is perhaps most prominently displayed in the eleventh-hour activities of the government before the surrender of Japan. Many in the Japanese military, including the all-powerful military leaders in the cabinet, wanted to keep fighting until the end and never surrender under any circumstances whatsoever. They saw Japan as unbeaten in a thousand years. Why end that now? Following the atomic detonation at Hiroshima, the emperor and civilian leaders called a cabinet meeting to discuss surrender, but the military refused to even attend. The government remained in limbo.

On 9 August there was a Supreme War Council meeting. This time the military leaders came because the massive Soviet invasion into Manchuria had begun. News of the second bomb dropped on Nagasaki came during the meeting. Even with these cataclysmic developments, some of the military representatives advocated no surrender unless there were certain conditions. But, unusually, the emperor at this point made a plea to halt the madness. At this, "they no longer blocked the civilians' efforts to make peace, although they had the power to do so."[31] Pape notes that "Hirohito's actions in August were the only direct political interventions of his reign."[32] It is remarkable that it took the unprecedented step of the emperor himself to put an end to the military's continued desire to keep fighting, despite two atomic weapons. Had he not done so, Japan might well have continued the war for some time to come. Even *after* surrender had finally been agreed to by the government, large elements of the military tried to resist it. On 14 August, there was an attempted coup by hundreds of army officers and men, who stormed the imperial palace, "aiming to subvert negotiations entirely and fight to the bitter end."[33] A recording of the speech announcing the decision had to be smuggled out of the palace. The following day at noon, 15 August 1945, the emperor's voice was broadcast to the nation, announcing surrender. It was the first time in history that a Japanese emperor had given a public speech, and Japanese civilians had never heard his voice. Around the country, people stopped what they were doing to listen, "stunned and dismayed."[34]

Japanese Excesses: Out-Group Dehumanization and Atrocities

In this chapter, I focus on Japanese *in*-group bias and American *out*-group bias, partly because they offer such striking examples of excess and partly to avoid simplistic stereotypes (that, at least in Western eyes, the Americans were always in the right and the Japanese were always the aggressors). Nevertheless, it would be remiss to end this section on Japan without some observations about out-group biases as well. Having stressed overzealous *in*-group behavior on the Japanese side, Japan's *out*-group perceptions also significantly damaged their military and strategic effectiveness, if not also helping to draw them into the war in the first place, and then prevent them from ending it for so long.

EXCESSIVE OUT-GROUP BIAS IN THE JAPANESE PUBLIC

The most obvious place to start would be the widespread maltreatment and death visited upon vast numbers of Asian peoples by the Japanese, which had a long history but rose to epic proportions in the 1930s. Although precise figures are not known, they are widely understood to be in the order of many millions of victims, especially in China.[35] While cataclysmic and unavoidably part of the story of out-group enmity, more relevant to the question of military effectiveness here are perceptions of the American adversary.

The first example is, ironically, the projection of tendencies toward extreme out-group aggression onto the Americans—a belief that they were fundamentally evil and depraved. The "Tokyo propaganda machine" had long informed Japanese soldiers and civilians alike that "if the Americans invaded their land, and were successful, the Japanese would become slaves. The Americans, said Radio Tokyo, would ravish the women and children and torture the rest."[36] There was a campaign to spread the idea that American soldiers in particular were "blood-sotted killers."[37] On Guadalcanal, the Japanese high command informed its soldiers that "the Americans on this island are not ordinary troops, but Marines, a special force recruited from jails and insane asylums for blood lust."[38] They warned that they would routinely mutilate and kill prisoners. Americans were also widely said to kill prisoners by "laying them on the ground and running them over with tanks and bulldozers."[39]

One might dismiss this as mantra that would hardly be believed. Yet, one wartime study found that 84 percent of captured Japanese soldiers "had expected to be killed or tortured by the Allies if taken prisoner."[40] Among Japanese civilians at large, in 1945, "more than two-thirds of the population expected enslavement, starvation, or annihilation if Japan were to lose the war."[41] Mass suicides by both servicemen and civilians to avoid being captured were common, and survivors often explicitly stated stories of American brutality as their motivation. It was a pattern repeated across the Pacific, from the Marianas to Okinawa, and one that increasingly involved civilians as U.S. forces approached the Japanese home islands. The first major such event was at Saipan, where "at the end of the battle hundreds of civilians had gathered on the cliffs at Marpi Point, the last remaining bit of territory held by the Japanese. There mothers had strangled their children or jumped with them into the sea. Soldiers had shot down civilians and then killed themselves. Most of the Japanese crowded together on that little bit of land had committed suicide rather than face capture by the Americans."[42]

On Geruma, in the Okinawan islands, American soldiers found "the bodies of hundreds of civilians and soldiers. Some had been strangled. Some had been killed. Some had been shot. It was the same on the other islands. In Tokashiki, the soldiers discovered one small valley where every person had either killed or been killed in this suicidal rampage. Whole families had committed suicide by grenade."[43] The indigenous Okinawans had long been viewed as inferior by mainland Japanese, and during the invasion the Japanese army treated them appallingly, including using civilians as human shields. In March 1945 the army urged them to commit mass suicide, apparently in part because they were concerned they might help the invaders. The explanation given to the Okinawans themselves was that they would "escape the horrors and humiliations the Americans had in store for them: rape, torture, and murder."[44]

Japanese military commanders sometimes ordered local civilians, as well as their soldiers, to commit suicide rather than surrender, but which Japanese soldiers often had to carry out, and by which means they "ended up slaughtering the very people they were presumedly [sic] protecting."[45] There was no conceivable means by which this behavior served to help Japan's cause. If anything it just brought down the wrath of the Americans ever harder upon them (film of civilians killing themselves or being killed by Japanese soldiers "became part of the regular indoctrination program for Marines").[46] Certainly, none of these people—whether soldiers or civilians—could contribute to the war effort now.

EXCESSIVE OUT-GROUP BIAS
IN THE JAPANESE MILITARY

Japan's excessive out-group prejudice is starkly illustrated by their own (actual) horrific treatment of prisoners of war. Compared to the 4 percent of British and Americans captured by Germans that died in captivity, for those captured by the Japanese the death toll was a shocking 27 percent (and 33 percent for Americans alone).[47] This amounted to some 36,000 Anglo-American POWs (compared to "only" somewhere around 9,000 in German captivity, where almost twice as many fell into enemy hands).[48] The Japanese regarded surrendering soldiers as cowards and thus special targets for abuse. Combatants and civilians alike were, in Lawrence James's words, "systematically humiliated and maltreated in what the victims interpreted as a form of racial revenge; and some were wantonly murdered."[49] From among those who survived emerged a steady stream of thousands of memoirs and books that described the brutality of Japanese slave labor and prisoner-of-war camps in all their horrific detail. If it did not negatively affect the Japanese military effort during the war, it certainly negatively affected sentiment toward Japan for many decades after.

Another important result of out-group bias among the Japanese military seems to have been to massively underestimate the resilience and determination of the Americans. The United States' "implacable resolution" and "commitment, indeed ruthlessness," were only finally impressed upon Japanese leaders toward the end of the war, as Japan fell into ruins under the relentless onslaught.[50] This underestimation of the out-group's willpower can help in understanding Japan's decision to attack the United States in the first place (expecting, as they did, a negotiated solution short of all-out war), as well as account for the prolongation of the war. It proved a remarkably persistent misperception. Evidence to the contrary was there to see from Wake Atoll, Guadalcanal, Midway, Iwo Jima, and any number of other battles. To maintain this belief beyond all the evidence implicates the workings of far too strong a bias in derogatory perceptions of the enemy other.

As many argue, Japan might conceivably have ended the war a whole year earlier in 1944, once it was already clear they could not win. However, with a powerful aversion to surrender and a belief in their superior resolve, they could cling to the belief that the United States, or its citizens and soldiers, would tire of the war and seek a negotiated resolution—allowing Japan to keep many of their possessions in Asia. This was a deeply flawed perception, reinforced if not generated by an excessive in-group/out-group bias, and it would bring horrendous further costs to both sides in the many more months of war to come.

EXCESSIVE OUT-GROUP BIAS IN JAPANESE LEADERS

Excessive out-group bias is perhaps most patently explicit among Japan's leaders themselves. Hanson wrote that "Japan would live and die by the race card—defining (and demonizing) America as 'white' and thus Japan as a kindred but clearly superior 'yellow' people."[51] As Dower was at pains to point out, racism can be found on both sides, but on the American side it was to a large extent elicited by the conflict, the treachery of Pearl Harbor, and the mounting atrocities committed by the Japanese foe. By contrast, Japanese racism was overt, institutionalized national policy, and not only preceded the conflict but underlay their entire strategy of territorial expansion—Japan's manifest destiny.

Having argued that their goal was to liberate Asian nations from white imperialist rule, Japan belied their own arguments in the horrific treatment they themselves directed at the variety of peoples within Japan's growing empire. Hanson wrote that "the entire creed of Japanese militarism rested on the implicit assumption of innate Japanese racial superiority over its 'inferior' Asian subject peoples."[52] Other Asians were seen and treated with even greater disdain than the Americans, and "Japan's armies had roamed Asia at will, killing on a Homeric scale."[53]

An indication of the extent of out-group sentiment was the willingness to develop and use chemical and biological weapons to indiscriminately kill adversaries. The Japanese had already used anthrax and plague bacteria against the Chinese, and during the war it made an industrial-scale effort to develop biological weapons in Harbin, Manchuria, accompanied by horrific human experiments.[54] They also deliberately targeted civilians, not just during military operations but in explicit acts of revenge. After the early American Doolittle air raid on Japan, when fifty civilians were killed, the Japanese avenged the deaths by killing tens of thousands of Chinese.[55] Over a period of many years, the Japanese armed forces, encouraged by the government and supported by the public, had taken out-group hostility to a level rarely matched in the annals of history and that continues to sour relations with neighbors to this day. It was excessive in the extreme—and was counterproductive to their national survival, let alone the war effort. Millions of Japanese themselves paid for it with their lives.

American Excesses: Pushing the Limits

On the American side, it is not hard to find instances in which in-group favoritism and out-group animosity certainly appeared excessive, as has been emphasized, for example, in John Dower's *War without Mercy*, although arguably they pale in comparison to Japanese excesses such as those outlined above.[56] What is harder to show is whether—seemingly excessive or not—this worked for or against the American war effort.

Amid the tide of Japanese atrocities around Asia, many cases of American brutality were reported as well. Scholars emphasize that no moral equivalence should be drawn, since Japanese atrocities were so prolific and premeditated whereas American atrocities were rarer and usually violated official policy.[57] Nevertheless, they did occur and the goal here is simply to show that, when they did, extreme out-group bias could be counterproductive, via their material as well as moral consequences.

EXCESSIVE OUT-GROUP BIAS IN
THE AMERICAN PUBLIC

Dower argued that "to the majority of Japanese, as to the Anglo-Americans, atrocities committed by one's own side were episodic, while the enemy's brutal acts were systematic and revealed a fundamentally perverse national character."[58] As predicted by the in-group/out-group bias, identical behavior was deplored when it was carried out by the enemy but excused or explained away when carried out by one's own side. Moreover, such behavior tended to be seen as representative or typical—but only of the other side. Each new event thus served to corroborate existing out-group prejudice.[59]

While the American public had little impact on the fast-moving and distant events on Pacific battlefields, they did elect and support political leaders at home who were running the war. One could argue, therefore, that any excesses of out-group bias among the public helped to facilitate unnecessarily brutal policies of the war being enacted or continued. For example, the firebombing of Japanese population centers might have been halted had there been sufficient public outcry in the United States. But there was none. Before the war, "while the nation was at peace, Americans repeatedly condemned the bombing of civilians—which was already happening around the globe—as fundamentally immoral. But after Pearl Harbor, ethical inhibitions were largely discarded."[60]

As the war progressed, sentiment became strong for the destruction not only of Japan's military but of the Japanese nation and its people as well. Reaching a crescendo in 1945, *Time* magazine "called the firebombing of Tokyo 'a dream come true,' because 'properly kindled, Japanese cities will burn like autumn leaves.'"[61] Opinion polls found that significant segments of the American public "consistently supported the 'annihilation' or 'extermination' of the Japanese as a people, while a comparable percentage were in favour of severe retribution after Japan had been defeated."[62] One poll in December 1944, asking what should be done with Japan after the war, found that 13 percent responded "kill all Japanese," and 33 percent advocated "destroying Japan as a political entity."[63] These polls are usually reported to illustrate the remarkable segments of the population that were extreme in their support for killing Japanese civilians, but it also reveals that "others"—in fact the majority—did not harbor beliefs quite as strong as that. For most, their views were still dominated by outrage and a willingness to support the necessary evils of war but fell short of outright genocide.

Nevertheless, support for extreme strategies persisted. A poll in March 1945 found that 30 percent of the American public even approved of "using poison gas against the Japanese," if it would shorten the war (65 percent disapproved).[64] More surprisingly still, *after* the war, 23 percent of Americans expressed a wish that the United States had dropped "many more" atomic bombs "before Japan had a chance to surrender."[65] If one sees the bombing campaign against Japanese cities as irrelevant to the defeat of Japan, then it can be considered an excess of out-group animosity implicitly supported, and thus permitted to continue, by the American public. At the time, however, the American public had little reason to know whether the bombing would contribute to the defeat of Japan, or at least end the war more quickly. The prevailing view was that it would—or at least might. Moreover, American leaders themselves were arguing that it was an important part of the strategy, so the public can hardly be implicated in the decision to pursue or continue the air offensive. Similar arguments go for other controversial strategies, such as the unrestricted submarine campaign against Japanese civilian as well as military shipping, and most obviously the nuclear attacks—about which the public knew nothing at all until after it had already happened.

What the public did know largely came from a government and media on a war footing. There was, therefore, the opportunity for vast manipulation of information and perceptions, arguably inflaming the in-group/out-group bias to unnatural proportions. Major propaganda campaigns were launched to remind people of the need for American unity and the defense of its liberal ideals, as well as to disparage the Japanese nation and people. The military commissioned Hollywood director Frank Capra to produce a series of films called "Why We Fight," which were shown to troops shipping out to war. They were so successful that they started to be played in public theaters as well, becoming "classics of wartime cinematic propaganda," one of which won an Academy Award.[66] The films emphasized the enemy's supposed deep-seated lust for power and their brutal treatment of populations elsewhere in Asia. They stressed the idea that Japanese civilians and soldiers were cut from the same cloth, essentialized in the stereotype of obedient masses "devoid of individual identity," fanatical, and brutal.[67]

Whether true or not, it raises the prospect that the public would have supported the war *less* had their in-group/out-group bias not been stoked by government and media rhetoric. Dower emphasized the powerful role of propaganda in the Pacific War, including evidence of the strategic use and timing of information to maximize effects at home. The U.S. government released information in a way that was "carefully orchestrated" to reveal Japanese outrages at propitious moments.[68] But since Dower's argument was to highlight racism on both sides—a controversial or misguided claim to many Americans—he may have pushed some of the points about American brutality and manipulation too hard, relative to those on the other side, in an effort to make the point.[69] For one thing, the propagandists in the United States never had to make anything up, as the Japanese continued to leave a trail of atrocities across Asia and the Pacific, not least the Rape of Nanking in 1937, the killing of millions of Chinese civilians throughout the 1930s and 1940s, and the brutal treatment of POWs, among a litany of others. After the news broke of the Bataan Death March in 1942, during which thousands of Americans and Filipinos had died or been executed, "the floodgates were opened, and a torrent of Japanese atrocity stories poured forth that continued unabated into the months and even years that followed Japan's surrender."[70]

Having emphasized the effect of Pearl Harbor in the previous chapter in triggering an immediate and massive antipathy toward the Japanese, anti-Japanese sentiment did not emerge out of nothing on 7 December 1941. Rather, the attack gave voice to an undercurrent of long-held animosity. As Dower documented, "In the United States and Britain, the Japanese were more hated than the Germans before as well as after Pearl Harbor, not least because of mounting press coverage of Japan's brutal actions elsewhere in Asia and especially China. On this, there was no dispute among contemporary observers. The Japanese were perceived as a race apart, even a species apart—and an overpoweringly monolithic one at that."[71] Posters in America depicted *Germans* in a variety of demeaning ways, but they "retained human form," whereas the Japanese were often depicted not as humans at all but rather as "smiling, brutal rat and monkey men."[72] Whatever boost it gave to public support, if the in-group/out-group bias was not excessive on its own, the wartime propaganda efforts certainly pushed it to new heights.

EXCESSIVE OUT-GROUP BIAS IN THE AMERICAN MILITARY

As for the American military, out-group animosity could sometimes contribute to behavior that was immediately counterproductive on the battlefield. For example, one soldier lamented his comrade shooting a Japanese soldier coming out of a pillbox with his hands on his head: "Not only was this a vicious thing to do but it was asinine. You can bet your life that none of the others are going to come out."[73] While Japanese soldiers would often rather die than surrender, many Marine units learned to avoid taking any prisoners anyway, given the knowledge that sometimes they would pretend to surrender and then kill their captors. Although this was "not official policy . . . over wide reaches of the Asian battleground it was everyday practice."[74] Even when prisoners *were* taken, they did not always survive. Bourke reports an intelligence memo saying "it was necessary to bribe troops with promises of ice cream and three days leave before they could be persuaded to keep prisoners alive."[75]

Suspicion of surrendering or wounded soldiers may have been vital to preserve the lives of American troops, who were frequently exposed to ambushes from fake surrenders and grenade-wielding or booby-trapped wounded soldiers. However, it could clearly be counterproductive as well. One consequence was a vicious circle by which one practice begat the other—Japanese soldiers were even less likely to surrender than they already were if they believed they might be killed anyway. Such practices could become habitual even when there was little danger, so that "actions that had been adopted as essential to survival," Linderman observed, "then became so ingrained that they persisted where survival was no longer at stake."[76] Apart from the ethical dimension and the blatant violation of the laws of war, prisoners could also be vital for obtaining intelligence, and this opportunity was often forsaken. Others would also argue that, irrespective of military efficacy, killing the wounded or prisoners was simply morally unacceptable under any circumstances and in its own way undermined the American cause.

In the fighting itself, military practice could at times become blurred with murderous vengeance. By one account, some soldiers tired of the mechanized slaughter of wave after wave of Japanese soldiers and, given the opportunity, preferred "choking them to death when they could have shot them."[77] Another soldier declared, "I had resigned from the human race . . . I just wanted to kill."[78] Japanese ears, fingers, and other body parts became prized trophies, not only among the soldiers themselves but also when mailed home to friends and family—a practice widely reported and "coveted for a time from war front to home front."[79] While not everyone engaged in the practice, many acquiesced. Dower notes that "it is virtually inconceivable, however, that teeth, ears, and skulls could have been collected from German or Italian war dead and publicized in the Anglo-American countries without provoking an uproar; and in this we have yet another inkling of the racial dimensions of the war."[80] While morally outrageous, such behavior was also hardly helpful to the cause, except to the extent that it may have instilled fear among Japanese soldiers or motivation to kill among Americans (many cited it as such). But it suggests that incentives other than merely military objectives were gathering momentum.

Certainly, out-group prejudice and animosity were reaching extreme levels. Linderman detailed how "successive stages in the dehumanization of the Japanese traced a series of culture-bound propositions that consecutively diminished the adversary."[81] The first was simply incredulity, and the idea that "nobody can understand the Japs," because their atrocities were often so arbitrary and sometimes even carried out with humor. Next was the idea that "the Japs are crazy," since their suicidal tactics and brutality must mean they are suffering some kind of "mental aberration." But gradually these notions changed into more explicit forms of dehumanization, the first being that "the Japs aren't human," with numerous manifestations of this sentiment among soldiers at the front. This became refined into the notion that "the Japs are animals." Many images emerged, including swarms of bees, jackals, lice, dogs, apes, and, most often, rats or monkeys. One soldier reported that Marines wished "they were fighting against Germans. They are human beings, like us. But the Japs are like animals."[82] While commonplace among the fighting men, the epithets extended to the top. General Holland Smith asserted that Japanese soldiers "were taught to live and die like animals."[83] Admiral Halsey referred to them as "little yellow monkeys."[84] And the tendency was not limited to Americans. British general Sir William Slim called the Japanese "the most formidable fighting insect in history."[85] Australian General

Sir Thomas Blamey, addressing troops on New Guinea, declared "we have to exterminate these vermin if we and our families are to live."[86] Even Churchill referred to the nation as the "Japanese dog."[87] Dower stressed how the Allies "consistently emphasized the 'subhuman' nature of the Japanese, routinely turning to images of apes and vermin to convey this."[88] Whether or not this facilitated military objectives (Halsey claimed that his virulent language was to help "undermine the idea of Japanese invincibility"), it also appeared to ramp up the violence for its own sake.[89]

Finally, the costs of the brutality and killing could be high for the individuals involved. "Whatever the provocation," Linderman found, "to dehumanize the enemy had placed American soldiers on the path to their own dehumanization."[90] Thousands of soldiers suffered mental breakdowns and battle fatigue, which potentially afflicted anyone irrespective of rank, age, or background. Military authorities believed soldiers could deal with 200–240 days in combat, but the experience of soldiers on the ground suggested much lower figures. Marine veteran Eugene Sledge, whose memoirs became widely read after the war, gave newcomers 15 days before noticing "the Stare" on their faces that tended to follow the harrowing conditions of frontline duty. A study by psychologists following the Normandy landings in Europe found that after 30 days of combat a "soldier's effectiveness began to decline precipitously," and by 45 days soldiers "were close to a vegetative state."[91] Brits typically aimed to rotate units out after 12 days of combat, while many American troops in Europe ended up having to endure around 60. But in the Pacific, "the average Marine rifleman serving from Pearl Harbor to the Japanese surrender passed 120 days in combat."[92] The consequences were striking. In the brutal fighting on Okinawa, for example, while the United States suffered over 8,000 killed and 32,000 injured, there were also a staggering 26,000 "psychiatric casualties."[93]

EXCESSIVE OUT-GROUP BIAS IN AMERICAN LEADERS

Of the major decisions taken by American leaders that are often argued to have been excessive, three stand out: the internment of Japanese civilians in the United States, the firebombing of cities and civilians in Japan, and the use of nuclear weapons. Before discussing each of those in turn, it is worth noting one excess that *might* have been committed but was ultimately withdrawn from becoming a systematic strategy. In a significant divergence from behavior in the European theater, chemical and biological weapons were considered for use against Japan. In the end they were not, "primarily because of strong opposition by Churchill," lest Hitler be minded to copy the strategy.[94] People are sometimes doubtful about whether this was a genuine possibility, but there was at least one "conspicuous" exception that shows it was possible, and that was the "use of asphyxial gases against Japanese soldiers—and island civilians—in Okinawa's caves."[95] This was a decision that came from "at least as high as theatre headquarters."⁹⁶ Fortunately, the Allies chose to make no systematic use of chemical or biological weapons elsewhere in the war, and we should remember that, despite the level of out-group hostility that pervaded and grew among exasperated Western Allies as they approached Japan, they retained some lines that were not crossed. However, for many, the treatment of Japanese civilians in the United States, the area bombing of civilian population centers in Japan, and the use of nuclear weapons represented strategies that pushed boundaries very hard.

First, let us consider internment. Much has been written on the fate of ethnic Japanese civilians in the United States in World War II. At home, "war hysteria was not excessive," wrote historian Andrew Sinclair, "except for the 112,000 Japanese-Americans who lost their property and were herded into camps."⁹⁷ A more recent account by Richard Reeves puts the figure at over 120,000.⁹⁸ Around 40,000 Japanese citizens were interned (immigrants born in Japan), along with 80,000 second- or third-generation Japanese Americans—U.S. citizens by birth, mainly on the West Coast. President Roosevelt enacted this policy by executive order, interning all ethnic Japanese for the entire war in "relocation centers," concerned that they may act as spies or saboteurs. This was an especially notable decision given that American citizens of *German* descent were largely left alone (even German POWs shipped to the United States were given considerable freedoms later on). People have put the discrepancy down to Pearl Harbor and/or racism.

Either way, such extreme action had to be justified, and it could not be done without a bit of psychological mind bending. One U.S. general remarked: "The very fact that no sabotage has taken place is a disturbing and confirming indication that such action will be taken."⁹⁹ Military psychologist Lawrence LeShan explored the many changes that a society undergoes in times of war, and noted the recurrent view that "moral standards are no longer applicable to our dealings with 'those people,' as they would only work to our disadvantage."¹⁰⁰ In the minds of many Americans in the 1940s, therefore, "it was seen as perfectly reasonable in World War II to put Japanese-Americans in 'relocation' camps without trial, and to confiscate their homes, farms, and stores. Since all 'Japanese' (including second- and third-generation American citizens) were seen as alike—devious, sinister, and ruthless—this procedure was perceived as not only acceptable but necessary."¹⁰¹

However, "there was not a single American of Japanese descent, alien or citizen, charged with espionage or sabotage during the war."¹⁰² Internment became widely regarded as a senseless and immoral policy, and any material advantages for the war effort appear to have been minimal or nonexistent, while the practical and human costs were high. At minimum, the considerable time, money, and effort plowed into the internment program could have been used for other urgent purposes. But in addition, many of these very individuals—most of them second-generation American-born citizens—would have carried on contributing to the American economy and the war effort as a whole, or indeed to America's own military or intelligence. Reeves wrote of the interned that "most of them, citizens and aliens alike, were fiercely patriotic."[103] Some Japanese American units were famously formed later in the war, and fought with distinction, including twenty-two men who received the Medal of Honor—although, in keeping with the point, most were awarded only years later.

Next, let us consider the bombing of Japan. In the previous chapter I reviewed evidence that strategic bombing, while it may have *contributed* to bringing about the surrender of Japan, was not decisive. While this could not be known to leaders at the time (who after all were prosecuting the same strategy in Europe, at great expense to both sides), scholars have since scrutinized whether, at least in hindsight, it was effective or excessive.[104] The logic of the so-called Douhet strategy was that if a nation suffers significant enough damage to its population and infrastructure, it will surrender, or its people will rise up against the government. Bob Pape argued that "if this model could succeed anywhere, it should have been in Japan."[105] This is because of the sheer level of destruction wrought, across a large proportion of the population up and down the country, which tested the theory to its limit. In the end over sixty Japanese cities had been subjected to saturation bombing, with almost half of their urban areas "burned to the ground."[106] Two-thirds of the total civilian population experienced air raids, and more than a third had bombs fall in their neighborhood. Though fewer bombs were dropped on Japan than on Germany, the densely packed wooden buildings and use of incendiary bombs meant that there were significantly more casualties: 900,000 Japanese (1.2 percent of the population), compared to 330,000 Germans (0.5 percent of the population).[107]

The height of the destruction came on the night of 9 March 1945, in the firebombing of Tokyo. A total of 334 B-29s bombed the city, killing 83,000 people and injuring 100,000 more—not dissimilar to the casualties in either of the later nuclear attacks—and wiping out 16 square miles (25 percent) of the city.[108] That raid "remains the most devastating air attack in history."[109] U.S. Air Force commander Curtis LeMay, widely known as the bullish and unrepentant commander of the bomber force, later said of the raid on Tokyo, "We knew we were going to kill a lot of women and kids when we burned that town. . . . Had to be done."[110] As destructive as it was, there were in fact many such firebombing raids, even if not killing as many people. More firebombings were carried out from 11 to 19 March, for example, on Nagoya, Osaka, and Kobe.[111] Over time, the air force had increased the proportion of incendiaries alongside conventional explosives, amplifying the overall effect as "the high-explosive bombs would break up structures so that the incendiaries could set the pieces on fire," often creating a firestorm.[112] Aircrews were instructed to drop their incendiary bombs into areas that were not already burning "in order to spread the blaze as far as possible."[113] In addition, nighttime raids meant less fighter cover and air defenses were less effective, allowing the air force to remove bombers' own armaments and increase the payload of bombs they could carry. In the Pacific theater, a contributing factor was interservice rivalry, which made it imperative that the young air force demonstrate its effectiveness in comparison to the powerful navy in particular. The switch to nighttime firebombing facilitated this demonstration, as tonnage of bombs dropped and square miles of cities visibly burned were considered more "impressive" and photographs of desolated cities "speak for themselves."[114] Chief of Staff of the Twentieth Air Force General Lauris Norstad found the results of the early firebombing raids "nothing short of wonderful."[115]

After this series of raids, the "fire blitz was temporarily halted [but] only because LeMay ran out of incendiary bombs." [116] For the next two months B-29s went back to bombing airfields and factories in Japan. But more was to come. The next major attacks between 14 May and 15 June were to "finish off" the six largest cities in Japan: Tokyo, Nagoya, Kobe, Osaka, Yokohama, and Kawasaki. They then moved on to second-tier cities (populations over 100,000), and 58 of 62 of these were firebombed. The next stage would have been to firebomb third-tier cities (with populations over 30,000), since there was nothing else left to destroy, but the war ended before this could be done. By 1945 Japan had been pummeled to oblivion. B-29 pilots called the missions to Japan the "milk run," escorted by fighters the whole way and with little opposition.

LeMay later famously said, "Killing Japanese didn't bother me very much at that time. It was getting the war over that bothered me. So I wasn't worried particularly about how many people we killed getting the job done."[117] He wasn't alone in advocating this aggressive stance. As we saw in polling data, some Americans even talked openly of eliminating the entire Japanese population, and such extreme views were not limited to lay opinion. Chairman of the War Manpower Commission Paul McNutt "told a public audience in April 1945 that he favored 'the extermination of the Japanese in toto,'" confirming that he did not mean just the military but the Japanese people as a whole.[118] An advisor to the State-War-Navy Coordinating Committee also contemplated the "annihilation of the Japanese as a race."[119] Roosevelt's son—a valued confidant of the president—proposed a continuation of the bombing "until we have destroyed about half the Japanese civilian population."[120]

Pape argues that the targeting of Japanese cities has been downplayed, both by the media at the time and by political leaders in their later reflections: "Churchill and Truman hardly mention it. They give the impression that countercity attacks were just under way when the war ended."[121] Yet the level of damage to urban areas was in Pape's assessment "extreme." After the war, the U.S. Strategic Bombing Survey reported that the whole air campaign (conventional and nuclear) had destroyed about 43 percent of Japan's 66 largest cities.[122] Somewhere around 22 million people were left homeless (around

30 percent of the Japanese population), with 40 percent of all houses in Japan destroyed.[123] There were almost a million civilian casualties, with around 400,000 killed.[124]

LeMay himself suggested that if Japan had somehow won the war, he probably would have been charged for war crimes. As it was, Japan had succumbed, but no one knew until much later, working through the data and archives, how little the bombing had affected the Japanese government's debates on the war and the decision to surrender.[125] As in Europe, the strategic bombing had "succeeded" in killing civilians of the enemy state in staggering numbers, but with little effect on the war. Pape, Rosen, Hasegawa, and others argue that the naval blockade, the Soviet entry into the war against Japan, and the threat of a U.S. invasion of the home islands would eventually have led to surrender *irrespective* of the air campaign. "'Morale' or terror bombing," Pape concluded, "under whatever name, is not only immoral but futile."[126]

Finally, let us consider the use of nuclear weapons. It remains a common belief, or argument, that the atomic bombs dropped on Japan ended or at least shortened the war. Advocates hold that it avoided an American invasion of Japan, as well as ended the firebombing raids, and thus ultimately saved hundreds of thousands more American and Japanese lives. Many believe, therefore, that it was a necessary evil.

However, others argue that no such weapon should have been used regardless of its contribution to the war because it was a qualitatively different means of mass destruction and simply morally unacceptable under any circumstances. Still others argue that it merely represented an irresistible "test" of the bomb, since Japan was going to surrender anyway because of some combination of the blockade, the impending invasion, and Soviet intervention. Stalin's reaction was notable. "War is barbaric," he said, "but using the A-bomb is a super-barbarity. And there was no need to use it. Japan was already doomed."[127] Of course, Stalin saw it as a message to him. The next day he initiated a massive effort to develop Soviet atomic weapons, codenamed "Task Number One."

In his study of the role of airpower, Pape shows that nearly all strategic bombing campaigns in history have failed. Air *support* to ground forces can be highly effective. But nations do not concede to strategic bombing offensives alone without a land invasion. However, Japan did. Given such a statistical outlier, it is tempting to suggest that the difference was the use of atomic weapons. Yet this turns out—with hindsight—to be unconvincing because of the synchronous effects of the blockade and the Soviet invasion of Manchuria. It is hard to disentangle which was the straw that broke the camel's back. Plus, as Pape and others have pointed out, it is also questionable because conventional bombing had created just as much damage, or more, well before these nuclear attacks. As Pape put it, "the 'hostage' was already dead."[128] Pape's famous argument is therefore that the strategic air offensive against Japan as a whole—*including* the atomic bombing itself—had little or no effect on the Japanese decision to surrender.[129] He contends that to have been effective as a strategy the nuclear attacks must have credibly threatened "vast future damage," with the time between strikes long enough for the effects to register. He argues neither criterion was fulfilled: "Without many more bombs—perhaps dozens—which the United States did not have, atomic bombing certainly could not have overshadowed the effects of [conventional B-29] incendiary attacks. In fact, no more bombs were on hand at the end of the war, and only two [more] were produced by the end of 1945."[130] Of course, Japan did not know this, but it meant the threat was hollow.[131]

As for the timing, the second bomb was dropped on Nagasaki with "barely sufficient time for the Japanese government to carry out a cursory investigation of the effects of a wholly revolutionary weapon [at Hiroshima], and not enough to develop a reasoned assessment of the danger it presented."[132] Certainly there was no time for Japanese civilians to discover or absorb the news of the atomic bombings, and therefore "much less were they pressing their government to capitulate because of them. If the Emperor had told them to fight on, the Japanese people would no doubt have fought on."[133] Pape reports that not until 10 August, *after* the second bomb was dropped, "did the investigators finally agree that Japan faced the prospect of an enemy equipped with atomic power."[134] That was too late for Nagasaki.

EXCESSIVE OUT-GROUP BIAS AND OVERALL AMERICAN MILITARY EFFECTIVENESS

In sum, it seems beyond doubt that during the Pacific campaign many aspects of out-group animosity reached extremes that were arguably counterproductive—among the public (e.g., in racist attitudes toward the Japanese), the military (e.g., in their treatment of prisoners), and leaders (e.g., in their decisions to intern Japanese Americans, to press as hard as they did with the devastating air offensive against Japanese cities, and to drop the atomic bombs). It is hard to say whether the effects of these excesses outweighed any positive effects that the in-group/out-group bias may have had on the war effort and military effectiveness, operating at the lower levels outlined in the previous chapter. But what is clear is that the in-group/out-group bias led or contributed to detrimental effects as well as advantageous ones. At the theoretical level, this is not surprising. As we have seen, biases tend to have an inverted U-curve of efficacy, meaning that they are effective in moderation, but not if they are too weak or too strong. There is a balance to be struck in order to milk the advantages of adaptive biases without overplaying one's hand. In the war against Japan, there was evidence of overkill.

Notably, on the American side there was little evidence of extreme manifestations of *in*-group bias (the extremes tended to be in out-group perceptions).

At times one can of course find examples of extraordinary hubris in American beliefs about their moral or material superiority, as well as extraordinary loyalty and sacrifice, but this did not seem to lead to pathologically counterproductive behavior. As Hanson stressed, whatever the level of groupishness among Americans, it was bounded by a powerful countercurrent of individualism, and this was critical to their success.[135] In the Japanese case, however, both in-group and out-group biases became extreme, with significant detrimental effects.

Conclusions

This chapter provides plentiful evidence that while the in-group/out-group bias may be useful *in moderation*, it can quickly become counterproductive and damaging in extremis. Both Japanese and American effectiveness were undermined when beliefs about their own in-group or enemy out-group became excessive. Moreover, regardless of the detrimental effects of the bias on *material* outcomes, excessive in-group exaltation and excessive out-group dehumanization raised *moral* questions that, in themselves, triggered blowback within the war and long after, if measured in slightly more ambiguous reputational and political costs among citizens, enemies, neighbors, and potential future allies.

On the American side, the strategic bombing offensive was played down, and the use of nuclear weapons came under sufficient enough scrutiny to generate a counternarrative justifying the bomb, to the extent that its dubious utility in ending the war became an established "myth," in Hasegawa's view, among Americans and Western allies.[136] But most authors point out that even this pales in comparison with the many millions that suffered and perished at the hands of the Japanese across Asia—long before and throughout the Pacific campaign. After the war, many Japanese atrocities were suppressed, and indeed "the Japanese have rewritten their history textbooks more than once under governmental supervision, first to erase their heinous behavior in East Asia during the 1930s and 1940s, and then to make concessions when the Korean, Chinese, and Philippine governments demonstrated that Japanese history books were guilty of whitewash and cover-up tactics."[137] A Japanese minister of justice claimed as recently as 1994 that Japanese soldiers "were not aggressors in World War II, committed no atrocities in the Chinese city of Nanking, and behaved no worse toward Korean and Chinese women than did U.S. and British soldiers."[138] He was forced to publicly retract the statement. To whatever extent the in-group/out-group bias exacerbated the excesses of prejudice, racism, and violence on both sides, they could clearly be counterproductive as well as immoral.

In a chapter with the goal to demonstrate the negative consequences of cognitive biases held to excess, we could have revisited the other cases too. We could have looked at excesses in Washington's overconfidence, which sometimes led to recklessness and disaster as well as bold feats. We could also have looked at excesses in the fundamental attribution error in Churchill and others who shunned peace efforts, which sometimes led to disastrous decisions as well as good ones (or indeed, the good side of Chamberlain's apparent *lack* of the FAE, which at least drove him to try to secure peace when others had given up). However, the Pacific War case is important because it forces a consideration of both material and moral dimensions of excessive biases. Biases may be excessive and "only" cause disaster, but sometimes excessive biases may be morally reprehensible regardless of whether they cause disasters or not. This is all too obvious in many aspects of the brutal war in the Pacific.

Finally, this chapter raises an additional theoretical point. The book's main argument is that biases can be good as well as bad in their effects on *material* outcomes. This suggests a parallel argument: Can biases can be *good* as well as bad in their effects on *moral* outcomes? That is, there is no reason to believe that biases cannot promote moral as well as immoral behavior, just as they promote good as well as bad performance. For example, overconfidence might make leaders strive for peace rather than war, even or especially against severe obstacles. The FAE might help diplomats be empathetic to the desires of other states, as well as suspicious of them, and thus more able to understand and resolve conflict. The in-group/out-group bias might lead citizens to reduce their self-interest for the good of a more broadly conceived in-group, allowing progress on poverty or climate change. In other words, cognitive biases might—under certain circumstances—make people irrationally determined and morally motivated to *avoid* war, to *end* conflict, or to *help* others. So while the book's main point is to challenge the idea that biases are always bad for states from a strategic, material perspective, it can also challenge the idea that biases are always bad for moral reasons as well.

As evolutionary anthropologists have argued, human moral inclinations themselves have evolved too—just like other human heuristics and biases—and these moral inclinations are highly adaptive for successful social interaction.[139] As an example, while the in-group/out-group bias can indeed exacerbate immoral outcomes such as prejudice in certain settings (as this chapter makes clear), it can also lead people to undertake extraordinary efforts in pursuing moralistic behavior, such as in the defense of their ideals, of justice, or of their group—even in situations of severe risk where rational actors might be expected to give up and turn their attention to self-preservation. Cognitive biases can, therefore, motivate *morally* advantageous behavior as well as *materially* advantageous behavior. This offers an additional perspective on strategic instincts for the field, although one that will have to wait for further exploration.

CHAPTER TEN

Guardian Angels

THE STRATEGIC ADVANTAGES
OF COGNITIVE BIASES

To be sane in a world of madmen is itself a kind of madness.

—JEAN-JACQUES ROUSSEAU

*System 1 [intuitive, unconscious thought] is indeed the origin of much
that we do wrong, but it is also the origin of most of what we do right—
which is most of what we do.*

—DANIEL KAHNEMAN

NIXON CALLED IT THE "MADMAN THEORY." By nurturing an image that
the U.S. president was obsessed with the threat of communism and crazy
enough to launch a nuclear strike to halt its spread, Nixon thought that Ho
Chi Minh could be forced to break the deadlock in Vietnam.[1] And it wasn't just
a theory. In October 1969 Nixon ordered the U.S. military into full global war
readiness alert, triggering nuclear-armed bombers and submarines to deploy
as if for war. Such extreme measures were supposed to be reserved for a pre-
lude to nuclear attack. Ho and the Soviets, however, did not buy the bluff—
they remained resilient, and the plan failed.

This anecdote demonstrates two things. First, crazy *behavior* does not
always imply irrationality of the actor or the strategy itself. Nixon dreamed
up his "madman theory" as a conscious plan, one that he deduced might alter
Ho's behavior. In that sense, it was perfectly rational. Although it did not succeed, it was not *necessarily* a bad idea. Indeed, it can be viewed as an example
of Thomas Schelling's theory of bargaining behavior: committing to carry out
some significant action unless the adversary concedes or compromises.[2] The
strategic logic of apparent non-rationality was also recognized by one of the

greatest strategists of all time. In his *Discourses on Livy*, Niccolò Machiavelli argued that it can be "a very wise thing to simulate craziness at the right time."[3] Machiavelli's example was sixth-century BC Junius Brutus, founder of Rome, who acted "crazily" in a series of important incidents as a strategy to ingratiate himself with allies and—seemingly—with the gods to help him in his plan to overthrow the last Roman king, Lucius Tarquinius Superbus. In Brutus's case, the plan worked. Sometimes, what looks like irrational judgment and decision-making can represent a deliberate strategy that might work where conventional strategies have failed.[4] This is precisely what cognitive biases are—violations of rationality on the face of it but actually smart heuristics in the service of strategic advantages.[5]

Second, *acting* crazy is not always convincing. Nixon had been fairly rational before. Why should Ho believe he was now mad enough to risk everything in a nuclear confrontation? While Brutus was evidently convincing, Nixon was evidently not convincing enough. The reason that cognitive biases can be so effective is because they are "real," not feigned. We do not *act* overconfident, *pretend* to be overly suspicious of adversaries, or *fake* devotion to our in-group and animosity toward out-groups. We actually believe it—and that is crucial to their effectiveness. Instead of *pretending* to be a little crazy, cognitive biases make us *actually* a little crazy. Just enough to give a convincing performance. Without having to fake it, our signals of intent are more credible; if we are sincerely committed, then there is no bluff to be called.[6] A conscious strategy of feigned craziness like Nixon's might be effective in principle, but if we don't believe the ruse ourselves we can hardly expect it to necessarily convince anyone else. An actor is always liable to give the game away through "behavioral leakage," signs of insincerity that reveal our true doubts and fears. Only by altering our beliefs and perceptions themselves can our behavior, and the signals it transmits to others, become fully reliable and credible. And if it is convincing, then it can change our adversaries' behavior as well as our own. This is the other key component of cognitive biases: distortions of reality that literally change our perceptions of the world, but all the better to succeed within it, especially in competition with other actors.

Human cognitive dispositions generate judgments and decisions that, compared to the expectations of rational choice theory, look a little crazy. However, while they may seem odd in the laboratory, in the real world they offer strategic advantages—not 100 percent of the time but, on average, over time.[7] Sometimes they will lead to mistakes, but—as Daniel Kahneman stressed in the quote that opened this chapter—most of the time our instinctive heuristics provide vital adaptive advantages as we navigate the stream of complex interactions in everyday life. The outstanding question of the book, however, has been: Do these biases offer strategic advantages in international politics as well?

The Success of Errors: A Summary of Findings

This book explored three examples of cognitive biases—overconfidence, the fundamental attribution error, and in-group/out-group bias—all of which: (a) are empirically pervasive and powerful; (b) have adaptive origins in human evolution; and (c) conceivably offer strategic advantages in international politics (Table 10.1). The argument is not that they will *always* be advantageous in every case and every situation: sometimes they will be advantageous and sometimes they will not. But an evolutionary perspective on these biases helps us to understand how and why, in principle, they can be useful, as well the contexts and conditions under which they are more or less likely to emerge and more or less likely to generate an advantage. In this light, all three biases are far from psychological mistakes or flaws. Rather, they are strategic instincts.

What was remarkable in the cases was the diversity of ways in which biases can turn out to be good instead of bad. In the first case, overconfidence is commonly cited as a cause of war and a reason Britain lost the American War of Independence, yet we find it in abundance on the winning American side as well—boosting ambition, resolve, and perseverance. In the second case, the fundamental attribution error is often blamed for threat inflation and crisis escalation, yet we find it embarrassingly absent in 1930s Britain when it would have helped to *avoid* the worst foreign policy disaster of the century at Munich—by boosting earlier and stronger threat detection, preparations for war, and alliance formation. In the final case, the in-group/out-group bias is commonly cast as the root of harmful prejudice, leading to senseless hubris and hostility, yet we find that in moderate doses it was a vital ingredient of the United States' effectiveness in the bitter Pacific War against Japan—boosting collective action, unit cohesion, and offensive action.

Table 10.1. Summary of the cases and strategic advantages of the three biases examined

Bias	Historical Case	Strategic Advantage	Behaviors Promoted
Overconfidence	American Revolution	Boldness	• Ambition • Resolve • Perseverance
Fundamental Attribution Error	Appeasement of Hitler *(Reverse case)*	Forewarning	• Threat detection • Preparation for war • Alliance formation
In-Group/ Out-Group Bias	Pacific Campaign of World War II	Military effectiveness	• Collective action • Unit cohesion • Offensive action

With each of these biases (as with many others), the literature typically looks at disaster X and points the finger at bias Y on side Z. Yet, when we look at bias Y on the *other side*, we find it there too. Or, when we look at some *other disaster*, we find the bias absent when it would have helped. Or, when we look at *success* instead of failure, we find bias Y helped the winning side just as much as it hurt the loser. Biases can be good as well as bad, and we need to pay more attention to whom and to what we attribute error and success.

There are many other cognitive biases that one could explore from an evolutionary perspective (such as cognitive dissonance, prospect theory, and negativity bias), and the general argument applies to them all.[8] If they have adaptive origins—that is, they evolved because they were useful problem-solving mechanisms—then they are candidates for strategic instincts, likely to continue lending advantages today whenever the situation is sufficiently analogous to those in which they evolved. This was argued to be the case for overconfidence, the fundamental attribution error, and in-group/out-group bias. Let us review why each one can be so effective.

BEING BOLD: ADAPTIVE OVERCONFIDENCE FROM ANCIENT ATHENS TO YORKTOWN

Overconfidence can be useful. Such a bias is initially puzzling because it leads to inaccurate assessments and, one would expect, more failures and greater costs as a result. However, theoretical models showed that, under uncertainty, if the benefit of the prize at stake is sufficiently greater than the cost of competition, overconfidence can in fact be a better strategy than unbiased or cautious strategies.[9]

While this may seem surprising, it conforms with the common intuition that boldness is an important ingredient of success, as numerous athletes, business leaders, and military strategists—not least Clausewitz himself—have long observed.[10] In competition with rivals, especially in the dangerous world of international relations and war, any competitive edge over and above material power alone can make the difference between victory and defeat. After his long experience in war and government, former U.S. Army general and secretary of state Colin Powell reflected on a key life lesson: "Perpetual optimism, believing in yourself, believing in your purpose, believing you will prevail, and demonstrating passion and confidence is a force multiplier."[11]

This has two important implications. First, if contested resources were sufficiently valuable compared to the costs of competing for them during human evolutionary history, we might expect humans to have evolved a bias toward overconfidence.[12] The experimental psychology literature has long demonstrated that humans *are* overconfident but has lacked an explanation for why.[13] Evolution offers an answer. A review of whether and which kinds of "false beliefs" could be biologically adaptive concluded that the most compelling candidate was "positive illusions"—inflated self-assessments, the illusion of control, and overoptimism (all forms of overconfidence).[14] Today, we retain deep-seated, evolved proximate mechanisms in our bodies and brains that give rise to overconfidence, even in situations where the costs of conflict have increased relative to the value of the reward, sometimes rendering overconfidence maladaptive. However, the argument of the book is that at other times, or even oftentimes, overconfidence remains highly advantageous.

Second, whether or not our bias toward overconfidence actually *evolved* (creationists read on), empirically it turns out to be a good strategy in a variety of contemporary situations in which the ratio of benefits to costs is large enough. This means that in many modern settings, bankers, businesspeople, lawyers, military commanders, politicians, and states do well and are rewarded if they are overconfident.[15] The precise mechanism by which overconfidence brings advantages in each case may vary, and often not be obvious even to the actors themselves, but if strategies that are successful spread—whether by trial and error, imitation, learning, or some form of selection—then more confident and decisive individuals will rise to the top of their professions at the expense of more cautious and hesitant ones. Leadership psychologist Mark van Vugt argues that, from a game theoretical perspective, an element of boldness is essential for leadership to emerge and function effectively and, empirically, there is a well-established association between leaders, boldness, and risk-taking.[16] Sometimes, this can be a catastrophic mix, as leaders that marshal great power may allow their hubris to run away with them, with equally great consequences for their own and others' welfare. Yet, boldness and risk-taking is often what helped leaders become leaders in the first place, and for many, it allowed them to achieve great things—even things that others thought were impossible. It certainly seems to have given George Washington the ambition and confidence, against all the odds, to carry the fight for American independence.

BEING SUSPICIOUS: ADAPTIVE ATTRIBUTION FROM ANCIENT TROY TO MUNICH

Suspicion can be useful. The fundamental attribution error (FAE) again appears puzzling because it conjures up enemies where there are none, exaggerates the severity of threats that are real, causes states to plow colossal resources into defense, and undermines potential cooperation. However, in an anarchic world where states have to fend for themselves, a state that assumes other states are accumulating power for nefarious purposes is less likely to be exploited, attacked, or destroyed than a state that gives them the benefit of the doubt. Where such threats are significant, suspicious states are more likely to survive.

While this may seem a gloomy picture of the world, it concurs with the common intuition to "err on the side of caution" when dealing with others, and only expose oneself to engagement and cooperation when one is sure of the other party's good intentions. In game theoretical models such as the prisoner's dilemma, getting this wrong incurs the "sucker's payoff"—the worst of all possible outcomes. Having extended an olive branch, it is easy for an adversary to bite your hand off. Precisely *because* of the problem that one can never be sure of the intentions of the other side, the safest strategy is to remain circumspect and assume the worst. Of course, if interactions are repeated over long periods of time, then incremental positive gestures that are reciprocated by the opponent can break out of this vicious circle, as long as actors can keep convincing each other, in a tit-for-tat manner, that they will continue to peacefully pursue mutual interests in the long run (the "shadow of the future"—the opportunity costs of failing to cooperate over long periods of time—makes that a good strategy, when it is possible).[17] But sustained cooperation is hard to achieve and highly fragile, especially when state leaders and policies keep changing on either side (a particular problem for democracies). This fundamental problem of never being sure of other states' intentions generates the "security dilemma" in international relations, whereby states feel compelled to arm themselves for their own protection but in so doing only end up reducing the security of others, exacerbating the incentive for all to arm further.[18] Excessive suspicion often appears to lead states to *inflate* external threats and *underestimate* their own threat to others—beyond whatever the real levels are.[19] While unfortunate and expensive, it does not alter the logic for an individual state: in the absence of better information, the only safe strategy is to assume the worst, or else. As Morgenthau observed, intentions are the hardest thing for states to assess, and yet vital.[20]

This has important implications. First, if threats from other actors were sufficiently severe during human evolutionary history, we might expect humans to have evolved a bias toward making dispositional attributions—assuming intent behind others' accumulation of power and threatening behavior, whatever the reality. The experimental psychology literature has long demonstrated that humans *are* biased toward making dispositional attributions—as manifested in the fundamental attribution error—but has lacked a clear explanation for why this is the case. Evolution offers an answer. The bias was named the "fundamental" attribution error because it is so pervasive and powerful that it appears to underlie many other psychological phenomena. This is suggestive of its crucial adaptive significance in our evolutionary past.[21] Today, we retain deep-seated, evolved proximate mechanisms that continue to give rise to the attribution error, whether or not it is appropriate to do so. However, the argument of the book is that at certain times, and perhaps most of the time, it is the right bias to have.

Second, whether or not our bias toward the fundamental attribution error actually *evolved*, it turns out to be a prudent strategy today. In many modern settings, military commanders, politicians, and states do well to assume other actors are behaving according to their intentions—particularly in the realm of security. As Philip Tetlock pointed out so succinctly, "Making dispositional attributions can be adaptive. One may make more Type I errors (false alarms of malevolent intent) but fewer Type II errors (missing the threats posed by predatory powers such as Hitler's Germany)."[22] Since the latter error is more costly than the former, this is the "right mistake" to make. In principle, therefore, such a bias can be advantageous, even or especially in international relations. States fear for their security in part because the fundamental attribution error encourages the assumption that other states have nefarious intentions. According to realist theories of international relations, and especially offensive realism, this is the assumption that states *should* make if they are to maximize their security and their chances of survival.[23] But sometimes they get it wrong. If only the FAE had been stronger in 1938, Britain might have been more wary of Hitler and avoided what many see as the worst foreign policy disaster of the twentieth century, in the capitulation of Munich.

BEING UNITED: ADAPTIVE GROUP BIAS FROM ANCIENT GAUL TO THE PACIFIC

Group bias can be useful. Perhaps especially in international relations, which is fundamentally the relations between national or other groups, the bias initially appears puzzling because it causes states—even small and weak ones—to believe they are materially or morally superior and special, to see enemies, rivals, and even allies as inferior or illegitimate, and to misunderstand others' goals, beliefs, and perspectives, all of which reduce opportunities for cooperation and increase the probability of conflict. However, in the merciless competition of feudal societies and the development of nation-states, a group that believed in its superior legitimacy, morals, and capabilities was more likely to cohere and bond into an effective unit, to fight harder for survival and independence, and to persist in the face of lethal rivals. As historians have suggested, the history of the state is largely the history of war.[24] Populations that failed to organize themselves into sufficiently coherent groups, or with a strong enough unifying identity, generally became subsumed by other groups that did, or disappeared altogether.

While this suggests a world made up of egoistic groups that see themselves as better than others, it nevertheless aligns with what we observe. Few nations believe themselves to be inferior to any others, while many see themselves as superior to all—and often overtly. Even among democracies, nationalist chauvinism is rampant and manifested in all manner of phenomena from beliefs in superior origins, cultures, and religions, to saber-rattling and vilification of other states in the causes of war, to territorial and trade barriers that privilege their own citizens and deny others.[25] While the excesses of such prejudice can be alarming, the basic logic of making in-group/out-group distinctions is a vital ingredient for groups to succeed, or indeed, for groups to exist at all. For states to form and function—in normal times—they have to generate an identity that binds them together and distinguishes them from others. When facing challenges—not least, in times of war—the in-group/out-group bias comes strongly to the fore to pull groups together and compete more effectively with rival groups.

This has important implications. First, if out-groups posed a significant threat and in-groups provided protection during human evolutionary history, we might expect humans to have evolved a bias toward favoring their own group and fearing others. The experimental psychology literature has long demonstrated that humans *are* biased toward groupish behavior—indeed, it is considered one of the strongest and most pervasive cognitive biases of all, which psychologist Susan Fiske called "the problem of the century."[26] Yet, we have lacked a clear explanation for why we have it. Evolution offers an answer. While the in-group/out-group bias may seem tragic today, it was highly adaptive in our evolutionary past.[27] Apart from accidents and diseases, the greatest danger to humans in our ancestral environment was not woolly mammoths or saber-toothed tigers; it was a much more dangerous predator: other humans. In small-scale societies similar to the social environments in which we evolved, out-group conflict accounts for around 15 percent of all male deaths (and a much greater percentage in some regions).[28] Archaeological and ethnographic studies reveal that human societies were strongly organized around maintaining a coherent and tightly bonded group, as well as preparations and defense against other groups. For example, there is widespread evidence of communal cohesion, group rituals, and powerful social norms, along with settlements having strategic locations, vantage points, and fortifications, and the societies themselves developing weapons, warriors, and coalitions in a setting of not infrequent conflict, injuries, and deaths.[29] In such an environment, in-group favoritism and out-group suspicion is a vital disposition for survival. Intergroup trade, marriage, and alliances were common, too, but often precisely because they helped maintain peace—or dominance—in the face of competition and war. Today, we retain deep-seated, evolved proximate mechanisms that give rise to the in-group/out-group bias, even though it often has negative consequences (both in excessive conformity to in-group norms and in excessive prejudice toward out-groups). However, the argument of the book is that under certain conditions, and especially when in lethal competition with rival groups, it can be a highly advantageous bias.

Second, whether or not the in-group/out-group bias actually *evolved*, it turns out to be an effective strategy today. For many modern groups—whether social movements, ethnic minorities, rebellions, or nations—they are more likely to succeed if they believe in, and rally their followers by emphasizing, their own group's distinctive identity, qualities, and cohesiveness, and contrast these with perceived deficiencies of their opponents. Paul Collier explains how popular rebellions, in particular, face immense obstacles to overcoming the collective action problem. An ad hoc collection of poorly armed, poorly equipped, and untrained civilians must not just fight but oust a powerful incumbent group—and one that will severely punish rebels who are caught or fail.[30] The in-group/out-group bias helps to overcome this problem by motivating individuals to join forces and fight collectively as a group, even in the face of hardship, injury, and death. Nation-states have gotten around the collective action problem by using professional armies, who follow their orders rather than their hearts. But in all-out wars of national survival, when millions of ordinary citizens are called up to serve, the in-group/out-group bias can become a powerful, even essential, motivator—helping to rally the nation and fight the enemy. It certainly provided tailwinds for the United States in World War II to finance, furnish, and fight the brutal Pacific campaign against Japan.

Pastures New: The Many Biases of Human Nature

This book focused on three specific cognitive biases, but the general argument applies to a whole range of human dispositions that, while typically assumed to be detrimental, actually represent adaptive traits that evolved because they were useful to us in the past. Where that is the case, there is no reason to assume they do not continue to help us today—even on the stage of international politics.

Many of these dispositions are general behavioral or emotional traits rather than cognitive biases per se. For example, take territoriality, anger, or aggression. These are often seen as detrimental phenomena, contributing to a variety of negative outcomes such as negotiation failure, escalation, and war. But like cognitive biases they evolved precisely because, under the right circumstances, they are highly adaptive traits.[31] Indeed, they are recurrent dispositions across the animal kingdom, and that is no accident of nature.[32] They may not always be desirable in modern, polite society, but when push comes to shove they are highly effective strategies for survival. And even where they increase the probability of conflict, that does not mean that they reduce performance within it or that conflict itself represents a poor choice of action. Charles Darwin, Robert Ardrey, and Robert Frank, among others, have explored the adaptive advantages of these three traits of human nature.[33] They showed that, while cooperation and nonviolence are all well and good, there are times when territoriality, anger, and aggression are highly advantageous traits: for example, when defending homeland, responding to treachery, and protecting kin. They may be conflictual strategies, but they are not always violent and simply represent tools for maintaining successful strategic interactions with others. Even cooperation, for example, can often only be sustained if cheats are punished, and punishment behavior itself appears to have evolved as an adaptation to promote cooperation in both animals and humans.[34] Territoriality, anger, and aggression might not be what we would call "nice" strategies, but evolution has found them to be effective. Over the eons, individuals that lacked them were more likely to end up homeless, exploited, or dead.

Shifting focus back to cognitive biases (rather than general behavioral or emotional traits), there are many other cognitive biases that get a bad rap for causing mayhem and disaster but on the whole are adaptive traits that help us out. If they have important adaptive functions, they may continue to lend strategic advantages today—again, not always, but under the right conditions. These may include, for example, "cognitive dissonance" (sticking to your guns in the face of negative feedback can be a good strategy if it helps in persevering with difficult tasks), "prospect theory" (taking risks when facing losses can be a good strategy if it offers a chance of prevailing in the face of otherwise certain defeat), and the "negativity bias" (overweighting bad information over good information can be a good strategy if it helps in preparing for downturns or disasters).[35] One could go on, identifying the good side of many dozens of biases that psychologists have identified in human judgment and decision-making and yet that social scientists have tended to invoke as liabilities. Their positive and negative effects would all have to be explored, of course. Perhaps they are only sometimes useful, and perhaps some of them are never useful. However, since human bodies, brains, and behavior are evolved adaptations, our natural instincts and dispositions generally tend to be things that help us, not hurt us. Certainly, there are many more potential strategic instincts out there ripe for study.

One might wonder, given so many biases apparently pulling our judgment and decision-making in different directions, what the overall effect is when all of the biases and their bad and good effects are summed together. Perhaps they just create chaos, or even cancel each other out. In fact, the three biases explored in this book—overconfidence, the fundamental attribution error, and in-group/out-group bias—appear to converge to amplify biases in a similar, hawkish direction, making us highly sensitive to threats, especially from out-groups, and yet believing we can prevail against them. In fact, this general pattern seems to apply to cognitive biases as a whole. Kahneman noted that, of the numerous biases in judgment and decision-making documented over the years, *all* of them tend to favor "hawkishness"—a tendency to favor bold or even aggressive rather than conciliatory behavior.[36] This is unlikely to be an accident. Instead, the broad tendency toward hawkishness suggests that, in competitive environments, a forward-leaning, proactive disposition is an adaptive one to have. Therefore, the combination of overconfidence, the fundamental attribution error, and in-group/out-group bias (or, in light of Kahneman's conclusion, any combination of biases) may contribute to an overall behavioral repertoire that tends to be preemptive rather than idle, suspicious rather than empathetic, and fearful of others rather than open-armed. In the struggle for power and survival among tribes, kingdoms, and states over the millennia, generosity and altruism have often emerged, but rarely have they overwhelmed the ubiquity of fear and conflict—phenomena that underlie international relations and continue to characterize the world around us. Evolving under the law of the jungle, as it were, our strategic instincts may have helped to create that very world, but however it came about, they are good instincts to have if we want to survive within it.

Evolution's Predictive Power: Explanation, Variation, and Insight

An evolutionary perspective on human behavior is compelling because it can explain otherwise puzzling behavior. Human beings systematically deviate from the rational choice expectation that they weigh up costs, benefits, and probabilities in their judgments and decision-making in an evenhanded manner. It's a reasonable starting assumption that they might do so, but it is wrong.[37] Actual human judgment and decision-making "biases" are therefore a puzzle—as well as a problem—for economists and political scientists who use rational choice as their baseline model of human behavior. Even where they accept that empirical violations are genuine and stem from the human mind, they cannot explain the origin or cause of why we commit those violations.[38]

However, an evolutionary perspective can explain this puzzle very easily. Biology opens up the "black box" of human judgment and decision-making, revealing a remarkably complex but systematic tactician inside. The first lesson is that no one should *expect* human beings to behave like rational computers in the first place. Instead, evolution has generated a brain that follows a range of behavioral dispositions and rules of thumb that are good strategies to pursue on average, over time. Underlying these dispositions and rules of thumb are cognitive heuristics and biases that, given the constraints of biology, offer a faster, more efficient, and more reliable way of making judgments and decisions, compared with trying to compute a perfect solution at every juncture using our general intelligence, especially when there is limited time and information. As the inhuman Architect of *The Matrix* observed of the all-too-human Neo, when confronted with a dilemma, "Already, I can see the chain reaction—the chemical precursors that signal the onset of an emotion, designed specifically to overwhelm logic and reason."[39] If cold, rational decision-making was the best way of making decisions in the real world, emotions would never have evolved. Neither would cognitive biases. We would all be Vulcans instead of humans. Research shows that emotions and heuristics not only guide but are essential *components of* our decision-making—even when it is rational—and without which we cannot make decisions at all.[40]

The revelation that comes from looking through an evolutionary lens, therefore, is seeing cognitive biases for what they are—not unfortunate errors but strategic instincts.

A second reason why an evolutionary perspective is compelling is because as well as explaining puzzling behavior, it can explain *variation* in that behavior. Our heuristics and biases are sometimes present and sometimes absent, sometimes weak and sometimes strong. Contrary to a common misconception—among social scientists in particular—evolved traits are not fixed; they vary. Evolutionary theory can explain this variation, and at different levels of scale. First, it can explain *individual variation* in behavior as natural variation among people given different genetic dispositions and life history strategies, and how these are expressed in interaction with their environment. Second, it can explain *contextual variation* in behavior as the contingent triggering of traits in different situations (whether those situations derive from individual, social, or physical variables). Third, it can explain *cultural variation* in behavior as physiological and psychological adaptations to different environments (whether this arises via genetic or cultural evolution).[41]

Having biases kick in *when*—and only when—they are useful is an essential feature of their strategic advantage. This is a recurrent feature of both physiological and psychological adaptations throughout nature. We are not angry all of the time, for example; we *become* angry when something triggers that response. Being angry all the time, or never, would be highly maladaptive.[42]

The same contingency is critical in cognitive biases too. For example, the Rubicon theory describes how overconfidence is muted when weighing up options but comes to the fore after a decision has been made.[43] The fundamental attribution error prompts us to attribute a rival's behavior to their disposition rather than their situational constraints, but this is reversed when the behavior at issue is good rather than bad.[44] The in-group/out-group bias is triggered and strengthened when individuals are primed into groups and becomes stronger still when they come into competition with other groups.[45]

The core argument of this book is that cognitive biases evolved in human ancestral environments because they provided adaptive advantages that were favored by natural selection, and these advantages can still accrue today—even in politics and international relations (indeed, perhaps especially in politics and international relations). This continued utility hinges, of course, on the adaptive problems of our past sufficiently resembling those of the present. They do not have to be a perfect match. But they must be close enough that the bias is similarly triggered and that the bias does a similar job of providing relevant advantages—like the peregrine falcons of chapter 2 (as cliff-dwelling aerial predators, finding themselves well adapted to life in modern cities with plentiful skyscrapers and pigeons). In any given domain or case, such parallel situations may or may not occur. However, rather than a problem, this in itself creates an opportunity. Because evolutionary biologists have developed theories about what problem set a given bias was originally designed to solve, this generates predictions for where and when that bias is likely to work well today (as an "evolutionary match") and where and when it is likely to fail (as an "evolutionary mismatch"). Overconfidence, the fundamental attribution error, and in-group/out-group bias all appear to offer powerful advantages in strategic competition with other actors, at least in some important situations and cases. Numerous other biases and other cases await testing, with applications to a wide range of topics in international relations.[46] Some time ago Schelling wrote of the "rationality of irrationality," in which rational behavior can sometimes fail while seemingly irrational behavior enjoys a competitive edge in strategic competition.[47] Evolution had discovered this too, but long before.

Error Management: A Unifying Theory of Adaptive Biases

Error management theory (EMT), introduced in chapter 1 and revisited throughout the book, offers an underlying logic for why cognitive biases of many different types may have evolved and why they may be advantageous.[48] The three biases in this book—overconfidence, the fundamental attribution error, and in-group/out-group bias—may appear to be disparate phenomena. But EMT offers a way to organize them into a common theory of adaptive biases. The adaptive nature of cognitive biases, and indeed evolved human dispositions in general, comes into view when we think of them not as errors in trying to reach perfect decisions but as heuristics that are effective in managing what are inevitable errors in the challenge of decision-making under uncertainty.

In a landmark review, psychologists Martie Haselton and Daniel Nettle identified the role of EMT in many psychological phenomena, which they grouped into three main categories of adaptive decision-making problems: (1) dangerous objects/people (and thus, including the in-group/out-group biases); (2) interpersonal perception (thus, including the fundamental attribution error); and (3) self-perception (thus, including overconfidence). Therefore, the biases explored in this book represent all three of these broad categories in which EMT has been argued to be adaptive.[49]

In the chapters on each bias, we considered whether the conditions for EMT—uncertainty and asymmetric costs—hold, both in the origins of the bias (making it adaptive) and in the prevailing conditions of the contemporary world (making it potentially adaptive still). Both conditions appear to be particularly salient to international relations. First, uncertainty about other states is rampant, about capabilities but especially about intentions. Second, the costs of errors can be both asymmetric and enormous, even in normal times but especially in times of crisis, when security and survival can be at stake. In an interesting additional point, Stephen Walt noted that "more than any other realm of public policy, international affairs demands a capacity to improvise, and to deal with events that were wholly unforeseen."[50] Biases, as opposed to rational deliberation, can be useful precisely because they enable faster intuitive judgments and decision-making in novel or unfamiliar situations—ones about which we benefit from a massive data set underlying our evolved dispositions (from the millions of interactions made over evolutionary time) but not in our conscious memory. It is that process of calibrating the unseen balance of false positive and false negative errors that underlies the logic of error management.

Even more intriguingly, one could imagine that the anarchy of international relations itself could have provided a selective environment for error management biases to arise. Anarchy in the international system is like anarchy in nature, in that there is no Leviathan to control or protect actors, so the strategies and behaviors that emerge are those that simply work best (and thus survive and spread).[51] States that get their positioning vis-à-vis other states wrong will have to change their approach or they will disappear—the failing strategy, ideas, or ideology, if not the state itself, will be selected out of the population. This is analogous to genes for a given trait being selected in or out of the population, whatever the fate of its bearers. Successful strategies can spread via direct selection (failing states die), by learning (failing states change their ways), or by imitation (failing states copy the strategies of more successful states). Whatever the mechanism, winning strategies spread. By this process, "biases" can emerge in state behavior to take advantage of balancing alternative possible errors.[52] These biases can emerge via the effects of human psychology, as argued in this book, but they could also emerge or be reinforced by institutional dispositions and historical experience that equally steer states and their leaders on courses that avoid the worst kinds of errors.

On the very last page of his famous *Perception and Misperception in International Politics*, the book that gave voice to the importance of psychology in international relations, Robert Jervis precisely foresaw the logic of EMT. After an exhaustive analysis of psychological dispositions, he arrived at the important outstanding question of when one misperception may be better or worse than another, and when a given misperception might in fact help states rather than hinder them. His book focused on the disastrous results of judgment and decision-making being derailed by psychological biases. "But," he ends the book, "we must note that the finding that a certain misperception is more common than its opposite does not necessarily mean that this distribution of errors is less than optimum. . . . we have to know about the costs of the misperception and the costs of the opposite error."[53] Jervis clearly recognized the logic of error management. His intuition was that, applied to assessments of threats at least, states have tended to be "excessively vigilant" and paid for it in unnecessary escalation, arms races, and war. One can certainly hypothesize that either error (excessive vigilance or excessive complacency) is the more significant, and I made the case in chapters 5 and 6 that states *should* be excessively vigilant, at least they should have been before the catastrophe at Munich. But interestingly, both of us are essentially arguing that a bias—rather than pure rationality—can be advantageous, whatever the direction in which the bias should lead us. The broader point here, therefore, is that error management theory offers a compelling and as yet unused lens through which to view the role of cognitive biases in international relations. The need to balance errors can demand a bias rather than accuracy.

Finally, it is vital to stress that the logic of EMT is that it gives rise to biases that work well *on average, over time*—that is, across numerous instances of judgment and decision-making. It does *not* say that a particular bias will always be advantageous in any given *single* case. Indeed, the whole point of the theory is to recognize that errors in both directions are inevitable and expected. The goal is simply to avoid the worst possible error as much as possible—steering into the wind to make sure one keeps moving in the direction one wants to go. Until now, we have tended to only look at the instances when states were blown onto the rocks and disaster ensued. But what about all the other times when they sailed close to the wind and in so doing accomplished great feats?

Implications for International Relations Theory

A critique of any evolutionary perspective on international relations—indeed of any psychological perspective—will come from neorealists (or "structural realists"), who argue that states just do whatever they must to survive and prosper given the anarchy of the international system. They are not necessarily biased, for good or ill, and we don't even need to look at the characteristics of individual states or their leaders to explain their behavior. However, as Joe Nye argues, any system, including the international system, has two elements: *structure* and *process*.[54] While we may agree that structure imposes similar constraints on all states, process accounts for the different ways in which individual actors react to those constraints—and here, psychology matters a lot.

Nye invokes an analogy to explain: "In the metaphor of a poker game, the structure refers to the players' cards and chips, while the process refers both to the formal rules and the informal customs or conventions that affect interactions among the players. Variations in the ability of the players to calculate odds, infer the strength of opponents' hands, or bluff are at the unit, or actor, level."[55] This is vitally important because wherever states' assessments of each other matter—just as for individuals in poker—cognitive biases at work in *making* those assessments will matter too. Thus, any strategic *advantages* that these cognitive biases may bring will also manifest themselves in the process of state interactions—even within a structural realist framework of international relations.

An evolutionary perspective is additionally important because it offers a deep understanding of the preferences and goals that guide that process. Nye argues that "neither game theory nor expected utility are really theories of international politics because they need to import theoretical assumptions about context" and thus, understanding "how preferences are formulated and how learning occurs may be more important than the actual choice."[56] Nye's suggestion is that neorealism and neoliberalism can be combined into a unified theory, with neorealism explaining the structural level of international politics and neoliberalism explaining the process level (largely on the basis of institutions and norms of behavior). However, institutions and norms are not enough on their own, because what generates those? In a somewhat similar manner, therefore, I would argue that *psychological* factors must also be brought within the bigger structural framework to help refine our understanding—but at that critical *process* level of the preferences and dispositions lying hidden at the heart of international relations theory. In his retrospective on the role of psychology in international relations Robert Jervis noted, "While many approaches to the study of politics take for granted actors' preferences and ideas about how to reach them, these are often the most important parts of the explanation for behavior, and it is doubtful that we can understand them without employing political psychology."[57] Indeed, *given* a certain distribution of power among states (the *structure* of the international system), and *given* the institutions and norms within which (or around which) states work, the leaders of those states still have to form strategies and choose from among them, which is inevitably influenced by psychological factors.

The added value of an evolutionary perspective is that: (a) it *does* explain the origins of our core preferences, and these are manifested in our evolved dispositions; and (b) rethinking biases *as adaptive*—as "strategic instincts"—draws our attention to the fact that while psychological factors will sometimes hinder states' endeavors, at other times they will help. They may even help to create or surmount the very structural and institutional obstacles that constrain us in the first place.

Implications for Current Affairs

Here, I look briefly at three contemporary challenges in international relations as a way of exploring how strategic instincts play a role in current affairs. None of these reflections represent policy advocacy. Rather, they are merely meant to show that, from the perspective of cognitive biases as adaptive, we can see and think about much-debated topics in a novel way.

CHINA: OVERCONFIDENCE AND THE CLASH OF THE TITANS

How might overconfidence help us in contemporary politics? Today, perhaps the biggest question facing international relations is the consequences of the rise of China. While the United States retains its hegemony in many spheres, these are diminishing, and some have already been lost. History tells a gloomy story about rising states.[58] They have rarely risen peacefully, either because they begin a quest for expansion or because other states act to prevent from them doing so, or from acquiring the ability to try. Normally, in such a context of rising tensions, overconfidence would be cited as an outright danger. The United States (or China) is likely to overestimate its own capabilities, exaggerate its level of control over events, and maintain overoptimistic predictions about the future, all of which would seem to increase the probability of deterrence failure, crisis, and war. Stephen Walt argues that the United States has already been lulled into believing that "China won't act like a great power" and that other states see the United States as a "benign hegemon"—aspects of wishful thinking that undermine American foreign policy.[59]

However, in this book I have argued that there are advantages of overconfidence. Even if the disadvantages are genuine and are likely to cause mistakes, the advantages could outweigh them, avoiding mistakes in the other direction that would be even more costly. It would be easy for a state to shrink back in the face of a rising power, anxious to avoid conflict and hesitant or unwilling to commit to the bold actions necessary to assert and preserve its position. This was certainly Chamberlain's problem in the 1930s, and Britain paid the price— losing its empire, bankrupting the nation, and nearly suffering an invasion of its homeland as well. As we have seen, overconfidence can serve to increase ambition, resolve, and perseverance, helping to exploit opportunities, deter enemies, attract allies, and provide a competitive edge in strategic interactions. While drawbacks of overconfidence certainly remain in the mix, all of these advantages could conceivably help the United States consolidate and preserve its position vis-à-vis China in the coming years.

If war ever occurs, then like the fledgling Continental Army in the American Revolution or U.S. forces in the last Pacific War, bold strategies and actions may again be distinct advantages—even necessities—enhancing daring and determination beyond whatever level they would otherwise be. But here the more pressing question is whether overconfidence might help in the hegemonic competition *short of war* that is already raging today. The answer is arguably yes, especially in the areas of strategic ambition, deterrence, and alliances.

First, significant political and academic voices call for a renewed American isolationism and a withdrawal of overseas deployments. Overreacting has only gotten the United States into trouble in the past, the argument goes, so it should retreat and let China's neighbors check its rise, and perhaps they would do so more effectively than America trying to do it from afar. But if the United States wants to be more ambitious, it will have to lean into significant headwinds and meet challenges where they arise. It must rely on itself and not others—even long-standing allies—who might just as well end up jumping or falling into China's growing sphere of influence. Overconfidence increases ambition, and where it occurs it is likely to encourage the United States to strengthen its security alliances and increase its military presence in the Asia-Pacific region, and to challenge and push back against Chinese expansion. For many, this seems a risky strategy of provocation. But it is exactly what successful great powers have often done in the past—although only those bold enough to draw a line in the sand and stand by it. Given the massive risks, and the massive costs any conflict could bring, even if such a strategy looks good on paper a rational actor may lack the nerve to see it through.[60]

Second, if deterrence is strong enough, China's military ambitions may be kept in check, and conflict may be averted, even without having to follow through on massive forward deployments across Asia. But how will this deterrence be maintained as China grows? Today, U.S. conventional and nuclear deterrence remains significant and credible, enjoying a massive numerical and technological advantage over China. But this will change over time as China's military and its arsenal continue their rapid expansion and innovation. At some point, U.S. conventional forces will be matched (especially in the region surrounding China as America's must be deployed far from home), and the U.S. nuclear arsenal will be rivaled by China's. We will then face something similar to the U.S.-Soviet standoff during the Cold War, where large nuclear arsenals with second-strike capability meant all-out war would lead to certain destruction for both sides. In those times, what came to dominate was not the military balance but psychological mettle. Both American and Soviet freedom of action around the world was significantly curtailed, for fear of escalation. It took a cool confidence to carry on conducting effective foreign policy and military operations in the face of massive risks and the world poised on a hair trigger. In such conditions, only the bold may prevail.

Finally, American confidence in its continued hegemony is critical to maintaining its network of alliances. As China grows, there are increasing economic and security incentives for its Asian neighbors to bandwagon with China, rather than balance against it. The argument is compelling: Why should Vietnam, say, remain allied to a distant America (which might or might not risk coming to the aid of a tiny ally, if it was ever threatened) when it has a bigger market and menace right on its doorstep? With two hegemons vying for allegiance, or at least compliance, the United States will need highly credible displays of commitment to face down a rising China and a clear capability and willingness to defend its allies in that goal. A rational actor might surmise that such promises are good to make but are hypothetical, and whether they will be binding at the brink of major war remains uncertain—and any such doubts are liable to being exposed. A less rational actor that is unconditionally convinced of its superiority—that is, an overconfident one—is likely to give the impression that it is a much more attractive and compelling ally. After all, who wants to follow leaders who doubt their own claim to leadership? In a kind of self-fulfilling prophecy, therefore, as long as America convinces itself and others that it has the upper hand over China, the task of preserving that advantage will be easier because it has more friends flocking to help.

Critically, we don't yet *know* whether China will seek to expand militarily, whether it can be deterred, and whether Asian states will remain allies or jump ship. But this is precisely the domain in which biases become important and useful. It is *because* of uncertainty, combined with the asymmetric costs of false positive and false negative errors, that a bias can be a good strategy—a rule of thumb that helps us aim high and end up at least punching our weight, if not above it. The last time the United States fought another superpower, George Washington's audacity and boldness certainly helped to overcome what was already a significantly stronger adversary.

NUCLEAR PROLIFERATION: MAKING USE OF THE FUNDAMENTAL ATTRIBUTION ERROR

How might the fundamental attribution error (FAE) help us in contemporary politics? Today, we are faced with the vital question of whether certain states—such as Iran—are developing nuclear weapons. This is a dilemma for international security because, if it is, then significant steps may be worth taking in order to prevent proliferation in the region. But if Iran is not developing nuclear weapons, then great risks and costs may be unnecessarily incurred, with economic sanctions and military action endangering stability in the region and having significant political consequences beyond. We just don't know.

However, what we do know is that the FAE will tend to make Western decision-makers: (a) *devalue the situational constraints* that motivate Iran's actions; and (b) *overvalue the dispositional factors* that motivate Iran's actions. In other words, Western states will tend to assume the worst and be *more likely to believe* that Iran is developing nuclear weapons rather than just nuclear power—whether it is or not. It is a compelling belief anyway, given Iran's desire for regional power and influence, as well as its hostility toward Israel, neighboring rivals, and the West. But many resist this view and give Iran the benefit of the doubt. A rational actor might sit on the fence, pending further information on both sides of the debate. As it stands, the United States along with the United Nations, International Atomic Energy Agency (IAEA), and European Union have indeed been assuming the worst, hence the diplomatic efforts and sanctions directed at Iran. To the extent that the FAE is at work in the minds of diplomats, decision-makers, and political leaders, we know that it would push in exactly that direction. This would typically be cited in international relations scholarship as a problem—heightening tensions when in fact the threat may be exaggerated or imagined. Moreover, following the debacle of inflated fears about weapons of mass destruction (WMD) in Iraq in 2003, people are especially skeptical of Western claims that other nations are developing WMD. They have cried wolf before.

However, the point of this book is to reconsider whether that decision—assuming the worst—is a good policy or not, and therefore whether the FAE is an advantageous bias in such settings. What if this case is more like Munich than Iraq? Or what if we can't tell which it is more like? I contend that in this case the FAE does indeed steer decision-making in the right, adaptive direction. Why? Because of the significant uncertainty about Iran's intentions, and because of the massive asymmetry in the costs of alternative possible errors for international security—an asymmetry magnified by nuclear weapons. If Iran becomes the first nation to develop nuclear weapons in the Persian Gulf, it introduces tremendous instability and dangers to the region, via: (1) escalation, accident, or the temptation to exploit a window of opportunity (while Iran has nuclear weapons and others do not); (2) proliferation among rivals in the region (most obviously Saudi Arabia but possibly others as well); and (3) setting a precedent that may derail non-proliferation efforts in other regions (if it happens in Iran, the dominoes of nuclear weapons development may fall elsewhere around the Middle East, Asia, and beyond). Where nuclear weapons are concerned, the costs of getting this wrong become extreme—and there is no going back.

For the United States, the cost of a false positive error (assuming a nuclear weapons program when there is none) is, in the big scheme of things, relatively low, but the cost of a false negative error (assuming no nuclear weapons program when there is one) is unacceptably high. In the case of nuclear proliferation, therefore, the best strategy is arguably one that assumes the worst and is therefore more motivated to enact whatever policies are necessary to prevent it—*even against evidence and assurances to the contrary* that may convince a rational actor. The FAE increases the probability that an Iranian nuclear weapons program remains *perceived* as a significant possibility, whether it is or not. Having set our smoke alarm to be highly sensitive to all possible instances of proliferation around the world, we are bound to end up panicking over some cases that prove to be false alarms (and we should expect them). But if we have a serious commitment to non-proliferation, then such mistakes may be worth it. They are necessary collateral if we are to avoid the much bigger, reverse mistake of allowing proliferation when it could have been prevented—such as in North Korea.

Each new leader comes afresh to the Iran crisis and often claims that, today, things are different, pointing to new words and promises. The gift of the FAE is to steel us against such hypothetical overtures and force us to give more weight to the longer-term dispositional behavior of the state, by which concrete actions, rather than words, reveal the true causes of behavior. Chamberlain was taken in by Hitler's word at Munich, and we should be glad of a bias that usually prevents us from being so gullible. While solutions are being sought, it gives us a healthy skepticism about other states' true intentions.

UNITED WE FALL? EUROPE AND THE IN-GROUP/OUT-GROUP BIAS

How might the in-group/out-group bias help us in contemporary politics? Today, group identities are under significant threat in at least two dimensions. First, there is a radical new *aggregation* of existing groups under super-group banners. This is sometimes explicit in the grouping of states into institutions such as the European Union, and sometimes implicit in the many ways globalization is breaking down the physical borders of societies and states. Second, at the same time there is a contrary *disaggregation* of existing groups under subgroup banners. This is sometimes explicit in the breaking up of former states such as Yugoslavia and the Soviet Union, and sometimes implicit in the devolution of powers to regional or local authorities, such as the autonomy given to the regions of the United Kingdom—with Wales, Scotland, and Northern Ireland now having their own parliaments.

Either way—whether reforming into super-groups or subgroups—what were once clearly defined national populations are bonding together or breaking up into bigger or smaller "groups" of people. These new groups may be salient to some aspects of life (such as political alignment or ethnic identity) and not to others (such as nationality or language). These shifting boundaries are reflected in political actions as well as political entities. Even when we fight wars today, for example, we increasingly do so as large coalitions of states, sometimes organized by the UN or NATO or some other supranational body, and sometimes encouraged at home by certain subnational factions or lobby groups and resisted by others. Moreover, often these wars are against subgroups within another state rather than the state itself. Whom exactly are we fighting? And who exactly are "we"? In the modern kaleidoscope of international politics and war, any biases toward in-group favoritism and out-group animosity might seem to be becoming irrelevant because there is no clear demarcation of the interacting groups on either side—they only add to the confusion. Certainly, the contemporary world appears to be an increasingly complicated picture of identities new and old, small and large, political and personal.

However, while in-group/out-group biases are often invoked as pernicious disrupters of politics and international relations, demanding policies that favor some in-group at the expense of some out-group, one might equally see them as continuing to have strategic advantages—vital forces that work to maintain group cohesion and cooperation at a relevant scale and to rein in new group divisions or agglomerations that are likely to undermine collective action. If humans did not have any in-group/out-group bias at all, and were happy to live as individuals without identification with anyone else, we would lose the advantages of the nation-state altogether—a political unit that works (at least in theory) because its people have shared identity, interests, and culture. There might be no enemies, but no friends either.

It is precisely *because* of shared identity that nation-states are able to justify and maintain a representative government (again, at least in theory) and generate large collective rewards from the coordinated actions of a more or less united group of people. The sum is much greater than its parts, but only when the parts have bonds holding them together. When necessary, they are thereby also able to unite to effectively compete with, deter, or fight other groups that threaten them—something human societies have been doing since time immemorial.

Yet, the question arises as to whether such in-group benefits and out-group competition can work at *any* scale. Is it effective regardless of the number of millions or billions of people that are binned into the same political unit? Or does its effectiveness depend on a workable threshold of group size? A group needs to be (or needs to be perceived as) small enough to credibly represent its citizens' interests and enforce social contracts (a nation of ten billion could hardly govern all within it), yet big enough to benefit from economies of scale and generate collective goods sufficiently greater than the sum of its parts (a nation of ten cannot field an army). Human nature has an in-group/out-group bias precisely because *some level* of in-group identification and *some level* of out-group distinction have proven useful and important, but only within reasonable limits.[61] They do not extend to arbitrarily large groups. Much of modern international relations comes down to testing the boundaries to which natural groupish instincts can be pushed, upward or downward, and what happens when they are pushed too far. Leaders have these in-group/out-group biases too, of course, and it is precisely their beliefs and intuitions about people's social glue and fear of out-groups that often propel them into positions of power, as well as guiding their policies on the right level of inclusion and exclusion in the groups they claim to represent.

The European Union is a case in point. It is a remarkable feat of political engineering, not just unifying disparate states to align common interests and principles but actually locking them together in economic and legal structures such that the fate and duties of one depend of the fate and duties of the others. In terms of the original idea to chain together states that had habitually made war on each other for centuries, it has proved successful so far—we've argued a lot and competed intensely but avoided war. But as numerous economic, legal, political, and social roots have gradually grown to solidify the union and spread to encompass virtually all aspects of government and life, the natural autonomy of national groups has been increasingly compromised. National governments are now often unable, whether they would like to or not, to introduce or alter key aspects of legislation on their own territory (the so-called democratic deficit, in which sovereign governments are no longer able to make all their own laws and therefore also their citizens are unable to vote for or against them). As the Union has deepened, every European state has endured or developed conflicting interests with the European Union on some issue or another. For some, this is a price worth paying. For others, the slide to a superstate has gone too far.

Without the in-group/out-group bias, the European Union would be free to grow inexorably into an "ever deeper union," unrestricted by groupish sentiment and expanding as far as rational actors calculate that the net benefits will reach. This may have many good consequences, as advocates argue. But it also has bad ones because, however good it looks on paper, it may fail dramatically in the eyes of the public. Again, there is inherent uncertainty as to the likelihood of different future scenarios, whether those scenarios are good or bad, and how good or bad they would be. But without (or even with) good information, there is an argument that intuition—our strategic instincts—is a good guide as to what level of group integration is likely to actually work, rather than what we might dream of.

As it is, *with* the in-group/out-group bias, the European Union has been repeatedly set back in its drive toward political union—whether by refusal to join in the first place (Norway, Switzerland), by rejection of the euro currency (Denmark, UK), by severe financial crises (Greece, Italy), or by upping sticks and defecting after decades of membership (Brexit). Perhaps people, and their leaders, have strategic instincts telling us when we are approaching the limit of what the all-too-human in-group/out-group bias will allow as a workable form of polity and government. Such large political structures, spanning massive cultural and linguistic divides, cut against the grain of a human nature shaped by millions of years of life in small-scale extended kin groups. United we may stand, but united too far, we may fall.

The united states of the European Union are, today, similar in population to the United States of America. So the unity of the latter might seem to herald an eventually similar success in the former, if only we keep trying. But these federations are very different beasts. The European Union stretches ancient group identifications far further than the unity that brought the young American states into alliance against the British Empire, or the later United States to victory over Japan, when Europe itself was consumed in one of its own bitter fights to the death. The in-group/out-group bias can be a powerful strategic instinct, but it has to be brought to bear at a relevant scale to avoid its dangers and reap its advantages.

Implications for the Future

In the future, how will our relatively stable, evolved human nature interact with a rapidly changing social and physical environment, a burgeoning population, and dwindling resources? The Age of Biology has significantly advanced our understanding of how our evolved traits affect our health, behavior, and thought. The question now is, will the social impacts of these dispositions get better or worse? Will our evolutionary legacy help or hinder cooperation and conflict? Will it assist or undermine our efforts to improve the human condition? An evolutionary perspective is useful because it allows us to anticipate the likely reactions of human physiology and behavior to future environments brought about by technological and social change. This offers insights for reducing sources of conflict, as well as identifying opportunities for promoting security, cooperation, and prosperity.

While there are reasons for optimism, therefore, staying aligned with the world we have created may be getting harder. As the scale, complexity, and technology of social and political interactions increase, misperception and misjudgment may become more difficult to avoid, even when we are aware of the biases we are prone to. Strategic instincts that served humans well in the past—and often still do so today—may ultimately prove to be maladaptive in the future, in a world that is becoming increasingly divorced from the one in which we evolved. Humans may be becoming, as the saying goes, fish out of water.

In some cases technology may allow us to mitigate the negative consequences of cognitive biases, for example by better and faster communications that can help to avoid misunderstanding and escalation. But on the other hand, better and faster communications could equally cause tensions to rise rather than fall, because increasing interactions with more and more others at faster and faster speeds can lead to confusion rather than clarity, the reinforcement and spread of extreme views in an increasingly interconnected world, and distant events made increasingly visceral by instant imagery and social media. Humans used to be significantly isolated from or ignorant about world events—George III had to wait several months to find out the latest news on the American Revolution (and by the time he got it the "news" was old). Today, news from around the globe is constantly beamed not just into our living rooms but into the smartphones in our pockets, wherever we are. Public opinion and political elites sometimes become animated by stimuli that, in the past, would never have even reached them. There is little opportunity for "cooling off" periods either. People expect and demand rapid responses. An evolutionary perspective can be helpful here because, by understanding the proximate physiological and psychological mechanisms through which individual human beings *actually* react to social stimuli empirically (rather than how they "should" react), it suggests novel ways to reduce mismatches between human behavior and our modern environment and engineer ways to align them instead.

Another change apart from technology is the social nature of international politics. In the past, nation-states were in greater danger from each other, as there were few international laws, institutions, or norms that constrained their behavior. States did what they liked, and often attacked and conquered other states at will. In such a world, any advantages of strategic instincts in navigating this cutthroat competition might have been more obvious. By contrast, in the contemporary world, states are more measured in their foreign policy behavior (at least in some states and in some respects). Economic, normative, and legal factors, as well as international institutions and sanctions, can deter or impede conflict that in former times might have gone unopposed. In this new world, there may be a greater premium on rationality. Negotiation and diplomacy through international institutions sometimes have greater sway than military power, or at least provide alternative options. However, while war may be in decline among states, competition is not.[62] States are always vying for advantage in other ways. The argument of this book is that cognitive biases offer a strategic edge in competition with other actors—whether that competition is war, coercion, deterrence, bargaining, trade, or diplomacy. I suspect that biases come to the fore in the urgency and lethality of crisis and war, when time is short and barriers break down, but their strategic advantages can shine in any kind of international interaction. This is an area ripe for further investigation.

Conclusion

This book is meant to be provocative. The international relations literature routinely invokes cognitive biases as decision-making "flaws" or "mistakes" that explain many foreign policy failures and disasters. I argue the opposite. Cognitive biases are advantageous "heuristics" or "strategic instincts" that help explain many foreign policy successes and victories. Furthermore, the international relations literature sees cognitive biases as violations of idealized, rational judgment and decision-making, resulting from computational constraints of the human brain. Instead, I argue that they are evolved, adaptive dispositions of human nature that were favored by natural selection, resulting from proximate physiological and neurological mechanisms in the brain. Biases are not decision-making problems; they are elegant *solutions* to decision-making problems. So I have tried to turn the literature on its head to suggest that when we look at international relations through an evolutionary lens, human judgment and decision-making biases emerge not as stupid mistakes but as strategic instincts.

This should not be a controversial conclusion. After all, it is hard to argue that a measure of boldness, a healthy level of suspicion, and a degree of unity are not highly adaptive strategies, especially in the competitive anarchy of international relations and most of all in times of war. Strategic instincts don't always work in every instance, but we should not expect them to. They are designed to work well on average, over time—not definitive solutions to a specific problem but broad strategies to help us deal effectively with a stream of fast-moving strategic interactions, which are typically conducted under uncertainty and with imperfect information. They are the dispositions that make us humans instead of Vulcans—and all the better for it. Evolution gave us the hard-won gift of strategic instincts, but in our elevation of the ideal of rational choice, as Einstein lamented, it is a gift we have strangely forgotten.

Introduction. Our Gift

The epigraph source is: A. Calaprice, *The Ultimate Quotable Einstein* (Princeton: Princeton University Press, 2011), 477. This quote may in fact have evolved from an amalgamation of what Bob Samples reported Einstein to have said and his own interpretation of it: B. Samples, *Metaphoric Mind: A Celebration of Creative Consciousness* (Reading, MA: Addison-Wesley, 1976), 26. For an investigation of its origins, see https://quoteinvestigator .com/2013/09/18/intuitive-mind/.

1. Full script available at http://www.chakoteya.net/StarTrek/14.htm.

2. J. Galef, "The Straw Vulcan," *Skepticon 4*, https://www.youtube.com/watch?v =FvinMc-koN4.

3. T. Gilovich, D. Griffin, and D. Kahneman, eds., *Heuristics and Biases: The Psychology of Intuitive Judgment* (Cambridge: Cambridge University Press, 2002); J. H. Kagel and A. E. Roth, eds., *The Handbook of Experimental Economics* (Princeton: Princeton University Press, 1995); S. T. Fiske and S. E. Taylor, *Social Cognition: From Brains to Culture*, 2nd ed. (New York: McGraw-Hill, 2013).

4. D. T. Kenrick and V. Griskevicius, *The Rational Animal: How Evolution Made Us Smarter than We Think* (New York: Basic Books, 2013), ix.

5. The increasing recognition and importance of cognitive biases in human judgment and decision-making has been demonstrated not least by the award of the Nobel Prize in recent years to behavioral economists Daniel Kahneman and Vernon Smith (in 2002) and Richard Thaler (in 2017).

6. J. Mercer, "Rationality and Psychology in International Politics," *International Organization* 59, no. 1 (2005): 77–106.

7. Note here that, of course, cognitive biases are not the only source of misperceptions, given that misperceptions can also arise (even in a perfectly rational actor) due to *incorrect* information or a *lack of* information, rather than whatever information is available being distorted by cognitive bias. See ibid.; B. Bueno de Mesquita, "The Contribution of Expected Utility Theory to the Study of International Conflict," *Journal of Interdisciplinary History* 18, no. 4 (1988): 629–52, 648–49.

8. M. Toda, "The Design of a Fungus Eater: A Model of Human Behavior in an Unsophisticated Environment," *Behavioral Science* 7, no. 2 (1962): 164–83, 165.

9. G. Gigerenzer and P. M. Todd, *Simple Heuristics That Make Us Smart* (Oxford: Oxford University Press, 2000); G. Gigerenzer, *Adaptive Thinking: Rationality in the Real World* (Oxford: Oxford University Press, 2002).

10. R. Jervis, *How Statesmen Think: The Psychology of International Politics* (Princeton: Princeton University Press, 2017), 6.

11. Ibid.

12. C. Jarrett, "A Journey in the Fast and Slow Lanes," *Psychologist* 25, no. 1 (2012): 14–15.

13. Jervis, *How Statesmen Think*, 6.

14. J. S. Levy, "Misperception and the Causes of War: Theoretical Linkages and Analytical Problems," *World Politics* 36, no. 1 (1983): 76–99, 77; italics in original. As a notable exception, Levy cites R. Jervis, *Perception and Misperception in International Politics* (Princeton: Princeton University Press, 1976).

15. Mercer, "Rationality and Psychology in International Politics," 77.

16. Ibid.

17. R. M. Hogarth, "Beyond Discrete Biases: Functional and Dysfunctional Aspects of Judgmental Heuristics," *Psychological Bulletin* 90, no. 2 (1981): 197–217.

18. E.g., J. Diamond, *Guns, Germs and Steel: A Short History of Everybody for the Last 13,000 Years* (London: Vintage, 1998); P. Turchin, *War and Peace and War: The Life Cycles of Imperial Nations* (New York: Pi Press, 2005); C. Tilly, *Big Structures, Large Processes, Hugh Comparisons* (New York: Russell Sage Foundation, 1989).

19. D. W. Larson, *Anatomy of Mistrust: U.S.-Soviet Relations during the Cold War* (Ithaca: Cornell University Press, 1997); G. Allison and P. Zelikow, *Essence of Decision: Explaining the Cuban Missile Crisis* (New York: Longman, 1999).

20. For the classic text, see S. E. Taylor, *Positive Illusions: Creative Self-Deception and the Healthy Mind* (New York: Basic Books, 1989).

21. G. A. Blainey, *The Causes of War* (New York: Free Press, 1973); S. Van Evera, *Causes of War: Power and the Roots of Conflict* (Ithaca: Cornell University Press, 1999); B. W. Tuchman, *The March of Folly: From Troy to Vietnam* (New York: Alfred A. Knopf, 1984).

22. E.g., J. Fallows, "Blind into Baghdad," *Atlantic Monthly* (January/February 2004): 53–74; B. Woodward, *State of Denial* (New York: Simon & Schuster, 2005); G. A. Akerlof and R. J. Shiller, *Animal Spirits: How Human Psychology Drives the Economy, and Why It Matters for Global Capitalism* (Princeton: Princeton University Press, 2009).

23. D. Nettle, "Adaptive Illusions: Optimism, Control and Human Rationality," in *Emotion, Evolution and Rationality*, ed. D. Evans and P. Cruse (Oxford: Oxford University Press, 2004); S. E. Taylor and D. A. Armor, "Positive Illusions and Coping with Adversity," *Journal of Personality* 64 (1996): 873–98; D. D. P. Johnson, *Overconfidence and War: The Havoc and Glory of Positive Illusions* (Cambridge, MA: Harvard University Press, 2004).

24. P. E. Tetlock, "Social Psychology and World Politics," in *Handbook of Social Psychology*, ed. D. Gilbert, S. Fiske, and G. Lindzey (New York: McGraw-Hill, 1998); E. E. Jones and V. A. Harris, "The Attribution of Attitudes," *Journal of Experimental Social Psychology* 3 (1967): 1–24.

25. This is an important amplifier of the "security dilemma" underlying international relations. When states arm to ensure their defense, other states can only assume they are arming to increase their offensive power, thus leading both states to arm further and ironically decreasing their security rather than increasing it. R. Jervis, "Cooperation under the Security Dilemma," *World Politics* 30, no. 2 (1978): 167–74.

26. D. G. Herrmann, *The Arming of Europe and the Making of the First World War* (Princeton: Princeton University Press, 1996).

27. M. G. Haselton and D. Nettle, "The Paranoid Optimist: An Integrative Evolutionary Model of Cognitive Biases," *Personality and Social Psychology Review* 10, no. 1 (2006): 47–66.

28. M. Hewstone, M. Rubin, and H. Willis, "Intergroup Bias," *Annual Review of Psychology* 53 (2002): 575–604; H. Tajfel, "Social Identity and Intergroup Behaviour," *Social Science Information* 13, no. 2 (1974): 65–93.

29. S. T. Fiske, "What We Know about Bias and Intergroup Conflict, Problem of the Century," *Current Directions in Psychological Science* 11, no. 4 (2002): 123–28; E. Staub and D. Bar-Tal, "Genocide, Mass Killing, and Intractable Conflict," in *Oxford Handbook of Political Psychology*, ed. D. O. Sears, L. Huddy, and R. Jervis (Oxford: Oxford University Press, 2003).

30. M. van Vugt, D. De Cremer, and D. Janssen, "Gender Differences in Competition and Cooperation: The Male Warrior Hypothesis," *Psychological Science* 18 (2007): 19–23; L. LeShan, *The Psychology of War: Comprehending Its Mystique and Its Madness* (New

York: Helios, 2002); R. J. Rielly, "Confronting the Tiger: Small Unit Cohesion in Battle," *Military Review* 80, no. 6 (2000): 61–65; R. A. Hammond and R. Axelrod, "The Evolution of Ethnocentrism," *Journal of Conflict Resolution* 50, no. 6 (2006): 926–36.

Chapter 1. Adaptive Biases: Making the Right Mistakes in International Politics

The epigraph sources are: L. Cosmides and J. Tooby, "Better than Rational: Evolutionary Psychology and the Invisible Hand," *American Economic Review* 84, no. 2 (1994): 327–32, 329; L. Freedman, "The Future of Strategic Studies," in *Strategy in the Contemporary World: An Introduction to Strategic Studies*, ed. J. Baylis, J. J. Wirtz, and C. S. Gray (Oxford: Oxford University Press, 2007), 362.

1. D. A. Welch, *Justice and the Genesis of War* (Cambridge: Cambridge University Press, 1993), 3.

2. B. W. Tuchman, *The March of Folly: From Troy to Vietnam* (New York: Alfred A. Knopf, 1984).

3. B. C. Rathbun, *Reasoning of State: Realists, Romantics and Rationality in International Relations* (Cambridge: Cambridge University Press, 2019); B. C. Rathbun, "The Rarity of Realpolitik: What Bismarck's Rationality Reveals about International Politics," *International Security* 43, no. 1 (2018): 7–55.

4. G. B. Shaw, *Man and Superman: A Comedy and a Philosophy* (1903; London: Penguin, 2000), 260.

5. R. Dunbar and L Barrett, eds., *Oxford Handbook of Evolutionary Psychology* (Oxford: Oxford University Press, 2009); D. M. Buss, *Evolutionary Psychology: The New Science of the Mind*, 6th ed. (New York: Routledge, 2019); R. Wright, *The Moral Animal: Why We Are the Way We Are: The New Science of Evolutionary Psychology* (New York: Random House, 1994); J. H. Barkow, L. Cosmides, and J. Tooby, eds., *The Adapted Mind: Evolutionary Psychology and the Generation of Culture* (Oxford: Oxford University Press, 1992); S. Pinker, *The Blank Slate: The Modern Denial of Human Nature* (New York: Penguin Putnam, 2002).

6. M. G. Haselton et al., "Adaptive Rationality: An Evolutionary Perspective on Cognitive Bias," *Social Cognition* 27 (2009): 733–63.

7. E.g., see T. C. Schelling, *The Strategy of Conflict* (Cambridge, MA: Harvard University Press, 1960); A. H. Kydd, *International Relations Theory: The Game-Theoretic Approach* (Cambridge: Cambridge University Press, 2015); M. A. Nowak, *Evolutionary Dynamics: Exploring the Equations of Life* (Cambridge, MA: Belknap Press of Harvard University Press, 2006).

8. D. Kahneman, *Thinking, Fast and Slow* (London: Allen Lane, 2011), 416.

9. T. D. Wilson, *Strangers to Ourselves: Discovering the Adaptive Unconscious* (Cambridge, MA: Belknap Press of Harvard University Press, 2004); M. Gladwell, *Blink: The Power of Thinking without Thinking* (New York: Little, Brown, 2005).

10. G. Gigerenzer, *Adaptive Thinking: Rationality in the Real World* (Oxford: Oxford University Press, 2002); G. Gigerenzer and P. M. Todd, *Simple Heuristics That Make Us Smart* (Oxford: Oxford University Press, 2000); Haselton et al., "Adaptive Rationality."

11. S. E. Taylor et al., "Portrait of the Self-Enhancer: Well Adjusted and Well Liked or Maladjusted and Friendless," *Journal of Personality and Social Psychology* 84, no. 1 (2003): 165–76; S. E. Taylor, *Positive Illusions: Creative Self-Deception and the Healthy Mind* (New York: Basic Books, 1989).

12. P. McLeod, N. Reed, and Z. Dienes, "Psychophysics: How Fielders Arrive in Time to Catch the Ball," *Nature* 426, no. 6964 (2003): 244–45; G. Gigerenzer and H. Brighton,

"*Homo Heuristicus*: Why Biased Minds Make Better Inferences," *Topics in Cognitive Science* 1 (2009): 107–43.

13. M. G. Haselton and D. Nettle, "The Paranoid Optimist: An Integrative Evolutionary Model of Cognitive Biases," *Personality and Social Psychology Review* 10, no. 1 (2006): 47–66; R. T. McKay and D. C. Dennett, "The Evolution of Misbelief," *Behavioral and Brain Sciences* 32 (2009): 493–561; D. D. P. Johnson et al., "The Evolution of Error: Error Management, Cognitive Constraints, and Adaptive Decision-Making Biases," *Trends in Ecology & Evolution* 28, no. 8 (2013): 474–81.

14. J. Ledoux, *The Emotional Brain: The Mysterious Underpinnings of Emotional Life* (New York: Simon & Schuster, 1998); D. Goleman, *Emotional Intelligence: Why It Can Matter More than IQ* (London: Bloomsbury, 1996); R. H. Frank, *Passions within Reason: The Strategic Role of the Emotions* (New York: Norton, 1988); R. L. Trivers, "The Elements of a Scientific Theory of Self-deception," *Annals of the New York Academy of Sciences* 907 (2000): 114–31; R. L. Trivers, *Deceit and Self-Deception: Fooling Yourself the Better to Fool Others* (London: Allen Lane, 2011); C. Darwin, *The Expression of the Emotions in Man and Animals* (1872; London: Penguin Classics, 2009). The role—and often advantages—of emotions and interpersonal interactions has been applied to international relations specifically. See T. H. Hall, *Emotional Diplomacy: Official Emotion on the International Stage* (Ithaca: Cornell University Press, 2019); M. Holmes, "The Force of Face-to-Face Diplomacy: Mirror Neurons and the Problem of Intentions," *International Organization* 67, no. 4 (2013): 829–61; M. Holmes, *Face-to-Face Diplomacy: Social Neuroscience and International Relations* (Cambridge: Cambridge University Press, 2018); N. J. Wheeler, *Trusting Enemies: Interpersonal Relationships in International Conflict* (Oxford: Oxford University Press, 2018); S. S. Wong, "Stoics and Hotheads: Leaders' Temperament, Anger, and the Expression of Resolve in Face-to-Face Diplomacy," *Journal of Global Security Studies* 4, no. 2 (2019): 190–208. Hall, for example, argues that states' strategic use of emotion, such as anger, sympathy, and guilt, can serve to signal and gain advantage via "emotional diplomacy" over and above rational behavior alone.

15. C. Peterson, *A Primer in Positive Psychology* (New York: Oxford University Press, 2006); C. Peterson and M. E. P. Seligman, *Character Strengths and Virtues: A Handbook of Classification* (New York: Oxford University Press, 2004); C. Peterson, "The Values in Action (VIA) Classification of Strengths: The Un-DSM and the Real DSM," in *A Life Worth Living: Contributions to Positive Psychology*, ed. M. Csikszentmihalyi and I. Csikszentmihalyi (Oxford: Oxford University Press, 2006). See also J. E. Gillham, ed., *The Science of Optimism and Hope: Research Essays in Honor of Martin E. P. Seligman* (Radnor, PA: Templeton Foundation, 2000).

16. R. el Kaliouby, "We Need Computers with Empathy," *Technology Review* 120, no. 6 (2017): 8.

17. G. Lawton, "The Grand Delusion: Head Full of Half-truths," *New Scientist* (2011): 39. See also T. Suddendorf, D. R. Addis, and M. C. Corballis, "Mental Time Travel and the Shaping of the Human Mind," *Philosophical Transactions of the Royal Society B* 364, no. 1521 (2009): 1317–24; D. L. Schacter, *Searching for Memory: The Brain, the Mind, and the Past* (New York: Basic Books, 1996).

18. L. Damisch, B. Stoberock, and T. Mussweiler, "Keep Your Fingers Crossed! How Superstition Improves Performance," *Psychological Science* 21, no. 7 (2010): 1014–20.

19. K. R. Foster and H. Kokko, "The Evolution of Superstitious and Superstitious-like Behaviour," *Proceedings of the Royal Society B: Biological Sciences* 276 (2009): 31–37.

20. D. S. Wilson, *Darwin's Cathedral: Evolution, Religion, and the Nature of Society* (Chicago: University of Chicago Press, 2002); D. D. P. Johnson, H. Lenfesty, and J. P. Schloss, "The Elephant in the Room: Religious Truth Claims, Evolution and Human Nature," *Philosophy, Theology and the Sciences* 1, no. 2 (2014): 200–231.

21. A. Norenzayan, *Big Gods: How Religion Transformed Cooperation and Conflict* (Princeton: Princeton University Press, 2013); D. D. P. Johnson, *God Is Watching You: How the Fear of God Makes Us Human* (New York: Oxford University Press, 2016).

22. A. W. Lo, *Adaptive Markets: Financial Evolution at the Speed of Thought* (Princeton: Princeton University Press, 2017); M. Shermer, *Mind of the Market: How Biology and Psychology Shape Our Economic Lives* (New York: Times Books, 2007).

23. T. C. Schelling, "Nuclear Strategy in the Berlin Crisis," in *The Development of American Strategic Thought: Writings on Strategy 1961–1969, and Retrospectives*, ed. M. Trachtenberg (New York: Garland Publishing, 1988), 18.

24. Schelling, *The Strategy of Conflict*, 18. See also A. T. Little and T. Zeitzoff, "A Bargaining Theory of Conflict with Evolutionary Preferences," *International Organization* 71, no. 3 (2017): 523–57.

25. L. Freedman, *Strategy: A History* (Oxford: Oxford University Press, 2013), 156–77.

26. A. R. Damasio, *Descartes' Error: Emotion, Reason and the Human Brain* (New York: Avon, 1994); R. McDermott, "The Feeling of Rationality: The Meaning of Neuroscientific Advances for Political Science," *Perspectives on Politics* 2, no. 4 (2004): 691–706; J. Mercer, "Rationality and Psychology in International Politics," *International Organization* 59, no. 1 (2005): 77–106.

27. M. J. Young et al., "Mad Enough to See the Other Side: Anger and the Search for Disconfirming Information," *Cognition and Emotion* 25, no. 1 (2011): 10–21.

28. Schelling, *The Strategy of Conflict*, 17.

29. Gigerenzer and Brighton, "*Homo Heuristicus*," 107.

30. Cosmides and Tooby, "Better than Rational."

31. Freedman, "The Future of Strategic Studies," 364.

32. C. von Clausewitz, *On War*, trans. M. Howard and P. Paret (1832; Princeton: Princeton University Press, 1976), 586.

33. L. Milevski, "The Idea of Genius in Clausewitz and Sun Tzu," *Comparative Strategy* 38, no. 2 (2019): 139–49.

34. Freedman, "The Future of Strategic Studies," 361. He also noted, "'Practical men' can expect to be judged by results. They will therefore tend to rely on what works for them. This may be intuition and hunch, or lessons drawn from searing experience or remembered bits of history. Such sources may be relied upon in preference to excellent information sources and exemplary staff work."

35. Ibid., 362.

36. R. M. Nesse, "Natural Selection and the Regulation of Defensive Responses," *Annals of the New York Academy of Sciences* 935 (2001): 75–85; D. M. Green and J. A. Swets, *Signal Detection Theory and Psychophysics* (Oxford: John Wiley, 1966); R. M. Nesse, "Natural Selection and the Regulation of Defenses: A Signal Detection Analysis of the Smoke Detector Problem," *Evolution and Human Behavior* 26 (2005): 88–105.

37. Haselton and Nettle, "The Paranoid Optimist"; Johnson et al., "The Evolution of Error."

38. D. Nettle, "Adaptive Illusions: Optimism, Control and Human Rationality," in *Emotion, Evolution and Rationality*, ed. D. Evans and P. Cruse (Oxford: Oxford University Press, 2004); Johnson et al., "The Evolution of Error."

39. Johnson et al., "The Evolution of Error."

40. McKay and Dennett, "The Evolution of Misbelief."

41. D. D. P. Johnson and J. H. Fowler, "Complexity and Simplicity in the Evolution of Decision-Making Biases," *Trends in Ecology & Evolution* 28, no. 8 (2013): 446–47.

42. D. Kahneman and A. Tversky, "Subjective Probability: A Judgment of Representativeness," in *Judgment under Uncertainty: Heuristics and Biases* (Cambridge: Cambridge University Press, 1982), 46.

43. Johnson et al., "The Evolution of Error"; Johnson and Fowler, "Complexity and Simplicity in the Evolution of Decision-Making Biases."

44. Cosmides and Tooby, "Better than Rational."

45. J. G. Neuhoff, "An Adaptive Bias in the Perception of Looming Auditory Motion," *Ecological Psychology* 13, no. 2 (2001): 87–110.

46. Haselton et al., "Adaptive Rationality"; Cosmides and Tooby, "Better than Rational."

47. D. T. Kenrick and V. Griskevicius, *The Rational Animal: How Evolution Made Us Smarter than We Think* (New York: Basic Books, 2013), 79.

48. S. N. Ghaemi, *A First-Rate Madness: Uncovering the Links between Leadership and Mental Illness* (New York: Penguin Press, 2011), 2.

49. A. M. Ludwig, *King of the Mountain: The Nature of Political Leadership* (Lexington: University Press of Kentucky, 2002). See also H. L. Abrams, "Disabled Leaders, Cognition and Crisis Decision Making," *Canadian Papers in Peace Studies*, Special issue: Proceedings of the 18th Pugwash Workshop on Nuclear Forces (1990): 136–49; R. McDermott, *Presidential Leadership, Illness, and Decision Making* (Cambridge: Cambridge University Press, 2007).

50. I. H. Robertson, *The Winner Effect: How Power Affects Your Brain* (London: Bloomsbury, 2012).

51. Ludwig, *King of the Mountain*, 226.

52. Ibid., 254.

53. Ibid.

54. For examples, see G. Allison and P. Zelikow, *Essence of Decision: Explaining the Cuban Missile Crisis* (New York: Longman, 1999); J. Snyder, *Myths of Empire: Domestic Politics and Political Ambition* (Ithaca: Cornell University Press, 1991).

55. Y. Dror, *Crazy States: A Counterconventional Strategic Problem* (Lexington, MA: Heath Lexington Books, 1971), xiii.

56. Ibid., 24–27.

57. As explored in chapter 2, not all traits imply adaptation, and alternative causes must be considered. However, adaptation is a good starting hypothesis to explore, as we are doing here, and represents the novel insight offered by an evolutionary approach. See G. C. Williams, *Adaptation and Natural Selection* (Princeton: Princeton University Press, 1966); P. W. Andrews, S. W. Gangestad, and D. Matthews, "Adaptationism: How to Carry Out an Exaptationist Program," *Behavioral and Brain Sciences* 25 (2002): 489–553.

58. E.g., P. E. Tetlock, "Social Psychology and World Politics," in *Handbook of Social Psychology*, ed. D. Gilbert, S. Fiske, and G. Lindzey (New York: McGraw Hill, 1998); L. Huddy, D. O. Sears, and J. S. Levy, *Oxford Handbook of Political Psychology*, 2nd ed. (New York: Oxford University Press, 2013).

59. Barkow, Cosmides, and Tooby, *The Adapted Mind*; Pinker, *The Blank Slate*; Wright, *The Moral Animal*; D. M. Buss, *The Handbook of Evolutionary Psychology* (New York: Wiley, 2005).

60. United States National Center for Health Statistics, www.cdc.gov/nchs/fastats /deaths.htm (2007).

Chapter 2. The Evolution of an Idea: Politics in the Age of Biology

The epigraph sources are: I. B. Neumann, "International Relations as a Social Science," *Millennium: Journal of International Studies* 43, no. 1 (2014): 330–50, 345; C. Darwin, *The Descent of Man* (New York: Penguin Classics, 1871), 398.

1. J. Stavridis, "The Dawning of the Age of Biology," *Financial Times*, 19 January 2014. The "Age of Biology" was also heralded by the Chief Scientific Adviser to the President of

the European Commission, Anne Glover, "The 21st Century: The Age of Biology," *OECD Forum on Global Biotechnology*, Paris, 12 November 2012. Others identified the beginning of the age some time ago. S. Toulmin, "The Age of Biology," *New York Review of Books*, 31 December 1964.

2. See, e.g., P. Cohen, "A Rising Call to Promote STEM Education and Cut Liberal Arts Funding," *New York Times*, 21 February 2016; A. Preston, "The War against the Humanities at Britain's Universities," *Guardian*, 29 March 2015; E. Delany, "Humanities Studies under Strain around the Globe," *New York Times*, 1 December 2013. Of course, as if to refute the claim, just this year American billionaire Stephen Schwarzman gifted £150 million to the University of Oxford—the university's largest-ever donation—for the humanities. However, the gift is so important and unusual precisely because such large-scale funding for the humanities is rare. Also, the purpose of the donation is to promote humanities research on the impact of a STEM phenomenon: artificial intelligence. So in some ways even this remarkable exception reinforces the point.

3. E. O. Wilson, *Consilience: The Unity of Knowledge* (London: Abacus, 1999).

4. For reviews, see J. H. Fowler and D. Schreiber, "Biology, Politics, and the Emerging Science of Human Nature," *Science* 322, no. 5903 (2008): 912–14; J. H. Barkow, *Missing the Revolution: Darwinism for Social Scientists* (Oxford: Oxford University Press, 2006).

5. J. H. Fowler, J. E. Settle, and C. T. Dawes, "The Heritability of Partisan Attachment," *Political Research Quarterly* 62, no. 3 (2009): 601–13; J. H. Fowler and C. T. Dawes, "Two Genes Predict Voter Turnout," *Journal of Politics* 70, no. 3 (2008): 579–94; J. H. Fowler, L. A. Baker, and C. T. Dawes, "Genetic Variation in Political Participation," *American Political Science Review* 102, no. 2 (2008): 233–48; J. R. Alford, C. L. Funk, and J. R. Hibbing, "Are Political Orientations Genetically Transmitted?" *American Political Science Review* 99, no. 2 (2005): 153–67.

6. D. R. Oxley et al., "Political Attitudes Vary with Physiological Traits," *Science* 321 (2008): 1667–70.

7. J. Haidt and J. Graham, "When Morality Opposes Justice: Conservatives Have Moral Intuitions That Liberals May Not Recognize," *Social Justice Research* 20, no. 1 (2007): 98–116.

8. G. E. Marcus, W. R. Neuman, and M. MacKuen, *Affective Intelligence and Political Judgement* (Chicago: University of Chicago Press, 2000); R. Jervis, *How Statesmen Think: The Psychology of International Politics* (Princeton: Princeton University Press, 2017); R. McDermott, "The Feeling of Rationality: The Meaning of Neuroscientific Advances for Political Science," *Perspectives on Politics* 2, no. 4 (2004): 691–706.

9. S. Pinker, *The Blank Slate: The Modern Denial of Human Nature* (New York: Penguin Putnam, 2002); R. Wright, *The Moral Animal: Why We Are the Way We Are: The New Science of Evolutionary Psychology* (New York: Random House, 1994).

10. K. N. Waltz, *Man, the State and War: A Theoretical Analysis* (New York: Columbia University Press, 1959); R. O. Keohane, *After Hegemony: Cooperation and Discord in the World Political Economy* (Princeton: Princeton University Press, 1986); A. Wendt, *Social Theory of International Politics* (Cambridge: Cambridge University Press, 1999). Waltz's subsequent *Theory of International Politics* explicitly dispensed with human nature entirely, in an effort to develop a theory deriving state behavior from the characteristics of the international system alone, regardless of factors acting at the state or individual level. K. N. Waltz, *Theory of International Politics* (New York: McGraw-Hill, 1979).

11. J. J. Mearsheimer, *The Tragedy of Great Power Politics* (New York: Norton, 2001); Waltz, *Theory of International Politics*; J. Mercer, "Rationality and Psychology in International Politics," *International Organization* 59, no. 1 (2005): 77–106; D. D. P. Johnson and B. A. Thayer, "The Evolution of Offensive Realism: Survival under Anarchy from the Pleistocene to the Present," *Politics and the Life Sciences* 35, no. 1 (2016): 1–26.

12. G. Rose, "Neoclassical Realism and Theories of Foreign Policy," *World Politics* 51, no. 1 (1998): 144–72. Even social theories of international relations are built on the social construction of human thought and behavior, not empirical psychology. See A. Wendt, "Anarchy Is What States Make of It: The Social Construction of Power Politics," *International Organization* 46, no. 2 (1992): 391–425.

13. Others have suggested this as well, such as B. A. Thayer, "Bringing in Darwin: Evolutionary Theory, Realism, and International Politics," *International Security* 25, no. 2 (2000): 124–51; J. R. Alford and J. R. Hibbing, "The Origin of Politics: An Evolutionary Theory of Political Behavior," *Perspectives on Politics* 2, no. 4 (2004): 707–23. It is not that political psychologists are unscientific but rather that they rely on psychology. The buck does not stop there, however. If we are to understand the origins and functions of human psychological dispositions and the mechanisms that underpin them, we need not just scientific approaches in general but evolutionary sciences in particular.

14. Even Daniel Kahneman and Amos Tversky, who are perhaps most famous for uncovering key psychological dispositions that are routinely applied in political science, did not embrace an evolutionary approach. Indeed, some of their work has been directly challenged by those with an evolutionary perspective, on the basis that many dispositions come and go depending on the evolutionary salience of the task and its presentation. See G. Gigerenzer, "How to Make Cognitive Illusions Disappear: Beyond 'Heuristics and Biases,'" in *European Review of Social Psychology*, vol. 2, ed. W. Stroebe and M. Hewstone (London: John Wiley & Sons, 1991).

15. This kind of logic can be found in numerous past and present work in psychology. Often, there is a nod to the possibility of an evolutionary origin and adaptive function, but this is by no means a universally applied framework.

16. Barkow, *Missing the Revolution.*

17. For the famous attack on "adaptationism," see S. J. Gould and R. C. Lewontin, "The Spandrels of San Marco and the Panglossian Paradigm: A Critique of the Adaptationist Programme," *Proceedings of the Royal Society of London. Series B, Biological Sciences* 205, no. 1161 (1979): 581–98. For the arguments in favor of deducing and testing adaptations, see G. C. Williams, *Adaptation and Natural Selection* (Princeton: Princeton University Press, 1966); P. W. Andrews, S. W. Gangestad, and D. Matthews, "Adaptationism: How to Carry Out an Exaptationist Program," *Behavioral and Brain Sciences* 25 (2002): 489–553; D. M. Buss, *Evolutionary Psychology: The New Science of the Mind*, 6th ed. (New York: Routledge, 2019).

18. J. Sidanius and R. Kurzban, "Evolutionary Approaches to Political Psychology," in *Handbook of Political Psychology*, ed. D. O. Sears, L. Huddy, and R. Jervis (Oxford: Oxford University Press, 2003), 157.

19. For reviews, see Pinker, *The Blank Slate*; Wright, *The Moral Animal*; D. M. Buss, *The Handbook of Evolutionary Psychology* (New York: Wiley, 2005); Fowler and Schreiber, "Biology, Politics, and the Emerging Science of Human Nature"; Barkow, *Missing the Revolution.*

20. L. Cronk and B. L. Leech, *Meeting at Grand Central: Understanding the Social and Evolutionary Roots of Cooperation* (Princeton: Princeton University Press, 2013).

21. P. H. Rubin, *Darwinian Politics: The Evolutionary Origin of Freedom* (New Brunswick, NJ: Rutgers University Press, 2002).

22. Alford and Hibbing, "The Origin of Politics"; J. R. Hibbing, K. B. Smith, and J. R. Alford, *Predisposed: Liberals, Conservatives, and the Biology of Political Differences* (New York: Routledge, 2013).

23. A. Todorov et al., "Inferences of Competence from Faces Predict Election Outcomes," *Science* 308 (2005): 1623–26.

24. D. D. P. Johnson and D. R. Tierney, *Failing to Win: Perceptions of Victory and Defeat in International Politics* (Cambridge, MA: Harvard University Press, 2006).

25. C. Boehm, *Hierarchy in the Forest: The Evolution of Egalitarian Behavior* (Cambridge, MA: Harvard University Press, 2001).

26. Sidanius and Kurzban, "Evolutionary Approaches to Political Psychology."

27. R. D. Sagarin and T. Taylor, eds., *Natural Security: A Darwinian Approach to a Dangerous World* (Berkeley: University of California Press, 2008); B. A. Thayer and V. M. Hudson, "Sex and the Shaheed: Insights from the Life Sciences on Islamic Suicide Terrorism," *International Security* 34, no. 4 (2010): 37–62; J. Orbell and T. Morikawa, "An Evolutionary Account of Suicide Attacks: The Kamikaze Case," *Political Psychology* 32, no. 2 (2011): 297–322.

28. G. Gigerenzer, *Adaptive Thinking: Rationality in the Real World* (Oxford: Oxford University Press, 2002); D. Nettle, "Adaptive Illusions: Optimism, Control and Human Rationality," in *Emotion, Evolution and Rationality*, ed. D. Evans and P. Cruse (Oxford: Oxford University Press, 2004).

29. K. Payne, *Strategy, Evolution, and War: From Apes to Artificial Intelligence* (Washington, DC: Georgetown University Press, 2018); D. D. P. Johnson and N. J. MacKay, "Fight the Power: Lanchester's Laws of Combat in Human Evolution," *Evolution and Human Behavior* 36, no. 2 (2015): 152–63.

30. M. van Vugt, "Evolutionary Origins of Leadership and Followership," *Personality and Social Psychology Review* 10, no. 4 (2006): 354–71; A. J. King, D. D. P. Johnson, and M. van Vugt, "The Origins and Evolution of Leadership," *Current Biology* 19, no. 19 (2009): 1591–1682.

31. D. D. P. Johnson, *Overconfidence and War: The Havoc and Glory of Positive Illusions* (Cambridge, MA: Harvard University Press, 2004); B. A. Thayer, *Darwin and International Relations: On the Evolutionary Origins of War and Ethnic Conflict* (Lexington: University Press of Kentucky, 2004); A. Gat, *War in Human Civilization* (Oxford: Oxford University Press, 2006); A. Gat, "So Why Do People Fight? Evolutionary Theory and the Causes of War," *European Journal of International Relations* 15, no. 4 (2009): 571–99.

32. D. D. P. Johnson and M. D. Toft, "Grounds for War: The Evolution of Territorial Conflict," *International Security* 38, no. 3 (2014): 7–38.

33. R. W. Wrangham, "Is Military Incompetence Adaptive?" *Evolution and Human Behaviour* 20 (1999): 3–17.

34. S. P. Rosen, *War and Human Nature* (Princeton: Princeton University Press, 2004).

35. D. S. Wilson, "A Tale of Two Classics: Biology vs. Economics," *New Scientist*, 21 March 2012.

36. R. Jervis, *System Effects: Complexity in Political and Social Life* (Princeton: Princeton University Press, 1997).

37. Barkow, *Missing the Revolution*.

38. See, e.g., D. Reiter and A. C. Stam, *Democracies at War* (Princeton: Princeton University Press, 2002).

39. E.g., G. Allison and P. Zelikow, *Essence of Decision: Explaining the Cuban Missile Crisis* (New York: Longman, 1999).

40. E.g., Jervis, *How Statesmen Think*; R. Jervis, *Perception and Misperception in International Politics* (Princeton: Princeton University Press, 1976); F. I. Greenstein, *The Presidential Difference: Leadership Style from F.D.R. to Bill Clinton* (New York: Free Press, 2000); R. McDermott, *Presidential Leadership, Illness, and Decision Making* (Cambridge: Cambridge University Press, 2007).

41. I. L. Janis, *Victims of Groupthink: Psychological Studies of Policy Decisions and Fiascoes* (Boston: Houghton Mifflin, 1972); P. A. Kowert, *Groupthink or Deadlock: When*

Do Leaders Learn from Their Advisors? (Albany: State University of New York Press, 2002); D. Kahneman and J. Renshon, "Why Hawks Win," *Foreign Policy*, no. 158 (2007): 34–38. For a review of Janis's "groupthink" specifically, see M. E. Turner and A. R. Pratkanis, "Twenty-Five Years of Groupthink Theory and Research: Lessons from the Evaluation of a Theory," *Organizational Behavior and Human Decision Processes* 73, no. 2–3 (1998): 105–15.

42. For a discussion of this and the methodological utility of divergences from commonly held biases, see C. D. Kaufmann, "Out of the Lab and into the Archives: A Method for Testing Psychological Explanations of Political Decision-Making," *International Studies Quarterly* 38 (1994): 557–86.

43. M. C. Horowitz, A. C. Stam, and C. M. Ellis, *Why Leaders Fight* (Cambridge: Cambridge University Press, 2015); G. Mukunda, *Indispensable: When Leaders Really Matter* (Boston: Harvard Business School Press, 2012).

44. Allison and Zelikow, *Essence of Decision*; R. N. Lebow, *Between Peace and War: The Nature of International Crisis* (Baltimore: Johns Hopkins University Press, 1981).

45. S. N. Ghaemi, *A First-Rate Madness: Uncovering the Links between Leadership and Mental Illness* (New York: Penguin Press, 2011); B. C. Rathbun, *Reasoning of State: Realists, Romantics and Rationality in International Relations* (Cambridge: Cambridge University Press, 2019).

46. B. R. Spisak et al., "Warriors and Peacekeepers: Testing a Biosocial Implicit Leadership Hypothesis of Intergroup Relations Using Masculine and Feminine Faces," *PLoS ONE* 7, no. 1 (2012): 30399.

47. I. H. Robertson, *The Winner Effect: How Power Affects Your Brain* (London: Bloomsbury, 2012).

48. J. S. Levy, "Misperception and the Causes of War: Theoretical Linkages and Analytical Problems," *World Politics* 36, no. 1 (1983): 76–99.

49. Greenstein, *The Presidential Difference*; McDermott, *Presidential Leadership, Illness, and Decision Making*; G. Chiozza and H. E. Goemans, *Leaders and International Conflict* (Cambridge: Cambridge University Press, 2011); E. A. Cohen, *Supreme Command: Soldiers, Statesmen, and Leadership in Wartime* (New York: Free Press, 2002); J. M. Post and A. George, *Leaders and Their Followers in a Dangerous World: The Psychology of Political Behavior*, 1st ed., Psychoanalysis and Social Theory (Ithaca: Cornell University Press, 2004); Jervis, *How Statesmen Think*; Horowitz, Stam, and Ellis, *Why Leaders Fight*.

50. Waltz, *Theory of International Politics*.

51. Waltz, *Man, the State and War*. Note that traits can be universal ("species-typical"), meaning all humans have them, but even universal traits can *vary* in their expression (this is especially the case for behavioral traits but also applies to physiological traits; for example, we all have hair, but hair color varies). Williams, *Adaptation and Natural Selection*; Andrews, Gangestad, and Matthews, "Adaptationism"; Barkow, *Missing the Revolution*.

52. J. D. Fearon, "Rationalist Explanations for War," *International Organization* 49, no. 3 (1995): 379–414.

53. R. H. Thaler, *Misbehaving: The Making of Behavioral Economics* (New York: W. W. Norton, 2016); Mercer, "Rationality and Psychology in International Politics."

54. Pinker, *The Blank Slate*.

55. Neumann, "International Relations as a Social Science," 345.

56. A point that authors have been at pains to emphasize, as often revealed in their book titles themselves; see, e.g., the full titles of Buss, *Evolutionary Psychology*; Wright, *The Moral Animal*; Barkow, *Missing the Revolution*. For a review of the sociobiology debate and the personalities involved, see U. Segerstrale, *Defenders of the Truth: The Sociobiology Debate* (Oxford: Oxford University Press, 2000). See also Pinker, *The Blank Slate*; Hibbing, Smith, and Alford, *Predisposed*.

57. Rosen, *War and Human Nature*; M. D. Toft, *The Geography of Ethnic Violence: Identity, Interests, and the Indivisibility of Territory* (Princeton: Princeton University Press, 2003); Thayer, *Darwin and International Relations*; Gat, "So Why Do People Fight?"

58. E. M. Hafner-Burton et al., "The Behavioral Revolution and International Relations," *International Organization* 71, no. S1 (Supplement) (2017): 1–31; Fowler and Schreiber, "Biology, Politics, and the Emerging Science of Human Nature."

59. Sagarin and Taylor, *Natural Security*; Payne, *Strategy, Evolution, and War.*

60. Buss, *Evolutionary Psychology*; R. Dunbar and L. Barrett, eds., *Oxford Handbook of Evolutionary Psychology* (Oxford: Oxford University Press, 2009); J. H. Barkow, L. Cosmides, and J. Tooby, eds., *The Adapted Mind: Evolutionary Psychology and the Generation of Culture* (Oxford: Oxford University Press, 1992); Pinker, *The Blank Slate.*

61. D. Kahneman, *Thinking, Fast and Slow* (London: Allen Lane, 2011); T. Gilovich, D. Griffin, and D. Kahneman, eds., *Heuristics and Biases: The Psychology of Intuitive Judgment* (Cambridge: Cambridge University Press, 2002).

62. R. Giphart and M. van Vugt, *Mismatch: How Our Stone Age Brain Deceives Us Every Day (And What We Can Do About It)* (London: Little, Brown Book Group, 2018).

63. L. Cosmides and J. Tooby, "Better than Rational: Evolutionary Psychology and the Invisible Hand," *American Economic Review* 84, no. 2 (1994): 327–32; M. G. Haselton et al., "Adaptive Rationality: An Evolutionary Perspective on Cognitive Bias," *Social Cognition* 27 (2009): 733–63.

64. M. G. Haselton and D. Nettle, "The Paranoid Optimist: An Integrative Evolutionary Model of Cognitive Biases," *Personality and Social Psychology Review* 10, no. 1 (2006): 47–66; D. D. P. Johnson et al., "The Evolution of Error: Error Management, Cognitive Constraints, and Adaptive Decision-Making Biases," *Trends in Ecology & Evolution* 28, no. 8 (2013): 474–81.

65. M. Toda, "The Design of a Fungus Eater: A Model of Human Behavior in an Unsophisticated Environment," *Behavioral Science* 7, no. 2 (1962): 164–83; Gigerenzer, *Adaptive Thinking.*

66. Gigerenzer, *Adaptive Thinking.*

67. One may wonder what the exact criteria are to deduce that a trait constitutes an adaptation. This has been a topic of long debate even among biologists. See, e.g., Andrews, Gangestad, and Matthews, "Adaptationism"; Williams, *Adaptation and Natural Selection.* In a review of this literature, anthropologist Richard Sosis offers a useful summary: "The burden of evidence required to demonstrate an adaptation is considerable and unfortunately there is no agreed-upon protocol for accepting and rejecting what counts as an adaptation. Andrews *et al.* (2002) review six evidentiary standards that have been employed by biologists to identify adaptations, including phylogenetic comparisons, fitness maximization, and beneficial effects in ancestral environments, but their thorough review also highlights the limitations of each of the approaches they discuss. Williams (1966), the recognized father of the adaptationist program, cautioned that alternative explanations for the emergence of trait characteristics must be eliminated, but he also recognized that there is no universal list of evidentiary standards that can be applied to all traits. He argued that adaptations should exhibit evidence of 'special design'; i.e., they should efficiently solve the adaptive problem they are purported to solve, and demonstrate reliability, economy and precision." R. Sosis, "The Adaptationist-Byproduct Debate on the Evolution of Religion: Five Misunderstandings of the Adaptationist Program," *Journal of Cognition and Culture* 9 (2009): 315–32, 324. In this book, I have followed Williams's approach, which retains broad consensus among evolutionary biologists.

68. S. J. Gould and S. Vrba, "Exaptation: A Missing Term in the Science of Form," *Paleobiology* 8 (1982): 4–15.

69. Technically, a given cognitive bias could also be an exaptation: a tendency that arose by chance, or for some unrelated reason in the past, but that happens to be useful today. This seems to have rarely been considered for cognitive biases, and may be unlikely or unusual, but is perhaps worthy of further investigation.

70. For some analysis of leadership and reproductive success, see A. M. Ludwig, *King of the Mountain: The Nature of Political Leadership* (Lexington: University Press of Kentucky, 2002); L. Betzig, *Despotism and Differential Reproduction: A Darwinian View of History* (New York: Aldine, 1986).

71. E. Mayr, "Cause and Effect in Biology," *Science* 134 (1961): 1501–6; N. Tinbergen, "On Aims and Methods in Ethology," *Zeitschrift für Tierpsychologie* 20 (1963): 410–33; T. C. Scott-Phillips, T. E. Dickins, and S. A. West, "Evolutionary Theory and the Ultimate-Proximate Distinction in the Human Behavioral Sciences," *Perspectives on Psychological Science* 6, no. 1 (2011): 38–47.

72. N. B. Davies, J. R. Krebs, and S. A. West, *An Introduction to Behavioural Ecology* (Chichester: Wiley Blackwell, 2012), 2.

73. T. Burnham and J. Phelan, *Mean Genes: From Sex to Money to Food, Taming Our Primal Instincts* (New York: Penguin, 2001); Giphart and van Vugt, *Mismatch*; M. Solinas et al., "Dopamine and Addiction: What Have We Learned from 40 Years of Research?" *Journal of Neural Transmission* 126, no. 4 (2019): 481–516.

74. T. Birkhead, J. Wimpenny, and B. Montgomerie, *Ten Thousand Birds: Ornithology since Darwin* (Princeton: Princeton University Press, 2014), 301–8; N. Davies, *Cuckoo: Cheating by Nature* (London: Bloomsbury, 2015).

75. A. L. George and A. Bennett, *Case Studies and Theory Development in the Social Sciences* (Cambridge, MA: MIT Press, 2004); J. Gerring, "What Is a Case Study and What Is It Good For?" *American Political Science Review* 98, no. 2 (2004): 341–54.

76. G. J. Vermeij, *Nature: An Economic History* (Princeton: Princeton University Press, 2004).

77. R. C. Lewontin, S. Rose, and L. J. Kamin, *Not in Our Genes: Biology, Ideology and Human Nature* (New York: Pantheon Books, 1984).

78. Pinker, *The Blank Slate*.

79. R. C. Lewontin, "Sociobiology as an Adaptationist Program," *Behavioral Science* 24, no. 1 (1979): 5–14.

80. D. S. A. Bell and P. K. MacDonald, "Correspondence: Start the Evolution without Us," *International Security* 26, no. 1 (2001): 187–94.

81. Fowler, Settle, and Dawes, "The Heritability of Partisan Attachment"; Alford, Funk, and Hibbing, "Are Political Orientations Genetically Transmitted?"

82. For examples relevant to politics, see M. Bang Petersen, "Evolutionary Political Psychology: On the Origin and Structure of Heuristics and Biases in Politics," *Political Psychology* 36, no. S1 (2015): 45–78; Fowler and Schreiber, "Biology, Politics, and the Emerging Science of Human Nature"; M. Horowitz, R. McDermott, and A. Stam, "Leader Age, Regime Type and Violence," *Journal of Conflict Resolution* 49, no. 5 (2005): 661–85; L. Laustsen and M. B. Petersen, "Perceived Conflict and Leader Dominance: Individual and Contextual Factors behind Preferences for Dominant Leaders," *Political Psychology* 38, no. 6 (2017): 1083–1101; A. C. Lopez, R. McDermott, and M. B. Petersen, "States in Mind: Evolution, Coalitional Psychology, and International Politics," *International Security* 36, no. 2 (2011): 48–83.

83. E.g., see M. A. Nowak, *Evolutionary Dynamics: Exploring the Equations of Life* (Cambridge, MA: Belknap Press of Harvard University Press, 2006); K. Sigmund, *Games of Life: Explorations in Ecology, Evolution and Behaviour* (London: Penguin, 1995); P. Turchin, *War and Peace and War: The Life Cycles of Imperial Nations* (New York: Pi Press, 2005).

84. Waltz, *Man, the State and War*; J. S. Nye, "Neorealism and Neoliberalism," *World Politics* 40, no. 2 (1988): 235–51, 241.

85. See, for e.g., Barkow, *Missing the Revolution*; Rosen, *War and Human Nature*; D. T. Kenrick and V. Griskevicius, *The Rational Animal: How Evolution Made Us Smarter than We Think* (New York: Basic Books, 2013).

86. Note that "epigenetics" has two meanings. Originally, it referred simply to the differential activity and expression of genes (that change aspects of an organism's phenotype without any change in the underlying genotype). In recent years, however, it has come to refer to changes in gene activity and expression that are in themselves *heritable* ("epigenetic inheritance"). For a review, see É. Danchin et al., "Beyond DNA: Integrating Inclusive Inheritance into an Extended Theory of Evolution," *Nature Reviews Genetics* 12 (2011): 475–86. For debates on the relative importance of epigenetic inheritance and other factors on evolution, see K. Laland et al., "Does Evolutionary Theory Need a Rethink?" *Nature* 514, no. 161–64 (2014).

87. R. McDermott et al., "Monoamine Oxidase A Gene (MAOA) Predicts Behavioral Aggression Following Provocation," *Proceedings of the National Academy of Sciences* 106, no. 7 (2009): 2118–23.

88. G. Frazzetto et al., "Early Trauma and Increased Risk for Physical Aggression during Adulthood: The Moderating Role of MAOA Genotype," *PLoS ONE* May, no. 5 (May 2007): e486; A. Caspi et al., "Role of Genotype in the Cycle of Violence in Maltreated Children," *Science* 297, no. 5582 (2002): 851–54.

89. For some reviews and perspectives, see Payne, *Strategy, Evolution, and War*; Hafner-Burton et al., "The Behavioral Revolution and International Relations"; Hibbing, Smith, and Alford, *Predisposed*; Thayer, *Darwin and International Relations*; A. C. Lopez, "The Hawkish Dove: Evolution and the Logic of Political Behavior," *Millennium: Journal of International Studies* 43, no. 1 (2014): 66–91; Gat, "So Why Do People Fight?"; McDermott, "The Feeling of Rationality"; Rosen, *War and Human Nature*.

Chapter 3. Fortune Favors the Bold: The Strategic Advantages of Overconfidence

The epigraph sources are: T. Roosevelt, *The Strenuous Life: Essays and Addresses* (1902; Boston: Vigeo Press, 2017), 2; C. von Clausewitz, *On War*, trans. M. Howard and P. Paret (1832; Princeton: Princeton University Press, 1976), 190.

1. Thucydides, R. B. Strassler, and R. Crawley, *The Landmark Thucydides: A Comprehensive Guide to the Peloponnesian War*, 1st Touchstone ed. (New York: Simon & Schuster, 1998), 16.

2. Ibid., 81.

3. Ibid., 83.

4. Ibid.

5. Ibid., 83–84.

6. J. S. Levy, "Misperception and the Causes of War: Theoretical Linkages and Analytical Problems," *World Politics* 36, no. 1 (1983): 76–99, 84.

7. D. Kagan, *The Outbreak of the Peloponnesian War* (Ithaca: Cornell University Press, 1969), 356.

8. Ibid.

9. P. de Souza, *The Peloponnesian War, 431–404 BC* (Oxford: Osprey, 2002), 7.

10. P. de Souza, *The Greek and Persian Wars, 499–386 BC* (Oxford: Osprey, 2003), 90.

11. de Souza, *The Peloponnesian War, 431–404 BC*, 75.

12. For a classic text, see S. E. Taylor, *Positive Illusions: Creative Self-Deception and the Healthy Mind* (New York: Basic Books, 1989). Note that "illusions" are distinct from

"delusions." In psychology, an *illusion* is defined as "a perception that is not true to reality, having been altered subjectively in the mind of the perceiver"; the definition of *delusion*, on the other hand, is a psychiatric term meaning "a belief held in the face of evidence to the contrary, that is resistant to all reason" (*Collins Dictionary*, 2019). While they may seem different in degree rather than in kind, positive illusions are within a "normal" range of beliefs held by mentally healthy people, whereas delusions are outside the "normal" range of beliefs and are held by mentally ill people. The definition of "illusion" used by Shelley Taylor (originally from the Random House *Dictionary of the English Language*, 1982) is: "A perception that represents what is perceived in a way different from the way it is in reality. An illusion is a false mental image or conception which may be a misinterpretation of a real appearance or may be something imagined. It may be pleasing, harmless, or even useful." S. E. Taylor et al., "Maintaining Positive Illusions in the Face of Negative Information: Getting the Facts without Letting Them Get to You," *Journal of Social and Clinical Psychology* 8 (1989): 114–29, 115.

13. While at least familiar, the term "overconfidence" can still be potentially misleading. The word can imply that we are referring to people or events that, *by definition*, are eventual losers, since "overconfidence" suggests they were *too* confident about the outcome of a given event (e.g., only the Athenians could be called "overconfident" in the Peloponnesian War, since they were the side that lost). Equally, the term can imply that we are ruling out people or events that, *as it turns out*, are eventual victors, since the successful outcome itself suggests that they were *not* "overconfident" after all (e.g., none of the Allied Powers could be called "overconfident" in 1914, since they won). Clearly, both of these interpretations would be false.

What is important is to separate overconfidence about *assessments* from overconfidence about *outcomes*. One can be overconfident and win or lose, just as one can be perfectly unbiased and still win or lose. Overconfidence simply describes one's assessment of the probability of an outcome (beliefs about an event), whatever happens in the end (the result of an event). The result in itself does not (and cannot) alter whether you were overconfident or not before it happened! Overconfidence therefore does not mean being "*too* confident" for some task (i.e., it is not that the task is impossible); rather, overconfidence means being "*more* confident than one ought to be," given the circumstances (i.e., the task is harder than it seems). Outcomes can be one important *indicator* of overconfidence, but a single instance of success or failure does not define it.

14. A distinction can be made between: (1) "overestimation" (exaggerating one's *performance*); (2) "overplacement" (exaggerating one's *performance relative to others*); and (3) "overprecision" (exaggerating certainty in the *accuracy* of one's beliefs, whatever those beliefs are). Each of these three forms of overconfidence can have their own causes and consequences. D. A. Moore and D. Schatz, "The Three Faces of Overconfidence," *Social and Personality Psychology Compass* 11, no. 8 (2017): e12331. See also P. E. Tetlock, *Expert Political Judgment: How Good Is It? How Can We Know?* (Princeton: Princeton University Press, 2005). Such distinctions highlight the point that "positive illusions" are about things going well, whereas "overconfidence" can mean unwarranted confidence that things will go *badly* as well as go well (for example, I could be overconfident that the stock market is going to rise, but I could equally be overconfident that the stock market is going to crash). However, I use "overconfidence" in the more common usage in which it implies unwarranted expectations about *positive* events or outcomes, as with positive illusions.

15. The notion of overconfidence is sometimes criticized because it appears to require post hoc judgments. Often we do not know the true likelihood of an outcome, and thus whether or not a given person's assessment of that outcome was overly confident. However,

this is not as large a problem as it may seem. Taking the example of war, although it is not easy to estimate each side's true likelihood of winning at the outbreak of a conflict, these estimates are not entirely subjective or arbitrary, for at least five reasons:

(1) *Outright hubris.* In many cases, overconfidence is so extreme (e.g., "we will win in a few days"), and so far removed from a reasonable assessment of the available evidence, that labeling it as overconfidence is straightforward.

(2) *Third parties.* The true likelihood of an outcome is usually estimated by many observers, both inside and outside the decision-making group and the states concerned, so estimates that are far more confident than the average are likely to be overconfident.

(3) *Process tracing.* There is often strong evidence that accurate or contrary information was available to leaders but was discounted or ignored out of hand, suggesting overconfident beliefs.

(4) *Hindsight.* The actual outcome is typically known, providing evidence about whether decision-makers made a good bet or not. If the tape of history were rerun, the outcome might be different on another occasion, but one data point is nevertheless better than none. On average, expecting X and gaining less than X implies overconfidence.

(5) *Mutual overconfidence.* When both or all sides think they will resoundingly crush their adversaries, this is a good sign that at least one of the sides is overconfident.

16. Taylor, *Positive Illusions.*

17. C. Peterson, *A Primer in Positive Psychology* (New York: Oxford University Press, 2006). The field of "positive psychology" emerged to counter what many saw as an undue focus in psychology and psychiatry on *disorders* and *abnormalities.* Instead, positive psychologists argue we should focus on the strengths of our psychological dispositions. C. Peterson and M. E. P. Seligman, *Character Strengths and Virtues: A Handbook of Classification* (New York: Oxford University Press, 2004); C Peterson, "The Values in Action (VIA) Classification of Strengths: The Un-DSM and the Real DSM," in *A Life Worth Living: Contributions to Positive Psychology,* ed. M. Csikszentmihalyi and I. Csikszentmihalyi (Oxford: Oxford University Press, 2006). See also J. E. Gillham, ed., *The Science of Optimism and Hope: Research Essays in Honor of Martin E. P. Seligman* (Radnor, PA: Templeton Foundation, 2000).

18. T. Sharot, *The Optimism Bias: A Tour of The Irrationally Positive Brain* (New York: Pantheon, 2011).

19. T. Sharot, C. W. Korn, and R. J. Dolan, "How Unrealistic Optimism Is Maintained in the Face of Reality," *Nature Neuroscience* 14, no. 11 (2011): 1475–79.

20. B. M. Barber and T. Odean, "Boys Will Be Boys: Gender, Overconfidence, and Common Stock Investment," *Quarterly Journal of Economics* 116 (2001): 261–92; C. Camerer and D. Lovallo, "Overconfidence and Excess Entry: An Experimental Approach," *American Economic Review* 89, no. 1 (1999): 306–18; U. Malmendier and G. Tate, "C.E.O. Overconfidence and Corporate Investment," *Journal of Finance* 60, no. 6 (2005): 2661–2700; D. Lovallo and D. Kahneman, "Delusions of Success: How Optimism Undermines Executives' Decisions," *Harvard Business Review* 81, no. 6 (2003): 56–63.

21. G. A. Akerlof and R. J. Shiller, *Animal Spirits: How Human Psychology Drives the Economy, and Why It Matters for Global Capitalism* (Princeton: Princeton University Press, 2009); G. Anderson, *Cityboy: Beer and Loathing in the Square Mile* (London: Headline, 2008); N. N. Taleb, *Fooled by Randomness: The Hidden Role of Chance in Life and in the Markets* (London: Penguin, 2007); N. Ferguson, *The Ascent of Money: A Financial History of the World* (New York: Penguin, 2008).

22. Sharot, *The Optimism Bias*; J. Burger and M. Palmer, "Changes in and Generalization of Unrealistic Optimism Following Experiences with Stressful Events: Reactions to the 1989 California Earthquake," *Personality and Social Psychology Bulletin* 18 (1992): 39–43; D. D. P. Johnson and S. A. Levin, "The Tragedy of Cognition: Psychological Biases and Environmental Inaction," *Current Science* 97, no. 11 (2009): 1593–1603; D. D. P. Johnson, *Overconfidence and War: The Havoc and Glory of Positive Illusions* (Cambridge, MA: Harvard University Press, 2004).

23. D. D. P. Johnson et al., "Overconfidence in Wargames: Experimental Evidence on Expectations, Aggression, Gender and Testosterone," *Proceedings of the Royal Society of London, Series B* 273, no. 1600 (2006): 2513–20.

24. Why did we only look at males? This was for three reasons. First, our previous experiments found very large differences between the sexes, and here we wanted to focus on other causal factors. Looking at only one sex maximized our sample size while removing one known source of variation. Second, we were also looking at certain genetic polymorphisms, one of which is easier to study in men than women. Third, believe it or not we have encountered difficulties publishing studies in political science journals that found sex differences in behavior!

25. D. D. P. Johnson et al., "Dead Certain: Confidence and Conservatism Predict Aggression in Simulated International Crisis Decision-Making," *Human Nature* 23, no. 1 (2012): 98–126.

26. And it specified, "Please circle your response, where 0 is very unlikely and 10 is very likely."

27. Hew Strachan, BBC 4, *In Our Time*, "Clausewitz and *On War*," aired on 17 May 2012, at time 07:00.

28. "The 1812 Overture," *Economist*, 7 January 2012, 39.

29. A. Roberts, *Waterloo: Napoleon's Last Gamble* (London: HarperCollins, 2005), 40.

30. Ibid., 41.

31. D. D. P. Johnson and D. R. Tierney, "The Rubicon Theory of War: How the Path to Conflict Reaches the Point of No Return," *International Security* 36, no. 1 (2011): 7–40; K. Macksey, *Military Errors of World War Two* (London: Cassell, 1987); B. W. Tuchman, *The March of Folly: From Troy to Vietnam* (New York: Alfred A. Knopf, 1984); Johnson, *Overconfidence and War*.

32. D. Ignatius, "James Clapper: We Underestimated the Islamic State's 'Will to Fight,'" *Washington Post*, 18 September 2014.

33. "France's Foreign Policy: Showing the Strain," *Economist*, 14 July 2011, 39–40, 39.

34. M. Waldman, "System Failure: The Underlying Causes of US Policy-making Errors in Afghanistan," *International Affairs* 89, no. 4 (2013): 825–43, 825.

35. L. Diamond, "What Went Wrong in Iraq," *Foreign Affairs* 83, no. 5 (2004): 34–56.

36. K. Phillips, "Hegemony, Hubris and Overreach," in *The Iraq War Reader: History, Documents, Opinions*, ed. M. L. Sifry and C. Cerf (New York: Touchstone, 2003), 633.

37. J. G. Stoessinger, *Why Nations Go to War* (New York: St. Martin's, 1998); S. Ganguly, *Conflict Unending: India-Pakistan Tensions since 1947* (New Delhi: Oxford University Press, 2001); R. N. Lebow, *Between Peace and War: The Nature of International Crisis* (Baltimore: Johns Hopkins University Press, 1981); Johnson, *Overconfidence and War*; D. Kahneman and J. Renshon, "Why Hawks Win," *Foreign Policy*, no. 158 (2007): 34–38; Tuchman, *The March of Folly*; R. K. White, *Nobody Wanted War: Misperception in Vietnam and Other Wars* (New York: Doubleday, 1968).

38. G. A. Blainey, *The Causes of War* (New York: Free Press, 1973), 35.

39. S. Van Evera, *Causes of War: Power and the Roots of Conflict* (Ithaca: Cornell University Press, 1999), 16.

40. R. Jervis, "War and Misperception," *Journal of Interdisciplinary History* 18, no. 4 (1988): 675–700, 676.

41. Levy, "Misperception and the Causes of War," 83.

42. Ibid., 84.

43. S. M. Walt, "International Relations: One World, Many Theories," *Foreign Policy*, no. 110 (1998): 29–46, 37.

44. I am grateful to Robert Jervis for this point. See also Jervis, "War and Misperception." For analyses of why we should expect this even among rational actors, see E. Van den Steen, "Rational Overoptimism (and Other Biases)," *American Economic Review* 94 (2004): 1141–51; D. Altman, "The Strategist's Curse: A Theory of False Optimism as a Cause of War," *Security Studies* 24, no. 2 (2015): 284–315.

45. R. A. Doughty, *Pyrrhic Victory: French Strategy and Operations in the Great War* (Cambridge, MA: Belknap Press, 2005), 1.

46. See, e.g., Blainey, *The Causes of War*; Van Evera, *Causes of War*; J. S. Levy and W. R. Thompson, *Causes of War* (Oxford: Wiley-Blackwell, 2010); White, *Nobody Wanted War*; Ganguly, *Conflict Unending*. There is plenty of disagreement over the *source* of this overconfidence. For example, is a given instance of overconfidence a result of a *cognitive bias* (that is, a distortion of good information)? Or a result of rational actors having *faulty information* (that is, an accurate assessment but based on poor intelligence)?

47. S. M. Walt, "Wishful Thinking: Top 10 Examples of the Most Unrealistic Expectations in Contemporary U.S. Foreign Policy," *Foreign Policy*, 29 April 2011, http://www.foreignpolicy.com/articles/2011/04/29/wishful_thinking.

48. S. M. Walt, *The Origins of Alliances* (Ithaca: Cornell University Press, 1987).

49. Van Evera, *Causes of War*.

50. B. W. Tuchman, *The Guns of August* (New York: Macmillan, 1962); Tuchman, *The March of Folly*.

51. Widely quoted although no source found.

52. Taylor, *Positive Illusions*; D. L. Feltz, S. E. Short, and P. J. Sullivan, *Self-efficacy in Sport* (Champaign, IL: Human Kinetics, 2008); A. D. Stajkovic and F. Luthans, "Self-efficacy and Work-Related Performance: A Meta-analysis," *Psychological Bulletin* 124 (1998): 240–61.

53. B. J. Zimmerman, "Self-efficacy and Educational Development," in *Self-efficacy in Changing Societies*, ed. A. Bandura (New York: Cambridge University Press, 1995).

54. A. Bandura and D. H. Schunk, "Cultivating Competence, Self-efficacy, and Intrinsic Interest through Proximal Self-motivation," *Journal of Personality and Social Psychology* 41 (1981): 586–98.

55. R. M. Kanter, *Confidence: How Winning Streaks and Losing Streaks Begin and End* (New York: Crown Business, 2004).

56. M. Fenton-O'Creevy, *Traders: Risks, Decisions and Management in Financial Markets* (Oxford: Oxford University Press, 2005).

57. J. M. Keynes, *The General Theory of Employment, Interest and Money* (London: Macmillan, 1936), 161–62.

58. E. Dimson, P. Marsh, and M. Staunton, *Triumph of the Optimists: 101 Years of Global Investment Returns* (Princeton: Princeton University Press, 2002).

59. Fred Perry quote given in Ronald Atkin, "Andy Murray Can Learn from the 1936 Wimbledon Champion Fred Perry," *Guardian*, 9 July 2012.

60. A. Salvador et al., "Anticipatory Cortisol, Testosterone and Psychological Responses to Judo Competition in Young Men," *Psychoneuroendocrinology* 28, no. 3 (2003): 364–75.

61. J. Taylor, "Confidence Matters for Athletes," *Huffington Post*, 24 February 2011.

62. S. E. Taylor and D. A. Armor, "Positive Illusions and Coping with Adversity," *Journal of Personality* 64 (1996): 873–98; R. F. Baumeister, "The Optimal Margin of Illusion," *Journal of Social and Clinical Psychology* 8 (1989): 176–89.

63. S. E. Taylor and J. D. Brown, "Positive Illusions and Well-Being Revisited: Separating Fact from Fiction," *Psychological Bulletin* 116, no. 1 (1994): 21–27, 22.

64. Ibid., 23.

65. S. E. Taylor and J. D. Brown, "Illusion and Well-Being: A Social Psychological Perspective on Mental Health," *Psychological Bulletin* 103 (1988): 193–210, 199.

66. S. C. Segerstrom, *Breaking Murphy's Law: How Optimists Get What They Want from Life—and Pessimists Can Too* (New York: Guilford Press, 2007).

67. C. Anderson et al., "A Status-Enhancement Account of Overconfidence," *Journal of Personality and Social Psychology* 103, no. 4 (2012): 718–35. Some studies find that even when people are revealed to have been overconfident, others still viewed them positively. J. A. Kennedy, C. Anderson, and D. A. Moore, "When Overconfidence Is Revealed to Others: Testing the Status-Enhancement Theory of Overconfidence," *Organizational Behavior and Human Decision Processes* 122, no. 2 (2013): 266–79.

68. R. T. McKay and D. C. Dennett, "The Evolution of Misbelief," *Behavioral and Brain Sciences* 32 (2009): 493–561.

69. J. C. Beck and M. Wade, *Got Game: How the Gamer Generation Is Reshaping Business Forever* (Boston: Harvard Business School Press, 2004), 164.

70. E. M. Rusli, N. Perlroth, and N. Bilton, "The Education of Mark Zuckerberg," *New York Times*, 12 May 2012.

71. D. T. Kenrick and V. Griskevicius, *The Rational Animal: How Evolution Made Us Smarter than We Think* (New York: Basic Books, 2013), 91.

72. D. Nettle, "Adaptive Illusions: Optimism, Control and Human Rationality," in *Emotion, Evolution and Rationality*, ed. D. Evans and P. Cruse (Oxford: Oxford University Press, 2004); M. G. Haselton and D. Nettle, "The Paranoid Optimist: An Integrative Evolutionary Model of Cognitive Biases," *Personality and Social Psychology Review* 10, no. 1 (2006): 47–66; R. L. Trivers, *Deceit and Self-Deception: Fooling Yourself the Better to Fool Others* (London: Allen Lane, 2011); R. W. Wrangham, "Is Military Incompetence Adaptive?" *Evolution and Human Behaviour* 20 (1999): 3–17.

73. Trivers, *Deceit and Self-Deception*; R. L. Trivers, "The Elements of a Scientific Theory of Self-Deception," *Annals of the New York Academy of Sciences* 907 (2000): 114–31; W. von Hippel and R. Trivers, "The Evolution and Psychology of Self-Deception," *Behavioral and Brain Sciences* 34 (2011): 1–56.

74. Wrangham, "Is Military Incompetence Adaptive?"

75. J. Tooby and L. Cosmides, "The Evolution of War and Its Cognitive Foundations," Institute for Evolutionary Studies Technical Report #88–1 (1988); J. Tooby and L. Cosmides, "Groups in Mind: The Coalitional Roots of War and Morality," in *Human Morality & Sociality: Evolutionary & Comparative Perspectives*, ed. H. Høgh-Olesen (New York: Palgrave MacMillan, 2010).

76. Source: scribbled down frantically in person by myself.

77. D. D. P. Johnson, N. B. Weidmann, and L.-E. Cederman, "Fortune Favours the Bold: An Agent-Based Model Reveals Adaptive Advantages of Overconfidence in War," *PLoS ONE* 6, no. 6 (2011): e20851.

78. L.-E. Cederman, "Endogenizing Geopolitical Boundaries with Agent-Based Modeling," *Proceedings of the National Academy of Sciences* 99, no. Supplement 3 (2002): 7296–7303; L.-E. Cederman, *Emergent Actors in World Politics: How States and Nations Develop and Dissolve* (Princeton: Princeton University Press, 1997).

79. D. D. P. Johnson and D. R. Tierney, "Bad World: The Negativity Bias in International Relations," *International Security* 43, no. 3 (2019): 96–140.

80. For full details of the methods and results, see the original journal article: Johnson, Weidmann, and Cederman, "Fortune Favours the Bold." Methods followed prior studies using this approach, such as in Cederman, *Emergent Actors in World Politics*. In each time step, all states synchronously executed five subprocedures: (1) *resource extraction phase*—the state extracts one unit of resources from each of its provinces and adds it to its current resource level (all states begin life with 10 units per province); (2) *decision phase*—states assess the probability p of defeating each neighbor and attack the state conferring the highest p (as long as p exceeds a given "attack threshold" w, with default $w = 0.5$); (3) *resource-allocation phase*—states divide resources among all "active fronts" (wars with neighboring states, whoever initiated them) in proportion to the size of each of those states; (4) *interaction phase*—war outcomes are determined by a commonly used logistic conflict success function; (5) *structural change phase*—the winning state gains a randomly selected adjacent province from the loser's territory. Provinces become independent states if their capital is: (a) captured; or (b) geographically cut off. Such "newborn" states inherit the strategy (α) of their former state. No other processes of geopolitical change, such as secession of a subset of a state, could occur in this model.

81. D. D. P. Johnson and J. H. Fowler, "The Evolution of Overconfidence," *Nature* 477 (2011): 317–20.

82. Nettle, "Adaptive Illusions"; Haselton and Nettle, "The Paranoid Optimist."

83. J. Maynard Smith and G. A. Parker, "The Logic of Asymmetric Contests," *Animal Behavior* 24 (1976): 159–75.

84. R. W. Wrangham, "The Evolution of Coalitionary Killing," *Yearbook of Physical Anthropology* 42 (1999): 1–30. For other factors that can make fighting cheaper, see D. D. P. Johnson and N. J. MacKay, "Fight the Power: Lanchester's Laws of Combat in Human Evolution," *Evolution and Human Behavior* 36, no. 2 (2015): 152–63; Tooby and Cosmides, "Groups in Mind."

85. Wrangham, "Is Military Incompetence Adaptive?"

86. Von Clausewitz, *On War*, 117.

87. Ibid., 86.

88. R. K. Herrmann and J. K. Choi, "From Prediction to Learning: Opening Experts' Minds to Unfolding History," *International Security* 31, no. 4 (2007): 132–61, 145.

89. Ibid.

90. K. Wang and J. L. Ray, "Beginners and Winners: The Fate of Initiators of Interstate Wars Involving Great Powers since 1495," *International Studies Quarterly* 38 (1994): 139–54.

91. Roosevelt, *The Strenuous Life: Essays and Addresses*, 2.

92. A. Carroll, ed., *War Letters: Extraordinary Correspondence from American Wars* (New York: Scribner, 2001), 240. Capitalization in the original, but I added some missing punctuation.

93. Von Clausewitz, *On War*, 190.

94. B. S. Lambeth, "Why Submariners Should Talk to Fighter Pilots," RAND Paper RP-864 (2000).

95. R. Collins, *Violence: A Micro-Sociological Theory* (Princeton: Princeton University Press, 2008), 398–99.

96. P. K. Davis, *Masters of the Battlefield: Great Commanders from the Classical Age to the Napoleonic Era* (Oxford: Oxford University Press, 2013), 413–14.

97. Roberts, *Waterloo: Napoleon's Last Gamble*, 119–20.

98. R. Greene, *The 48 Laws of Power* (New York: Penguin, 1998), 233.

99. William Shakespeare, *Henry V*, Act IV, scene I.

100. Actually, this quote is widely attributed to Goethe but in fact appears to come from Scottish mountaineer W. H. Murray, inspired by Goethe's *Faust* and given in Goethe's style. https://www.thoughtco.com/goethe-quote-may-not-be-his-4070881.

101. Widely attributed but no source found.

102. Virgil, *The Aeneid* (London: Penguin Classics, 2003).

103. Roberts, *Waterloo: Napoleon's Last Gamble*, 87.

104. A. J. King, D. D. P. Johnson, and M. van Vugt, "The Origins and Evolution of Leadership," *Current Biology* 19, no. 19 (2009): 1591–1682.

105. T. Judge et al., "Personality and Leadership: A Qualitative and Quantitative Review," *Journal of Applied Psychology* 87 (2002): 765–80.

106. M. van Vugt, "Evolutionary Origins of Leadership and Followership," *Personality and Social Psychology Review* 10, no. 4 (2006): 354–71.

107. G. Barlow, W. Rogers, and N. Fraley, "Do Midas Cichlids Win through Prowess or Daring? It Depends," *Behavioral Ecology and Sociobiology* 19 (1986): 1–18; D. D. P. Johnson and M. D. Toft, "Grounds for War: The Evolution of Territorial Conflict," *International Security* 38, no. 3 (2014): 7–38.

108. H. A. Kissinger, *White House Years* (Boston: Little, Brown, 1979), 316, 318.

109. Ibid., 321.

110. Cited in C. Lamb, "Belief Systems and Decision Making in the Mayaguez Crisis," *Political Science Quarterly* 99, no. 4 (1984–85): 681–702, 685.

111. J. D. Kertzer, *Resolve in International Politics* (Princeton: Princeton University Press, 2016).

112. Ibid., 165.

113. T. C. Schelling, *The Strategy of Conflict* (Cambridge, MA: Harvard University Press, 1960); Kertzer, *Resolve in International Politics*. Although see also J. Mercer, *Reputation and International Politics* (Ithaca: Cornell University Press, 1996).

114. Kertzer, *Resolve in International Politics*.

115. Wrangham, "Is Military Incompetence Adaptive?"

116. Ibid.

117. D. Reiter and A. C. Stam, "Democracy and Battlefield Military Effectiveness," *Journal of Conflict Resolution* 42, no. 3 (1998): 259–77.

118. Johnson and Tierney, "The Rubicon Theory of War."

119. P. M. Gollwitzer, "Mindset Theory of Action Phases," in *Handbook of Theories of Social Psychology*, ed. P. A. M. Van Lange, A. W. Kruglanksi, and E. T. Higgins (London: Sage, 2011); H. Heckhausen and P. M. Gollwitzer, "Thought Contents and Cognitive Functioning in Motivational versus Volitional States of Mind," *Motivation and Emotion* 11, no. 2 (1987): 101–20.

120. Note that this is a *relative* change: in psychological experiments, even subjects who were setting goals—as well as control subjects who were neither setting nor implementing goals—exhibited positively biased self-perceptions. The point is that the level of positive illusions varied among groups and *increased* dramatically in an implemental mind-set. S. E. Taylor and P. M. Gollwitzer, "The Effects of Mindset on Positive Illusions," *Journal of Personality and Social Psychology Bulletin* 69 (1995): 213–26.

121. Heckhausen and Gollwitzer, "Thought Contents and Cognitive Functioning in Motivational versus Volitional States of Mind," 103.

122. Taylor and Gollwitzer, "The Effects of Mindset on Positive Illusions," 221.

123. Ibid., 223.

124. Maynard Smith and Parker, "The Logic of Asymmetric Contests"; J. Maynard Smith and G. R. Price, "The Logic of Animal Conflict," *Nature* 246 (1973): 15–18. See also D. Tingley and B. Walter, "Can Cheap Talk Deter? An Experimental Analysis," *Journal of Conflict Resolution* 55, no. 6 (2011): 994–1018. Although they argue that it can work the other way around: rational actors can use cheap talk to exploit *less* rational actors! For the role of cheap talk, see also R. F. Trager, "Diplomatic Calculus in Anarchy: How Diplomacy Matters," *American Political Science Review* 104, no. 2 (2010): 347–68.

125. J. H. Poole, "Announcing Intent: The Aggressive State of Musth in African Ele-phants," *Animal Behaviour* 37 (1989): 140–52.

126. Maynard Smith and Parker, "The Logic of Asymmetric Contests."

127. Wrangham, "Is Military Incompetence Adaptive?"; Trivers, *Deceit and Self-Deception*; von Hippel and Trivers, "The Evolution and Psychology of Self-deception"; Johnson, *Overconfidence and War*, 11–13.

128. Schelling, *The Strategy of Conflict*; R. Jervis, "Deterrence and Perception," *International Security* 7, no. 3 (1983): 3–30. See also Trager, "Diplomatic Calculus in Anarchy." Tingley and Walter, "Can Cheap Talk Deter?"

129. Roberts, *Waterloo: Napoleon's Last Gamble*, 114.

130. Baumeister, "The Optimal Margin of Illusion"; Johnson, *Overconfidence and War*.

131. Baumeister, "The Optimal Margin of Illusion."

132. Greene, *The 48 Laws of Power*, 230.

133. C. Cotton and C. Liu, "100 Horsemen and the Empty City: A Game Theoretic Examination of Deception in Chinese Military Legend," *Journal of Peace Research* 48, no. 2 (2011): 217–23.

134. Johnson and Fowler, "The Evolution of Overconfidence"; Johnson, Weidmann, and Cederman, "Fortune Favours the Bold."

135. J. J. Mearsheimer, *The Tragedy of Great Power Politics* (New York: Norton, 2001); E. Labs, "Beyond Victory: Offensive Realism and the Expansion of War Aims," *Security Studies* 6, no. 4 (1997): 1–49; P. Liberman, *Does Conquest Pay? The Exploitation of Occupied Industrial Societies* (Princeton: Princeton University Press, 1998); I. Morris, *War! What Is It Good For? Conflict and the Progress of Civilization from Primates to Robots* (London: Profile Books, 2015).

136. Walt, "International Relations."

137. Wang and Ray, "Beginners and Winners."

138. I. Arreguin-Toft, *How the Weak Win Wars: A Theory of Asymmetric Conflict* (Cambridge: Cambridge University Press, 2005); D. Lindley and R. Schildkraut, *Is War Rational? The Extent of Miscalculation and Misperception as Causes of War* (Philadelphia: American Political Science Association Conference, 2006).

139. P. Feaver and C. Gelpi, *Choosing Your Battles: American Civil-Military Relations and the Use of Force* (Princeton: Princeton University Press, 2004).

140. Walt, "Wishful Thinking." See section 2. The examples he gives are as follows: "In 1999, the Clinton administration thought a few days of air strikes would cause Slobodan Milosevic to fold—in fact, it took weeks of bombing and Russian diplomatic intercession to end the Kosovo War. In 2002, the Bush administration assumed that the rapid ouster of the Taliban would solve our problems in Afghanistan, and in 2003 it thought toppling Saddam Hussein would trigger a radical transformation of the whole Middle East. More recently, the Obama administration's decision to intervene in Libya seems to have been based on the hope that Muammar al-Qaddafi's support would quickly dissolve as soon as NATO jumped into the fray. It might have been nice if it had, but it was wishful thinking to assume it." As with Kosovo, NATO did achieve their primary aims in the end, but it took a lot longer than expected.

141. R. Draper, *Dead Certain: The Presidency of George W. Bush* (New York: Free Press, 2007); B. Woodward, *State of Denial* (New York: Simon & Schuster, 2005); J. Fallows, "Blind into Baghdad," *Atlantic Monthly* (January/February 2004): 53–74.

142. Phillips, "Hegemony, Hubris and Overreach," 633.

143. "How to Save the Euro," *Economist*, 17 September 2011, 11–12.

144. M. MacMillan, *The War That Ended Peace: How Europe Abandoned Peace for the First World War* (London: Profile Books, 2014); H. Strachan, *The Outbreak of the First*

World War (New York: Oxford University Press, 2004); Van Evera, *Causes of War*; Blainey, *The Causes of War*.

145. Johnson, *Overconfidence and War*.

146. Walt, "International Relations," 37.

147. Mearsheimer, *The Tragedy of Great Power Politics*; Labs, "Beyond Victory"; C. Layne, *The Peace of Illusions: International Relations Theory and American Grand Strategy in the Post–Cold War Era* (Ithaca: Cornell University Press, 2005).

148. K. N. Waltz, "Nuclear Myths and Political Realities," *American Political Science Review* 84, no. 3 (1990): 731–45, 734.

149. Ibid.

150. K. Woods, J. Lacey, and W. Murray, "Saddam's Delusions: The View from the Inside," *Foreign Affairs* 85, no. 3 May/June (2006): 2–26.

151. Schelling, *The Strategy of Conflict*.

152. Johnson and Tierney, "The Rubicon Theory of War."

153. T. Garton Ash, *The Polish Revolution: Solidarity* (New Haven: Yale University Press, 2002), 351.

154. This is widely attributed to Mandela but there is no established source. See https://quoteinvestigator.com/2016/01/05/done/.

155. J. Vandemoortele, "Ambition Is Golden: Meeting the Millennium Development Goals," *Development* 48 (2005): 5–11.

156. Camerer and Lovallo, "Overconfidence and Excess Entry."

157. Thucydides, Strassler, and Crawley, *The Landmark Thucydides*, 85.

Chapter 4. The Lion and the Mouse: Overconfidence and the American Revolution

The epigraph sources are: Public Affairs Office, U.S. Naval Academy, https://www.usna.edu/PAO/faq_pages/JPJones.php; J. J. Ellis, "Sit Down, You're Rocking the Boat," review of D. H. Fischer, *Washington's Crossing*, *New York Times*, 15 February 2004.

1. A. J. O'Shaughnessy, *The Men Who Lost America: British Leadership, the American Revolution and the Fate of the Empire* (New Haven: Yale University Press, 2013), 5.

2. J. A. Morrison, "Before Hegemony: Adam Smith, American Independence, and the Origins of the First Era of Globalization," *International Organization* 66 (2012): 395–428, 402.

3. O'Shaughnessy, *The Men Who Lost America*, 4.

4. B. W. Tuchman, *The March of Folly: From Troy to Vietnam* (New York: Alfred A. Knopf, 1984), 228. Today's equivalent comes from entering Tuchman's figure of £100 million into the Bank of England's "Inflation Calculator" from 1783 to 2019 (the latest year available). See https://www.bankofengland.co.uk/monetary-policy/inflation/inflation-calculator. Other sources put the original figure even higher at £165 million: see J. L. Smith, "How Was the Revolutionary War Paid For?" *Journal of the American Revolution*, 23 February 2015 (online journal without volume, issue, or page numbers). Historical GDP figures are from www.UKpublicspending.co.uk.

5. France already "owned" about a third of the current-day United States (which for a time was ceded to Spain), and the Louisiana Purchase, in which the French sold this huge central part of the continent to the United States, did not take place until 1803. Other regions that comprise today's United States still belonged to Spain, Mexico, and Great Britain well into the nineteenth century.

6. J. Ferling, *Almost a Miracle: The American Victory in the War of Independence* (New York: Oxford University Press, 2007), 562, 573.

7. Morrison, "Before Hegemony," 422.

8. L. James, *Raj: The Making and Unmaking of British India* (London: St. Martin's Griffin, 2000).

9. O'Shaughnessy, *The Men Who Lost America*, 5.

10. W. C. Martel, *Victory in War: Foundations of Modern Military Policy* (Cambridge: Cambridge University Press, 2006), 106.

11. Tuchman, *The March of Folly*, 130.

12. Ibid.

13. Ibid., 205.

14. Ibid., 206.

15. Ellis, "Sit Down, You're Rocking the Boat."

16. J. E. Ferling, *The First of Men: A Life of George Washington* (Oxford: Oxford University Press, 2010).

17. Morrison, "Before Hegemony," 401.

18. O'Shaughnessy, *The Men Who Lost America*, 4.

19. A. Sinclair, *A Concise History of the United States* (Stroud: Sutton, 1999), 38.

20. L. James, *The Illustrated Rise and Fall of the British Empire* (London: Little, Brown, 1999), 54.

21. O'Shaughnessy, *The Men Who Lost America*, 5.

22. J. J. Ellis, *His Excellency: George Washington* (New York: Vintage, 2004), 87.

23. D. Marston, *The American Revolution, 1774–1783* (Oxford: Osprey Publishing, 2002), 39–40. See also N. Philbrick, *Bunker Hill: A City, A Siege, A Revolution* (New York: Viking, 2006), 267.

24. Philbrick, *Bunker Hill*, 260.

25. James, *The Illustrated Rise and Fall of the British Empire*, 56. As we shall see later (see chapter 7 on the in-group/out-group bias), it is precisely the personal dangers and costs of joining a revolution against a powerful incumbent that can easily undermine it. Howe's proclamation might well have been perceived as the last chance for any reprieve. Those who fought on were going to *have* to win now, because failure would mean punishment, imprisonment, or death.

26. Ferling, *The First of Men*, 181.

27. E.g., see R. Powell, "Bargaining Theory and International Conflict," *Annual Review of Political Science* 5 (2002): 1–30.

28. Tuchman, *The March of Folly*, 217.

29. Ibid.

30. Ferling, *Almost a Miracle*, 277.

31. Ibid., 278.

32. Critics have noted that Howe was too busy enjoying himself with his mistress in Philadelphia, but it also seems to stem from Howe's aversion to attacking any well-entrenched opposition. Ibid., 288–89.

33. Tuchman, *The March of Folly*, 225.

34. Morrison, "Before Hegemony," 412. Morrison's argument is that it was not military defeats that ended the war but rather an eventual change in Britain's (indeed, Shelburne's) beliefs. Influenced by Adam Smith, he may have become persuaded that Britain's acceptance of American independence, under a free trade agreement, would have economically benefited Britain far more than continued military occupation and management, let alone war. However, whether this is true or not, it could not be known to Washington at the time. Even if this argument is correct, therefore, the puzzle remains as to what kept Washington going, regardless of what Shelburne thought.

35. James, *The Illustrated Rise and Fall of the British Empire*, 55.

36. O'Shaughnessy, *The Men Who Lost America*, 359.

37. Ibid.

38. Ferling, *The First of Men*, 149.

39. J. Merriman, *Modern Europe: From the Renaissance to the Present* (London: Norton, 1996), 477–78.

40. Tuchman, *The March of Folly*; P. Mackesy, *The War for America, 1775-1783* (Cambridge, MA: Harvard University Press, 1964).

41. O'Shaughnessy, *The Men Who Lost America*, 12.

42. James, *The Illustrated Rise and Fall of the British Empire*, 55.

43. Ferling, *Almost a Miracle*, 565–66.

44. Philbrick, *Bunker Hill*, 238–39.

45. O'Shaughnessy, *The Men Who Lost America*. See also Mackesy, *The War for America, 1775-1783*; J. Shy, *A People Numerous and Armed: Reflections on the Military Struggle for American Independence* (Ann Arbor: University of Michigan Press, 1990).

46. Merriman, *Modern Europe*, 478.

47. Philbrick, *Bunker Hill*, 241.

48. Ferling, *Almost a Miracle*, 570.

49. A. Rose, *Washington's Spies: The Story of America's First Spy Ring* (New York: Bantam Books, 2006).

50. Philbrick, *Bunker Hill*, 262.

51. Martel, *Victory in War*, 106.

52. Philbrick, *Bunker Hill*, 262.

53. Sinclair, *A Concise History of the United States*, 38.

54. Ibid., 42.

55. James, *The Illustrated Rise and Fall of the British Empire*, 56.

56. Ibid.

57. R. M. Calhoon, "Loyalism and Neutrality," in *A Companion to the American Revolution*, ed. J. P. Greene and J. R. Pole (Oxford: Blackwell, 2000), 246.

58. P. Albury, *The Story of the Bahamas* (London: Macmillan, 1975), 96.

59. Philbrick, *Bunker Hill*, 245.

60. Marston, *The American Revolution, 1774-1783*, 23.

61. Ferling, *Almost a Miracle*, 564; Marston, *The American Revolution, 1774-1783*, 81–82.

62. Although these were not unusual among colonial soldiers often raised for specific tasks on a kind of contract. Tuchman, *The March of Folly*, 145.

63. Ibid., 225.

64. Ferling, *Almost a Miracle*, 568.

65. Although it should be noted of course that the British victory in the French and Indian War was aided by many thousands of provincial and Native American soldiers. Ibid.

66. Tuchman, *The March of Folly*, 215.

67. Marston, *The American Revolution, 1774-1783*, 50.

68. Ibid., 51.

69. O'Shaughnessy, *The Men Who Lost America*, 159.

70. Marston, *The American Revolution, 1774-1783*, 66.

71. J. T. Flexner, *Washington: The Indispensable Man* (New York: Back Bay Books, 1974), 139.

72. Marston, *The American Revolution, 1774-1783*.

73. O'Shaughnessy, *The Men Who Lost America*, 249.

74. Tuchman, *The March of Folly*, 208.

75. Ferling, *The First of Men*; E. G. Lengel, *General George Washington: A Military Life* (New York: Random House, 2005).

76. Flexner, *Washington*.

77. R. Shenkman, *Presidential Ambition: Gaining Power at Any Cost* (New York: Harper Collins, 1999), 1.

78. Ibid., 66.

79. F. Alexander et al., eds., *Oxford Encyclopedia of World History* (Oxford: Oxford University Press, 1998), 716, entry, "George Washington."

80. Philbrick, *Bunker Hill*, 239.

81. R. M. Utley and W. E. Washburn, *Indian Wars* (New York: Mariner, 2002), 80.

82. Shenkman, *Presidential Ambition*, 1.

83. Ibid.

84. Ibid.

85. Ibid., 2.

86. Ibid., 3.

87. Ferling, *The First of Men*, 112–13. Washington also had John Adams to thank for lobbying for his cause, against some opposition, and despite an existing competent commander in Artemas Ward. Not least among the arguments, as Ferling put it, "What better way was there to nationalize the struggle than to appoint a southerner as commander of the army" [then massed in New England] (112). While Ward graciously gave way in Boston to the new commander, "betraying none of the prideful biliousness that had charactered [*sic*] Washington's behavior at his own downgrading by [Virginia governor Robert] Dinwiddie twenty years before" (128), Washington himself "depicted Ward as fat, lazy, and incompetent, and as too inert to remove himself 'from the smoke of his own chimney'" (250).

88. Shenkman, *Presidential Ambition*, xviii.

89. Ellis, *His Excellency*, 74.

90. D. H. Fischer, *Washington's Crossing* (New York: Oxford University Press, 2004), 13.

91. Philbrick, *Bunker Hill*, 237.

92. Lengel, *General George Washington*, 80.

93. R. M. Kanter, *Confidence: How Winning Streaks and Losing Streaks Begin and End* (New York: Crown Business, 2004), 318.

94. G. A. Blainey, *The Causes of War* (New York: Free Press, 1973), 42.

95. Ibid.

96. Merriman, *Modern Europe*, 478.

97. Tuchman, *The March of Folly*, 148.

98. Ellis, *His Excellency*, 74. He goes on: "Despite all his mistakes, events seemed to align themselves with his own instincts. He began the war at the siege of Boston determined to deliver a decisive blow against more disciplined and battle-tested British regulars. He ended it at the siege of Yorktown doing precisely that."

99. Ferling, *The First of Men*, 132.

100. Ibid., 145.

101. Lengel, *General George Washington*, 366.

102. James, *The Illustrated Rise and Fall of the British Empire*, 56.

103. Ellis, "Sit Down, You're Rocking the Boat."

104. Tuchman, *The March of Folly*, 214.

105. Lengel, *General George Washington*, 366.

106. Ferling, *The First of Men*, 145.

107. Ibid., 319.

108. Ibid.

109. Ibid.

110. Marston, *The American Revolution, 1774–1783*, 29.

111. Ferling, *The First of Men*, 275.

112. Martel, *Victory in War*, 105.

113. James, *The Illustrated Rise and Fall of the British Empire*, 56.

114. Ferling, *Almost a Miracle*, 562. Farewell Orders of 2 November 1783.

115. N. Ferguson, *Colossus: The Rise and Fall of the American Empire* (New York: Penguin, 2004), 304. This is the source for all figures in this paragraph. Ferguson's table of data excludes the 2003 Iraq War and the ongoing war in Afghanistan.

116. Circa 1780 the population was around 3 million; in 1940 it was around 130 million; in 1970 it was around 200 million. Martel's study of victory in war noted that, in the American Revolution, "British human and material losses, though not catastrophic, were demoralizing. However, the price paid in human losses on the American side was extremely high: almost seven thousand killed in combat out of a population of three million." That figure would correspond to an even higher 0.23 percent killed. Martel, *Victory in War*, 105.

117. Other wars had higher numbers of total casualties (including killed in action, plus wounded, plus "other"). However, the extent of such "other" deaths is not known, or at least is not reported in the above sources, for the American Revolution.

118. Shenkman, *Presidential Ambition*, xvi.

119. Sinclair, *A Concise History of the United States*, 45.

120. Tuchman, *The March of Folly*, 221.

121. J. Ferling, *A Leap in the Dark: The Struggle to Create the American Republic* (New York: Oxford University Press, 2003).

122. Sinclair, *A Concise History of the United States*, 46.

123. Ferling, *A Leap in the Dark*, xiii.

124. See, e.g., Mackesy, *The War for America, 1775–1783*.

125. Tuchman, *The March of Folly*.

126. Ibid., 128.

127. Blainey, *The Causes of War*, 42. See also J. D. Fearon, "Rationalist Explanations for War," *International Organization* 49, no. 3 (1995): 379–414; S. Van Evera, *Causes of War: Power and the Roots of Conflict* (Ithaca: Cornell University Press, 1999).

128. Tuchman, *The March of Folly*, 145.

129. Van Evera, *Causes of War*, 17.

130. Ibid. Italics in original.

131. R. Leckie, *George Washington's War: The Saga of the American Revolution* (New York: Harper Perennial, 1993), 149.

132. Tuchman, *The March of Folly*, 206.

133. R. Raphael and M. Raphael, *The Spirit of '74: How the American Revolution Began* (New York: New Press, 2015), 198.

134. B. Davis, *Black Heroes of the American Revolution* (Orlando, FL: Harcourt, 1976), 15.

135. Philbrick, *Bunker Hill*, 326.

136. According to Tuchman, "No minister of a British government from 1763 to 1775, much less before or after, ever visited the trans-Atlantic provinces upon which they felt the empire depended." Tuchman, *The March of Folly*, 194.

137. Ibid., 229.

138. Ibid., 201.

139. Ibid., 229.

140. O'Shaughnessy, *The Men Who Lost America*.

141. James, *The Illustrated Rise and Fall of the British Empire*, 55.

142. Ibid., 56.

143. Marston, *The American Revolution, 1774–1783*, 52.

144. Ferling, *Almost a Miracle*, 288.

145. Tuchman, *The March of Folly*, 215.

146. Lengel, *General George Washington*, 105.

147. Fischer, *Washington's Crossing*, 243, 235, 335.

148. Morrison, "Before Hegemony."

149. Ellis, "Sit Down, You're Rocking the Boat."

Chapter 5. Hedging Bets: The Strategic Advantages of Attribution Error

The epigraph sources are: H. J. Morgenthau, *Politics among Nations* (1948; New York: McGraw-Hill, 1993), 5; R. Jervis, *Perception and Misperception in International Politics* (Princeton: Princeton University Press, 1976), 424.

1. Smyrnaeus Quintus (fourth century AD), *The Fall of Troy*, Project Gutenberg, Book XII (penultimate paragraph). Odd punctuation in the original.

2. I. Scopelliti et al., "Individual Differences in Correspondence Bias: Measurement, Consequences, and Correction of Biased Interpersonal Attributions," *Management Science* 64, no. 4 (2018): 1879–1910.

3. R. Jervis, "Cooperation under the Security Dilemma," *World Politics* 30, no. 2 (1978): 167–74.

4. E.g., see J. M. Cavanaugh, "From the 'Red Juggernaut' to Iraqi WMD: Threat Inflation and How It Succeeds in the United States," *Political Science Quarterly* 122, no. 4 (2007): 555–84; C. Kaufmann, "Threat Inflation and the Failure of the Marketplace of Ideas: The Selling of the Iraq War," *International Security* 29, no. 1 (2004): 5–48; A. T. Thrall and J. K. Cramer, eds., *American Foreign Policy and the Politics of Fear: Threat Inflation since 9/11* (New York: Routledge, 2009).

5. For key works in the development of attribution theory, see H. H. Kelley and J. L. Michela, "Attribution Theory and Research," *Annual Review of Psychology* 31, no. 457–501 (1980); B. Weiner, *Human Motivation: Metaphors, Theories and Research* (Newbury Park, CA: Sage Publications, 1992).

6. The fundamental attribution error has also been variously called the "attribution effect," the "actor-observer bias," and the "correspondence bias," the latter in reference to the fact that people assume others' behavior "corresponds" to that person's unique dispositions. For further definitions of situational and dispositional attributions, see L. Ross, "The Intuitive Psychologist and His Shortcomings: Distortions in the Attribution Process," in *Advances in Experimental Social Psychology*, ed. L. Berkowitz (New York: Academic Press, 1977); D. T. Gilbert and P. S. Malone, "The Correspondence Bias," *Psychological Bulletin* 117, no. 1 (1995): 21–38.

7. For a retrospective, see J. M. Darley and J. Cooper, *Attribution and Social Interaction: The Legacy of Edward E. Jones* (Washington, DC: American Psychological Association Press, 1998). For the classic study, see E. E. Jones and V. A. Harris, "The Attribution of Attitudes," *Journal of Experimental Social Psychology* 3 (1967): 1–24. For more recent analyses, see P. W. Andrews, "The Psychology of Social Chess and the Evolution of Attribution Mechanisms: Explaining the Fundamental Attribution Error," *Evolution and Human Behavior* 22 (2001): 11–29.

8. See also P. E. Tetlock, "Accountability: A Social Check on the Fundamental Attribution Error," *Social Psychology Quarterly* 48 (1985): 227–36.

9. F. Heider, *The Psychology of Interpersonal Relations* (New York: John Wiley & Sons, 1958).

10. E. E. Jones, "The Rocky Road from Acts to Dispositions," *American Psychologist* 34, no. 2 (1979): 107–17, 114.

11. Ross, "The Intuitive Psychologist and His Shortcomings." How "fundamental" it really is has been challenged by some scholars. Other criticisms have arisen because situation and disposition are not always perfectly separable. For example, if A does something

"for money" (at first glance situational), it is possible that this partly reflects disposition as well, because A "values money" (dispositional). This is sometimes a concern in experimental designs and indeed a possible explanation for instances where there is a lack of clear results (the two causes may be conflated). However, the key interest is how much weight people give to one or the other explanation, and they need not be mutually exclusive. For a discussion of these issues as they pertain to international relations, see D. Heradstveit and G. M. Bonham, "Attribution Theory and Arab Images of the Gulf War," *Political Psychology* 17, no. 2 (1996): 271–92, 276–77.

12. Gilbert and Malone, "The Correspondence Bias," 21.

13. S. Milgram, *Obedience to Authority: An Experimental View* (1974; New York: HarperCollins, 2004).

14. Jones, "The Rocky Road from Acts to Dispositions," 115–16. Interestingly, this could be one reason why the role of anarchy in international relations is, for many, hard to grasp or difficult to believe, and people—even whole disciplines—often intuitively prefer "Great Man" or at least social theories that emphasize the roles of individuals, personalities, and politics.

15. Ibid., 116.

16. R. M. Kramer, "The Sinister Attribution Error: Paranoid Cognition and Collective Distrust in Organizations," *Motivation and Emotion* 18 (1994): 199–230.

17. When I submitted this book manuscript to Princeton (and after having already written that paragraph), there was a deathly silence from the editor. I started to get really worried, and as the days went by my anxiety mounted that perhaps after all the hard work they hated it. Eventually I wrote again to sheepishly inquire. An apologetic email shot back saying that they were delighted to receive the manuscript and had merely been busy, and the secretary to whom I'd addressed the email had left to another job. Phew! Just the sinister attribution error in action.

18. Jervis, *Perception and Misperception in International Politics.*

19. D. M. Taylor and V. Jaggi, "Ethnocentrism and Causal Attribution in a South Indian Context," *Journal of Cross-Cultural Psychology* 5, no. 2 (1974): 162–71.

20. The FAE may be exaggerated by the "halo effect"—our favorable impressions of friends and our unfavorable impressions of foes. The FAE interacts with this such that an enemy acting in a friendly manner tends to be seen as merely forced by circumstances to be friendly, while maintaining their internal dispositional intentions. See, e.g., D. Heradstveit, *The Arab-Israeli Conflict: Psychological Obstacles to Peace* (Oslo: Norwegian University Press, 1979).

21. In line with the expectation of rational choice theory, the so-called "law of uncommon effects" in psychology had suggested that "one should not explain with dispositions that which has already been explained by the situation." Gilbert and Malone, "The Correspondence Bias," 22. See also E. E. Jones and K. E. Davis, "From Acts to Dispositions: The Attribution Process in Person Perception," in *Advances in Experimental Social Psychology*, ed. L. Berkowitz (San Diego: Academic Press, 1965).

22. Jones and Harris, "The Attribution of Attitudes."

23. Gilbert and Malone, "The Correspondence Bias," 24.

24. Ibid., 22.

25. Ibid., 21.

26. Jones, "The Rocky Road from Acts to Dispositions," 107.

27. Morgenthau, *Politics among Nations*, 5.

28. K. Yarhi-Milo, *Knowing the Adversary: Leaders, Intelligence Organizations, and Assessments of Intentions in International Relations* (Princeton: Princeton University Press, 2014), 1.

29. R. K. Herrmann and J. K. Choi, "From Prediction to Learning: Opening Experts' Minds to Unfolding History," *International Security* 31, no. 4 (2007): 132–61, 145.

30. J. L. Richardson, *Crisis Diplomacy: The Great Powers since the Mid-Nineteenth Century* (Cambridge: Cambridge University Press, 1994).

31. Jervis also noted that *power* has an important interaction with attributions of causes of behavior. When strong actors comply with something, it suggests they must have done so because of their "values and desires" (since they could hardly be compelled to do anything). When a weak actor complies, by contrast, we assume "compulsion from the environment." Jervis, *Perception and Misperception in International Politics*, 36. We are, therefore, likely to assign dispositional causes to the behavior of large, especially hegemonic, powers and situational causes to small states.

32. Yarhi-Milo, *Knowing the Adversary*, 249.

33. Ibid.

34. Jones, "The Rocky Road from Acts to Dispositions," 107–8.

35. Gilbert and Malone, "The Correspondence Bias," 35.

36. In fact, it is often groups—such as the people or governments of other nations—to which our FAE bias applies (*"they"* did X because of Y), and the FAE can operate powerfully in group settings. Indeed, psychologists have proposed the "Ultimate Attribution Error," which is similar to the FAE except that it describes our particularly strong tendency to attribute dispositional motives to entire groups as well as mere individuals within them. T. F. Pettigrew, "The Ultimate Attribution Error: Extending Allport's Cognitive Analysis of Prejudice," *Personality and Social Psychology Bulletin* 5, no. 4 (1979): 461–76. Although for a critical review and discussion of this concept, see M. Hewstone, "The 'Ultimate Attribution Error'? A Review of the Literature on Intergroup Causal Attribution," *European Journal of Social Psychology* 20 (1990): 311–35.

37. Though for an argument that even cheap talk can be effective, see R. F. Trager, "Diplomatic Calculus in Anarchy: How Diplomacy Matters," *American Political Science Review* 104, no. 2 (2010): 347–68.

38. It is important to note that situational causes can be just dangerous—an aggressive state is a threat regardless of whether the cause of its aggression is being forced into war by circumstances or by design. Indeed, a Waltzian realist would argue that all state behavior has a situational cause in the anarchic international system, and threats are therefore always the result of states being forced into action because of their environment. K. N. Waltz, *Theory of International Politics* (New York: McGraw-Hill, 1979). However, that is not how most statesmen (or scholars) think. Instead, they expend great effort trying to work out the intentions of other states. Moreover, dispositional causes still arguably represent a much more important threat, because while situational causes can be observed, measured, and altered, dispositional causes are hard to discern, let alone understand or change, as Morgenthau stressed. Morgenthau, *Politics among Nations*. The FAE is therefore critical in shaping our assessments of other states' dispositions, over and above their situation.

39. A related phenomenon is the "spotlight effect": we tend to think we are being closely observed and scrutinized and that others will notice everything about us. In fact people will generally not notice the details, or even much at all. T. Gilovich, V. H. Medvec, and K. Savitsky, "The Spotlight Effect in Social Judgment: An Egocentric Bias in Estimates of the Salience of One's Own Actions and Appearance," *Journal of Personality and Social Psychology* 78, no. 2 (2000): 211–22.

40. J. S. Levy and W. R. Thompson, *Causes of War* (Oxford: Wiley-Blackwell, 2010), 136.

41. Jervis, *Perception and Misperception in International Politics*, 34–35.

42. D. D. P. Johnson and D. R. Tierney, "In the Eye of the Beholder: Victory and Defeat in U.S. Military Operations," in *Understanding Victory and Defeat in Contemporary War*, ed. J. Angstrom and I. Duyvesteyn (London: Routledge, 2007), 63.

43. E. Becker, *When the War Was Over: Cambodia and the Khmer Rouge Revolution* (New York: PublicAffairs, 1986), 195.

44. Ibid.

45. Ibid.

46. Ibid., 195–96.

47. Heradstveit, *The Arab-Israeli Conflict.*

48. D. W. Larson, *Anatomy of Mistrust: U.S.-Soviet Relations during the Cold War* (Ithaca: Cornell University Press, 1997).

49. A. Thalis, "Threat or Threatened? Russia in the Era of NATO Expansion," *Quarterly Access* 11, no. 1 (2018): 8–15, 9.

50. S. Atran, "Genesis of Suicide Terrorism," *Science* 299 (2003): 1534–39.

51. D. D. P. Johnson and S. A. Levin, "The Tragedy of Cognition: Psychological Biases and Environmental Inaction," *Current Science* 97, no. 11 (2009): 1593–1603, 1597.

52. M. E. Price and D. D. P. Johnson, "The Adaptationist Theory of Cooperation in Groups: Evolutionary Predictions for Organizational Cooperation," in *Evolutionary Psychology in the Business Sciences*, ed. G. Saad (Heidelberg: Springer, 2011); L. Cronk and B. L. Leech, *Meeting at Grand Central: Understanding the Social and Evolutionary Roots of Cooperation* (Princeton: Princeton University Press, 2013); E. Ostrom, *Governing the Commons: The Evolution of Institutions for Collective Action* (Cambridge: Cambridge University Press, 1990).

53. S. M. Walt, "Wishful Thinking: Top 10 Examples of the Most Unrealistic Expectations in Contemporary U.S. Foreign Policy," *Foreign Policy*, 29 April 2011, http://www.foreignpolicy.com/articles/2011/04/29/wishful_thinking.

54. Heider, *The Psychology of Interpersonal Relations.*

55. Gilbert and Malone, "The Correspondence Bias," 34.

56. Ibid., 35.

57. Ibid. See also R. E. Nisbett, *The Geography of Thought: How Asians and Westerners Think Differently . . . and Why* (Yarmouth, ME: Nicholas Brealey Publishing, 2003).

58. Gilbert and Malone, "The Correspondence Bias," 32.

59. Ibid.

60. Although they have a footnote (p. 22) saying that though the bias may be useful, they "continue the tradition" of referring to them as errors!

61. M. C. Corballis, *The Recursive Mind: The Origins of Human Language, Thought, and Civilization* (Princeton: Princeton University Press, 2011); R. I. M. Dunbar, "The Social Brain: Mind, Language, and Society in Evolutionary Perspective," *Annual Review of Anthropology* 32 (2003): 163–81.

62. M. G. Haselton and D. Nettle, "The Paranoid Optimist: An Integrative Evolutionary Model of Cognitive Biases," *Personality and Social Psychology Review* 10, no. 1 (2006): 47–66.

63. L. Cosmides, "The Logic of Social Exchange: Has Natural Selection Shaped How Humans Reason? Studies with the Wason Selection Task," *Cognition* 31 (1989): 187–206; J. M. Bering, "The Existential Theory of Mind," *Review of General Psychology* 6 (2002): 3–24; A. H. Harcourt and F. B. M. d. Waal, eds., *Coalitions and Alliances in Humans and Other Animals* (Oxford: Oxford University Press, 1992).

64. A. C. Lopez, R. McDermott, and M. B. Petersen, "States in Mind: Evolution, Coalitional Psychology, and International Politics," *International Security* 36, no. 2 (2011): 48–83.

65. Haselton and Nettle, "The Paranoid Optimist."

66. Jervis, *Perception and Misperception in International Politics*, 424. Jervis himself noted that, while the logic is correct, the empirical balance of costs between the two alternative errors is debatable, and he suspects that states incur high costs for overestimating threats.

67. E. R. May, "Capabilities and Proclivities," in *Knowing One's Enemies: Intelligence Assessment before the Two World Wars*, ed. E. R. May (Princeton: Princeton University Press, 1984), 503.

68. Ibid.

69. Gilbert and Malone, "The Correspondence Bias," 35. Elsewhere they also note, "The time and energy that one saves by using such heuristics is probably worth the cost of their rare failures" (32).

70. Haselton and Nettle, "The Paranoid Optimist."

71. P. E. Tetlock, "Social Psychology and World Politics," in *Handbook of Social Psychology*, ed. D. Gilbert, S. Fiske, and G. Lindzey (New York: McGraw-Hill, 1998), 877. He goes on: "A balanced appraisal of the fundamental attribution 'error' hinges on our probability estimates of each logically possible type of error (false alarms and misses) as well as on the political value we place on avoiding each error—all in all, a classic signal detection problem" (877). What is odd is that this important insight has not been pursued more. See also the same realization on the very last page of Jervis, *Perception and Misperception in International Politics*, 424.

72. Jones, "The Rocky Road from Acts to Dispositions," 116. Although he noted that this in itself does not necessarily suggest anything about why dispositional attributions are better than situational ones.

73. Ibid.

74. For the inflation of threats, see Thrall and Cramer, *American Foreign Policy and the Politics of Fear*; Cavanaugh, "From the 'Red Juggernaut' to Iraqi WMD"; J. K. Cramer, *National Security Panics: Threat Inflation and US Foreign Policy Shifts* (New York: Routledge, forthcoming); Jervis, *Perception and Misperception in International Politics*.

75. R. K. Betts, *Analysis, War and Decision: Why Intelligence Failures Are Inevitable* (Washington, DC: Brookings Institution, 1978), 75. Italics in original.

76. D. D. P. Johnson and E. M. P. Madin, "Paradigm Shifts in Security Strategy: Why Does It Take Disasters to Trigger Change?" in *Natural Security: A Darwinian Approach to a Dangerous World*, ed. R. D. Sagarin and T. Taylor (Berkeley: University of California Press, 2008).

77. P. Tetlock, "Why Foxes Are Better Forecasters than Hedgehogs," Seminars about Long-Term Thinking, Long Now Foundation, San Francisco, 26 January 2007.

78. Larson, *Anatomy of Mistrust*.

79. S. S. Montefiore, *Stalin: The Court of the Red Tsar* (London: Weidenfeld & Nicolson, 2003).

80. H. Blum, *The Eve of Destruction: The Untold Story of the Yom Kippur War* (New York: HarperCollins, 2003).

81. R. Betts, *Surprise Attack: Lessons for Defense Planning* (Washington, DC: Brookings Institution Press, 1983); Johnson and Madin, "Paradigm Shifts in Security Strategy"; S. Van Evera, foreword to *American Foreign Policy and the Politics of Fear: Threat Inflation since 9/11*, ed. A. T. Thrall and J. K. Cramer (New York: Routledge, 2009); D. D. P. Johnson and D. R. Tierney, "Bad World: The Negativity Bias in International Relations," *International Security* 43, no. 3 (2019): 96–140.

82. Tetlock, "Social Psychology and World Politics," 877.

83. Ibid.

84. J. J. Mearsheimer, *The Tragedy of Great Power Politics* (New York: Norton, 2001); D. D. P. Johnson and B. A. Thayer, "The Evolution of Offensive Realism: Survival under Anarchy from the Pleistocene to the Present," *Politics and the Life Sciences* 35, no. 1 (2016): 1–26.

85. R. M. Kramer, "Paranoid Cognition in Social Systems: Thinking and Acting in the Shadow of Doubt," *Personality and Social Psychology Review* 2, no. 4 (1998): 251–75.

86. A. M. Ludwig, *King of the Mountain: The Nature of Political Leadership* (Lexington: University Press of Kentucky, 2002).

87. Ibid.

88. Ibid., 248.

89. Gilbert and Malone, "The Correspondence Bias," 33–35. Gilbert and Malone expanded in some detail on the conditions in which the FAE may be advantageous, or at least lead to no harm. They grouped them into three categories (as briefly summarized the main text).

First, there are what they called *self-induced constraints*. Here, "people seek situations that will 'push' them in the same direction as do their own dispositions" (33). This may be the case for states and decision-makers, who sometimes significantly shape the politics, people, and nations surrounding them. History, then, may lead to a convergence of disposition and situation, in which the FAE generates correct inferences after all.

Seccond, there may be *superfluous constraints*. Sometimes the situation only forces an actor to do what he would have done anyway. In such cases, situational and dispositional causes will be indistinguishable and FAE will not be an "error."

Finally, there may be *omnipresent constraints*. There are two elements to this. (a) If the behavior of interest always occurs only in a limited set of circumstances, then situational factors may not change between them and disposition is a good predictor of behavior. Gilbert and Malone note that social roles were probably more fixed in our hunter-gatherer past, such that dispositional attributions were generally more likely to be correct. In today's world, by comparison, people move much more often between different roles, increasing the opportunities for incorrect attributions. (b) If situations persist for a very long time, then they may actually generate dispositions (behavioral tendencies) that fit the circumstances.

90. If these are only loose correlations, situation could of course be a more accurate predictor of behavior than disposition but, as discussed, disposition might nevertheless dominate if it carries other advantages, such as simplicity and salience in focusing on human actors, rather than having to keep track of and understand many complex situational factors.

91. M. A. Nowak, "Five Rules for the Evolution of Cooperation," *Science* 314 (2006): 1560–63.

92. K. Sigmund, "Punish or Perish? Retaliation and Collaboration among Humans," *Trends in Ecology & Evolution* 22, no. 11 (2007): 593–600.

93. M. E. Price, L. Cosmides, and J. Tooby, "Punitive Sentiment as an Anti–Free Rider Psychological Device," *Evolution and Human Behavior* 23 (2002): 203–31.

94. Cosmides, "The Logic of Social Exchange"; C. Boehm, *Hierarchy in the Forest: The Evolution of Egalitarian Behavior* (Cambridge, MA: Harvard University Press, 2001).

95. E.g., L. Mealey, C. Daood, and M. Krage, "Enhanced Memory for Faces of Cheaters," *Ethology and Sociobiology* 17 (1996): 119–28.

96. R. Kurzban and M. R. Leary, "Evolutionary Origins of Stigmatization: The Functions of Social Exclusion," *Psychological Bulletin* 123 (2001): 187–208.

97. J. L. Barrett, "Exploring the Natural Foundations of Religion," *Trends in Cognitive Sciences* 4, no. 1 (2000): 29–34.

98. K. R. Foster and H. Kokko, "The Evolution of Superstitious and Superstitious-Like Behaviour," *Proceedings of the Royal Society B: Biological Sciences* 276 (2009): 31–37.

99. C. K. Morewedge, "Negativity Bias in Attribution of External Agency," *Journal of Experimental Psychology* 138, no. 4 (2009): 535–45.

100. Jervis, "Cooperation under the Security Dilemma." For debates on the security dilemma, see also C. L. Glaser, "The Security Dilemma Revisited," *World Politics* 50, no. 1 (1997): 171–201; E. B. Montgomery, "Breaking out of the Security Dilemma: Realism,

Reassurance, and the Problem of Uncertainty," *International Security* 31, no. 2 (2006): 151–85; R. L. Schweller, "Neorealism's Status Quo Bias: What Security Dilemma?" *Security Studies* 5, no. 3 (1996): 90–121; S. Tang, "The Security Dilemma: A Conceptual Analysis," *Security Studies* 18, no. 3 (2009): 587–623.

101. Herrmann and Choi, "From Prediction to Learning," 155.

102. Jervis, *Perception and Misperception in International Politics*, 33.

103. Haselton and Nettle, "The Paranoid Optimist."

104. Waltz, *Theory of International Politics*.

105. Jervis, *Perception and Misperception in International Politics*.

106. S. M. Walt, *The Origins of Alliances* (Ithaca: Cornell University Press, 1987). Walt laid out four criteria in particular that influence evaluations of a potential threat: its strength, its geographical proximity, its offensive capabilities, and—critically—its offensive *intentions*.

107. Quoted in Gilbert and Malone, "The Correspondence Bias," 23.

108. Ibid.

109. Morgenthau, *Politics among Nations*; R. Niebuhr, *Christian Realism and Political Problems* (New York: Charles Scribner's Sons, 1953).

110. Waltz, *Theory of International Politics*; S. M. Walt, "International Relations: One World, Many Theories," *Foreign Policy*, no. 110 (1998): 29–46.

111. G. Rose, "Neoclassical Realism and Theories of Foreign Policy," *World Politics* 51, no. 1 (1998): 144–72; E. M. Hafner-Burton et al., "The Behavioral Revolution and International Relations," *International Organization* 71, no. S1 (Supplement) (2017): 1–31; R. McDermott, *Political Psychology in International Relations* (Ann Arbor: University of Michigan Press, 2004).

112. R. H. Thaler, *Misbehaving: The Making of Behavioral Economics* (New York: W. W. Norton, 2016).

113. A. A. Agrawal, "Phenotypic Plasticity in the Interactions and Evolution of Species," *Science* 294 (2001): 321–26.

114. Cited in Gilbert and Malone, "The Correspondence Bias," 23.

115. Yarhi-Milo, *Knowing the Adversary*, 254.

116. C. H. Achen and L. M. Bartels, *Democracy for Realists: Why Elections Do Not Produce Responsive Government* (Princeton: Princeton University Press, 2016), 15. Naturally, an academic debate has sprung up as to the veracity of the most extreme claims. A. Fowler and A. B. Hall, "Do Shark Attacks Influence Presidential Elections? Reassessing a Prominent Finding on Voter Competence," *Journal of Politics* 80, no. 4 (2018): 1423–37.

117. R. E. Riggio and H. R. Riggio, "Social Psychology and Charismatic Leadership," in *Social Psychology and Leadership*, ed. C. Hoyt, D. Forsyth, and A. Goethals (New York: Praeger Perspectives, 2008), 32–33.

118. Ibid.

119. L. Fisher, "Deciding on War against Iraq: Institutional Failures," *Political Science Quarterly* 118, no. 3 (2003): 389–410.

120. Kaufmann, "Threat Inflation and the Failure of the Marketplace of Ideas." Note that past instances of threat inflation, such as Iraqi WMD in 2003, do not mean the assumption of threat is a bad strategy in general. They only represent one instance of failure (a single false positive) in a broader picture of numerous estimates of threats over time. The aim is to reduce the chance of making the most costly errors, and this may best be achieved by overestimating threats all the time. Doing so increases false positives, but this is worth it if it serves to decrease false negatives that incur even greater costs.

121. R. Jervis, *How Statesmen Think: The Psychology of International Politics* (Princeton: Princeton University Press, 2017); Larson, *Anatomy of Mistrust*; Heradstveit and Bonham, "Attribution Theory and Arab Images of the Gulf War"; B. Silverstein, "Enemy

Images: The Psychology of U.S. Attitudes and Cognitions Regarding the Soviet Union," *American Psychologist* 44 (1989): 903–13.

122. B. Fung, "America's Worst Nicknames," *Foreign Policy*, 15 July 2010. Interestingly, Castro's "Empire" charge seemed to emphasize the (situational) fragility of empires as well as their predatory disposition.

123. Morgenthau, *Politics among Nations*.

124. L. F. Richardson, *Arms and Insecurity: A Mathematical Study of the Causes and Origins of War* (Pacific Grove, CA: Boxwood Press, 1978).

Chapter 6. Know Your Enemy: Britain and the Appeasement of Hitler

The epigraph sources are: J. Garnett, "The Causes of War and the Conditions of Peace," in *Strategy in the Contemporary World*, ed. J. Baylis (New York: Oxford University Press, 2012), 33; Halifax's response, when asked whether he regretted the Munich agreement: E. R. May, *Lessons of the Past: The Use and Misuse of History in American Foreign Policy* (Oxford: Oxford University Press, 1973), 18.

1. W. K. Wark, *The Ultimate Enemy: British Intelligence and Nazi Germany, 1933–1939* (Ithaca: Cornell University Press, 1985), 18; R. Overy, *1939: Countdown to War* (London: Penguin, 2010).

2. Wark, *The Ultimate Enemy*, 234.

3. Ibid., 228.

4. J. Keegan, *The Second World War* (London: Penguin, 2005), 37.

5. Wark, *The Ultimate Enemy*, 229.

6. P. Neville, *Winston Churchill: Statesman or Opportunist?* (London: Hodder & Stoughton, 1996), 65.

7. Wark, *The Ultimate Enemy*, 231.

8. Ibid., 20.

9. Ibid., 237.

10. Ibid., 234.

11. Keegan, *The Second World War*, 39.

12. Wark, *The Ultimate Enemy*, 232.

13. A. J. P. Taylor, *The War Lords* (London: Penguin, 1977); J. Record, *The Specter of Munich: Reconsidering the Lessons of Appeasing Hitler* (Dulles, VA: Potomac Books, 2007).

14. Neville, *Winston Churchill*, 85.

15. M. Fulbrook, *A Concise History of Germany* (Cambridge: Cambridge University Press, 1995), 193.

16. Wark, *The Ultimate Enemy*, 228.

17. Ibid., 224.

18. Ibid., 22. This echoes criticisms made of U.S. intelligence prior to our own era's major intelligence failure: 9/11 and the threat of Al Qaeda.

19. K. Yarhi-Milo, *Knowing the Adversary: Leaders, Intelligence Organizations, and Assessments of Intentions in International Relations* (Princeton: Princeton University Press, 2014), 47.

20. R. G. Vansittart, *Black Record: Germans Past and Present* (London: Hamish Hamilton, 1941).

21. Yarhi-Milo, *Knowing the Adversary*, 65.

22. Wark, *The Ultimate Enemy*, 225.

23. K. S. Davis, *FDR: Into the Storm, 1937–1940: A History* (New York: Random House, 1993), 345.

24. Neville, *Winston Churchill*, 60.

25. M. Lee, ed., *Chambers British Biographies: The 20th Century* (Edinburgh: Chambers, 1993), 100.

26. J. Merriman, *Modern Europe: From the Renaissance to the Present* (London: Norton, 1996), 1237.

27. D. C. Watt, "British Intelligence and the Coming of the Second World War in Europe," in *Knowing One's Enemies: Intelligence Assessment before the Two World Wars*, ed. E. R. May (Princeton: Princeton University Press, 1984), 268.

28. S. Budiansky, *Air Power: The Men, Machines, and Ideas That Revolutionized War, from Kitty Hawk to Gulf War II* (New York: Viking, 2004), 186–87.

29. Ibid., 187. MacDonald was prime minister from 1931 to 1935.

30. Wark, *The Ultimate Enemy*, 235–36.

31. Watt, "British Intelligence and the Coming of the Second World War in Europe," 243.

32. Budiansky, *Air Power*, 189.

33. Ibid.

34. Winston Churchill, "The Sinews of Power," speech at Fulton, Missouri, 5 March 1946.

35. Neville, *Winston Churchill*, 67.

36. Ibid., 62.

37. Wark, *The Ultimate Enemy*, 233. Italics added.

38. Ibid., 224.

39. Ibid., 236.

40. Yarhi-Milo, *Knowing the Adversary*, 93.

41. Fulbrook, *A Concise History of Germany*, 187.

42. P. Marsh, *The Chamberlain Litany: Letters within a Governing Family from Empire to Appeasement* (London: Haus Publishing, 2010). For a discussion of Chamberlain's reading of *Mein Kampf*, see C. Hastings, "Pre War Prime Minister Chamberlain Made Study of Hitler," *The Sunday Times* (London), 7 March 2010.

43. Yarhi-Milo, *Knowing the Adversary*, 86.

44. Fulbrook, *A Concise History of Germany*, 187–88.

45. Ibid., 188.

46. Ibid., 190.

47. Yarhi-Milo, *Knowing the Adversary*, 57.

48. Merriman, *Modern Europe*, 1232.

49. Watt, "British Intelligence and the Coming of the Second World War in Europe," 250.

50. A. Stein, *Why Nations Cooperate: Circumstance and Choice in International Relations* (Ithaca: Cornell University Press, 1990), 75. Italics added.

51. Ibid. He goes on: "he made his contingent decision in 1938 based on his mistaken belief that Hitler would be a cooperator in the future" (75–76).

52. L. James, *The Illustrated Rise and Fall of the British Empire* (London: Little, Brown, 1999), 275.

53. Yarhi-Milo, *Knowing the Adversary*, 72.

54. Ibid., 87.

55. R. N. Lebow, *Between Peace and War: The Nature of International Crisis* (Baltimore: Johns Hopkins University Press, 1981), 36.

56. Ibid.

57. Garnett, "The Causes of War and the Conditions of Peace," 33.

58. James, *The Illustrated Rise and Fall of the British Empire*, 275.

59. Neville, *Winston Churchill*, 90. And as Neville notes, while we can all agree that "ultimately Churchill was right and Chamberlain was wrong," the ongoing question is whether—whatever Hitler's intentions—there was a viable alternative policy that Britain could have followed.

60. Yarhi-Milo, *Knowing the Adversary*, 91.

61. Budiansky, *Air Power*, 187.

62. Ibid.

63. Ibid.

64. Watt, "British Intelligence and the Coming of the Second World War in Europe," 266.

65. Fulbrook, *A Concise History of Germany*, 188.

66. Record, *The Specter of Munich*, 29.

67. Lebow, *Between Peace and War*, 35.

68. Ibid.

69. Yarhi-Milo, *Knowing the Adversary*, 68.

70. Ibid., 68–69.

71. Ibid., 72.

72. Ibid., 69.

73. Ibid.

74. Ibid., 80.

75. Ibid., 90.

76. Ibid., 92.

77. Ibid., 99.

78. Interestingly, given that interactions with Hitler and his advisors could be somewhat unpleasant and hostile, one might imagine that such personal meetings would *increase* dispositional attributions. This suggests that the countervailing factors affecting Chamberlain, that Yarhi-Milo identifies, must have been especially strong.

79. Neville, *Winston Churchill*, 62.

80. Yarhi-Milo, *Knowing the Adversary*, 97.

81. Ibid., 47.

82. Neville, *Winston Churchill*, 63.

83. Yarhi-Milo, *Knowing the Adversary*, 97.

84. Ibid., 67.

85. Ibid., 78.

86. Ibid., 77.

87. Ibid., 76.

88. Ibid., 99.

89. Ibid., 88–89.

90. Ibid., 77, 89.

91. Ibid., 77.

92. K. Feiling, *The Life of Neville Chamberlain* (London: Macmillan, 1946).

93. Yarhi-Milo, *Knowing the Adversary*, 87.

94. D. D. P. Johnson, *Overconfidence and War: The Havoc and Glory of Positive Illusions* (Cambridge, MA: Harvard University Press, 2004).

95. J. R. M. Butler, *Lord Lothian, Philip Kerr, 1882–1940* (London: Macmillan, 1960), 226. Italics added.

96. Yarhi-Milo, *Knowing the Adversary*, 92.

97. Wark, *The Ultimate Enemy*, 233.

98. J. F. Kennedy, *Why England Slept* (New York: Wilfred Funk, 1940); W. S. Churchill, *While England Slept: A Survey of World Affairs, 1932–1938* (1938; New York: Ishi Press, 2016). One interesting possibility is that *other states* were bound—by the FAE itself—to see *Britain* as dragging its feet. There were many factors that made dealing with Hitler a

complex challenge, and the FAE may have made outsiders tend to see Britain's slow preparation itself as dispositional—a lack of concern about the German threat rather than a
grindingly slow reaction to a set of interacting historical, economic, and political circumstances in Britain and Europe. In support of this, France followed a somewhat similar
policy of appeasement toward Hitler, sharing much of the geographical and historical experience of Britain. Both were strongly aware of the role of situational factors constraining
their own behavior (such as perceived unpreparedness for war), which may have been less
obvious to others. As I go on to argue, however, there were still big differences between
Britain and France in their perceptions of Hitler's intentions.

99. R. J. Young, "French Military Intelligence and Nazi Germany, 1938–1939," in *Knowing One's Enemies: Intelligence Assessment before the Two World Wars*, ed. E. May (Princeton: Princeton University Press, 1984), 307.

100. P. Jackson, *France and the Nazi Menace: Intelligence and Policy Making, 1933–
1939* (Oxford: Oxford University Press, 2000).

101. W. L. Shirer, *The Collapse of the Third Republic: An Inquiry into the Fall of France
in 1940* (New York: Simon & Schuster, 1969), 339.

102. B. Thatcher, *Rise and Decline: Where We Are and What We Can Do About It* (Lulu
.com, 2017), 238.

103. D. N. Lammers, *Explaining Munich: The Search for Motive in British Policy*
(Stanford: Hoover Institution, 1966), 4.

104. Merriman, *Modern Europe*, 1230.

105. Yarhi-Milo, *Knowing the Adversary*, 97.

106. Lammers, *Explaining Munich*.

107. Merriman, *Modern Europe*, 1237.

108. S. S. Montefiore, *Stalin: The Court of the Red Tsar* (London: Weidenfeld & Nicolson, 2003), 272.

109. Merriman, *Modern Europe*, 1237.

110. Montefiore, *Stalin*, 272–73.

111. Ibid., 273.

112. Ibid., 274.

113. After the pact was signed, Stalin crowed, "Of course it's all a game to see who can
fool whom. I know what Hitler's up to. He thinks he's outsmarted me but actually it's I
who's tricked him." Ibid., 276.

114. Keegan, *The Second World War*, 35.

115. Yarhi-Milo, *Knowing the Adversary*, 246–47.

116. Fulbrook, *A Concise History of Germany*, 189.

117. D. Dutton, *Neville Chamberlain* (London: Arnold, 2001), 12.

118. Ibid.

119. Marsh, *The Chamberlain Litany*, 288.

120. Yarhi-Milo, *Knowing the Adversary*, 70.

121. Overy, *1939*, 28–29.

122. Keynes, interview with the *New Statesman*, 28 January 1939, in J. M. Keynes,
The Collected Writings of John Maynard Keynes (Cambridge: Cambridge University Press,
1998), 21:499.

123. L. S. Amery, *My Political Life*, vol. 3, *The Unforgiving Years* (London: Hutchinson,
1955), 292. It was Amery who, in 1940, gave the famous rousing speech calling for Chamberlain to leave office, ending with Cromwell's words: "Depart, I say, and let us have done
with you. In the name of God, go!"

124. N. M. Ripsman and J. S. Levy, "Wishful Thinking or Buying Time? The Logic of
British Appeasement in the 1930s," *International Security* 33, no. 2 (2008): 148–81. See
also some critiques and Ripsman and Levy's response in a subsequent issue of the journal.

A. Barros et al., "Correspondence: Debating British Decisionmaking toward Nazi Germany in the 1930s," *International Security* 34, no. 1 (2009): 173–98. See also Layne, who argues Britain was trying to balance against Germany but that Chamberlain "was playing a weak hand, and did the best that he could with the cards he was dealt." C. Layne, "Security Studies and the Use of History: Neville Chamberlain's Grand Strategy Revisited," *Security Studies* 17 (2008): 397–437, 397.

125. J. J. Mearsheimer, *The Tragedy of Great Power Politics* (New York: Norton, 2001), 165.

126. Ibid.

127. Neville, *Winston Churchill*, 84.

128. Barros et al., "Correspondence."

129. Neville, *Winston Churchill*, 84. Italics in original.

130. Marsh, *The Chamberlain Litany*.

131. S. G. Walker, *Role Theory and the Cognitive Architecture of British Appeasement Decisions: Symbolic and Strategic Interaction in World Politics* (New York: Routledge, 2013); Neville, *Winston Churchill*.

132. B. C. Rathbun, *Reasoning of State: Realists, Romantics and Rationality in International Relations* (Cambridge: Cambridge University Press, 2019), 245.

133. For an analysis of prospects of victory in 1938, see K. Ben-Arie, "Czechoslovakia at the Time of 'Munich': The Military Situation," *Journal of Contemporary History* 25, no. 4 (1990): 431–46, 439, 443; H. Ragsdale, *The Soviets, the Munich Crisis, and the Coming of World War II* (Cambridge: Cambridge University Press, 2004), xix; W. Murray, *The Change in the European Balance of Power, 1938–1939: The Path to Ruin* (Princeton: Princeton University Press, 1984), 150.

134. Editorial, *The Times*, 1 October 1938.

135. Lebow, *Between Peace and War*, 37.

136. Watt, "British Intelligence and the Coming of the Second World War in Europe," 263. Fulbrook concurs, saying that "Hitler himself at the time was bitterly disappointed at his bloodless success, feeling cheated of a potentially successful war." Fulbrook, *A Concise History of Germany*, 191. See also D. C. Copeland, *The Origins of Major War* (Ithaca: Cornell University Press, 2000), 133.

137. D. D. P. Johnson and D. R. Tierney, *Failing to Win: Perceptions of Victory and Defeat in International Politics* (Cambridge, MA: Harvard University Press, 2006), 9.

138. Fulbrook, *A Concise History of Germany*, 191. German citizens themselves were relieved by the avoidance of war, and Hitler's popularity rose further as a result.

139. P. Hoffmann, *German Resistance to Hitler* (Cambridge, MA: Harvard University Press, 1988), 98.

140. May, *Lessons of the Past*, 130.

141. A. Sinclair, *A Concise History of the United States* (Stroud: Sutton, 1999), 165.

142. A. T. Thrall and J. K. Cramer, eds., *American Foreign Policy and the Politics of Fear: Threat Inflation since 9/11* (New York: Routledge, 2009); C. Kaufmann, "Threat Inflation and the Failure of the Marketplace of Ideas: The Selling of the Iraq War," *International Security* 29, no. 1 (2004): 5–48.

143. Watt, "British Intelligence and the Coming of the Second World War in Europe," 268.

Chapter 7. United We Stand: The Strategic Advantages of Group Bias

The epigraph sources are: *The Liberty Song*, 1768. J. Dickinson, *The Writings of John Dickinson* (Bedford, MA: Applewood Books, 1895), 432; A. C. Grayling, *War: An Enquiry* (New Haven: Yale Univeristy Press, 2017), 3.

1. J. Caesar, *The Gallic War* (Oxford: Loeb Classic Library, 1989).

2. J. J. Norwich, *France: A History from Gaul to Gaulle* (London: John Murray, 2018), 3.

3. Ibid., 1.

4. Dickinson, *The Liberty Song*, 1768.

5. D. O. Sears, L. Huddy, and R. Jervis, *Oxford Handbook of Political Psychology* (Oxford: Oxford University Press, 2003); P. E. Tetlock, "Social Psychology and World Politics," in *Handbook of Social Psychology*, ed. D. Gilbert, S. Fiske, and G. Lindzey (New York: McGraw-Hill, 1998); D. Kahneman, P. Slovic, and A. Tversky, *Judgment under Uncertainty: Heuristics and Biases* (Cambridge: Cambridge University Press, 1982); M. Hewstone, M. Rubin, and H. Willis, "Intergroup Bias," *Annual Review of Psychology* 53 (2002): 575–604; M. B. Brewer, "The Psychology of Prejudice: Ingroup Love or Outgroup Hate," *Journal of Social Issues* 55, no. 3 (1999): 429–44.

6. H. Tajfel, "Social Identity and Intergroup Behaviour," *Social Science Information* 13, no. 2 (1974): 65–93; J. C. Turner, "A Self-Categorization Theory," in *Rediscovering the Social Group: A Self-Categorization Theory*, ed. J. C. Turner et al. (Oxford: Basil Blackwell, 1987).

7. S. T. Fiske, "What We Know about Bias and Intergroup Conflict, Problem of the Century," *Current Directions in Psychological Science* 11, no. 4 (2002): 123–28.

8. N. Dasgupta and A. G. Greenwald, "On the Malleability of Automatic Attitudes: Combating Automatic Prejudice with Images of Admired and Disliked Individuals," *Journal of Personality and Social Psychology* 81 (2001): 800–814; J. Sidanius and R. Kurzban, "Evolutionary Approaches to Political Psychology," in *Handbook of Political Psychology*, ed. D. O. Sears, L. Huddy, and R. Jervis (Oxford: Oxford University Press, 2003); R. Kurzban, J. Tooby, and L. Cosmides, "Can Race Be Erased? Coalitional Computation and Social Categorization," *Proceedings of the National Academy of Sciences* 98, no. 26 (2001): 15387–92; Hewstone, Rubin, and Willis, "Intergroup Bias."

9. Hewstone, Rubin, and Willis, "Intergroup Bias"; Fiske, "What We Know about Bias and Intergroup Conflict"; S. T. Fiske and S. E. Taylor, *Social Cognition: From Brains to Culture*, 2nd ed. (New York: McGraw-Hill, 2013).

10. R. J. Robinson and D. Keltner, "Defending the Status Quo: Power and Bias in Social Conflict," *Personality and Social Psychology Bulletin* 23 (1997): 1066–77; Fiske, "What We Know about Bias and Intergroup Conflict"; Tajfel, "Social Identity and Intergroup Behaviour"; Hewstone, Rubin, and Willis, "Intergroup Bias"; Fiske and Taylor, *Social Cognition*.

11. M. Sherif et al., *Intergroup Conflict and Cooperation: The Robbers Cave Experiment* (Norman, OK: University Book Exchange, 1961).

12. Fiske and Taylor, *Social Cognition*; Sears, Huddy, and Jervis, *Oxford Handbook of Political Psychology*.

13. P. Molenberghs et al., "Seeing Is Believing: Neural Mechanisms of Action-Perception Are Biased by Team Membership," *Human Brain Mapping* (2012).

14. L. Cronk and B. L. Leech, *Meeting at Grand Central: Understanding the Social and Evolutionary Roots of Cooperation* (Princeton: Princeton University Press, 2013), 27.

15. Hewstone et al. noted that much of the research on intergroup bias has been "directed at its relatively mild forms," which may have inadvertently emphasized its positive in-group effects and downplayed its negative out-group effects and created a "mismatch" between the somewhat banal effects debated in the labs and journals and the severe and "striking social problems" that it should be addressing in the real world, such as intergroup conflict and genocide. Hewstone, Rubin, and Willis, "Intergroup Bias," 594. See also Fiske, "What We Know about Bias and Intergroup Conflict"; E. Staub and D. Bar-Tal, "Genocide, Mass Killing, and Intractable Conflict," in *Oxford Handbook of Political Psychology*, ed. D. O. Sears, L. Huddy, and R. Jervis (Oxford: Oxford University Press, 2003).

16. D. L. Hamilton and T. K. Trolier, "Stereotypes and Stereotyping: An Overview of the Cognitive Approach," in *Prejudice, Discrimination and Racism*, ed. J. R. Dovidio and S. L. Gaertner (Orlando, FL: Academic Press, 1986); D. Druckman, "Nationalism, Patriotism and Group Loyalty: A Social Psychological Perspective," *Mershon International Studies Review* 38, no. 1 (1994): 43–68. Subjects have even been found to judge other individuals in their own group as better than the group's average, even when they are anonymous strangers assigned to groups randomly. Y. Klar and E. E. Giladi, "No One in My Group Can Be below the Group's Average: A Robust Positivity Bias in Favor of Anonymous Peers," *Journal of Personality and Social Psychology* 73, no. 5 (1997): 885–901; Y. Klar, "Way Beyond Compare: Nonselective Superiority and Inferiority Biases in Judging Randomly Assigned Group Members Relative to Their Peers," *Journal of Experimental Social Psychology* 38, no. 5 (2002): 331–51; Y. Klar, "When Standards Are Wide of the Mark: Nonselective Superiority and Inferiority Biases in Comparative Judgements of Objects and Concepts," *Journal of Experimental Psychology* 131, no. 4 (2002): 538–51.

17. D. J. Goleman, "What Is Negative about Positive Illusions? When Benefits for the Individual Harm the Collective," *Journal of Social and Clinical Psychology* 8, no. 2 (1989): 190–97, 194.

18. R. F. Baumeister and J. M. Boden, "Aggression and the Self: High Self-Esteem, Low Self-Control, and Ego Threat," in *Human Aggression: Theories, Research, and Implications for Social Policy*, ed. R. G. Geen and E. Donnerstein (San Diego: Academic Press, 1998), 115, 116; J. M. Rabbie, "Group Processes as Stimulants of Aggression," in *Aggression and War*, ed. J. Groebel and R. A. Hinde (Cambridge: Cambridge University Press, 1989).

19. R. W. Wrangham and M. L. Wilson, "Collective Violence: Comparisons between Youths and Chimpanzees," *Annals of the New York Academy of Sciences* 1036 (2004): 233–56.

20. B. Meier and V. Hinsz, "A Comparison of Human Aggression Committed by Groups and Individuals: An Interindividual-Intergroup Discontinuity," *Journal of Experimental Social Psychology* 40, no. 4 (2004): 551–59.

21. I. L. Janis, *Victims of Groupthink: Psychological Studies of Policy Decisions and Fiascoes* (Boston: Houghton Mifflin, 1972). Paul t'Hart points out that the groupthink phenomenon can indeed spawn overoptimism, but this tends to occur when the decision is seen as a potential opportunity. If the decision is already seen as very risky, then groupthink may result in collective avoidance instead. P. t'Hart, *Groupthink in Government: A Study of Small Groups and Policy Failure* (Amsterdam: Swets and Zeitlinger, 1990).

22. Goleman, "What Is Negative about Positive Illusions?" 194.

23. D. A. Welch, *Justice and the Genesis of War* (Cambridge: Cambridge University Press, 1993).

24. Wrangham and Wilson, "Collective Violence," 249.

25. R. D. Ashmore et al., "An Experimental Investigation of the Double Standard in the Perception of International Affairs," *Political Behavior* 1, no. 2 (1979): 123–35. For some other examples, see M. Cinnirella, "A Social Identity Perspective on European Integration," in *Changing European Identities: Social Psychological Analyses of Social Change*, ed. G. M. Breakwell and E. Lyons (Oxford: Butterworth Heinemann, 1996); V. D. Volkan, "The Need to Have Enemies and Allies: A Developmental Approach," *Political Psychology* 6, no. 2 (1985): 219–47; B. Silverstein, "Enemy Images: The Psychology of U.S. Attitudes and Cognitions Regarding the Soviet Union," *American Psychologist* 44 (1989): 903–13.

26. S. Van Evera, "Hypotheses on Nationalism and War," *International Security* 18, no. 4 (1998): 5–39, 27.

27. N. C. Meier, *Military Psychology* (New York: Harper, 1943), 9.

28. R. F. Inglehart, M. Moaddel, and M. Tessler, "Xenophobia and In-Group Solidarity in Iraq: A Natural Experiment on the Impact of Insecurity," *Perspectives on Politics* 4, no. 3 (2006): 495–505. The authors also considered cultural heritage and economic insecurity

as alternative causes, but these factors could not explain such high levels of groupishness in Iraq, leaving insecurity generated by the invasion and civil conflict as the most plausible explanation.

29. L. LeShan, *The Psychology of War: Comprehending Its Mystique and Its Madness* (New York: Helios, 2002); See also Van Evera, "Hypotheses on Nationalism and War."

30. Hewstone, Rubin, and Willis, "Intergroup Bias"; M. Brewer, "The Importance of Being We: Human Nature and Intergroup Relations," *American Psychologist* 62, no. 8 (2007): 728–38; J. Greene, *Moral Tribes: Emotion, Reason and the Gap between Us and Them* (New York: Penguin, 2013).

31. Fiske and Taylor, *Social Cognition*, 283.

32. H. Tajfel and J. C. Turner, "The Social Identity Theory of Intergroup Behavior," in *Psychology of Intergroup Relations*, ed. S. Worchel and W. G. Austin (Chicago: Nelson-Hall Publishers, 1986); Fiske and Taylor, *Social Cognition*.

33. Fiske, "What We Know about Bias and Intergroup Conflict." At the time she was referring to the twentieth century, although it could well be described as the problem of this century so far as well.

34. S. P. Huntington, *The Clash of Civilizations and the Remaking of World Order* (New York: Touchstone, 1997); R. D. Petersen, *Understanding Ethnic Violence: Fear, Hatred, and Resentment in Twentieth-Century Eastern Europe* (Cambridge: Cambridge University Press, 2002); M. D. Toft, *The Geography of Ethnic Violence: Identity, Interests, and the Indivisibility of Territory* (Princeton: Princeton University Press, 2003).

35. B. F. Walter and J. L. Snyder, *Civil Wars, Insecurity, and Intervention* (New York: Columbia University Press, 1999); Petersen, *Understanding Ethnic Violence*.

36. For data, debates, and further literature on the role of ethnic groups in the causes of conflict, see J. D. Fearon and D. D. Laitin, "Ethnicity, Insurgency, and Civil War," *American Political Science Review* 97, no. 1 (2003): 75–90; L.-E. Cederman, N. B. Weidmann, and K. S. Gleditsch, "Horizontal Inequalities and Ethno-nationalist Civil War: A Global Comparison," *American Political Science Review* 105, no. 3 (2011): 478–495; Toft, *The Geography of Ethnic Violence*.

37. D. Wilkinson, *Deadly Quarrels: Lewis F. Richardson and the Statistical Study of War* (Berkeley: University of California Press, 1980).

38. M. MacMillan, *The War That Ended Peace: How Europe Abandoned Peace for the First World War* (London: Profile Books, 2014); S. Van Evera, *Causes of War: Power and the Roots of Conflict* (Ithaca: Cornell University Press, 1999).

39. Van Evera, *Causes of War*, 25.

40. S. Weintraub, *Silent Night: The Remarkable Christmas Truce of 1914* (London: Simon and Schuster, 2001), 6.

41. Ibid.

42. Ibid.

43. G. Martel, *The Origins of the First World War* (Harlow: Longman, 1987), 90.

44. P. M. Kennedy, "Great Britain before 1914," in *Knowing One's Enemies: Intelligence Assessment before the Two World Wars*, ed. E. R. May (Princeton: Princeton University Press, 1984), 191.

45. Ibid., 191–92.

46. Van Evera, *Causes of War*, 25.

47. Ibid.

48. Ibid.

49. N. M. Naimark, *The Russians in Germany: A History of the Soviet Zone of Occupation, 1945–1949* (Cambridge, MA: Belknap Press of Harvard University Press, 1995), 114.

50. J. Merriman, *Modern Europe: From the Renaissance to the Present* (London: Norton, 1996), 1254.

51. J. Hughes-Wilson, *Military Intelligence Blunders* (New York: Carroll & Graf, 1999), 110.

52. Ibid.

53. Ibid.

54. J. Keegan, *The Second World War* (London: Penguin, 2005), 259.

55. W. I. Miller, *The Mystery of Courage* (Cambridge, MA: Harvard University Press, 2000), 72–73.

56. Fiske, "What We Know about Bias and Intergroup Conflict"; Hewstone, Rubin, and Willis, "Intergroup Bias"; Staub and Bar-Tal, "Genocide, Mass Killing, and Intractable Conflict."

57. Grayling, *War: An Enquiry*, 3.

58. M. A. Nowak, "Five Rules for the Evolution of Cooperation," *Science* 314 (2006): 1560–63; T. Burnham and D. D. P. Johnson, "The Biological and Evolutionary Logic of Human Cooperation," *Analyse & Kritik* 27, no. 1 (2005): 113–35; E. Fehr and U. Fischbacher, "The Nature of Human Altruism," *Nature* 425 (2003): 785–91; Cronk and Leech, *Meeting at Grand Central*.

59. E. Ostrom, *Governing the Commons: The Evolution of Institutions for Collective Action* (Cambridge: Cambridge University Press, 1990); E. Ostrom, J. Walker, and R. Gardner, "Covenants with and without a Sword: Self Governance Is Possible," *American Political Science Review* 86 (1992): 404–17; M. Olson, *The Logic of Collective Action: Public Goods and the Theory of Groups* (Cambridge, MA: Harvard University Press, 1965).

60. L. H. Keeley, *War before Civilization: The Myth of the Peaceful Savage* (Oxford: Oxford University Press, 1996); S. LeBlanc and K. E. Register, *Constant Battles: The Myth of the Peaceful, Noble Savage* (New York: St. Martin's Press, 2003); A. Gat, *War in Human Civilization* (Oxford: Oxford University Press, 2006); J. Guilaine and J. Zammit, *The Origins of War: Violence in Prehistory* (Oxford: Blackwell, 2004); B. A. Thayer, *Darwin and International Relations: On the Evolutionary Origins of War and Ethnic Conflict* (Lexington: University Press of Kentucky, 2004).

61. S. Bowles, "Group Competition, Reproductive Leveling, and the Evolution of Human Altruism," *Science* 314 (2006): 1569–72.

62. Keeley, *War before Civilization*.

63. R. W. Wrangham, "The Evolution of Coalitionary Killing," *Yearbook of Physical Anthropology* 42 (1999): 1–30; R. W. Wrangham and D. Peterson, *Demonic Males: Apes and the Origins of Human Violence* (London: Bloomsbury, 1996); E. O. Wilson, *The Insect Societies* (Cambridge, MA: Harvard University Press, 1971).

64. M. M. McDonald, C. D. Navarrete, and M. van Vugt, "Evolution and the Psychology of Intergroup Conflict: The Male Warrior Hypothesis," *Philosophical Transactions of the Royal Society B* 367, no. 1589 (2012): 670–79; R. W. Wrangham, "Is Military Incompetence Adaptive?" *Evolution and Human Behaviour* 20 (1999): 3–17; J. Tooby and L. Cosmides, "Groups in Mind: The Coalitional Roots of War and Morality," in *Human Morality & Sociality: Evolutionary & Comparative Perspectives*, ed. H. Høgh-Olesen (New York: Palgrave MacMillan, 2010).

65. R. W. Wrangham and L. Glowacki, "Intergroup Aggression in Chimpanzees and War in Nomadic Hunter-Gatherers: Evaluating the Chimpanzee Model," *Human Nature* 23 (2012): 5–29; J. Manson and R. W. Wrangham, "Intergroup Aggression in Chimpanzees and Humans," *Current Anthropology* 32, no. 4 (1991): 369–90; Wrangham, "The Evolution of Coalitionary Killing"; N. A. Chagnon, *Noble Savages: My Life among Two Dangerous Tribes—The Yanomamo and the Anthropologists* (New York: Simon & Schuster, 2014).

66. S. Hearne, *A Journey from Prince of Wales's Fort in Hudson's Bay to the Northern Ocean, 1769, 1770, 1771, 1772* (Toronto: Macmillan Co. of Canada [available in eHRAF, group ND07, Chipewyan, Chapter VI, Transactions at the Coppermine River], 1958); this quote and the ones that follow are from this work.

67. A. P. Vayda, "Primitive Warfare," in *War: Studies from Psychology, Sociology and Anthropology*, ed. A. P. Vayda (New York: Basic Books, 1968); Keeley, *War before Civilization*; LeBlanc and Register, *Constant Battles*; Gat, *War in Human Civilization*; Wrangham and Peterson, *Demonic Males*.

68. D. D. P. Johnson, "Gods of War: The Adaptive Logic of Religious Conflict," in *The Evolution of Religion: Studies, Theories, and Critiques*, ed. J. Bulbulia et al. (Santa Margarita, CA: Collins Foundation Press, 2008); D. D. P. Johnson and Z. Reeve, "The Virtues of Intolerance: Is Religion an Adaptation for War?" in *Religion, Intolerance and Conflict: A Scientific and Conceptual Investigation*, ed. S. Clarke, R. Powell, and J. Savulescu (Oxford: Oxford University Press, 2013).

69. R. D. Alexander, *The Biology of Moral Systems* (Aldine, NY: Hawthorne, 1987).

70. F. L. Roes and M. Raymond, "Belief in Moralizing Gods," *Evolution and Human Behavior* 24 (2003): 126–35.

71. A. W. Johnson and T. Earle, *The Evolution of Human Societies: From Foraging Group to Agrarian State* (Palo Alto, CA: Stanford University Press, 2000); G. Barker, *The Agricultural Revolution in Prehistory: Why Did Foragers Become Farmers?* (Oxford: Oxford University Press, 2006); Gat, *War in Human Civilization*.

72. Alexander, *The Biology of Moral Systems*.

73. Ibid.; Greene, *Moral Tribes*.

74. Ostrom, *Governing the Commons*; J. H. Kagel and A. E. Roth, eds., *The Handbook of Experimental Economics* (Princeton: Princeton University Press, 1995); Olson, *The Logic of Collective Action*.

75. Ostrom, Walker, and Gardner, "Covenants with and without a Sword"; E. Fehr and S. Gächter, "Altruistic Punishment in Humans," *Nature* 415 (2002): 137–40.

76. M. van Vugt, D. De Cremer, and D. Janssen, "Gender Differences in Competition and Cooperation: The Male Warrior Hypothesis," *Psychological Science* 18 (2007): 19–23.

77. I. Eshel and L. L. Cavalli-Sforza, "Assortment of Encounters and Evolution of Cooperativeness," *Proceedings of the National Academy of Sciences (PNAS)* 79, no. 4 (1982): 1331–35; R. A. Hammond and R. Axelrod, "The Evolution of Ethnocentrism," *Journal of Conflict Resolution* 50, no. 6 (2006): 926–36; M. Nowak and K. Sigmund, "Evolution of Indirect Reciprocity," *Nature* 437 (2005): 1291–98.

78. R. Sosis, H. Kress, and J. Boster, "Scars for War: Evaluating Alternative Signaling Explanations for Cross-Cultural Variance in Ritual Costs," *Evolution and Human Behavior* 28 (2007): 234–47.

79. S. Bowles, "Did Warfare among Ancestral Hunter-Gatherers Affect the Evolution of Human Social Behaviors?" *Science* 324 (2009): 1293–98; D. S. Wilson and E. Sober, "Reintroducing Group Selection to the Human Behavioural Sciences," *Behavioral and Brain Sciences* 17, no. 4 (1994): 585–654.

80. S. A. West, C. El Mouden, and A. Gardner, "16 Common Misconceptions about the Evolution of Cooperation in Humans," *Evolution and Human Behavior* 32 (2011): 231–62; Tooby and Cosmides, "Groups in Mind."

81. O. Smirnov et al., "'Heroism' in Warfare as a Functionally Specific Form of Altruism," *Journal of Politics* 69, no. 4 (2007): 927–40; J. Orbell and T. Morikawa, "An Evolutionary Account of Suicide Attacks: The Kamikaze Case," *Political Psychology* 32, no. 2 (2011): 297–322.

82. R. Dawkins, *The Selfish Gene* (Oxford: Oxford University Press, 1976), 124.

83. For some contrasting perspectives, see J. W. Dower, *War without Mercy: Race and Power in the Pacific War* (New York: Pantheon, 1986); J. Bourke, *An Intimate History of Killing: Face to Face Killing in Twentieth Century Warfare* (London: Granta Books, 1999); J. A. Lynn, *Battle: A History of Combat and Culture* (New York: Basic Books, 2004).

84. J. Diamond, *Guns, Germs and Steel: A Short History of Everybody for the Last 13,000 Years* (London: Vintage, 1998).

85. B. R. Ferguson, "Tribal Warfare," in *The Encyclopedia of War*, ed. G. Martel (Hoboken, NJ: Wiley-Blackwell, 2012), 2238.

86. R. W. Wrangham, *The Goodness Paradox: How Evolution Made Us Both More and Less Violent* (London: Profile Books, 2019); C. Boehm, *Hierarchy in the Forest: The Evolution of Egalitarian Behavior* (Cambridge, MA: Harvard University Press, 2001).

87. Lynn points out that atrocities tend to occur outside of actual combat, when one side has overwhelming power against vulnerable others. Lynn, *Battle*.

88. M. Potts and T. Hayden, *Sex and War: How Biology Explains Warfare and Terrorism and Offers a Path to a Safer World* (Dallas: Benbella Books, 2008), 289.

89. B. J. Bushman et al., "When God Sanctions Killing: Effect of Scriptural Violence on Aggression," *Psychological Science* 18, no. 3 (2007): 204–7. Their sample sizes were: Joshua = 1,066, Lin = 168.

90. Wrangham and Glowacki, "Intergroup Aggression in Chimpanzees and War in Nomadic Hunter-Gatherers"; Wrangham, "The Evolution of Coalitionary Killing"; Gat, *War in Human Civilization*.

91. Orbell and Morikawa, "An Evolutionary Account of Suicide Attacks," 319.

92. Lynn, *Battle*, 251–56.

93. M. G. Haselton and D. Nettle, "The Paranoid Optimist: An Integrative Evolutionary Model of Cognitive Biases," *Personality and Social Psychology Review* 10, no. 1 (2006): 47–66, 53. *Within* a group, they argue, such asymmetries would not hold as strongly since constantly assuming aggressive intent within groups would lead to high levels of internal conflict. This aligns with Richard Wrangham's argument that, compared to other primates, human aggression *within* groups has evolved to become moderated, whereas aggression *between* groups has evolved to become exaggerated. Wrangham, *The Goodness Paradox*. See also Boehm, *Hierarchy in the Forest*.

94. Cronk and Leech, *Meeting at Grand Central*, 182.

95. Haselton and Nettle, "The Paranoid Optimist." See also C. L. Fincher et al., "Pathogen Prevalence Predicts Human Cross-Cultural Variability in Individualism/Collectivism," *Proceedings of the Royal Society, B* 275, no. 1640 (2008): 1279–85.

96. L. Rozsa, "Spite, Xenophobia, and Collaboration between Hosts and Parasites," *Oikos* 91, no. 2 (2000): 396–400, 396.

97. M. Ignatieff, *The Lesser Evil: Political Ethics in an Age of Terror* (Princeton: Princeton University Press, 2005), 1.

98. Olson, *The Logic of Collective Action*; Cronk and Leech, *Meeting at Grand Central*.

99. R. Boyd, "The Puzzle of Human Sociality," *Science* 314, no. 5805 (2006): 1555; J. Henrich et al., "In Search of Homo Economicus: Behavioural Experiments in 15 Small-Scale Societies," *American Economic Review* 91, no. 2 (2001): 73–78.

100. P. Collier, "Doing Well out of War: An Economic Perspective," in *Greed and Grievance: Economic Agendas in Civil Wars*, ed. M. Berdal and D. Malone (Boulder, CO: Lynne Rienner, 2000), 99.

101. Ibid., 100.

102. The problem is made even harder because governments often actively work to suppress not only political discontent itself but public knowledge that it exists at all. This means that discontent can build even though no one is aware of others' similar sentiments. This "creates an illusion of a citizenry that is satisfied with the status quo . . . [and] prevents people from realizing that their own revolutionary acts will be joined by more such acts." Cronk and Leech, *Meeting at Grand Central*, 166. An in-group/out-group bias can help to overcome this thorny problem—overwhelming the "silence of the majority" with the salience of the group.

103. A. Sinclair, *A Concise History of the United States* (Stroud: Sutton, 1999), 37.

104. Ibid., 38.

105. Ibid., 41. Italics in original.

106. LeShan, *The Psychology of War*, 111.

107. Lynn, *Battle*; R. J. Rielly, "Confronting the Tiger: Small Unit Cohesion in Battle," *Military Review* 80, no. 6 (2000): 61–65; H. Whitehouse et al., "Brothers in Arms: Libyan Revolutionaries Bond like Family," *Proceedings of the National Academy of Sciences (PNAS)* 111, no. 50 (2014): 17783–85.

108. D. D. P. Johnson, "Leadership in War: Evolution, Cognition, and the Military Intelligence Hypothesis," in *The Handbook of Evolutionary Psychology*, ed. D. M. Buss (New York: Wiley, 2015).

109. D. J. Goldhagen, *Hitler's Willing Executioners: Ordinary Germans and the Holocaust* (New York: Vintage, 1997).

110. J. M. Post and A. George, *Leaders and Their Followers in a Dangerous World: The Psychology of Political Behavior*, 1st ed., Psychoanalysis and Social Theory (Ithaca: Cornell University Press, 2004).

111. J. Snyder, *From Voting to Violence: Democratization and Nationalist Conflict* (New York: W. W. Norton, 2000), 18.

112. Melvin Konner specifically considered whether xenophobia served an adaptive logic for the Nazis: "have modern genocides been maladaptive for the perpetrators, regardless of how maladaptive we think they have been for the species—not to mention how immoral they are? These things are difficult to measure. Germans as a group probably did not gain a net benefit from Nazism, because they paid such a high price in the war. Nevertheless, we see a resurgent and successful Germany in which many perpetrators' descendants are doing well. . . . Meanwhile, the Jews in those countries [referring to Germany and some other states] are gone, having been murdered together with their children and grandchildren, most leaving no descendants, and many non-Jews (reparations aside) have long since occupied and benefited from their homes, stores, property, wealth, etc." M. Konner, "Is Xenophobia Now Maladaptive? Group Commitments in a Globalized World," *Psychology Today*, 2 September 2012.

113. Hewstone, Rubin, and Willis, "Intergroup Bias," 594.

114. Staub and Bar-Tal, "Genocide, Mass Killing, and Intractable Conflict," 726.

115. Ibid., 727.

116. S. L. A. Marshall, *Men against Fire: The Problem of Battle Command* (1947; Norman: University of Oklahoma Press, 2000).

117. F. Smoler, "The Secret of the Soldiers Who Didn't Shoot," *American Heritage* 40, no. 2 (1989): 37–45.

118. D. Grossman, *On Killing: The Psychological Cost of Learning to Kill in War and Society* (New York: Back Bay Books, 1996).

119. National Center for PTSD, U.S. Department of Veterans Affairs, https://www.ptsd.va.gov/index.asp.

120. R. Collins, *Violence: A Micro-sociological Theory* (Princeton: Princeton University Press, 2008); Bourke, *An Intimate History of Killing*.

121. Van Evera, "Hypotheses on Nationalism and War"; LeShan, *The Psychology of War*.

122. For models that demonstrate this effect, see Hammond and Axelrod, "The Evolution of Ethnocentrism."

123. D. D. P. Johnson et al., "The Evolution of Error: Error Management, Cognitive Constraints, and Adaptive Decision-Making Biases," *Trends in Ecology & Evolution* 28, no. 8 (2013): 474–81.

124. W. B. Swann et al., "What Makes a Group Worth Dying For? Identity Fusion Fosters Perception of Familial Ties, Promoting Self-Sacrifice," *Journal of Personality and Social Psychology* 106, no. 6 (2014): 912–26.

125. Whitehouse et al., "Brothers in Arms."

126. H. Whitehouse and J. A. Lanman, "The Ties That Bind Us: Ritual, Fusion, and Identification," *Current Anthropology* 55, no. 6 (2014): 674–95.

127. Hewstone, Rubin, and Willis, "Intergroup Bias"; Staub and Bar-Tal, "Genocide, Mass Killing, and Intractable Conflict."

128. See the many such phenomena in, e.g., J. Baylis, S. Smith, and P. Owens, eds., *The Globalization of World Politics: An Introduction to International Relations*, 6th ed. (Oxford: Oxford University Press, 2013).

129. J. Diamond, *Collapse: How Societies Choose to Fail or Succeed* (New York: Penguin, 2005); T. M. Fazal, *State Death: The Politics and Geography of Conquest, Occupation, and Annexation* (Princeton: Princeton University Press, 2007).

130. K. N. Waltz, *Theory of International Politics* (New York: McGraw-Hill, 1979); J. J. Mearsheimer, *The Tragedy of Great Power Politics* (New York: Norton, 2001).

131. A. Wendt, *Social Theory of International Politics* (Cambridge: Cambridge University Press, 1999).

132. J. Mercer, "Anarchy and Identity," *International Organization* 49, no. 2 (1995): 229–52.

133. Thayer, *Darwin and International Relations*; Haselton and Nettle, "The Paranoid Optimist"; McDonald, Navarrete, and van Vugt, "Evolution and the Psychology of Intergroup Conflict"; Wrangham and Peterson, *Demonic Males*.

134. D. D. P. Johnson and B. A. Thayer, "The Evolution of Offensive Realism: Survival under Anarchy from the Pleistocene to the Present," *Politics and the Life Sciences* 35, no. 1 (2016): 1–26.

135. Wrangham, "Is Military Incompetence Adaptive?"; R. L. Trivers, "The Elements of a Scientific Theory of Self-Deception," *Annals of the New York Academy of Sciences* 907 (2000): 114–31; Goleman, "What Is Negative about Positive Illusions?"

136. Pew Research Center, Global Attitudes and Trends, "U.S. Views of China Turn Sharply Negative amid Trade Tensions," 13 August 2019, https://www.pewresearch.org /global/2019/08/13/u-s-views-of-china-turn-sharply-negative-amid-trade-tensions/.

137. Volkan, "The Need to Have Enemies and Allies," 219; Druckman, "Nationalism, Patriotism and Group Loyalty"; R. K. White, *Nobody Wanted War: Misperception in Vietnam and Other Wars* (New York: Doubleday, 1968).

138. G. Allison and P. Zelikow, *Essence of Decision: Explaining the Cuban Missile Crisis* (New York: Longman, 1999).

139. LeShan, *The Psychology of War*, 110–11.

140. Even in its most extreme and abhorrent forms, the in-group/out-group bias may turn out to aid the interests of its bearers. Indeed, as Mel Konner somberly concluded: "So, alas, I cannot conclude that genocide is any less adaptive for the perpetrators now than it was in most of human history. If we consider the human species as a whole, I certainly think it is maladaptive, but that is not the way we usually calculate reproductive advantage, because it is advantage gained by individuals and, perhaps, groups that has up to now always determined what would evolve. For the forseeable future too, some groups will still seek success at the expense of other groups." Konner, "Is Xenophobia Now Maladaptive?"

141. R. R. Hassin et al., "Subliminal Exposure to National Flags Affects Political Thought and Behavior," *Proceedings of the National Academy of Sciences (PNAS)* 104, no. 50 (2007): 19757–19761.

142. R. Giphart and M. van Vugt, *Mismatch: How Our Stone Age Brain Deceives Us Every Day (And What We Can Do About It)* (London: Little, Brown Book Group, 2018).

Chapter 8. No Mercy: The Pacific Campaign of World War II

The epigraph sources are: H. M. Smith and P. Finch, *Coral and Brass* (New York: Charles Scribner's Sons, 1949), 10; H. Afflerbach and H. Strachan, eds., *How Fighting Ends: A History of Surrender* (Oxford: Oxford University Press, 2012), 202.

1. J. W. Dower, *War without Mercy: Race and Power in the Pacific War* (New York: Pantheon, 1986), 10.

2. A. Iriye, *Pearl Harbor and the Coming of the Pacific War: A Brief History with Documents and Essays* (Boston: Bedford/St. Martin's, 1999); D. Kahn, "Pearl Harbor as an Intelligence Failure," in *Pearl Harbor and the Coming of the Pacific War: A Brief History with Documents and Essays*, ed. A. Iriye (Boston: Bedford/St. Martin's, 1999).

3. G. A. Blainey, *The Causes of War* (New York: Free Press, 1973), 167.

4. R. Wohlstetter, *Pearl Harbor: Warning and Decision* (Stanford: Stanford University Press, 1962), 3.

5. Blainey, *The Causes of War*, 167.

6. S. Budiansky, *Air Power: The Men, Machines, and Ideas That Revolutionized War, from Kitty Hawk to Gulf War II* (New York: Viking, 2004), 255.

7. D. Kahn, "The United States Views Germany and Japan in 1941," in *Knowing One's Enemies: Intelligence Assessment before the Two World Wars*, ed. E. May (Princeton: Princeton University Press, 1984), 497.

8. Ibid., 500. See also Wohlstetter, *Pearl Harbor*.

9. S. Van Evera, *Causes of War: Power and the Roots of Conflict* (Ithaca: Cornell University Press, 1999), 22.

10. Budiansky, *Air Power*, 255.

11. J. Hughes-Wilson, *Military Intelligence Blunders* (New York: Carroll & Graf, 1999), 113.

12. Quoted in Budiansky, *Air Power*, 255.

13. Blainey, *The Causes of War*, 168.

14. Ibid., 169.

15. Kahn, "Pearl Harbor as an Intelligence Failure," 166.

16. Van Evera, *Causes of War*, 21.

17. Dower, *War without Mercy*; M. Hastings, *Nemesis: The Battle for Japan, 1944–1945* (London: William Collins, 2016).

18. K. Macksey, *Military Errors of World War Two* (London: Cassell, 1987), 148.

19. Ibid., 149.

20. T. V. Paul, *Asymmetric Conflicts: War Initiation by Weaker Powers* (Cambridge: Cambridge University Press, 1994), 73.

21. Van Evera, *Causes of War*, 27.

22. B. Posen, *The Sources of Military Doctrine: France, Britain, and Germany between the World Wars*, Cornell Studies in Security Affairs (Ithaca: Cornell University Press, 1984), 20.

23. G. F. Linderman, *The World within War: America's Combat Experience in World War II* (Cambridge, MA: Harvard University Press, 1997), 153.

24. D. Tierney, *How We Fight: Crusades, Quagmires, and the American Way of War* (New York: Little, Brown, 2010), 164.

25. Figures on rates of attrition are from N. Ferguson, *Colossus: The Rise and Fall of the American Empire* (New York: Penguin, 2004), 304. See also D. Brinkley and M. E. Haskew, *The World War II Desk Reference* (New York: Castle Books, 2008), 433.

26. W. I. Miller, *The Mystery of Courage* (Cambridge, MA: Harvard University Press, 2000), 66.

27. J. A. Lynn, *Battle: A History of Combat and Culture* (New York: Basic Books, 2004), 247.

28. Ibid.

29. Dower, *War without Mercy*, 64.

30. Ibid.

31. E. P. Hoyt, *The Kamikazes* (London: Guild, 1983).

32. Quote is from J. Merriman, *Modern Europe: From the Renaissance to the Present* (London: Norton, 1996), 1286. Figures are from J. Keegan, *The Second World War* (London: Penguin, 2005), 566–73.

33. Ibid., 1256.

34. Dower, *War without Mercy*, 36.

35. V. D. Hanson, *Carnage and Culture: Landmark Battles in the Rise of Western Power* (New York: Anchor, 2001), 354.

36. Ibid., 365.

37. Ibid.

38. A. Sinclair, *A Concise History of the United States* (Stroud: Sutton, 1999), 169.

39. Hanson, *Carnage and Culture*, 362.

40. Ibid., 341.

41. Sinclair, *A Concise History of the United States*, 170.

42. Hanson, *Carnage and Culture*, 341.

43. Ibid., 362.

44. T. G. Mahnken, *Uncovering Ways of War: U.S. Intelligence and Foreign Military Innovation, 1918–1941* (Ithaca: Cornell University Press, 2002); Budiansky, *Air Power*.

45. Sinclair, *A Concise History of the United States*, 171.

46. Ibid.

47. Figures are from Ferguson, *Colossus*, 304. See also Brinkley and Haskew, *The World War II Desk Reference*, 433.

48. Tierney, *How We Fight*.

49. Ibid., 154.

50. Ibid., 155.

51. Lynn, *Battle*, 252; Linderman, *The World within War*.

52. Linderman, *The World within War*, 2–3.

53. Ibid., 5.

54. Ibid., 7.

55. W. Murray and A. R. Millett, *A War to Be Won: Fighting the Second World War* (Cambridge, MA: Harvard University Press, 2000), 520.

56. J. Bourke, *An Intimate History of Killing: Face to Face Killing in Twentieth Century Warfare* (London: Granta Books, 1999), 146. Stouffer's study was conducted in 1944–45.

57. Linderman, *The World within War*, 350.

58. Smith and Finch, *Coral and Brass*, 130.

59. Ibid.

60. Ibid. Casualty figures from M. G. Walling, *Bloodstained Sands: U.S. Amphibious Operations in World War II* (Oxford: Osprey Publishing, 2017), 332.

61. Miller, *The Mystery of Courage*, 68.

62. Hastings, *Nemesis*.

63. Brinkley and Haskew, *The World War II Desk Reference*; Keegan, *The Second World War*.

64. C. L. Symonds, *World War II at Sea* (Oxford: Oxford University Press, 2018).

65. Hanson, *Carnage and Culture*, 363.

66. Ibid., 364.

67. D. Horner, *The Second World War (I): The Pacific* (Oxford: Osprey, 2002).

68. Hanson, *Carnage and Culture*, 355.

69. Ibid.

70. Ibid.; Hastings, *Nemesis*.

71. Budiansky, *Air Power*.

72. Hanson, *Carnage and Culture*, 351; A. Kernan, *The Unknown Battle of Midway* (New Haven: Yale University Press, 2005).

73. Hanson, *Carnage and Culture*, 351.

74. Ibid., 341.

75. Dower, *War without Mercy*, 73.

76. Hanson, *Carnage and Culture*, 364.

77. L. Saad, "A Country Unified after Pearl Harbor," *Gallup Vault*, 5 December 2016. Interestingly, even Roosevelt's spike was at the low end compared to other wartime rallies. J. Green, "What Explains FDR's Puny Poll Bounce after Pearl Harbor?" *Atlantic*, 4 May 2011.

78. Hanson, *Carnage and Culture*, 367.

79. Dower, *War without Mercy*.

80. Ibid., 12.

81. Ibid., 12n10.

82. Keegan, *The Second World War*, 259.

83. Linderman, *The World within War*, 174.

84. Quoted in Dower, *War without Mercy*, 33.

85. Ibid.

86. Ibid., 36.

87. Ibid.

88. Van Evera, *Causes of War*, 28.

89. Sinclair, *A Concise History of the United States*, 167.

90. D. Tierney, "Pearl Harbor in Reverse: Moral Analogies in the Cuban Missile Crisis," *Journal of Cold War Studies* 9, no. 2 (2007): 49–77.

91. Tierney, *How We Fight*, 154.

92. Ibid., 156.

93. Ibid., 154.

94. F. Ninkovich, *The Wilsonian Century: U.S. Foreign Policy since 1900* (Chicago: University of Chicago Press, 1999), 136.

95. Linderman, *The World within War*, 178.

96. R. A. Pape, *Bombing to Win: Air Power and Coercion in War* (Ithaca: Cornell University Press, 1996), 26.

97. Harry S. Truman, "Radio Address to the American People after the Signing of the Terms of Unconditional Surrender by Japan," 1 September 1945, https://www.trumanlibrary.org.

98. P. Neville, *Winston Churchill: Statesman or Opportunist?* (London: Hodder & Stoughton, 1996), 125.

99. Horner, *The Second World War (I)*, 29.

100. Neville, *Winston Churchill*, 125.

101. L. James, *The Illustrated Rise and Fall of the British Empire* (London: Little, Brown, 1999), 281.

102. Keegan, *The Second World War*, 257.

103. Linderman, *The World within War*, 155.

104. Tierney, *How We Fight*, 164.

105. Ibid., 165.

106. Dower, *War without Mercy*, 41.

107. Tierney, *How We Fight*, 158.

108. Budiansky, *Air Power*, 336.

109. Tierney, *How We Fight*, 158.

110. Dower, *War without Mercy*, 53.

111. Linderman, *The World within War*, 169.

112. Ibid., 154.

113. M. A. Hill, "Lessons of Bataan," in *How the Jap Army Fights*, ed. P. W. Thompson and H. Doud (New York: Penguin Books/Infantry Journal, 1942), 155. Italics in original.

114. Ibid.

115. Ibid. Italics in original.

116. Ibid., 158.

117. S. L. A. Marshall, *Men against Fire: The Problem of Battle Command* (1947; Norman: University of Oklahoma Press, 2000); Bourke, *An Intimate History of Killing*, 63–64.

118. D. Grossman, *On Killing: The Psychological Cost of Learning to Kill in War and Society* (New York: Back Bay Books, 1996).

119. Hill, "Lessons of Bataan," 158.

120. Bourke, *An Intimate History of Killing*, 100. Bourke notes that Marshall's insights about "psychological principles of group dynamics transformed military training regimes in Britain, America, and Australia."

121. R. J. Rielly, "Confronting the Tiger: Small Unit Cohesion in Battle," *Military Review* 80, no. 6 (2000): 61–65.

122. Lynn, *Battle*.

123. Linderman, *The World within War*, 161.

124. Ibid., 173.

125. Keegan, *The Second World War*, 292.

126. Linderman, *The World within War*, 159.

127. Ibid., 173.

128. Ibid., 175.

129. Dower, *War without Mercy*, 53.

130. Ibid., 55.

131. Ibid.

132. Linderman, *The World within War*, 173.

133. Dower, *War without Mercy*, 33.

134. Lynn, *Battle*, 229.

135. Ibid.

136. Bourke, *An Intimate History of Killing*, 146.

137. Ibid.

138. Lynn, *Battle*, 252; Linderman, *The World within War*.

139. Dower, *War without Mercy*, 11.

140. Tierney, *How We Fight*, 166.

141. Pape, *Bombing to Win*, 90.

142. Dower, *War without Mercy*, 56–57.

143. T. Hasegawa, *Racing the Enemy: Stalin, Truman, and the Surrender of Japan* (Cambridge, MA: Harvard University Press, 2006), 291.

144. Dower, *War without Mercy*, 56.

145. Ibid., 57.

146. Linderman, *The World within War*, 178.

147. Hanson, *Carnage and Culture*, 381.

148. Linderman, *The World within War*, 177.

149. Pape, *Bombing to Win*, 99.

150. Pape, *Bombing to Win*, 100.

151. S. P. Rosen, *Winning the Next War: Innovation and the Modern Military* (Ithaca: Cornell University Press, 1991).

152. Rosen, *Winning the Next War*, 130–47; Pape, *Bombing to Win*.

153. Pape, *Bombing to Win*, 99.

154. Rosen, *Winning the Next War*, 143–44.

155. Pape, *Bombing to Win*, 100.

156. Hoyt, *The Kamikazes*, 291.

157. Pape, *Bombing to Win*, 100.

158. Ibid.

159. Rosen, *Winning the Next War*; Pape, *Bombing to Win*.

160. Dower, *War without Mercy*, 38.

161. Ibid., 39.

162. Ibid., 40.

163. Hasegawa, *Racing the Enemy*, 103.

164. For extensive reviews and viewpoints, see T. D. Biddle, *Rhetoric and Reality in Air Warfare: The Evolution of British and American Ideas about Strategic Bombing, 1914–1945* (Princeton: Princeton University Press, 2004); Pape, *Bombing to Win*; A. B. Downes, *Targeting Civilians in War* (Ithaca: Cornell University Press, 2008); J. A. Warden, *The Air Campaign: Planning for Combat* (Washington, DC: National Defense University Press, 1988); Hasegawa, *Racing the Enemy*.

165. Pape, *Bombing to Win*, 102. By Pape's figures, 1.36 million tons of bombs were dropped on Germany.

166. Ibid.

167. Ibid., 131.

168. Ibid., 92.

169. Ibid., 88.

170. Ibid., 26.

171. Pape's book is largely about how strategic bombing does not work, at least on its own; see ibid. Although for arguments about how the air campaign did have at least some important strategic effects on the war effort, see Warden, *The Air Campaign*; A. Roberts, *The Storm of War: A New History of the Second World War* (London: Allen Lane, 2009); Hastings, *Nemesis*.

172. Pape, *Bombing to Win*, 87.

173. Hoyt, *The Kamikazes*, 291–92.

174. A. J. P. Taylor, *The War Lords* (London: Penguin, 1977), 186.

175. Years later, based on the experiences of the Pacific campaign up to that point, such as the 20:1 ratio of Japanese to American losses, Rufus Miles calculated that U.S. casualties might actually have been a maximum of 20,000 combat deaths. R. E. Miles Jr., "Hiroshima: The Strange Myth of Half a Million American Lives Saved," *International Security* 10 (1985): 121–40.

176. Hasegawa, *Racing the Enemy*, 103–4.

177. W. C. Martel, *Victory in War: Foundations of Modern Military Policy* (Cambridge: Cambridge University Press, 2006), 139.

178. Pape, *Bombing to Win*, 91–95.

179. Budiansky, *Air Power*, 334.

180. Hasegawa, *Racing the Enemy*.

181. D. C. Copeland, *The Origins of Major War* (Ithaca: Cornell University Press, 2000), 157. Stimson said this on 14 May 1945. Pape put the same point in political science

language: with so many reasons to drop the bomb, the decision to use it was "overdetermined." Pape, *Bombing to Win*, 94.

182. Budiansky, *Air Power*, 334.

183. R. Shenkman, *Presidential Ambition: Gaining Power at Any Cost* (New York: Harper Collins, 1999), 320.

184. Pape, *Bombing to Win*, 105.

185. Ibid., 94. In fact, as per a Schelling strategy of deterrence. T. C. Schelling, *The Strategy of Conflict* (Cambridge, MA: Harvard University Press, 1960).

186. Tierney, *How We Fight*, 165.

187. Pape, *Bombing to Win*, 128.

188. Shenkman, *Presidential Ambition*, 318.

189. Hasegawa, *Racing the Enemy*, 299.

190. R. K. Betts, *Nuclear Blackmail and Nuclear Balance* (Washington, DC: Brookings Institution Press, 1987), 34.

191. Tierney, *How We Fight*, 158.

192. Pape, *Bombing to Win*, 128. See also Hasegawa, *Racing the Enemy*.

193. Tierney, *How We Fight*, 158.

194. Dower, *War without Mercy*, 11.

195. Iriye, *Pearl Harbor and the Coming of the Pacific War*; S. D. Sagan, "The Origins of the Pacific War," *Journal of Interdisciplinary History* 18, no. 4 (1988): 893–922.

196. Dower, *War without Mercy*, 29. See also p. 14. Italics added.

197. R. Kurzban, J. Tooby, and L. Cosmides, "Can Race Be Erased? Coalitional Computation and Social Categorization," *Proceedings of the National Academy of Sciences* 98, no. 26 (2001): 15387–92.

198. Hanson, *Carnage and Culture*.

199. Ibid., 387.

200. Ibid., 370.

201. B. W. Tuchman, *The March of Folly: From Troy to Vietnam* (New York: Alfred A. Knopf, 1984), 201.

202. E. N. Luttwak, *Strategy: The Logic of War and Peace* (Cambridge, MA: Belknap Press, 2001), 249. According to Luttwak, "There were no genuinely decisive battles in the Pacific war. The only difference that the naval and ground battles of the Coral Sea, Midway, New Guinea, and Guadalcanal could make was to change the speed of Japan's decline toward complete defeat. None of those battles, dramatic as they were, could be decisive at the level of grand strategy because none of them could have changed the outcome of the war, as some of the German-Soviet battles on the eastern front could have done."

203. Hanson, *Carnage and Culture*, 385.

Chapter 9. Overkill: The Limits of Adaptive Biases

The epigraph sources are: Plato, *The Republic*, trans. B. Jowett (New York: Cosimo Classics, 2008), 223; A. Calaprice, *The Ultimate Quotable Einstein* (Princeton: Princeton University Press, 2011), 274.

1. V. D. Hanson, *Carnage and Culture: Landmark Battles in the Rise of Western Power* (New York: Anchor, 2001), 361.

2. T. Hasegawa, *Racing the Enemy: Stalin, Truman, and the Surrender of Japan* (Cambridge, MA: Harvard University Press, 2006); H. P. Bix, *Hirohito and the Making of Modern Japan* (New York: HarperCollins, 2001).

3. Hanson, *Carnage and Culture*, 361.

4. J. W. Dower, *War without Mercy: Race and Power in the Pacific War* (New York: Pantheon, 1986), 8.

5. D. Horner, *The Second World War (I): The Pacific* (Oxford: Osprey, 2002), 13.

6. Dower, *War without Mercy*, 30.

7. Ibid., 31.

8. R. A. Pape, *Bombing to Win: Air Power and Coercion in War* (Ithaca: Cornell University Press, 1996), 109.

9. J. Keegan, *The Second World War* (London: Penguin, 2005), 242.

10. M. Hastings, *Nemesis: The Battle for Japan, 1944–1945* (London: William Collins, 2016), 53.

11. Hanson, *Carnage and Culture*, 387.

12. Ibid., 375.

13. Ibid., 380.

14. Ibid., 375.

15. Hastings, *Nemesis*, 52.

16. G. F. Linderman, *The World within War: America's Combat Experience in World War II* (Cambridge, MA: Harvard University Press, 1997), 150.

17. Kenneth Davis, quoted in ibid., 161.

18. Ibid., 165.

19. Hanson, *Carnage and Culture*, 367.

20. W. I. Miller, *The Mystery of Courage* (Cambridge, MA: Harvard University Press, 2000), 68.

21. Hastings, *Nemesis*, 61.

22. Hanson, *Carnage and Culture*, 387.

23. Hastings, *Nemesis*, 40.

24. Pape, *Bombing to Win*, 130.

25. Hasegawa, *Racing the Enemy*; Hastings, *Nemesis*.

26. Dower, *War without Mercy*, 68.

27. Bix, *Hirohito and the Making of Modern Japan*.

28. S. Budiansky, *Air Power: The Men, Machines, and Ideas That Revolutionized War, from Kitty Hawk to Gulf War II* (New York: Viking, 2004), 335.

29. Ibid.

30. W. Murray and A. R. Millett, *A War to Be Won: Fighting the Second World War* (Cambridge, MA: Harvard University Press, 2000), 520.

31. Pape, *Bombing to Win*, 124.

32. Ibid., 131.

33. Ibid., 125.

34. Ibid., 130.

35. Dower, *War without Mercy*; Hastings, *Nemesis*.

36. E. P. Hoyt, *The Kamikazes* (London: Guild, 1983), 255.

37. Linderman, *The World within War*, 153.

38. Ibid., 153.

39. Dower, *War without Mercy*, 61.

40. Ibid., 68.

41. Pape, *Bombing to Win*, 130.

42. Hoyt, *The Kamikazes*, 255. See also Dower, *War without Mercy*, 45.

43. Hoyt, *The Kamikazes*, 255.

44. R. L. Trivers, *Deceit and Self-Deception: Fooling Yourself the Better to Fool Others* (London: Allen Lane, 2011), 229.

45. Dower, *War without Mercy*, 46.

46. Ibid., 45.

47. D. Brinkley and M. E. Haskew, *The World War II Desk Reference* (New York: Castle Books, 2008), 427–28.

48. Dower, *War without Mercy*, 48. Dower has exactly the same *percentages* as Brinkley and Haskew, but the total numbers that died in captivity differ between the two sources (the latter report 19,500 Anglo-American deaths, with those in German captivity not stated; Dower reports 35,756 died in Japanese captivity and 9,348 died in German or Italian captivity).

49. L. James, *The Illustrated Rise and Fall of the British Empire* (London: Little, Brown, 1999), 281.

50. Hastings, *Nemesis*, 590.

51. Hanson, *Carnage and Culture*, 367.

52. Ibid., 368.

53. Hastings, *Nemesis*, 18.

54. J. D. Moreno, *Mind Wars: Brain Research and National Defense* (New York: Dana Press, 2006), 166.

55. W. E. Grunden, *Secret Weapons and World War II: Japan in the Shadow of Big Science* (Lawrence: University Press of Kansas, 2005).

56. Dower, *War without Mercy*.

57. Ibid.

58. Ibid., 61.

59. In fact, Dower noted several patterns that were precisely reflected as mirror images of each other, strongly indicative of classic in-group/out-group effects: "First, they followed predictable patterns of contrariness, in which each side portrayed the other as its polar opposite: as darkness opposed to its own radiant light. Second, the positive self-images of one side were singled out for ridicule and condemnation by the other. Self-stereotypes fed hostile stereotypes: the group became the herd, for example, while the individualist became the egoist. Third, and scarcely acknowledged during the war years, a submerged strata of common values developed in the very midst of the polemics each side employed against the enemy. Each raised the banner of liberation, morality, and peace. Whatever their actual deeds may have been, moreover, they condemned atrocities, exploitation, and theories of racial supremacy. Fourth, policies and practices that became fixated on exterminating the enemy—and verged, for some participants, on the genocidal—followed depiction of the enemy as incorrigibly evil (or base, or mad)." Ibid., 28–29.

60. D. Tierney, *How We Fight: Crusades, Quagmires, and the American Way of War* (New York: Little, Brown, 2010), 157.

61. Ibid., 165.

62. Dower, *War without Mercy*, 53.

63. Ibid.

64. National World War II Museum, New Orleans, "Should We Use Poison Gas? How Public Opinion Influenced Military Policy on Poison Gas in World War II," 5 May 2018, https://www.nationalww2museum.org/war/wwii-polls/roper-polls-poison-gas.

65. Tierney, *How We Fight*, 165.

66. Dower, *War without Mercy*, 15.

67. Ibid., 19.

68. Ibid., 43.

69. See, e.g., J. A. Lynn, *Battle: A History of Combat and Culture* (New York: Basic Books, 2004).

70. Dower, *War without Mercy*, 51.

71. Ibid., 8.

72. Linderman, *The World within War*, 168.

73. Dower, *War without Mercy*, 63.

74. Ibid., 68.

75. J. Bourke, *An Intimate History of Killing: Face to Face Killing in Twentieth Century Warfare* (London: Granta Books, 1999), 172–73.

76. Linderman, *The World within War*, 178.

77. Ibid., 179.

78. Dower, *War without Mercy*, 63–64. Quote runs across page.

79. Linderman, *The World within War*, 181.

80. Dower, *War without Mercy*, 66.

81. Linderman, *The World within War*, 161.

82. Ibid., 168.

83. H. M. Smith and P. Finch, *Coral and Brass* (New York: Charles Scribner's Sons, 1949), 9.

84. Linderman, *The World within War*, 169.

85. Hastings, *Nemesis*, 52.

86. Dower, *War without Mercy*, 71.

87. James, *The Illustrated Rise and Fall of the British Empire*, 280.

88. Dower, *War without Mercy*, 9.

89. Lynn, *Battle*, 228.

90. Linderman, *The World within War*, 184.

91. Ibid., 356.

92. Ibid.

93. Ibid. Keegan and others put the number of Americans killed higher, at 12,000 or more, as well as a corresponding higher number of casualties. See Keegan, *The Second World War*, 566–73.

94. Pape, *Bombing to Win*, 103; Hastings, *Nemesis*, 7.

95. Linderman, *The World within War*, 177.

96. Ibid.

97. A. Sinclair, *A Concise History of the United States* (Stroud: Sutton, 1999), 171.

98. R. Reeves, *Infamy: The Shocking Story of the Japanese American Internment in World War II* (New York: Henry Holt, 2015).

99. Trivers, *Deceit and Self-Deception*, 153.

100. L. LeShan, *The Psychology of War: Comprehending Its Mystique and Its Madness* (New York: Helios, 2002), 115.

101. Ibid.

102. Reeves, *Infamy*, xiv.

103. Ibid.

104. T. D. Biddle, *Rhetoric and Reality in Air Warfare: The Evolution of British and American Ideas about Strategic Bombing, 1914-1945* (Princeton: Princeton University Press, 2004); A. B. Downes, *Targeting Civilians in War* (Ithaca: Cornell University Press, 2008); Pape, *Bombing to Win*; J. A. Warden, *The Air Campaign: Planning for Combat* (Washington, DC: National Defense University Press, 1988).

105. Pape, *Bombing to Win*, 129.

106. Ibid.

107. Ibid.

108. A. Roberts, *The Storm of War: A New History of the Second World War* (London: Allen Lane, 2009), 571, 575-77.

109. Pape, *Bombing to Win*, 103.

110. Budiansky, *Air Power*, 338.

111. Pape, *Bombing to Win*, 103.

112. Ibid.

113. Budiansky, *Air Power*, 338.

114. Pape, *Bombing to Win*, 93–94.

115. Ibid., 94.

116. Ibid., 104.

117. Budiansky, *Air Power*, 338.

118. Dower, *War without Mercy*, 55.

119. N. Ferguson, *Colossus: The Rise and Fall of the American Empire* (New York: Penguin, 2004), 71.

120. Dower, *War without Mercy*, 55.

121. Pape, *Bombing to Win*, 104.

122. J. J. Mearsheimer, *The Tragedy of Great Power Politics* (New York: Norton, 2001), 102, 440n52.

123. Sinclair, *A Concise History of the United States*, 174.

124. Brinkley and Haskew, *The World War II Desk Reference*, 433–34; see also Pape, *Bombing to Win*, 129.

125. Hasegawa, *Racing the Enemy*; Pape, *Bombing to Win*.

126. Pape, *Bombing to Win*, 135.

127. S. S. Montefiore, *Stalin: The Court of the Red Tsar* (London: Weidenfeld & Nicolson, 2003), 445.

128. Pape, *Bombing to Win*, 88.

129. Ibid., 105; Hasegawa, *Racing the Enemy*.

130. Pape, *Bombing to Win*, 106.

131. The strategy could be said to have worked if the Japanese incorrectly assumed the United States had many more bombs—they had no way of knowing. But again, this is not necessarily supported by the evidence. Hasegawa, *Racing the Enemy*.

132. Pape, *Bombing to Win*, 106.

133. Budiansky, *Air Power*, 339. Pape notes that "because the Japanese government tightly controlled information, news of the bombings spread slowly and the war ended before much of the population learned what had really happened at Hiroshima and Nagasaki." Pape, *Bombing to Win*, 105.

134. Pape, *Bombing to Win*, 115.

135. Hanson, *Carnage and Culture*.

136. Hasegawa, *Racing the Enemy*.

137. M. Kammen, "Some Patterns and Meanings of Memory Distortion in American History," in *Memory Distortion: How Minds, Brains, and Societies Reconstruct the Past*, ed. D. L. Schacter (Cambridge, MA: Harvard University Press, 1995), 336.

138. Ibid.

139. C. Boehm, *Moral Origins: The Evolution of Virtue, Altruism, and Shame* (New York: Basic Books, 2012); J. Haidt, "The New Synthesis in Moral Psychology," *Science* 316 (2007): 998–1002; R. Wright, *The Moral Animal: Why We Are the Way We Are: The New Science of Evolutionary Psychology* (New York: Random House, 1994); R. D. Alexander, *The Biology of Moral Systems* (Aldine, NY: Hawthorne, 1987).

Chapter 10. Guardian Angels: The Strategic Advantages of Cognitive Biases

The epigraph sources are: K. N. Waltz, *Man, the State and War: A Theoretical Analysis* (New York: Columbia University Press, 1959), 181; D. Kahneman, *Thinking, Fast and Slow* (London: Allen Lane, 2011), 416.

1. S. D. Sagan and J. Suri, "The Madman Nuclear Alert: Secrecy, Signaling, and Safety in October 1969," *International Security* 27, no. 4 (2003): 150–83; W. Burr and J. Kimball, *Nixon's Nuclear Specter: The Secret Alert of 1969, Madman Diplomacy, and the Vietnam War* (Lawrence: University of Kansas Press, 2015).

2. T. C. Schelling, *The Strategy of Conflict* (Cambridge, MA: Harvard University Press, 1960), 16–20.

3. N. Machiavelli, *Discourses on Livy*, trans. H. C. Mansfield and N. Tarcov (1517; Chicago: University of Chicago Press, 1996), 213; this is in fact in the title of Book 3, Chapter 2.

4. See also S. N. Ghaemi, *A First-Rate Madness: Uncovering the Links between Leadership and Mental Illness* (New York: Penguin Press, 2011).

5. G. Gigerenzer and P. M. Todd, *Simple Heuristics That Make Us Smart* (Oxford: Oxford University Press, 2000); G. Gigerenzer, *Adaptive Thinking: Rationality in the Real World* (Oxford: Oxford University Press, 2002); D. T. Kenrick and V. Griskevicius, *The Rational Animal: How Evolution Made Us Smarter than We Think* (New York: Basic Books, 2013).

6. R. L. Trivers, *Deceit and Self-Deception: Fooling Yourself the Better to Fool Others* (London: Allen Lane, 2011); R. L. Trivers, "The Elements of a Scientific Theory of Self-Deception," *Annals of the New York Academy of Sciences* 907 (2000): 114–31.

7. G. Gigerenzer and H. Brighton, "*Homo Heuristicus*: Why Biased Minds Make Better Inferences," *Topics in Cognitive Science* 1 (2009): 107–43; L. Cosmides and J. Tooby, "Better than Rational: Evolutionary Psychology and the Invisible Hand," *American Economic Review* 84, no. 2 (1994): 327–32.

8. J. Cooper, *Cognitive Dissonance: 50 Years of a Classic Theory* (New York: Sage, 2007); D. Kahneman and A. Tversky, "Prospect Theory: An Analysis of Decisions under Risk," *Econometrica* 47 (1979): 263–91; R. F. Baumeister et al., "Bad Is Stronger than Good," *Review of General Psychology* 5, no. 4 (2001): 323–70.

9. D. D. P. Johnson and J. H. Fowler, "The Evolution of Overconfidence," *Nature* 477 (2011): 317–20; D. D. P. Johnson, N. B. Weidmann, and L.-E. Cederman, "Fortune Favours the Bold: An Agent-Based Model Reveals Adaptive Advantages of Overconfidence in War," *PLoS ONE* 6, no. 6 (2011): e20851; D. Nettle, "Adaptive Illusions: Optimism, Control and Human Rationality," in *Emotion, Evolution and Rationality*, ed. D. Evans and P. Cruse (Oxford: Oxford University Press, 2004).

10. C. von Clausewitz, *On War*, trans. M. Howard and P. Paret (1832; Princeton: Princeton University Press, 1976). For a range of examples, see R. Greene, *The 48 Laws of Power* (New York: Penguin, 1998); R. M. Kanter, *Confidence: How Winning Streaks and Losing Streaks Begin and End* (New York: Crown Business, 2004); S. E. Taylor, *Positive Illusions: Creative Self-Deception and the Healthy Mind* (New York: Basic Books, 1989).

11. C. Powell, *It Worked for Me: In Life and Leadership* (New York: Harper Collins, 2012), 27.

12. D. D. P. Johnson, *Overconfidence and War: The Havoc and Glory of Positive Illusions* (Cambridge, MA: Harvard University Press, 2004); R. W. Wrangham, "Is Military Incompetence Adaptive?" *Evolution and Human Behaviour* 20 (1999): 3–17; Nettle, "Adaptive Illusions"; M. G. Haselton and D. Nettle, "The Paranoid Optimist: An Integrative Evolutionary Model of Cognitive Biases," *Personality and Social Psychology Review* 10, no. 1 (2006): 47–66.

13. Taylor, *Positive Illusions*; S. E. Taylor and J. D. Brown, "Positive Illusions and Well-being Revisited: Separating Fact from Fiction," *Psychological Bulletin* 116, no. 1 (1994): 21–27; C. Peterson, *A Primer in Positive Psychology* (New York: Oxford University Press, 2006); T. Sharot, *The Optimism Bias: A Tour of The Irrationally Positive Brain* (New York: Pantheon, 2011).

14. R. T. McKay and D. C. Dennett, "The Evolution of Misbelief," *Behavioral and Brain Sciences* 32 (2009): 493–561.

15. Sharot, *The Optimism Bias*; Johnson, *Overconfidence and War*.

16. M. van Vugt and A. Ahuja, *Selected: Why Some People Lead, Why Others Follow, and Why It Matters* (New York: Harper Business, 2011); M. van Vugt, "Evolutionary Origins of Leadership and Followership," *Personality and Social Psychology Review* 10, no. 4 (2006): 354–71.

17. R. Axelrod, *The Evolution of Cooperation* (London: Penguin, 1984); R. O. Keohane, *After Hegemony: Cooperation and Discord in the World Political Economy* (Princeton: Princeton University Press, 1986).

18. R. Jervis, "Cooperation under the Security Dilemma," *World Politics* 30, no. 2 (1978): 167–74.

19. A. T. Thrall and J. K. Cramer, eds., *American Foreign Policy and the Politics of Fear: Threat Inflation since 9/11* (New York: Routledge, 2009); J. K. Cramer, *National Security Panics: Threat Inflation and US Foreign Policy Shifts* (New York: Routledge, forthcoming); R. Jervis, *Perception and Misperception in International Politics* (Princeton: Princeton University Press, 1976).

20. H. J. Morgenthau, *Politics among Nations* (1948; New York: McGraw-Hill, 1948).

21. Haselton and Nettle, "The Paranoid Optimist."

22. P. E. Tetlock, "Social Psychology and World Politics," in *Handbook of Social Psychology*, ed. D. Gilbert, S. Fiske, and G. Lindzey (New York: McGraw-Hill, 1998), 877.

23. J. J. Mearsheimer, *The Tragedy of Great Power Politics* (New York: Norton, 2001).

24. C. Tilly, *Coercion, Capital, and European States, AD 990–1990* (Oxford: Blackwell, 1990); P. Turchin et al., "War, Space, and the Evolution of Old World Complex Societies," *Proceedings of the National Academy of Sciences (PNAS)* 110, no. 41 (2013): 16384–89; I. Morris, *War! What Is It Good For? Conflict and the Progress of Civilization from Primates to Robots* (London: Profile Books, 2015).

25. See, e.g., S. Van Evera, "Hypotheses on Nationalism and War," *International Security* 18, no. 4 (1998): 5–39.

26. S. T. Fiske, "What We Know about Bias and Intergroup Conflict, Problem of the Century," *Current Directions in Psychological Science* 11, no. 4 (2002): 123–28.

27. J. Sidanius and R. Kurzban, "Evolutionary Approaches to Political Psychology," in *Handbook of Political Psychology*, ed. D. O. Sears, L. Huddy, and R. Jervis (Oxford: Oxford University Press, 2003).

28. R. D. Alexander, *The Biology of Moral Systems* (Aldine, NY: Hawthorne, 1987); L. H. Keeley, *War before Civilization: The Myth of the Peaceful Savage* (Oxford: Oxford University Press, 1996); S. Bowles, "Did Warfare among Ancestral Hunter-Gatherers Affect the Evolution of Human Social Behaviors?" *Science* 324 (2009): 1293–98.

29. Keeley, *War before Civilization*; A. Gat, *War in Human Civilization* (Oxford: Oxford University Press, 2006); J. Guilaine and J. Zammit, *The Origins of War: Violence in Prehistory* (Oxford: Blackwell, 2004); S. A. LeBlanc and K. E. Register, *Constant Battles: The Myth of the Peaceful, Noble Savage* (New York: St. Martin's Press, 2003); R. W. Wrangham and L. Glowacki, "Intergroup Aggression in Chimpanzees and War in Nomadic Hunter-Gatherers: Evaluating the Chimpanzee Model," *Human Nature* 23 (2012): 5–29.

30. P. Collier, "Doing Well out of War: An Economic Perspective," in *Greed and Grievance: Economic Agendas in Civil Wars*, ed. M. Berdal and D. Malone (Boulder, CO: Lynne Rienner, 2000).

31. R. W. Wrangham and D. Peterson, *Demonic Males: Apes and the Origins of Human Violence* (London: Bloomsbury, 1996); D. M. Buss and T. K. Shackelford, "Human Aggression in Evolutionary Psychological Perspective," *Clinical Psychological Review* 17, no. 6 (1997): 605–19; A. Sell, J. Tooby, and L. Cosmides, "Formidability and the Logic of Human Anger," *Proceedings of the National Academy of Sciences* 106, no. 35 (2009): 15073–78; D. D. P. Johnson and M. D. Toft, "Grounds for War: The Evolution of Territorial Conflict," *International Security* 38, no. 3 (2014): 7–38; D. M. T. Fessler and K. J. Haley, "The Strategy of Affect: Emotions in Human Cooperation," in *The Genetic and Cultural Evolution of Cooperation*, ed. P. Hammerstein (Cambridge, MA: MIT Press, 2003).

32. N. B. Davies, J. R. Krebs, and S. A. West, *An Introduction to Behavioural Ecology* (Chichester: Wiley Blackwell, 2012).

33. C. Darwin, *The Expression of the Emotions in Man and Animals* (1872; London: Penguin Classics, 2009); R. Ardrey, *The Territorial Imperative: A Personal Inquiry into the Animal Origins of Property and Nations* (1966; New York: Kodansha America, 1997); R. H. Frank, *Passions within Reason: The Strategic Role of the Emotions* (New York: Norton, 1988).

34. T. H. Clutton-Brock and G. A. Parker, "Punishment in Animal Societies," *Nature* 373 (1995): 209–16; K. Sigmund, "Punish or Perish? Retaliation and Collaboration among Humans," *Trends in Ecology & Evolution* 22, no. 11 (2007): 593–600.

35. R. McDermott, J. H. Fowler, and O. Smirnov, "On the Evolutionary Origin of Prospect Theory Preferences," *Journal of Politics* 70, no. 2 (2008): 335–50; D. D. P. Johnson and D. R. Tierney, "Bad World: The Negativity Bias in International Relations," *International Security* 43, no. 3 (2019): 96–140.

36. D. Kahneman and J. Renshon, "Why Hawks Win," *Foreign Policy*, no. 158 (2007): 34–38; C. Shea, "The Power of Positive Illusions," *Boston Globe*, 26 September 2004.

37. R. H. Thaler, *Misbehaving: The Making of Behavioral Economics* (New York: W. W. Norton, 2016).

38. R. Jervis, *How Statesmen Think: The Psychology of International Politics* (Princeton: Princeton University Press, 2017).

39. Internet Movie Database, www.imdb.com/title/tt0234215/characters/nm0048127.

40. A. R. Damasio, *Descartes Error: Emotion, Reason and the Human Brain* (New York: Avon, 1994); R. McDermott, "The Feeling of Rationality: The Meaning of Neuroscientific Advances for Political Science," *Perspectives on Politics* 2, no. 4 (2004): 691–706; J. Mercer, "Rationality and Psychology in International Politics," *International Organization* 59, no. 1 (2005): 77–106.

41. D. M. Buss, *Evolutionary Psychology: The New Science of the Mind*, 6th ed. (New York: Routledge, 2019); Kenrick and Griskevicius, *The Rational Animal*; R. Dunbar and L. Barrett, eds., *Oxford Handbook of Evolutionary Psychology* (Oxford: Oxford University Press, 2009).

42. Frank, *Passions within Reason*; Fessler and Haley, "The Strategy of Affect."

43. D. D. P. Johnson and D. R. Tierney, "The Rubicon Theory of War: How the Path to Conflict Reaches the Point of No Return," *International Security* 36, no. 1 (2011): 7–40.

44. D. T. Gilbert and P. S. Malone, "The Correspondence Bias," *Psychological Bulletin* 117, no. 1 (1995): 21–38.

45. M. Hewstone, M. Rubin, and H. Willis, "Intergroup Bias," *Annual Review of Psychology* 53 (2002): 575–604.

46. J. H. Barkow, *Missing the Revolution: Darwinism for Social Scientists* (Oxford: Oxford University Press, 2006); M. Bang Petersen, "Evolutionary Political Psychology: On the Origin and Structure of Heuristics and Biases in Politics," *Political Psychology* 36, no. S1 (2015): 45–78.

47. Schelling, *The Strategy of Conflict*. See also L. Freedman, *Strategy: A History* (Oxford: Oxford University Press, 2013), ch. 13.

48. Note that much of the error management theory literature focuses on the fact that cognitive biases evolved due to the balancing of errors given the prevailing costs and benefits in our evolutionary past. This means that, today, we may behave *as if* the same costs and benefits occur in similar decision-making domains (or even in completely different domains). Whether that assumption is correct or not is an empirical question. Sometimes costs and benefits will be approximately the same (at least relative to each other) and the bias will continue to be useful. In other settings the costs and benefits may have changed considerably so that the bias no longer provides any advantage, or even tends to lead to the more costly type of error instead.

49. Haselton and Nettle, "The Paranoid Optimist."

50. S. M. Walt, "Wishful Thinking: Top 10 Examples of the Most Unrealistic Expectations in Contemporary U.S. Foreign Policy," *Foreign Policy*, 29 April 2011, http://www .foreignpolicy.com/articles/2011/04/29/wishful_thinking.

51. D. D. P. Johnson and B. A. Thayer, "The Evolution of Offensive Realism: Survival under Anarchy from the Pleistocene to the Present," *Politics and the Life Sciences* 35, no. 1 (2016): 1–26; W. R. Thompson, ed., *Evolutionary Interpretations of World Politics* (New York: Routledge, 2001).

52. For a model in which irrationality brings advantages, and biases evolve among actors, see A. T. Little and T. Zeitzoff, "A Bargaining Theory of Conflict with Evolutionary Preferences," *International Organization* 71, no. 3 (2017): 523–57.

53. Jervis, *Perception and Misperception in International Politics*, 424.

54. J. S. Nye, "Neorealism and Neoliberalism," *World Politics* 40, no. 2 (1988): 235–51.

55. Ibid., 249.

56. Ibid., 248. See also H. Simon, "Human Nature in Politics: The Dialogue of Psychology with Political Science," *American Political Science Review* 79 (1985): 293–304.

57. Jervis, *How Statesmen Think*, 5.

58. P. Kennedy, *Rise and Fall of the Great Powers: Economic Change and Military Conflict from 1500 to 2000* (New York: Knopf, 2010).

59. Walt, "Wishful Thinking."

60. S. G. Brooks, G. J. Ikenberry, and W. C. Wohlforth, "Don't Come Home, America: The Case against Retrenchment," *International Security* 37, no. 3 (2012/2013): 7–51.

61. Indeed, evolutionary anthropologists find that group size has been a critical influence on social and cognitive evolution and the development of human societies and civilizations. See, for example, R. I. M. Dunbar, "The Social Brain: Mind, Language, and Society in Evolutionary Perspective," *Annual Review of Anthropology* 32 (2003): 163–81; Alexander, *The Biology of Moral Systems*.

62. S. Pinker, *The Better Angels of Our Nature: Why Violence Has Declined* (New York: Viking, 2011).

INDEX

Page numbers in *italics* refer to tables and figures

A NOTE ON THE TYPE

THIS BOOK has been composed in Miller, a Scotch Roman typeface designed by Matthew Carter and first released by Font Bureau in 1997. It resembles Monticello, the typeface developed for The Papers of Thomas Jefferson in the 1940s by C. H. Griffith and P. J. Conkwright and reinterpreted in digital form by Carter in 2003.

Pleasant Jefferson ("P. J.") Conkwright (1905–1986) was Typographer at Princeton University Press from 1939 to 1970. He was an acclaimed book designer and AIGA Medalist.

The ornament used throughout this book was designed by Pierre Simon Fournier (1712–1768) and was a favorite of Conkwright's, used in his design of the *Princeton University Library Chronicle*.